Misunderstood Stories

Misunderstood Stories

Theological Commentary on Genesis 1–11

ROBERT GNUSE

CASCADE Books • Eugene, Oregon

MISUNDERSTOOD STORIES
Theological Commentary on Genesis 1–11

Copyright © 2014 Robert Gnuse. All rights reserved. Except for brief quotations in critical publications or reviews, no part of this book may be reproduced in any manner without prior written permission from the publisher. Write: Permissions. Wipf and Stock Publishers, 199 W. 8th Ave., Suite 3, Eugene, OR 97401.

Cascade Books
An Imprint of Wipf and Stock Publishers
199 W. 8th Ave., Suite 3
Eugene, OR 97401

www.wipfandstock.com

ISBN 13: 978-1-62564-007-9

Cataloguing-in-Publication data:

Gnuse, Robert Karl.

    Misunderstood stories : theological commentary on Genesis 1–11 / Robert Gnuse.

    xviii + 286 p. ; 23 cm. Includes bibliographical references and indexes.

    ISBN 13: 978-1-62564-007-9

    1. Bible. O.T.—Genesis, I–XI—Commentaries. 2. Bible—Theology. I. Title.

BS1235.3 G58 2014

Manufactured in the U.S.A.

To Beth, Becky, Chris, Riley, Jake, and Adam

Contents

Preface ix
Introduction xi

1. Ancient Near Eastern Creation Accounts   1
2. Cosmic Creation   13
3. Creation of Humanity   32
4. Creation of the Adam   48
5. The Garden   57
6. The Adam in the Garden   72
7. Creation of the Woman   82
8. Origin of Evil according to the Ancients   92
9. Sin in the Garden   98
10. Divine Pronouncements   114
11. Divine Blessings and Exile from the Garden   131
12. Cain and Abel   141
13. The Family of Cain   158
14. The Family of Seth   170
15. Ancient Flood Accounts   180
16. The Giants   193
17. The Flood   201
18. Covenant with Noah   217
19. Noah and His Sons   225
20. Genealogies   240

21 History behind Babel   248
22 The Tower of Babel and Beyond   257
23 Conclusion   274

Bibliography   279

Preface

THE STORIES IN GENESIS 1–11 are archetypal narratives that speak boldly of the human condition and have inspired artists, writers, preachers, Sunday School teachers, and countless people over the years. I have seen numerous movies and television shows (often science fiction) that have taken themes or plots from these stories. With all this attention it still amazes me how many people "get the story wrong," that is, they misconstrue details in the biblical text. On a deeper level many people fail to understand the real message of these narratives, focusing upon divine judgment rather than divine grace and forgiveness, or more insidiously, using these stories to justify the institution of slavery and the denigration of African Americans or women. That's why I wrote this popular theological commentary—to primarily address what are the theological messages in these texts. I hope that readers at all levels may be able to read this book and say, "I didn't know that!" I hope that readers may come away with a deeper appreciation of the powerful and positive nature of the message found in these biblical texts.

Behind every book that is written there is an author who has been supported by other people. I credit my wife, Beth, with patience as I have worked on this book for the past ten years at home as well as at the office. I would like to thank Loyola University for the sabbaticals in the fall 2003 semester and fall 2011 semester when I researched and wrote this work. I would like to thank the Deutscher Akademischer Austauschdienst for the research grant in fall 2005, and the Fachbereich Evangelische Theologie of Philipps Universität in Marburg where some of the research for this book was undertaken. I would like to thank the Interlibrary Loan Department of Loyola University for obtaining many of these volumes for me over the past few years. I would like to thank the library staff at New Orleans Baptist Theological Seminary for the use of their facilities over the years. Finally, I would like to thank Cascade Books for their willingness to publish this work.

Introduction

ONCE UPON A TIME there was a country priest who read the Bible very closely. He studied Hebrew at Oxford University, so he read the biblical text in the original languages and found teachings in the Bible that other preachers, theologians, and church hierarchs of the age ignored. In particular, in Genesis 1 he read that God had made "man" in his image, and then made "man" into male and female. This indicated to him that men and women were equal, for both were made at the same time in the image of God. But what impressed him more was that the "image of God" was something attributed only to kings in his age. If all people were made in the royal "image of God," then all people should be equal in the social realm. Perhaps, he thought, there should be no kings and all people should have the power to elect members of the parliament, not just the nobles. These were heady thoughts for the priest to entertain, and they were dangerous ideas to preach in the church. But he did both. For twenty years he proclaimed his message in rural villages of northern England, and eventually he preached in London. A chronicler from that era recorded part of one of his sermons,

> My good friends, things cannot go well in England, nor ever will until everything shall be in common; when there shall be neither vassal nor Lord and all distinctions leveled, when the Lords shall be no more masters than ourselves. How ill have they used us? And for what reason do they thus hold us in bondage? Are we not all descended from the same parents, Adam and Eve? And what can they show or what reasons give, why they should be more masters than ourselves? . . . But it is from us and our labor that everything comes with which they maintain their pomp. (Bobrick 60; Cohn 199)

The country priest, along with Jack Straw and Wat Tyler, led the peasants in a revolution against his oppressive government. After his followers seized the city of London and forced King Richard to negotiate with them, the king promised to end serfdom and the oppressive taxes. But when the peasants, believing that they had obtained these rights, dispersed to their homes, the king declared, "serfs you were, and serfs you will remain." For such is the way of kings. The leaders of the uprising, including the young priest, were executed, and the revolution failed. The year was 1381 and the priest's name was John Ball (Bobrick 59–62). We refer to the various peasants' uprisings in Europe in our world history textbooks, and we casually mention the John Ball uprising in 1381 and move along in our historical overviews. But this was a dramatic moment in human history. Had Ball lived in America four centuries later, he would be lauded as one of the founding fathers during the American Revolution. He would be called a patriot, not just another failed revolutionary peasant.

What is most striking is that he read the Bible, Genesis 1 in particular, and that inspired him to revolt. He saw the deeper meaning of Genesis 1, which speaks of the man and the woman made in the image of God and the implication of the universal human equality. Why did not more clergy discover this message in the Bible? Why did it take almost two thousand years for democracy to emerge in a Christian culture that supposedly used the Bible as its primary source for theology, ethics, worship, and Christian faith? Maybe the most brutal question is: Why do not all Christians today still not see this message of universal human equality and the concomitant concept of the equality of men and the women? Is it because we quote the Bible, but do not really read it? Oh, to be sure, we biblical scholars know this message of human equality and comment upon it in our learned commentaries and scholarly articles, but it has not yet infiltrated half of the churches in Christendom.

Throughout the Bible one can find a message of human dignity and equality before God. Though there are passages that admit the existence of the institutions of slavery and kingship and acknowledge distinctions between people on the basis of class, wealth, and sex, one senses that the texts speak of these matters in a concessive fashion, that is, these social distinctions are viewed as part of a world order that will someday be no more. For too long the institutional Church has allowed the concessive mode of discourse to become the normative mode of preaching for human society, and social realities that were meant to be changed by the people of God were ironically reinforced by the institutional churches.

We could review the entire biblical tradition to explicate those passages that speak of human dignity and equality or the imperative to move in such directions, but that would be an expansive work. This book seeks to focus upon the Primeval History in Genesis 1–11, for seldom do biblical scholars and theologians turn to these texts for inspiration for social reform. Yet these are the passages that have so often inspired children's stories, great artwork, and literature by famous authors. These are the passages that too often have been used consciously and unconsciously to legitimate oppression and the subordination of certain people. I would maintain that within these passages there are clarion statements for human equality and a subtle critique of the institution of kingship. To be sure, biblical scholars have focused upon these themes in scholarly discussion, though often in a tangential way, as the scholars seek to elucidate other topics. Feminist scholars have been especially adroit at unveiling the egalitarian images as they pertain to women. But I believe there are more pervasive egalitarian themes, as well as anti-royal themes, which by implication are egalitarian, to be found within these texts. These themes deserve greater attention than have been accorded them in the past.

Often scholars pay attention to the details of the biblical text, such as reconstructing the exact form of the original Hebrew to help create excellent English translations. Or they attempt to reconstruct how our present text evolved in oral and written form, which I must admit I find fascinating. The evolution of the text has probably consumed more energy of scholars in the past century than any other aspect of study. In regard to Genesis 1–11 in particular, scholars have determined that most of this narrative came together as part of a larger epic in Genesis, Exodus, and Numbers, which they call the Yahwist (so-called because it tends to favor the sacred name, Yahweh, for God). Then at some later time priests edited these books to create our present Pentateuch. We call their additions the Priestly texts. Thus, Genesis 1–11 appears to be a Yahwist narrative with Priestly additions (though not all agree with this model). In the past generation scholars have spent great time and energy attempting to locate when the greater Yahwist and Priestly traditions arose in fixed form. This is a fascinating debate, but the average reader of the Bible finds it somewhat boring. Undue attention to the Hebrew text or the development of the narratives can dull our senses to the powerful religious message found in these accounts.

As small children we were entertained (or maybe terrified) by some of the stories found in Genesis 1–11. We heard them in Jewish and Christian Sunday Schools. (Yes, my Christian friends, Jews do sometimes have religious education for children on Sundays—it keeps them out of the competition's schools!) These stories are among the best known stories in the Bible. When taught to small children, they are used to emphasize basic religious truths: obey God, keep God's laws, have the courage to stand apart from the values of society in your devotion to God, etc. (avoid young ladies with apples). Sometimes the stories are used to teach things that are really inappropriate and are not really taught by the text: that women are meant to be subordinate to men, that the first sin was the act of sex, that the woman and not the man was responsible for bringing sin into the world, that the sin of Ham destined Africans to be slaves and inferior as a race. We shall endeavor to show that the text is saying something different and far more theologically profound.

The point I wish to make is that these texts say a great deal about the dignity and equality of all human beings. Sometimes scholarly works just do not get that message across very well with all the other profound intellectual insights that need to be made in one book. I must admit that a number of the scholarly and technical works gave me the information with which I wrote this book! Nevertheless, sometimes scholars write really dull books, which would put most average people to sleep. These books sometimes put me to sleep, too. (I actually have fallen asleep reading stuff that I have written.) That is why I chose to write this book. It has a minimum of scholarly jargon and I focus on the theological and existential messages of these texts in a bold and clear fashion.

People in churches and Sunday Schools for years have heard these stories. But they do not walk away with the realization that these accounts testify to divine love and forgiveness, human freedom, responsibility, and equality. Over the years and still today too many leaders in the church, Protestant and Catholic alike, talk more about sin and judgment, and overlook the powerful message of grace and forgiveness in the text. Talk about sin and guilt is deemed necessary by clergy to get people to repent for their sins, to commit themselves to a moral life, and above all, to join the church of the preacher who used this message of guilt and judgment in the first place. Clergy sometimes tell the stories in a certain way to have psychological power over people by manipulating human guilt. I am a clergyman, so I speak from years of professional observation.

These biblical texts have been used too many times to oppress people. We have been told that the woman was created after man, and that is why women are inferior to men. We have been told that the woman was created to be man's helper, and that is why women serve men. We have been told that the woman was tempted first because she was weaker, and that is why women are subordinate to men. We have been told that the man and the woman ate an apple in the garden. We have been told that the man and the woman in the garden were naturally immortal and they lost that immortality when they ate the apple. We have been told that the three curses placed upon the man, the woman, and the snake are binding and unchangeable curses that prescribe the nature of reality. We have been told that Noah cursed Ham, and that is why African people were meant to be slaves. All of these statements are false, and these are issues we must talk about in this book. Some, like the belief that the fruit in the garden was an apple, are simply silly mistakes. But other popular misconceptions, such as those that tell why Africans are meant to be inferior to white people and why women are meant to be subordinate to men, are evil and insidious. They abuse the Bible by using it as a tool to oppress people.

We have been betrayed by too many popular preachers and televangelists, as well as by pious and well intentioned, albeit ill-informed, Sunday School teachers. The Bible proclaims a message about human dignity and equality, about divine grace and forgiveness, and that message must be proclaimed loudly. To be sure, seminaries teach what the text really says, and scholarly commentaries explicate in detail what the text really says, but somehow the message does not seem to reach people. Whatever the reason, this book is dedicated to telling the story about some very powerful biblical narratives and the message they have to tell us.

We shall seek to reconstruct how the original readers or listeners might have understood the message of the biblical text. Some pious Christians believe that we should stress how people hear the text by the power of the Holy Spirit today. That may be a nice pious approach and helps to strengthen the faith of many people. But the Bible is authoritative religious literature, often used by ecclesiastical authorities to generate official theological positions of the church. We need to strive to discern the original meaning in order to understand the message of the text for us today, since over the years many different, sometimes bizarre, ways of interpreting the text have arisen. When it comes to creating and articulating the views of the church and generating educational literature, scholars have a responsibility to determine what the text originally meant and then move to a discussion of what it means for the modern age.

When these texts first spoke to a people of God, they addressed a dramatic situation. Contemporary scholars suggest that these passages were penned by a Yahwist Historian and a Priestly Editor who lived in the late sixth and the fifth centuries BCE. They addressed Judeans who had been exiled to Babylon after the destruction of Jerusalem in 586 BCE and perhaps the few returning exiles who trudged back to Jerusalem in small groups in the years after 539 BCE. The vast majority of Judeans remained in exile in Babylon for centuries after 539 BCE, so this literature spoke to them and addressed their religious and psychological needs.

Issues and needs that the authors had to address were several: 1) What was the place of Judeans in the world in the light of their relationship with God? The Primeval History in Genesis 1–11 told a story of humanity that ultimately led to the call of Abraham and the beginning of the Israelite and Judean people. 2) Why had God let them be destroyed as a kingdom?

Painful as it was to say this, exilic theologians like Ezekiel the prophet and the Deuteronomistic History in Joshua, Judges, Samuel, and Kings, told them that breaking the Law of God led to punishment and destruction of the kingdom. 3) Was divine judgment the ultimate message from God for them? No! The stories in the Primeval History spoke of judgment, but the final word in every story was about divine love and forgiveness. The man and woman in the garden would be given names, clothing, and children. Cain would receive a mark to protect him. Noah and his family would be saved out of the flood. Shem and Japheth would be blessed. Out of the Babel dispersion Abraham would be called. Divine grace was always the final word in each story. 4) How should Judeans relate to foreigners? The Primeval History implied that all people were the people of God, thus Judeans should relate to them appropriately. 5) Where was God for exiled Judeans? Judeans should have patience; God will always act in time. God is present for people, involved in the process of their lives. As God cared to find the man a "helper," as God cared to provide for Noah in the flood, so God will provide for them. As God "grieved" over humanity and their sinfulness in Genesis 1–11, God still "grieves" over his people, the Judean exiles. This especially spoke to exiles (McKeown 51–52). 6) What would be their future hope? There would be a return, and the curses of the garden would be overcome, as well as the curse on the land from which they were exiled.

In addition to answering these questions, the author makes other strong statements. The Primeval History speaks of the equality of all people before God and the equality of men and women with each other. The narrative attacks in straightforward, but sometimes in subtle fashion, the prerogatives of kings. The implication is that the kings of foreign countries, who bestride the folk of so many lands, are but fools who someday will be toppled. Our own kings, says the biblical author, whose folly led to our exile, will be replaced by better rulers in the future.

These messages lie within the text, but they too often have not been heard by Christians over the past two thousand years, or at least they have not been emphasized enough. Perhaps because we tell these stories as children's stories, the powerful political messages cannot be heard. Perhaps because scholars have addressed scholarly issues, these messages were not stressed enough. There have been some fine textbooks in recent years meant to redress this inequity. But this textbook attempts to be as thorough as possible in treating those chapters, more so than previous works, without being too turgid. It is impossible to be thorough and include all the scholarly references; there are simply too many. So I apologize if not all the fine scholarship generated on these passages is included. But I have chosen those that I believe to be most relevant for the theological exposition of these passages.

Perhaps, if the message of these texts can be clearly communicated to the modern audience, the power of the text can be released once more (as it was in 1381).

1

Ancient Near Eastern Creation Accounts

THERE ARE SEVERAL ANCIENT Near Eastern myths that recount the creation of the world and the creation of people. It is difficult to say which texts were available to our biblical authors, but it appears that the authors were reacting against narrative motifs and ideologies found in many of those ancient narratives. Genesis 1 speaks of cosmic creation, and Genesis 2 describes more directly the creation of people. The two chapters come from separate authors, and each author appears to be reacting against specific texts and concepts.

Before we can consider the meaning of Genesis 1–2, we need to observe those ancient Near Eastern narratives. In the past some scholars have said that the biblical authors copied ancient accounts and changed a little here and there. This underestimates the creativity of the biblical authors and does not take into account the serious differences between the ancient Near Eastern creation accounts and Genesis 1–2. Others emphasized the differences between Genesis 1–2 and those other accounts, and they declared that the biblical narratives were not influenced significantly by other creation stories. That is incredibly naïve and overlooks the great similarities between Genesis 1–2 and the other narratives. Most scholars today assume that the authors of Genesis 1–2 knew those other accounts and set forth similar versions of creation with modifications as a critical intellectual response. I also believe the biblical authors were more sophisticated than to merely report what they thought happened at the beginning of the world. They were serious theologians responding to the underlying religious and political thought behind ancient Near Eastern creation narratives. Biblical authors affirmed that the God of the Judeans was the only God in the universe, and they provided veiled ridicule of polytheism and various gods important to other ancient Near Easterners. Their critique also entailed veiled political criticism of foreign kings and priests, as well as their symbols of imperial might.

Our biblical authors also debated the ancient predecessor texts in terms of their anthropology, that is, how they envisioned people. Whereas ancient accounts, especially those from Mesopotamia, viewed people as the slaves of the gods, biblical authors affirmed human freedom, dignity, equality, and responsibility. I believe the most important issues addressed by the biblical authors were in the narratives about the creation of people. Herein we can observe creativity and subtle sarcasm as they assaulted the beliefs of the Mesopotamians and affirmed a worldview that influenced the development of our modern intellectual assumptions. Thus, Genesis 1–2 is more than just another story about the creation of the world; it is a manifesto about the value of the human person.

We may outline the ancient Near Eastern stories or myths in several categories: 1) the creation of the cosmos, 2) the creation of humanity, 3) the paradise or primeval garden, 4) the tree of life and the tree of the knowledge of good and evil, and 5) the origin of mortality, evil, and suffering. In this chapter we shall discuss myths about the creation of the world and the creation of humanity; in later chapters we shall review those concerning the garden, the trees, mortality, evil, and suffering.

We know that not all the ancient accounts have been recovered by us, and that in the future we may be fortunate to discover more in the sands of the Middle East. But those in our possession may either be ones with which the biblical authors were familiar or they may be close enough in content to merit our consideration. We have valuable creation narratives from both Egypt and Mesopotamia, but the ones from Mesopotamia appear to be the stories most akin to what we observe in the biblical text.

The oldest Mesopotamian myths are written in Sumerian, a language totally unrelated to any other in the ancient Near East. Sumerians were culturally predominant in Mesopotamia from 3200–2000 BCE, when many of the Sumerian myths originated. But the language continued to be used as a religious language and scribes learned it and copied texts in this tongue until the second century BCE. Later myths, and especially longer epics, were written in Akkadian, a Semitic language that became more extensively used after the rise of Sargon the Great and the Akkadian Empire around 2400 BCE. Akkadian would continue to be used as a legal, political, and international language until around 1000 BCE.

The oldest well-developed creation account may be a Sumerian myth titled *Enki and the World Manor*, or *Enki and the Ordering of the World*. Copies date to about 2000 BCE, but it is older than that. Ea or Enki is described as creating nature, civilization, and worship, even though Enlil is recognized as the ruler deity. Created items expressly mentioned in the narrative include the plow and sacred shrines with their rituals. Though this poetic account originally was quite long, much of it has been destroyed (Beyerlin 78–80).

Another Sumerian account dating from about 1600 BCE, which we call the *Eridu Genesis*, tells the story of creation, the flood, and leading personages. The inclusion of all three of these categories makes the work quite similar to Genesis 1–11, except that it lacks the biblical emphasis on human sin (Jacobsen 527–29). In *Eridu Genesis* the mother goddess, Nintur, brings people from a nomadic existence to a land where they can build cities and cult places. This narrative may parallel the Genesis 11 account of how people came to settle in Shinar to build a city and a tower. Nintur creates kingship and then the first cities, which are assigned to their respective deities. That kingship is created before cities, tells us this is a myth of political legitimation for the power of kings (Hallo and Younger 1:513–15).

A third Sumerian tale is the story of *Enki and Ninmah*, who appear together in a number of Sumerian myths. In the primordial time the younger gods do manual labor for the senior gods, including digging canals. The junior gods complain to Enki and his mother Nammu, saying the work is too much for them. At Nammu's insistence, Enki obtains the assistance of Ninmah and a number of birth goddesses in order to make humanity. They nip off bits of clay taken from the underground watery abyss, the Apsu, and shape them to make human beings. The clay figurines are implanted in the birth goddesses, where they develop and are born. The mother goddess is told that she "must give life to the limbs." Subsequently Enki and Ninmah are at a banquet drinking beer and they engage in a contest in which Ninmah makes a creature and Enki finds a place for it in the world. Ninmah makes beings who are crippled in their hands, blind, crippled in their feet, men continually discharging semen, infertile women, and beings lacking sex organs. Enki finds roles for each of them in society: a musician, a servant of the king, a courtier, a weaver of cloth, and a metal-smith. Enki creates two extremely sickly creatures that Ninmah cannot place in the created order, and then he makes an *umul*, an immature fetus, to mock Ninmah's empty womb. Enki wins the contest, but in so doing, he and Ninmah introduce birth defects and human ailments into the world (Beyerlin 76–77; Van Seters 54–55; Kramer and Maier 31–37; Frymer-Kensky 73–74; Hallo and Younger 1:516–18). This last half of the myth may explain how human suffering entered the world, and as such would contrast with Genesis 3. In Mesopotamia suffering originates because the good gods got drunk and accidentally created these things; but in the biblical account it is the result of human free will that sin and suffering enter the world. Ninmah goes by a number of different names: Nintur, Nintu, Ninhursaga, Mami, Aruru, Belet-ili, all of whom are goddesses who shape babies in the womb. Once these were separate goddesses, but they were merged into one deity by 2000 BCE (Simkins 57).

There are also a few other short creation texts that refer to the origin of humanity. A bilingual Sumerian and Akkadian text found in north Mesopotamia, or Assyria, tells a short version of the creation of people. It states that the major gods make humanity from the blood of slain craftsmen gods, and their purpose is to do farming, build temples, and render worship to the gods. Two people are named, Ullegarra and Annegarra.

In a Chaldean Babylonian text dating to the sixth century BCE there is reference to how Anu creates the heavens, and Ea or Enki creates a number of deities who are the patrons of farming, religion, crafts, and the arts. Ea also creates a king to maintain the temples and finally people to do the service of the gods (Van Seters 59–60). In the latter story we have the interesting creation of a king separate from common humanity. In the creation of the Adam in Genesis 1–2 there are hints that the Adam is to be seen as a king, or more likely, as general humanity who now replace kings in the world.

To reinforce this critical observation there is yet another Chaldean text worth mentioning. In this account Ea and a mother goddess create people, but they take special time to create a king, who will be different from the rest of humanity. The text has Ea speak to Belet-ili and tell her,

> "You have created the common people, now construct the king, distinctively superior person. With goodness envelop his entire being. Form his features harmoniously; make his body beautiful." . . . The great gods gave the king the task of warfare. Anu gave him the crown; Enlil gave him the throne. Nergal gave him weapons; Ninurta gave him glistening splendor. Belet-ili gave him a beautiful appearance. Nusku gave him instruction and counsel and stands at his service. (Van Seters 61)

This account legitimates not only kings but also the entire institution of kingship itself. It is most significant that this creation account of the king is given such special attention. It implies that the biblical author, who may have been familiar with such stories, not only deliberately omitted such a story about kings, but may have intended the audience to sense that the

Adam was both a common human being and a king at the same time, thus implying that all people were kings (Fitzpatrick 149).

There is also a Chaldean Babylonian text from the sixth century BCE, *The Creation of the World by Marduk*, which may reflect an older version of creation perhaps taught at Eridu, a sacred Sumerian shrine down deep in the south of Mesopotamia. The first eleven lines of the account tell us what did not exist, comparable to the brief descriptions in Gen 1:2 about the "formless void" and Gen 2:5 about the lack of vegetation. In lines 20–27 we are told how Marduk creates the earth, and with the help of the goddess Aruru, he creates people. Then subsequently he creates animal life, the Tigris and Euphrates Rivers, vegetation, cities, and civilized life. The references to divine conflict and the death of an evil god to create humanity is lacking in this version (Van Seters 60; Blenkinsopp 2011:60). What is significant about this account is the list of things created, which is reminiscent of the things created in Genesis 1, even though they are not in the same order.

Perhaps the most significant account concerning the creation of the world among Mesopotamian myths is the *Enuma Elish*. Its title comes from the opening words, "When on high." It describes the theogony (a genealogy) of the gods and the creation of the world, but the most important purpose it served was to recall the rise of Marduk to supremacy in the divine realm. Marduk was the patron deity of Babylon. As a deity, Marduk did not function as an important god in the Mesopotamia pantheon until the rise of Babylon as a significant power center under Hammurabi (1792–1750 BCE) after which he was called a "great god." Under later Kassite rulers in Babylon, Marduk was elevated even more. Nebuchadnezzar I (1124–1103 BCE) exalted Marduk as the "king of the gods," and perhaps the *Enuma Elish* was created at this time (if not during the earlier time of Hammurabi). We believe the narrative was recited on the fourth day of the New Year Festival (or perhaps on the fourth day of every month) in the Babylonian temple, the Esagila, from at least the seventh century BCE onward. In Assyria the narrative was recited with the name of the Assyrian god Ashur replacing that of Marduk. The text runs about nine hundred lines on seven tablets. Our best copy comes from the library of the Assyrian king, Ashurbanipal (668–626 BCE), who created a library of ancient texts in the city of Ashur. Most of our textual fragments date between 750 and 200 BCE (Beyerlin 81–84; Lambert 527; Hallo and Younger 1:390–402).

The myth begins with the words, "When on high neither the heavens had been named, nor the earth below pronounced by name." The words remind us of the language of Gen 1:1, as we shall discuss later.

The story runs as follows. The old god Apsu, the god of the fresh or sweet waters below the earth, and Tiamat, the goddess of the salt waters of the great oceans, create the divine couple Lahmu and Lahamu, who give birth to Anshar and Kishar, who give birth to Anu, who gives birth to Nudimmud-Ea (or Enki). Apsu and Tiamat go to rest once the other gods are created, but they are disturbed by the noise created by the younger gods. So Apsu decides to kill them. But Ea or Enki with the help of his vizier Mummu defends the junior gods; he slays Apsu with a magic spell and sets up his abode on Apsu's body. This is why Ea or Enki, also a god of the sweet water, draws his source of sweet waters from the deep sweet waters of the depths below the earth, the "Apsu." After this initial victory more gods are born, including Marduk, the son of Ea and Damkina, who is described as a beautiful and powerful deity. Marduk then creates streams or waves to aggravate Tiamat.

Tiamat is encouraged by the lesser gods to take up the fight after Apsu's demise. Tiamat then decides to act after these gods encourage her to avenge Apsu. She creates eleven monsters and takes as her aide and boyfriend, the god Kingu, to whom she gives the Tablets of Destiny. The gods, including Anu and Ea, go forth to fight, but when they see her, they return afraid. Marduk is willing to fight, if the other gods make him king over them. Marduk demonstrates his power by making images (either a robe or a stellar constellation) disappear with a verbal command and by bringing them back into existence with a verbal command. One is reminded somewhat of God bringing creation into being by commands in Genesis 1. Marduk then creates a special bow for the battle.

Marduk rides forth into battle with a chariot drawn by Killer, Relentless, Trampler, and Swift; he is armed with the weapons called Smiter and Combat. He carries a net, the four winds of the heavens, and seven special winds. Marduk faces Tiamat on the field of battle and they hurl insults at each other before their one-on-one combat. One is reminded of the confrontation of David and Goliath in 1 Sam 17:8–10 and other biblical accounts (2 Sam 5:6–8; 1 Kgs 20:1–11; 2 Kgs 18:19–37), as well as the various heroes who fight each other in Homer's *Iliad*. Marduk's insults enrage Tiamat, who in turn attacks Marduk and leaves her specially created serpent monsters behind. When Tiamat opens her mouth to roar, Marduk casts his net over her and hurls the four winds of the heavens (north, south, east, and west) into her mouth to distend her body (what a cheater!). He shoots arrows of lightning bolts into her with his bow and then takes all of her demon prisoners captive. He also seizes the Tablets of Destiny from Kingu. Marduk takes Tiamat's body, crushes her skull with his mace, and cuts her in half like a "dried fish." Half of her becomes the firmament and the waters above the firmament; the other half becomes the world and the waters below the world. Mountains hold the firmament in place. Her spit becomes the clouds and her tail becomes the Milky Way. The Tigris and the Euphrates Rivers flow out of her eyes through holes bored in the mountains. Out of the death of the goddess comes the life of the world. All this imagery is described in very poetic fashion.

As Marduk creates the world, he engages in the following steps: 1) Tiamat's body is split to create the waters above the heaven and the waters below the earth. 2) A great void is created in-between to keep the waters separate, and this void must be maintained by the subsequent actions of Marduk. Marduk builds his abode on the grave of Apsu, as Ea had done previously. 3) Heavenly bodies are created: the sun, the moon, and thirty-six stars to regulate the seasons. He creates seven-day cycles for the month, reminiscent of the biblical week or Sabbath. Most importantly he creates the year. 4) Physical features of the earth are created out of Tiamat's physical body also. Thus, the Tigris and Euphrates Rivers are said to flow out of her eyes. 5) Man is created by Marduk and a mother goddess out of the blood of Kingu, the defeated evil god. References to clay are omitted in the story, but perhaps the author assumes the audience knows that clay was involved in the process. People are created to serve the gods by providing food and drink. 6) Babylon is created on the earth by the gods to be in the center of the universe, and this is where the assembly of the gods will meet. Its construction takes one year. (Nippur, the sacred town of Enlil, is thus displaced as the great cultic center.) 7) In gratitude the gods build a temple for Marduk, the Esagila or Esangila, with an accompanying ziggurat. This parallels Marduk's temple in the heavens, the Esharra. The gods mold bricks for a year before the temple is built. The gods are able to travel from the divine realm, the heavenly Esarra, down to the underworld, reminding us of Jacob's ladder in Gen 28:10–22. The gods meet at a banquet, admire Marduk's bow of war, proclaim him king, take a loyalty oath, and proclaim his fifty names (which is a long list indeed). Marduk places his bow of war in the heavens, where it becomes the star Sirius. 8) Marduk can now rest after his victory, and the other gods may also rest because human beings have been created to serve them (Pritchard 60–72; Beyerlin 82–84; Lambert 526–28; Matthews and Benjamin 9–18; Hallo and Younger 1:390–402).

We need to consider closely the creation of people in this narrative. After Marduk creates the world, the god who allied himself with Tiamat is brought forward. Kingu is led forth with a rope in his nose, and after he is executed, Ea (Enki) takes his blood and out of it makes humanity (Pritchard 68; Matthews and Benjamin 17; Beyerlin 84). Since humanity is created out of the blood of an evil, defeated god, people must forever serve the gods on the temple manor. One senses that this narrative in particular justifies why people must serve the gods by being obedient to the temple priests and by rendering sacrifice and temple taxes. The story legitimates the power of priests and the entire cultic system. Furthermore, when the *Enuma Elish* was performed, the king of Babylon played the role of Marduk, so the king was the representative of the high god. In everyday life the king was the person most responsible for providing order in society, comparable to how Marduk won cosmic order in battle. Hence, the power of the king was legitimated tremendously by this myth and its ritual performance during the *Akitu* Festival. The myth taught people obedience to both priests and kings.

The *Akitu* Festival was celebrated twice during the year. The most important performance occurred during the first month of the year, *Nisanu*, in the spring when the rivers flooded. The flooding of the rivers was seen as Tiamat's attempt to re-emerge and destroy created order with water every year. The festival was also celebrated in the fall, during the seventh month of the year, *Tashritu* (Sparks 632). The Judeans called these two months *Nisan* and *Tishri* and celebrated both as New Year's festivals at various times in their history, which is an interesting coincidence. I believe the *Enuma Elish* may have been the most powerful myth used for the legitimation of power in the hands of priests and kings in ancient Mesopotamia.

An older Mesopotamia account, which is as extensive as the *Enuma Elish*, is an account called the *Atrahasis Epic*. This epic is also written in Akkadian. It may be five hundred years older than *Enuma Elish* and may have been a primary source for the *Enuma Elish*. According to the text the scribe who wrote this was named Ku-Aya, and he functioned during the reign of Ammi-Saduqa, the great-great-grandson of Hammurabi. Thus, the text comes from the mid-second millennium BCE from the court of Amorite Babylon. *Atrahasis Epic* may have been more known and it may have been publicly performed, while the *Enuma Elish* may have been more of an internal political document for the Babylonian court and Babylonian intelligentsia. But that is highly speculative.

Atrahasis Epic is more expansive in its plot, for it includes narratives about the creation of the world, the creation of human beings, and the flood. So we shall discuss the remainder of the epic in a later chapter. The epic is named after Atrahasis, the person who survives the flood.

The story line runs as follows: There is a three-tiered universe in which Anu is in the heavens, Enlil on the earth, and Enki is down in the Apsu, the deep waters. Enlil puts the *Igigi*, the junior gods, to work, while the high gods, the *Anunnaki*, rest. (This rest foreshadows the biblical Sabbath.) After forty years lesser gods go on strike, burn their tools, refuse to work, and surround Enlil's house, the temple Ekur in Nippur. They are tired of serving the higher gods. Although Enlil appeals to Anu to punish them, Anu says their demands are justified. Their "strike" is resolved by creating human beings to do the work they once did. Upon the advice of Ea or Enki humans are created out of the body and blood of the deity who led the revolt, We or We-ila or Aw-ilu. His flesh and especially his blood are mixed with clay and the spit of the gods to produce people. Spit can symbolize semen. The spirit of the deity remains in people as a source of life and perhaps gives humanity a rebellious spirit. Ea or Enki takes charge of creating the humans, and fourteen birth goddesses assist in the process of human gestation. Seven pairs of people are created by the goddess Nintu-Mami (who is also called Belet-ili), working in conjunction with Enki. She prepares the clay mixture, then Enki stomps the clay with his feet. Nintu-Mami utters an incantation and pinches off little pieces of clay by which to make people. She rejoices when she has completed making humans, and we are reminded of Eve's cry of success when Cain is born. Enki and Nintu-Mami take them to the "House of Destiny" where the birth goddesses are located. Eventually the clay lumps become people and populate the earth. Enlil creates the different classes in society with these couples, but unfortunately that portion of the ancient text is lost, so we do not know what the classes are. Obviously this narrative becomes social legitimation for the different classes in early second millennium BCE Amorite Babylonian society (Lambert and Millard 23; Matthews and Benjamin 31–35; Batto 1992:63). The account of human creation is longer than the narrative in the *Enuma Elish*. Unlike the *Enuma Elish* this account contains no theogony, or birth sequence of the various generations of the gods, nor does it contain a cosmogonic conflict, an account of a great battle between Marduk and Tiamat. Instead, Anu, Enlil, and Enki, the three great Sumerian gods divide responsibilities among the gods. The narrative then moves to the flood account (Lambert and Millard 5–10; Van Seters 47–54; Matthews and Benjamin 31–35; Hallo and Younger 1:450–52).

Enuma Elish is more relevant for our discussion of Genesis 1, but *Atrahasis Epic* is more relevant for the discussion of Genesis 2. The *Enuma Elish* appears to be aware of the *Atrahasis Epic* and perhaps was written to describe the cosmic creation before the events told in the *Atrahasis Epic*. If so, the *Enuma Elish* bears the same relationship to the *Atrahasis Epic* as Genesis 1 bears to Genesis 2, for Genesis 1 appears to have been created after Genesis 2 and was designed to complement that earlier story.

As Genesis 1 seems to react against the *Enuma Elish*, Genesis 2 may react more to the *Atrahasis Epic*. Genesis 1 tells the story of cosmic creation, as does *Enuma Elish*, and Genesis 2 focuses more upon the creation of humanity, as does *Atrahasis Epic*. In fact, we could make a further generalization. The Priestly Editors are responsible for Genesis 1, the genealogy of Seth, and the dramatic elements in the flood narrative that hearken back to Genesis 1. The Priestly version of the flood reverses the creation events to bring watery chaos back upon the earth and repeats the creative events of Genesis 1 to remove the floodwaters. The Priestly Editors critique *Enuma Elish* with their version of the world's origin and a flood narrative with creation language. The Yahwist narrative is the core account into which the Priestly material has been placed. The Yahwist Historian critiques the *Atrahasis Epic*, which like the Yahwist, tells the story of human creation, human development and culture, and the flood. Placing Priestly material into the Yahwist Epic to create our final biblical text produces a rather wide-ranging critique of the Mesopotamian epic tradition and ideology.

An interesting observation to make is that in both of the Mesopotamian accounts, and to a certain degree in the biblical account, the world is primarily created out of water. If we look to Greece, we discover that the early philosophers, the pre-Socratics, likewise believed the world to be made out of water. Thales (624–546 BCE) and Anaximander (610–546 BCE) both stated that the primary element out of which all things came was water. Perhaps, our biblical author might have been familiar with the somewhat contemporary speculations of these Greek thinkers who lived in Ionia or western Turkey, which was part of the Persian Empire by the late sixth and fifth centuries BCE, as were Judeans in both Babylon and Jerusalem.

Greek accounts also contain elements of the conflict imagery found in Mesopotamian myths. In Hesiod's *Theogony* (823–825, 881–885) the high god Zeus establishes cosmic order after defeating Typhon. The biblical author of Genesis 1 could have been familiar with this older Greek tradition (Blenkinsopp 2011:32).

Egyptian accounts of creation have not been preserved for us very well, since most of our Egyptian texts come from temples and tombs especially, and thus the literature from Egypt tends to reflect the concerns that would be related to funerary issues. We know that the Egyptians had creation accounts, but we do not have a continuous, intact account. It seems that Egyptians did not see the need to recount an entire creation narrative (Simkins 65).

A short reference to creation is found in *The Creation by Atum*, also know as the *Heliopolitan Cosmogany*. The text comes from the Egyptian Sixth Dynasty in the twenty-fourth century BCE. In the beginning of the text we are told that Atum-Kheprer was on the first hillock of dirt arising out of the primeval ocean and that he spit out the first gods, Shu and Tefnut (Pritchard 3). Shu (male) is the firmament and Tefnut (female) is the earth or moisture. Some commentators suggest that the deity masturbated or sneezed rather than spit in this creative act, for we find that allusion in other fragmentary texts (Hallo and Younger 1:7–10, 12–14, 24–25; Simkins 66).

A significant account is the fragmentary *Theology of Memphis*, which is recorded on an eighth century BCE basalt stone by Pharaoh Shabaka. There is a dispute as to whether this account should be dated to the late eighth century BCE or whether it is older in the form in which we now have it. It portrays the god Ptah as the creator, and it has the rather sophisticated image of creation by the spoken word (if we understand the text correctly). At one point the text says that, "each word of god came about through what was devised by the heart and commanded by the tongue." His heart becomes the god Thoth and his tongue becomes the god Horus. This words "heart" and "tongue" occur repeatedly in the text. When Ptah finishes, the text says, "So Ptah rested after he had made all things and all the words of god" (Pritchard 4-6; Beyerlin 4-5; Hallo and Younger 1:21-23; Westermann 8; Mullen 95). It is interesting to note that in the previous text Atum creates the gods with his spit or semen, but in this text Ptah does it with his spoken word. Not only do we have the apparent reference to creation "by word" as in Genesis 1 but also the allusion to the deity resting after the creative process was finished. It might appear that the biblical author was familiar with Egyptian texts and images as well as the Mesopotamian material against which he was directly reacting. Scholars have observed that this text would not have been known outside of Egypt until the seventh or sixth centuries BCE, placing it at the time when Genesis 1 was generated (Smith 42).

A *Cosmogony of Thebes* can be considered a creation text, although it does not really describe creation. The text comes from the time of Ramses II (1290-1224 BCE). This text reflects upon the nature of Atum as the creator. Atum self-evolved and created the world by speaking, and subsequently remained separate from the world. It makes reference to how he was not created in the same way that he created Shu and Tefnut, by sneezing or ejaculation. This is somewhat close to a concept of creation out of nothing; however, it refers to the deity, not the world (Hallo and Younger 1:24-26).

In a work called the *Hymn to Ptah*, the god Ptah is described as fashioning the world on a potter's wheel. This reminds us of allusions to how the god Khnum fashions pharaoh on a potter's wheel (Hallo and Younger 1:20-21; Simkins 66-67).

Egypt has no story of how common people were crafted by divine hands. The gods in Egypt take time only to make divine pharaohs. We have an image of the ram-headed God Khnum making Pharaoh Amenhotep III on a potter's wheel from around 1400 BCE (Hamilton 157). The narrative about creation of common humanity in the Bible stands in stark contrast to this Egyptian artistic tradition.

Most of the references to creation found in Egyptian texts are brief allusions describing the majesty of gods like Amun, Re, and Ptah. Whereas the Mesopotamian accounts spoke more of world and human origins, the Egyptian accounts spoke of divine origins (Walton 2011:22, 29). We find continuity between some of these Egyptian images and the biblical text, but there is not the same degree of similarity we find between Mesopotamian and biblical texts. Some of the themes in our Egyptian narratives that recur in the biblical text include the following: 1) There is interest in light as an important aspect of the created order, as with day one in Genesis 1. 2) There is chaos before the creative acts begin, and it is usually seen as water or flooded land. 3) There is a concept of a firmament, or at least the god Shu, who is the firmament, and the firmament is often mentioned as the first act of creation. 4) Various texts mention how pharaoh is made in the image of the creator god, such as Khnum, who creates the pharaoh prior to his royal birth. 5) Pharaoh is created out of clay by the deity. However, there ultimately is no single narrative that we can point to in the Egyptian tradition that is parodied by the biblical author, as is the case with the Mesopotamian *Enuma Elish* and *Atrahasis Epic*.

We turn our attention now directly to Genesis 1. We will pay particular attention to those passages in which polytheism and concomitant political values are debunked.

2

Cosmic Creation

GENESIS 1 MAY HAVE been written sometime in the sixth to fifth century BCE, though an oral form may have existed for years before that. Our author would have been familiar with the politics and religious beliefs of the Chaldean Babylonian Empire (605–540 BCE). Under the leadership of Nebuchadnezzar II the Chaldeans destroyed the city of Jerusalem, burned the Temple, and dragged upper and middle class citizens of Jerusalem into exile to Babylon in 586 BCE. Beginning in 539 BCE and for centuries thereafter Judeans returned to Jerusalem in small groups; but most of the Judeans continued to live in and around Babylon where they were surrounded by Babylonian culture and religious values. Though we speak of the Babylonian Exile as lasting from 586 BCE to 539 BCE, I refer to Judeans and biblical authors living in Babylon as still being Babylonian exiles even after 539 BCE. Though Persia ruled Babylon after 540 BCE, Judeans living there were still surrounded predominantly by Babylonians. Biblical authors in the sixth and fifth centuries BCE recall how the Chaldean Babylonians declared that their god, Marduk, was superior to the god of the Judeans, Yahweh, by virtue of their military conquest in 586 BCE. Perhaps many Judeans in exile felt that was the case and slowly faded into the Babylonian populace and disappeared forever. Biblical authors had to attack Babylonian beliefs in order to encourage Judeans to retain their ethnic identity. ("Judeans" refers to the people of ancient Judea. We use the term "Jews" here for the ethnic and religious group after the fall of the second Jerusalem Temple in 70 CE and the development of rabbinic tradition. "Israelites" refers to those of the northern kingdom who were conquered by the Assyrians in 722

BCE [see 2 Kings 17], but it was also adopted by Judeans, and later Jews, as a group identifier; see, for example, Ezek 9:8; Matt 8:10; and the Mishnah.)

When I speak of an author being an exilic author, it means that the author lives in either the sixth or the fifth century BCE. Even if Genesis 1 was written in the fifth century BCE after exiles began to return to Judah, it still responds to Babylonian culture and religious beliefs, even though Judeans were under Persian rule by the fifth century BCE. Persian rulers sponsored a Judean return to Jerusalem to become a bulwark against the Greek merchant presence on the coastline. Persians were also monotheists, like the biblical authors. So Judean authors were more prone to direct their critique against Babylonian beliefs rather than Persian beliefs. Furthermore, under Persian rule Babylonians still lauded the superiority of their own culture, religious beliefs, and customs (Beaulieu 58), so that Judeans still encountered this rhetoric in Babylon well into the Persian era.

Our biblical author declares the superiority of the God of the Judeans over the gods of the Babylonians, for the religious imagery of superiority was used in the political rhetoric of the Chaldean Babylonians (or any Mesopotamian empire) to psychologically subdue conquered subjects. Babylonians lauded the supremacy of their gods to enhance the power of the king who represented those gods. Foreign peoples were forced to work on building projects, recognize the authority of the Babylonian gods, and participate in the religious rituals of the Babylonians, especially the New Year's Festival, which was dedicated to the god Marduk. This festival would continue to be celebrated in Mesopotamia and Babylon until the second century CE. Our biblical author creates a resistance document that assails the religious and political beliefs of the conquerors and lauds the God of the conquered. This is true intellectual guerilla warfare, as the oppressed speak out against oppressors.

The imagery of creation in Genesis 1 may speak to Judeans in exiles in an additional way. In the process of creating the world, God brings forth created order of out chaos and formless waste. Perhaps this said to Judeans that God would bring them out of the chaos of exile to their home in Palestine and Jerusalem once more (Brown 2010:48).

This passage is a great hymn. It uses exalted language and has a beautiful hymnic structure. The first three days are paralleled with the second three days. Powerful symbolism abounds in the passages. Subtle religious polemic occurs, as the biblical author assaults polytheism. People are described in exalted fashion more than in any other ancient text. In seven days the cosmos is created, and the culmination is the Sabbath, a sacred day for Judeans (and later Jews) forever. The number seven or multiples thereof recur in subtle fashion throughout the hymn. God "sees" creation seven times, creation is discerned as "good" seven times, the word "earth" occurs twenty-one times, and the name "God" appears thirty-five times. The text is powerful.

Genesis 1:1–25

(1) In the beginning when God created the heavens and the earth, (2) the earth was a formless void and darkness covered the face of the deep, while a wind from God swept over the face of the waters. (3) Then God said, "Let there be light"; and there was light. (4) And God saw that the light was good; and God separated the light from the darkness. (5) God called the light Day, and the darkness he called Night. And there was evening and there was morning, the first day. (6) And God said, "Let there be a dome in the midst of the waters, and let it separate the waters from the waters." (7) So God made the dome and separated the waters that were under the dome from the waters that were above the dome. And it was so. (8) God called the dome Sky. And there was evening and there was morning, the second day. (9) And God said, "Let the waters under the sky be gathered together into one place, and let the dry land appear." And it was so. (10) God called the dry land Earth, and the waters that were gathered together he called Seas. And God saw that it was good. (11) Then God said, "Let the earth put forth vegetation; plants yielding seed, and fruit trees of every kind on earth that bear fruit with the seed in it." (12) The earth brought forth vegetation: plants yielding seed of every kind, and trees of every kind bearing fruit with the seed in it. And God saw that it was good. (13) And there was evening and there was morning, the third day. (14) And God said, "Let there be lights in the dome of the sky to separate the day from the night; and let them be for signs and for seasons and for days and years, (15) and let them be lights in the dome of the sky to give light upon the earth." And it was so. (16) God made the two great lights—the greater light to rule the day and the lesser light to rule the night—and the stars. (17) God set them in the dome of the sky to give light upon the earth, (18) to rule over the day and over the night, and to separate the light from the darkness. And God saw that it was good. (19) And there was evening and there was morning, the fourth day. (20) And God said, "Let the waters bring forth swarms of living creatures, and let birds fly above the earth across the dome of the sky." (21) God created the great sea monsters and every living creature that moves, of every kind, with which the waters swarm, and every winged bird of every kind. And God saw that it was good. (22) God blessed them, saying, "Be fruitful and multiply and fill the

> *waters in the seas, and let birds multiply on the earth." (23) And there was evening and there was morning, the fifth day. (24) And God said, "Let the earth bring forth living creatures of every kind: cattle and creeping things and wild animals of the earth of every kind." And it was so. (25) God made the wild animals of the earth of every kind, and the cattle of every kind, and everything that creeps upon the ground of every kind. And God saw that it was good.*

"In the beginning"—one of the most famous lines of the biblical text sets the stage for the story of humankind's early moments. God begins to create the heavens and the earth, and this will lead to dramatic events involving God and humanity in an on-going story of human achievement, human failure, human sin, and most importantly, divine response.

The Hebrew word for "beginning" (*bereshith*) lacks the definite article, the letter *heh*, which would be attached to the front of the word. Thus, the Hebrew word means, "beginning" not "the beginning." We should translate "at the beginning of . . ." rather than "in *the* beginning." This was noted already by medieval rabbis like Rashi (1040–1105) and ibn Ezra (1092–1167) (Smith 44; Blenkinsopp 2011:30). The implication is that Genesis 1 is describing the "beginning" of God's creative process, not the absolute "beginning" of the world. It refers to an early period of time in which God began to work, such as those seven days, but it is not a point in time. The meaning is that when God began to create, "in the beginning of God's creative activity," there was a formless void there already. There could have been matter before God started to work. Genesis 1:1 refers to the primordial past, not the very beginning of time. There is creation out of chaos, not creation out of nothing (Smith 44–46; Walton 2011:126–27; Blenkinsopp 2011:30–31).

Furthermore, *bereshith* is an adverb, and it is followed by the verb, "he created" or *bara'* in the Hebrew. "Beginning" modifies the verb "creating." When these two words are combined with the word "God" we have a translation that would read something like this, "At the beginning of God's creating," or more properly in English, "When God first began to create . . ." If we translate it this way, we have a subordinate clause that anticipates that the main clause will be forthcoming. We shall discuss this later.

There is another significant issue connected to these first three words. To begin a sentence with the adverb followed by the verb is not proper Hebrew syntax. The sentence usually should begin with the verb. This sequence is grammatically appropriate in Akkadian, the Mesopotamian language in which the *Enuma Elish* is written. In fact, the two words *Enuma Elish* are an adverbial form that means "when on high." It appears that our biblical author might be deliberately imitating the beginning of the *Enuma Elish* to alert the audience that Genesis 1 is a parody on that Mesopotamian narrative. David Tsumura has carefully analyzed the vocabulary of Genesis 1 to demonstrate that the imagery of divine conflict with chaos is not to be found therein, nor is the language directly related to the vocabulary of *Enuma Elish* (Tsumura 2005:1–140). But he has missed the subtlety of the biblical author who responds to the Mesopotamian accounts by removing the imagery of chaos while flirting with the language of those Mesopotamian accounts. So Tsumura's carefully crafted arguments actually support the thesis of this commentary, for the biblical author has cast out the image of a divine battle with chaos in this narrative.

Victor Hamilton observes further interesting similarities between Genesis 1 and the *Enuma Elish*. 1) Gen 1:1 is an initial statement (a protasis), as are lines 1–2 of the *Enuma Elish*, which requires a concluding statement. 2) Gen 1:2 is a parenthetical clause, as are lines 3–8 of the *Enuma Elish*, which describe the nature of the world before creative activity begins. 3) Gen 1:3 is the statement that continues or concludes the thought of Gen 1:1 (an apodosis), as is line 9 of the *Enuma Elish*, which tells of the beginning of the creative process. 4) The *Enuma Elish*, line 9, says, "Then were the gods formed within these two." Genesis 1:3 says, "Then God said, 'Let there be light!'" (Hamilton 104).

The expression "heavens and the earth" was a stereotypic expression used by the ancients, especially in Mesopotamia, to begin their accounts of creation. A Sumerian text perhaps from the late third millennium BCE entitled, *Gilgamesh, Enkidu, and the Underworld* states the world was created "when the heaven had been separated from the earth, when the earth had come down from heaven" (Beyerlin 74; Walton 2009:36). Another text, a hymn in praise of the mattock, a tool used in farming and building construction, refers to creation by saying, "Enlil hastened to divide the heaven from the earth." In two Sumerian accounts called *Lugalbanda and the Mountain Cave* and *Silver and Copper* the heavens were separated from the earth (Beyerlin 75; Walton 2009:37). The most famous line is the beginning of the Akkadian epic, the *Enuma Elish*. It begins, "When on high the heaven had not been named, Firm ground below had not been called by name" (Pritchard 60–61). In all of these instances the sequence is "heaven" and "earth," as is the wording in Genesis 1. In Hittite literature the god Ubelluri declares that earth and heaven were cut apart with a copper cutting tool by the gods (Walton 2009:36).

We have two fragmentary papyri from Egypt that have portions of various creation accounts on them. The first comes from the Nineteenth Dynasty (1305–1185 BCE). The deity declares, "I am he who made the earth . . . I am he who made the heaven" (Pritchard 13). In another hymn, two successive verses begin with the expression, "when the heaven had not yet come into being, when the earth had not yet come into being" (Beyerlin 6–7). In another hymn to the god Re, we find the statement, "When I come, the day begins . . . There were no heavens and no earth (Matthews and Benjamin 7).

In the Egyptian hymns and the *Enuma Elish*, the language speaks negatively about how all these things had not yet been created. The language in Gen 2:5 follows that pattern when it says that God began creative work before any plant or herb developed.

Even closer to the biblical literature might be the texts from the West-Semitic realm of Syria-Palestine. In the ancient city of Ugarit, in south Syria, there are references to "heaven" and "earth" as two ancient primordial deities (Smith 49). If the biblical author was familiar with these references, then God's creation of "heaven and earth" as non-deities is a monotheistic critique of polytheism.

Hence, the introductory language to creation accounts in both Genesis 1 and Genesis 2 uses the language of the ancient world. This may not have any real theological significance, but it should be an initial alert to us to watch for other language in the biblical accounts that might come from the ancient world, and in those instances we may notice some truly significant variations.

In an interesting Egyptian account titled *The God and His Unknown Name of Power*, we find many of the same created components that were mentioned in Genesis 1. The text reads, "The spell of the divine god, who came into being by himself, who made heaven, earth, water, the breath of life, fire, gods, men, small and large cattle, creeping things, birds, and fishes, the king of men and gods at one time, . . ." We see references to "heaven" and "earth," "birds" and "fishes" of the fifth day, "creeping things" of the sixth day, "cattle" of the sixth day, and the "breath of life" which occurs in Genesis 2 with the creation of the man. We also notice the reference to the "king of men," which is distinctly missing in the Genesis 1 or Genesis 2 account. Instead the biblical text has the creation of a simple man and woman, not royalty. Herein we encounter some of the biblical text's subtle anti-royal imagery.

According to Gen 1:1, God "in the beginning" creates "the heavens and the earth." In Gen 2:4b it states, "In that day that the LORD God made the earth and the heavens." "Earth" is placed before "heavens." The biblical text reverses the terms, but this encourages us to recognize two different creation accounts. These accounts do not contradict, but complement each other: the former speaks of cosmic creation, the latter of human creation. The former uses elevated and liturgical poetry, the latter uses folksy language in prose style. The former places animal creation before that of humans, the latter places the creation of humanity first. The former speaks of the cosmos; the latter speaks of the sacred garden. Yet these differences pale before the similarities. Both accounts speak highly of humanity. In Genesis 1 people are made in the "image" and "likeness" of God and are called upon to "rule" creation, terms that describe the actions of kings. In Genesis 2 humanity tends the "garden," another function of kings, and by naming the animals the human being is graced and permitted to become a co-creator with God. This high calling of humanity is comparable to Ps 8:5, which declares that people are meant to be a little less than God or the angels. Genesis 3 then speaks of how the man and the woman tragically alienated themselves from God. Too often in the Christian tradition we emphasize the alienation and do not focus enough on the initial high calling. Nor have we cared to pay attention to the language that speaks of the equality between the man and the woman.

Christians often view the first line in Gen 1:1 as an absolute description of the total beginning of everything, a "creation out of nothing," or in the famous Latin expression, a *creatio ex nihilo*. We moderns are immediately reminded of the "big bang theory," wherein the universe exploded out of an infinitesimally small neutron ball to become the ever-expanding universe that exists today and is currently fifteen billion years old. It is nice to compare the modern theory of the "big bang" with the imagery in Gen 1:1, for both are equally dramatic. However, the biblical author did not envision reality the same way we do, for the biblical author was inspired to use the language and understanding of that day and age to effectively communicate to those people.

As noted above, many commentators point out that the expression "In the beginning God created the heavens and the earth" is a dependent temporal clause. In fact, both the *Enuma Elish* and *Atrahasis Epic* begin with dependent temporal clauses, so our biblical author was using the literary style of that age. As a dependent temporal clause the expression is best translated, "When God was creating the heavens and the earth at the beginning." The main clause or the primary thought then follows. But commentators and translations disagree on where the main clause begins.

If verse 2 is the main or primary clause, the meaning is as follows, "The earth was a formless void when God began creating." That would imply that formless matter existed at the beginning of the creation process. We are told what existed before God gives order and shape to the world (Simpson 466; Speiser 1964:12; Westermann 37; Sparks 630; Batto 2004:168). However, it might leave the possibility that the formless matter was an initial creative act by God. This is the general sense of the New English Bible, the New American Bible, and the Good News Bible.

Some commentators and translations suggest that verse 3 is the primary clause upon which Gen 1:1 is dependent, so that the understanding is as follows: "When God said, 'Let there be light,' in the beginning of the creation of heaven and earth when there was a formless void." This would clearly imply that there were raw materials that pre-existed before the creative activity, for reference to them occurs as part of the pre-conditional statement to the very first divine command. This reflects the sense of the translation by the Jewish Publication Society and the New Revised Standard Version (Smith 45). Our text above is the New Revised Standard Version, and this may not be too clear to readers, since verse 3 begins as a separate sentence so as not to make the first three verses read in cumbersome fashion in English. But if you read verses 1–3 as one sentence, you will capture the sense of the text.

A third option is to see the first words of Gen 1:1 as a main clause summarizing all of the creation narrative in verses 2–31, and it would render the Hebrew thus: "In the beginning God created heaven and earth." Genesis 1:1 is thus translated as a complete sentence. Since "formless void" follows that heading, one would still assume that chaos was created at the beginning of the creative process. Thus, God first creates chaos and then structures it (Simpson 468).

A fourth option is the traditional Christian and Jewish understanding that views Gen 1:1 as a separate act of creation. This would assume that God creates the raw materials of the cosmos in Gen 1:1, and then God begins to work with the "formless void" or raw materials in the subsequent verses. There could be a break in time between the creation of the raw materials and the first day. Translations that render Gen 1:1 as a single sentence support the understanding of creation out of nothing (Wenham 1987:11).

The King James Version, Revised Standard Version, Jerusalem Bible, New International Version, Revised English Bible, New Jerusalem Bible, and Contemporary English Version all translate Gen 1:1 with one sentence and thus imply either of these last two options. Creation out of nothing was first affirmed by 2 Macc 7:28 and Wis 11:17, texts that arose rather late in the biblical period and reflect Hellenistic Greek influence.

Most translators assume that God began to work with something already there, "the origins of which are of no apparent interest" (Fretheim 342). There could be a good theological reason for that. The common understanding of people in that ancient age was that there was existing matter created out of the very substance of the gods themselves or from the body of an evil, defeated goddess. The creator deity then took this matter and formed it into the existing world that lies before us now. Our biblical author is a monotheist and hence does not wish to refer to the gods from whom the formless mass of the world originated. God simply comes to this matter and begins to shape and create it in a meaningful fashion.

If we read verse 1 and verse 2 together smoothly, we can sense that this is what the author is saying. We read, "When God created the heavens and the earth, the earth was a formless void." God did not create the "formless void" at that point; rather, God encountered the "formless void" and began to shape it. God shaped inert matter. Though that does not sound too dramatic to us, it was a revolutionary statement in its age. The biblical author describes the formless matter as a thing, thus ignoring the gods and dismissing them from the universe.

The text reads that the earth was a "formless void." The old King James Version reads, "without form and void," so as to reflect the use of two Hebrew words: *tohu* and *bohu*. In the past linguists assumed that the first word meant watery chaos and the second word meant desert. These would be the threatening forces that people in Palestine faced: the winter rains that threatened to destroy the fall crops with floods from the Mediterranean Sea in the west and the summer wind or sirocco that threatened to destroy the spring crops from the Syrian and Arabian deserts in the east. Israelites or Judeans would be reminded that God protects them from the recurrent forces of nature threatening to destroy their food. This imagery could imply that Israel, like the world, was created as an ordered cosmos out of the chaos around it. But God can defeat the chaos with but a simple command and thus protect the people.

David Tsumura, however, points out that the first word actually means desert. He appeals to the use of the word "wilderness" in Deut 32:10 and an equivalent word, *thw*, in Syrian Ugaritic texts from 1400 BCE that means "desert." He prefers to translate this expression as "not yet productive earth," rather than chaos (Tsumura 1989:17–19, 2005:1–84; also Smith 57–59). Thus, if both words really mean the same thing, the translation of "formless void" is probably a better translation. More recently John Walton also suggests that the word chaos is too strong a translation, rather *tohu* simply means pre-creation formless matter (Walton 2009:140–44). The word is used in Job 6:18; 12:24; Ps 107:40; Isa 24:10; 45:18–19; Jer 4:23 to mean wastelands; but in Isa 29:11; 34:11; 40:17; 40:23; 41:29; 44:9; 49:4; 59:4 it seems to mean worthless or foolish. So the caveat of Tsumura and Walton has merit, but I still believe that in the context of Genesis 1 the word alludes to chaos because of the other imagery we encounter in Genesis 1. The biblical author hints that the forces of chaos in Mesopotamian literature are simply a mere formless void, but the author wishes us to think of the image of chaos so as to debunk it.

In the Mesopotamian stories the good creator god, be he Enlil, Marduk, or whomever, defeats the god or goddess of chaos in battle, often with the aid of wind and lightning. Once slain, the evil deity could be used to create the world. Our biblical author gives but a casual nod to this understanding by wryly saying, "darkness covered the face of the deep." The word for "deep" (*tehom* in Hebrew) is related to the name of the Mesopotamian goddess of chaos, Tiamat. The word *tehom* occurs thirty-five times in the Bible, and in thirty-four instances the word lacks the Hebrew article *he* prefacing the word. The preface *he* means "the," and we would translate this as "the ocean." But when that particle "the" is missing, one assumes that the word is a name. If *tehom* is a name in those thirty-four instances, it strongly implies that "deep" or "waters" should be personified, and thus related to the Mesopotamian Tiamat. *Tehom* is Ms. Ocean. In Gen 1:1 *tehom* lacks the article and is a name, but it is obvious that "Ms. Ocean" is no longer a goddess; she is just a thing. Our author thereby hints at divine personification, but then rejects the notion. The "wind from God swept over the face of the waters" is but a token reference to the great battle between the creator deity and the chaos goddess spoken of by Mesopotamians (Gunkel 106; Kselman 87; Hamilton 110). Tsumura adamantly proclaims that the word refers merely to water, not a chaos beast, and he is correct (Tsumura 2005:36–76), but he fails to appreciate that the biblical author deliberately debunks the notion of chaos in opposition to God by alluding to it. No fantastic battle is described. There is merely wind blowing over the water. In Ps 104:6–7 the poet declares that the "waters" flee from the "rebuke" of God, which is another poetic way of speaking about this creative process; but the waters are still a thing, not a goddess. The Israelites and the Judeans tell us the story and indicate that those Babylonians are confused and that the ocean is not really a goddess.

The expression "wind from God" may also be translated as "the spirit of God," a term that elsewhere in the Old Testament denotes God in person. The Hebrew word for "wind" or "spirit" is *ruach*. Some commentators believe this may be a being within the divine being (McKeown 26). It may mean "force" or "power," as it seems to imply in Job 26:13. In Ps 104:3 the word means the "wind" that God rides upon. In Dan 7:2 the four winds of the heavens stir up the seas, and this appears to be the same image we have in Gen 1:2, thus implying "wind." Mark Smith suggests that in Gen 1:2 the word means both "wind" and the "breath" that comes from God (Smith 56). Whatever the meaning, it is an expression that refers to God in a most powerful and direct fashion, which makes the wind a creative force from God. Commentators love to express how this implies the personal interaction of

God with the world (Fretheim 343). Eventually in the New Testament the term will refer to the third person of the Trinity, the Holy Spirit. With this single line the biblical author has criticized the Mesopotamian myths, for what the Mesopotamians perceive to have been a great and deciding battle was nothing more than God doing the preparatory work for the real creative activity. God was simply moving across the inert waters or perhaps stirring them like batter being prepared for baking. This is biblical sarcasm at its best; it is a way to refute the existence of the gods and demythologize the story of creation. Perhaps our biblical may have taken a cue from Egyptian accounts where the divine wind functions positively to divide the sky and the earth in the creative process (Walton 2009:146–52). At any rate, the biblical author counters the idea of divine combat with this portrayal of the divine wind.

After having dismissed the significance of the ancient Mesopotamian stories of combat between the good creator god and the evil goddess of water, or theomachies, as we sometimes call them, our author moves to the real story of creation. "Let there be light," says God, and the distinction between light and darkness is established. Our author just took another critical shot at Mesopotamian myths. For in those accounts the evil deity is defeated by being cut in half, and the result is two bodies of water, one of which becomes the oceans surrounding the land and reaching under the continents and the other is the water in the heavens above. For our biblical author that important division of water occurs on the second day, but the first day sees the separation of light and darkness. Perhaps our author has drawn this imagery from Egypt where the interplay of light and darkness in the divine realm is extremely important. The creation of light is often the first creative act in Egyptian accounts (Walton 2009:153–54). The sun god Re brings light and life during the day, but in the night the sun is hidden and the temporary chaos of darkness rules the land. The biblical idea of a clear division between day and night, between light and darkness, certainly reminds us of Egyptian themes. But most likely the biblical author draws upon Egyptian themes to criticize Mesopotamian concepts, because so much of the rest of Genesis 1–11 takes aim at Mesopotamian belief.

The biblical author may be attacking one particular Mesopotamian belief. In the *Enuma Elish* Marduk is the source of light and that light is separate from the sun. We immediately note that light is created on the first day, while the sun is created on the fourth day. Could this biblical sequence be an allusion to the light that comes exclusively from Marduk? If so, it is worth noting that light is a created object in the biblical text, unconnected to the divine (Smith 77–78).

There is yet another possibility. In the later years of the Judean monarchy the sun may have been worshipped as a symbol for God. Related to that there might have been a specific piety that venerated the light that came from the sun. Mark Smith believes that Ezek 8:16 alludes to this piety when it speaks of twenty-five devotees facing the light of the rising sun in the Temple precincts (Smith 84). The author of Genesis 1 may wish to disconnect light from God by describing it as a created object on day one; then the additional disconnection between God and the sun is made on day four. This is a monotheistic critique that attacks not the other gods but the connection of physical images with the one God of the Judeans.

In this first creative act the biblical author uses the word *bara'* as the verb for "create." Commentators wax eloquent over the meaning of this word. They speak of how the word is used only of God and implies effortless and powerful creative ability, something beyond human capacity (Isa 40:26, 28; 42:5; 47:7, 12, 18). It often refers to creating living beings, a divine act, and it describes the emergence of something new or an act of salvation (as in Isaiah 40–55, the oracles of another monotheist). Generally, it appears to be an exilic or post-exilic word (after 586 BCE), and it is found most frequently in Isaiah 40–55 and Genesis 1 (Skinner 15; Richardson 46–47; Vawter 39; Westermann 99; Löning and Zenger 21; Cotter 15; McKeown 20).

On the second day we see the imagery of Mesopotamian mythology come to the fore and receive its due response from the biblical author. In the *Enuma Elish* Marduk fought the seven-headed dragon goddess, Tiamat, who was made of water. (That's quite the image, isn't it? If she breathed fire, why didn't she put herself out?) Marduk split her like a fish into two parts that became the waters above and below the firmament, as well as the land of Mesopotamia. It is this image that our biblical author alludes to in Genesis 1 when it says that God separated the waters. In earlier Mesopotamian myths the hero deity is the Sumerian god Enlil, and in later Assyrian myths the hero is Ninurta. Mesopotamians re-enacted this myth for centuries during the New Year's celebration, the *Akitu* Festival, to insure stability for the cosmos against Tiamat, the chaos that threatened to destroy the created order each year with the flooding waters of the Tigris and Euphrates Rivers. The good god brought order and salvation each year with the defeat of the evil waters. (Israel's story of salvation also involves water, the waters that drowned pharaoh and his soldiers in the story of Exodus 14–15, the "sea crossing"!) The image of Tiamat, the threatening dragon, emerges in the poetry of the Old Testament, for therein she is sometimes called Tannin, Leviathan, and Rahab (or sometimes just the "sea"). Tiamat also influences the image of the ten-headed beast in Daniel 7 and the various beasts in the New Testament book of Revelation. But here in Genesis 1 Tiamat is no beast; she is just a thing, the waters. God did not engage in any combat to create the world; God spoke and things happened. It is a story about creation by word, not creation by combat.

Like the actions of Marduk in *Enuma Elish*, God cuts or "separates" the water and places some under the firmament and some above the firmament. The actions are the same as Marduk's, but the God of the Bible does it with so much ease, because God is the only God. The firmament is described with a Hebrew word that means "hard bowl." The word comes from the verb "to stamp" or "to spread," implying that the firmament may be stretched out like a tent or more likely hammered out like a burnished metal bowl (Simpson 472; Vawter 44; Wenham 1987:20; Hamilton 122). This was the perception of the universe shared by Israelites and by many ancients. The dome above us holds back the waters that can be either gentle rains or fierce storms. There are holes in the firmament that allow the water to fall as rain or to allow light from the divine realm to pass through. For the Mesopotamians that light comes from the gods; for the biblical author it comes from God. Thus ends the second day.

This day was the part of the story wherein the biblical author could deny the existence of the chaos goddess and state that the singular God of Israel had so much power that creation occurred with a spoken word and not a momentous struggle. Elsewhere, however, biblical authors are not shy to praise the God of Israel for winning this momentous struggle against the force of evil symbolized by Tannin, Rahab, Leviathan, or the ocean (Job 26:7–13; 38:1–11; Pss 74:12–17; 89:9–10; 104:6–8; 148:6–7; Prov 8:22–31). But here our author wants to make a special hard, monotheistic statement.

On the third day God separates the land and the water beneath the firmament. Marduk undertakes a similar action in the *Enuma Elish*. The separation of land from water might be seen as a significant action by people who live in swamplands; for there the distinction between muddy soil and water can be vague. This is certainly true in south Mesopotamia, and it was especially true in the early years of settlement in that region from about 6000 BCE onward as people began farming in those marshlands and draining them. Separation of land and water would remind the inhabitants of that region of their own struggle to separate tillable land from watery swamp. It has been suggested if the Garden of Eden is to be located in south Mesopotamia, perhaps the description of the early stages of creation may reflect the imagery of that region too.

I have a poetic vision of how the first days of Genesis 1 might apply to life in south Mesopotamia. When you awaken early in the morning, the light is dim with the first pink light of the sun in the east, which appears before the sun peeks above the horizon. At this time you distinguish only the light in the sky, and the rest of your world is wrapped in darkness—Day One. As the light becomes bright, you distinguish the vast expanse of the sky above and the swampland beneath you—Day Two. With increasing light from the east you distinguish water from solid land, and thus it is safer to walk—Day Three. When the sun finally rises over the horizon, you observe the light of the sun while the light of the moon begins to be overwhelmed—Day Four. The daylight now enables you to see the birds of the air as they fly in the early morning sky and you are equally aware of where the water is that contains the fish and other sea creatures—Day Five. Finally, the farms come to life with the livestock and the people moving around in their little villages—Day Six. We cannot state that Genesis 1 actually has such a scenario in mind, but the accounts that lie behind Genesis 1, which came from Mesopotamia, might have envisioned just such a process—a panorama of life that occurred every morning. One then could poetically suggest that the reverse process occurred every evening—hence, evening and morning. It is a fascinating thought.

The third day also sees the creation of plants and fruit trees. The plants are made "according to their kind" according to the literal reading of the Hebrew. The same expression is used on day six to refer to animals. Some scholars have suggested that "kind" refers to a distinct category of plant or animal, comparable to our notion of species or genus. However, the more logical reading is provided by our translation above, which views the term not as a term of individual distinction, but rather as a comprehensive term that simply means generically "every kind" or "every type" of plant and animal. It is simply a way of saying "all of them," God created every plant and animal, because God is the only deity who exists. It is a monotheistic affirmation (Neville 209–26). Polytheistic thought attributes different plants and animals to the creative activity of various deities.

God does two creative acts on this day. It seems God is behind on the work schedule, and so overtime has to be put in on this day. The third day records two creative acts of God, and day six also records two such creative acts. It appears that at one time the creation account of Genesis 1 described the eight creative acts of God. Then subsequently the week format was introduced into the story, and this forced the eight creative acts of God into six days. This was noticed as early as 1798 by an Old Testament scholar named Ilgen (Gunkel 119–20). In Mesopotamian accounts the divine creator made the world in eight creative acts. This inclines us even more to look to Mesopotamian accounts as the inspiration for our biblical author. (If the eight creative acts of God existed for some period of time as an independent story before another author placed the account into the six-day format, then we need to speak of more than one author for Genesis 1.)

As day four begins, the focus of the creative process is upon animals and the environmental stage of the world. We now notice a structural format in these six days. In the first three days God creates the categories of the world stage, and in each of the three final days God creates those things that specifically fit the first three days (Brown 2010:38–39; Middleton 74–77). Thus, on the first day God creates light and darkness, and on the fourth day God creates the sun and the moon to rule over the times of light (daytime) and darkness (nighttime). On the second day God separates the waters above the firmament from the waters below the firmament, and on the fifth day God creates the birds that fly toward the firmament above and the sea creatures that swim in the waters below the firmament. On the first part of the third day God separates the dry land from the water, and on the first part of the sixth day God creates land animals that live on that specially separated land. On the second half of the third day God creates plants and fruit trees, and on the second half of the sixth day God creates people who will grow and eat the plants. This parallel suggests that people were created to be vegetarians. (God will permit people to eat meat only after Noah comes out of the ark. In Gen 9:34 God says, "and just as I gave you the green plants, I give you everything. Only you shall not eat flesh with its life, that is, its blood.") In reviewing the format of the creative acts of God, the first three days emphasize creation by separation of the world elements, and the final three days describe the creation of those things to be placed in the categories thus separated.

People often wonder how light could be created on the first day, if the sun was not created until the fourth day. Given the structural format described above, it is logical. The sun is created on the fourth day to fit into the universal category of light that was created on the first day. Furthermore, the ancients also realized that the light of the early morning appeared before the sun actually arose, so that it was totally logical to them that there would be light before the actual sun. They believed that light existed in the universe that was separate from the sun, the moon, and the stars. (Ironically our modern science also acknowledges that light energy exists in the universe separate from those things.)

On the fourth day God creates the sun, moon, and the stars. In this part of the narrative we begin to notice a serious polemic against the gods of the foreign kingdoms. The sun and the moon are referred to as the "greater light" and the "lesser light." This is an insult. Our author will not call them the "sun" and the "moon," they are the "big light bulb" and the "little light bulb." Since the sun and the moon are routinely seen by the ancients as deities, the text clearly indicates that these celestial lights are objects, not gods. The stars, too, were associated with various deities by the ancients. Our author ridicules them as mere objects, demoted to created matter, created after the sun and moon, and their only purpose is to provide additional light and indicate the seasons for planting (Fritsch 24; Richardson 52; Vawter 48; Westermann 133; Wenham 1987:21; McKeown 24; Good 14–15). Our biblical author "has cleared the sky of heathen gods and the human mind of false theories regarding the beginning of things" (Fritsch 21). It also interesting to observe that the sequence of creation is sun, moon, and stars, and that is the reverse of the sequence in the *Enuma Elish*, where stars, moon, and sun are created (Hamilton 128).

There may be more to this polemic. The sun and the moon were special gods for the Mesopotamians; they were the gods Shamash (sun), the god of justice, and Sin (moon), the patron deity of the old and revered city of Ur. During the sixth century BCE both of these deities took on special significance for Chaldean Babylonian kings. The sun god was a patron deity of the royal Chaldean kings in general, and the last Chaldean king, Nabonidus, was a devout devotee of Sin. In fact, Nabonidus may have worshipped Sin exclusively, and he built ziggurats in various cities to the glory of Sin. The ziggurats he built may have inspired the Tower of Babel story. The author of Genesis 1 perhaps was a priest who lived in exile in Babylon in the late sixth or fifth centuries BCE, close to the time of Nabonidus. (This would place our priest slightly after the author of the prophetic oracles in Isaiah 40–55, which remind us of Genesis 1). If so, the author of Genesis 1 made a strong religious and political critique of the Chaldean rulers who held Judeans prisoner in exile. Their gods do not exist; only the god of the Judeans is truly God. The author also may be attacking the institution of kingship in general by attacking the deities who patronize kings.

The sun and the moon are important to our author, if indeed our author is a priest, for the sun and moon delineate time. Periods of time are important and sacred for priests; they tell the representatives of God when sacrifices and sacral duties are to be performed. For Mesopotamians the year was the important sacred period of time. Every spring in the New Year Festival Mesopotamians re-enacted the creation of the world, providing sacrifices to Marduk so he might win the battle against Tiamat and chaos once again. Genesis 1 proposes a different cycle of time as important and sacred. God creates the world in six days and rests on the seventh, thus creating the Sabbath as the important unit of sacred time. While the Mesopotamians spoke of the cosmic year, Judeans observed the sacred week. This is why the eight creative acts of God had to be crunched into six days. Genesis 1 is really about the creation of the Sabbath as much as it is a story about the creation of the world.

On day five God creates the birds that fly near and the fish that swim in the two great bodies of water separated on day two. But our biblical author adds, almost as if it were an afterthought, a reference to the "great sea monsters" that swim in the ocean. This is another pot-shot at polytheistic Mesopotamian beliefs. The Hebrew word is *tannin*, which sounds like Tunnan or Tunnanu, a term for the cosmic ocean defeated by the storm god Baal in the fourteenth century BCE north Canaanite or Syrian version of the battle between the gods (Hurowitz 46). In Ps 74:13–14 the *tannin* has multiple heads, which hints at the great dragon or seven-headed beast Tiamat. In other biblical texts *tannin* is portrayed as a threatening cosmic beast, Job 7:12; Isa 27:1; 51:9. But in Genesis 1 *tannin* is simply a benign animal, as in Ps 148:7 where the creature simply praises God. One could imagine Judeans in exile pressured by Babylonians to participate in the New Year Festival, but Genesis 1 bluntly says there is no Tiamat and sea monsters are just created animals. God did not fight rebellious sea monsters; God simply spoke the word and they were created. They are God's great "rubber duckies" in the ocean, obeying divine commands; they are not horrific threats to created order. The mention of such creatures is delayed until day five to further denigrate their significance (Walton 2009:66–67).

Once we have discovered that there is a spoof on the persona of Tiamat on the fifth day, we turn back to earlier passages in Genesis 1 to summarize the allusions to Tiamat. With this reference in verse 21, we are more confident in saying that there are references elsewhere to her. In Gen 1:1 the earth is a "formless void," *tohu* and *bohu* in Hebrew. If *tohu* refers to watery chaos, then *tohu* might be allusion to Tiamat, which declares her to be inanimate. In Gen 1:2, the "face of the deep" and the "face of the waters" are allusions to Tiamat. The Hebrew word for "deep" is *tehom*, which elsewhere in the Old Testament means the great chaotic waters that could oppose God. In Gen 1:2 the *tehom* are a thing, not a goddess of chaos. The Hebrew word for "waters" is *mayim*, which is not as dramatic a word as *tehom*, but nonetheless it can also refer to great cosmic powers that oppose God. Finally, the creative activity of the second day, which splits the waters, indicates that they are inanimate, not a powerful goddess.

What is important about day five is that God gives a command to the creatures of the ocean and to the birds of the air to "be fruitful and multiply." Together with God the denizens of the sky and the oceans create life; the world cooperates with God in the production of life. There is no combat between God and the world, as in Mesopotamia, but a cooperative process of life creation (Brown 2010:40,–41). The oceans have been a teeming source of life for people for centuries, but in the modern age we are killing the oceans. Created by God to be givers of life, the oceans are experiencing "dead zones" devoid of fish life, as in the Gulf of Mexico, created by the pollution of people. In addition, the Gulf of Mexico, south of where I live, has fought a battle with millions of barrels of oil spewed forth from a drilling well explosion in 2010. Can we not hear the oceans cry aloud to us as we strangle them with our pollution? The skies of America once were filled with beautiful birds, until we shot too many species into extinction. The skies of our land are now filled with pollution, bringing us the life giving oxygen for our bodies that now is tinged with carcinogens. Can we not hear the skies cry aloud to us also? Created by God to bring forth life, the oceans and the skies have been assaulted by humanity and their life giving capacity has been choked. As Genesis 1 tells the story, there is no conflict between God and nature, and likewise there should be no conflict between humanity and nature (Brown 1999:45). But we seem to have declared war on nature anyway.

On the sixth day God makes the animals in the first half of the day, and then in the latter half of the day God creates humanity. The text declares that God makes both the wild animals and the cattle or domesticated farm animals (the word for cattle can refer to all livestock in general). The biblical text devotes special attention to the creation of humanity. At this point the biblical author really moves to a very different theological discussion, one that highlights the equality of people and the value of people in the created order. Our story thus switches from being one about the creation of the cosmos and the affirmation of monotheism to a narrative that theologizes about the value and dignity of people.

Up to this point our author has made a powerful statement about how the universe was created by one God, the deity worshipped by Israelites and Judeans. Genesis 1 takes special effort to attack the existence of the other gods and affirm monotheism (Gunkel 103–33). Mesopotamian stories highlight the conflict between the creator god and the evil goddess of water; the world was created by divine combat. German scholars years ago created a term, *Chaoskampf*, "the battle against chaos," to describe the actions of the good creator god in Mesopotamian accounts. By way of contrast, the biblical author declares that there is no battle, but rather God creates by merely speaking the divine "Word." The God of the Judeans is so powerful that simply the spoken word suffices to create the world. The forces of chaos are impotent before the majestic God; no resistance is possible. Creation by Word replaces Creation by Combat.

The text also declares that the world is "good," and this refrain occurs every day. The world does not fight or oppose God; it is "good." The world works together with God in producing life once creation is accomplished. The sun and the moon are commissioned by God to govern the rhythm of life in the world; the sky, the oceans, and the earth are commissioned by

God to "multiply" and to teem with life (Brown 1999:38–41). God has created the world to be a smooth-running operation; now a creature must be created to work with this "good" natural order.

3

Creation of Humanity

Genesis 1:26—2:4a

(26) Then God said, "Let us make humankind in our image, according to our likeness; and let them have dominion over the fish of the sea, and over the birds of the air, and over the cattle, and over all the wild animals of the earth, and over every creeping thing that creeps upon the earth." (27) So God created humankind in his image, in the image of God he created them; male and female he created them. (28) God blessed them, and God said to them, "Be fruitful and multiply, and fill the earth and subdue it; and have dominion over the fish of the sea and over the birds of the air and over every living thing that moves upon the earth." (29) God said, "See, I have given you every plant yielding seed that is upon the face of all the earth, and every tree with seed in its fruit; you shall have them for food. (30) And to every beast of the earth, and to every bird of the air, and to everything that creeps on the earth, everything that has the breath of life, I have given every green plant for food." And it was so. (31) God saw everything that he had made, and indeed, it was very good. And there was evening and there was morning, the sixth day.

(2:1) Thus the heavens and the earth were finished, and all their multitude. (2) And on the seventh day God finished the work that he had done, and he rested on the seventh day from all the work that he had done. (3) So God blessed the seventh day and hallowed it, because on it God rested from all the work that he had done in creation.

Creation of Humanity

THE CREATION OF PEOPLE begins a separate story after the account of cosmic creation. The cosmic creation narrative declares that there is one God, and the creation of humanity narrative declares that people have dignity and equality; and both were radical statements in the first millennium BCE. Scholars sometimes have concluded that originally these were two separate stories crafted brilliantly by the Priestly Editors of Genesis 1 (Westermann 143).

God begins the task by speaking in the first person plural, "Let us make humanity." This expression has puzzled commentators for years. It will occur again in Genesis 3 and 11. Years ago it was assumed that this account had a polytheistic origin, either in Israel or another culture, such as Mesopotamia. It seemed logical that God was talking to the other deities, so the phrase was viewed as a holdover from the polytheistic origins of an old story (Gunkel 96; Skinner 31; Simpson 483). But if the biblical author were monotheistic, such old remnants of blatant polytheism should have been removed.

Some commentators have suggested that this is the "plural of majesty" (Westermann 144–45). Since the word for God is *ĕlohim*, and that word is plural, even though we translate it into English in the singular; nevertheless, in normal Hebrew grammar and syntax there are situations in which the corresponding verb forms which accompany *ĕlohim* will be in the plural. Thus, we translate literally the Hebrew that says, "and God said, 'Let us,'" but the real meaning is that God actually says, "Let me." We read a plural, but the meaning is singular, for the word *ĕlohim* is a plural with singular meaning. However, there are many instances in the Hebrew Bible where the word *ĕlohim* is used in a singular sense and no such translation is used. Most commentators think that this "plural of majesty" interpretation is a little over-rationalized. However, it has been pointed out that in the ancient Near East one can find examples of where a single deity (such as in the wisdom literary work, *Babylonian Theodicy*) or the Egyptian pharaoh (in the Amarna letters of the fourteenth century BCE) is addressed in the plural (van der Toorn 360). Such examples are too rare, I believe, to explain its presence here in Genesis 1.

A related concept is that the expression is a "deliberative" or "cohortative" use of the verb; that is, God is dramatically saying "let me do this," or "I am surely going to do this," and the plural is used to stress the intensity of the divine statement (Vawter 54; Cotter 17). That seems more logical, even if it is a modern rationalization.

It is worth observing that the people who build the tower of Babel in Genesis 11 use the verb form "let us" to describe their activity. The biblical author may place the verb form on their lips to contrast their arrogance in human construction with the truly creative power of God in creating humanity. Thus, Genesis 1 and 11 would be bookends for the entire Primeval History—from the creation of the world by God to the failed creation of a tower by people. I suspect that this might really be the best interpretation of the expression—it is a literary and theological device of the biblical author.

Most contemporary commentators, however, suspect that indeed God is talking to someone else, and these are the "heavenly host," God's divine assistants (Skinner 31; Batto 2004:173; Middleton 55–58). I would certainly not exclude this as an implied meaning of the biblical author in Genesis 1. Who are the "heavenly host," these beings so often mentioned throughout the rest of the Hebrew Bible? Later Jews and Christians would say that they are the angels. But who were the angels originally? The concept of angels develops for Judeans in the post-exilic period. In pre-exilic texts the "heavenly host" are the lesser deities who serve God. Originally they were once gods in the minds of many ancient Israelites. But as monotheism slowly arose, they were denigrated to divine assistants to God and their names were deliberately suppressed, so that they became a "nameless lump" of beings subordinate to the one God. Eventually they evolved into angels, but originally they were the other gods (Baal, El, Asherah, Anat, Astarte, the sun, the moon, Mot, etc.). Thus, we somewhat come back to the first position that God is indeed addressing other gods. But there is a difference. The "heavenly host" are actually beings subordinated to God in a conscious process by which monotheism is affirmed over polytheism. This is not simply a holdover from a polytheistic past that the author forgot to omit; it is a conscious and aggressive subordination of the other gods. Notice how God speaks to these beings in Gen 1:26, but we hear no more from them. That alone tells us of their subordinate and insignificant status compared to the one God. In later years, when monotheism has triumphed, then it is safe to give these "angels" names. The triumph of monotheism can be dramatic. (We see grumpy old deities putting on choir robes, wings, and halos, arguing over who gets a trumpet or a harp, as they assume their newer lower status.)

There is finally the old traditional suggestion that the plural discourse reflects the members of the Trinity speaking to each other. This is the imposition of later Christian theology into the text. The original biblical author did not have a concept of Trinity, nor was he or she mindlessly inspired by God to insert some divine truth into the text that would make no sense to people until six hundred years later with the emergence of Christianity.

God decides to make people in the "image" of God and in the "likeness" of God. The word "image" or *selem* in the Hebrew is found thirty-one times in the Old Testament. In eighteen instances it means an idol: Num 33:52; 2 Kgs 11:18; 2 Chron 23:17; Ezek 7:20; 16:17; Amos 5:20; and

Daniel 3 contains twelve instances used in reference to the statue built by Nebuchadnezzar [vv. 1 (twice), 2, 3 (twice), 5, 7, 10, 12, 14, 15, 18]. In five instances it merely means a statue; all of these are in Daniel 2 [vv. 31 (twice), 32, 34, 35]. In three instances it means a physical representation of a person (Ezek 23:14) or an object (1 Sam 6:5, 11). Once it means "shadow" (Ps 73:20). Finally, four usages are found in the Primeval History (Gen 1:26, 27; 5:3; 9:6) where it refers to the "image of God."

One would be tempted to conclude that "image" means physical likeness or portrayal, most notably a statue. That would imply human beings were physically made to appear like God. One notes that Seth is said to be in the "image" of Adam in Gen 5:3, and that might imply similar appearance. The man in the garden on the mountain in Ezek 28:12 is said to be beautiful; perhaps the "image could allude to beauty likened to that of God (Blenkinsopp 2011:26). Elsewhere, God is said to have bodily parts (Simpson 484; Fritsch 25–26). This would seem to justify a human representation of God in art. But since Israelites condemned that, we should be reluctant to jump to the conclusion of similar physical appearance.

Some commentators like the idea that "image" might imply "shadow" in the Genesis passages. "Shadow" is related to the concept of "image," in that an "image" casts a "shadow" and the shadow itself can be understood as the image. This might not be as offensive as the notion of an actual statue. Sculpted statues also cast images. If people are the "shadow" of God, perhaps this does not imply that humans are physically like God in appearance. This would avoid the impulse to portray God in human form. This line of argument also views the word "likeness," or *demuth*, as a similitude, something which resembles something else without necessarily being identical to it (Vawter 55; Wenham 1987:29).

Another theory suggests that people were designed to be the "statues" of God "to the world," that is, the physical representatives of God in the world (without actually looking like God). Their representation of God to the world would be a symbolic way of speaking of their rule over the world. One commentator suggests that if the "image" obliquely alludes to images in the ancient world, perhaps the biblical author implies that men and women are the true image or presence of God in the world, not idol statues. This would be a critique of idols similar to that of the prophet Second Isaiah (Isaiah 40–55) who was contemporary with the author of Genesis 1 and likewise came from a priestly background (Middleton 207–9; Blenkinsopp 2011:28). I suspect this is true, but there is more to the image than that.

Perhaps the use of the term "image" those four times in Genesis is unique, especially since it is the fuller expression, "image of God," and not just the word "image" by itself. Since half of our references to "image" come from the book of Daniel (seventeen), and only ten references occur outside the book of Daniel and Genesis, we must admit that we really do not have many texts by which to make a conclusive argument for the meaning of the word.

If we turn to the parallel word "likeness," or *demuth* in the Hebrew, we encounter an even more elusive word. It occurs twenty-five times in the Old Testament, primarily in the book of Ezekiel. Once it is used to indicate the incomparable nature of God (Isa 40:13), and sixteen times it is used by Ezekiel to describe some awesome visionary image that appears to be "like" something [Ezek 1:5 (twice), 10, 13, 16, 22, 26 (three times), 28; 8:2; 10:1, 10, 21, 22; 23:15]. Elsewhere the word is found in 2 Kgs 16:10; Isa 13:4; Ps 58:4; Dan 10:16; and 2 Chron 4:3. Obviously the word "likeness" lacks concreteness in reference to appearance. It means that something looks "like" something else, especially in a transcendent vision. Three instances of "likeness" are in Gen 1:26; 5:1, 3, where it is paired with "image." Pairing "likeness" with "image" gives us the feeling that "image" in these Genesis passages is a vague and ethereal representation. Thus, we are less inclined to say that the "image of God" implies that people physically look like God. This opens up the possibility of a great theological debate.

Christians have declared that being in the "image" and "likeness" of God makes humanity special and different from the animal realm. Some have equated these terms with human reason, saying that animals have only instinct. This is not a good argument, since now zoologists speak of animal intelligence and maintain it is simply less complex than human intelligence. The first century CE Jewish philosopher Philo (*On the Creation* 69–71) and the fifth century CE Christian theologian Augustine (*Confessions* 13,22) both opined the image alluded to human freedom. Other Christians have declared that the categories of Genesis 1 refer to the presence of the human soul in people, which animals are said to lack. This is probably not a good argument either, since the Old Testament authors do not clearly speak of the human soul as a separable and well defined entity; rather, the word for soul, *nephesh*, might be better understood to refer to the life force within people or their personal identity. Other various proposals have been propounded: these terms refer to special spiritual qualities, our ability to rule the world, our personhood in its entirety, the blessed nature of human existence, or our ability to dialogue with God (Westermann 149–55; Fretheim 345; Blenkinsopp 2011:26–28).

I believe our biblical author uses the terms "likeness" and "image" because they have been taken from the political language of that day and age, and their use betokens a very profound message that the biblical author seeks to communicate. The terms, or the equivalent cognates, are used in

Egypt, Mesopotamia, and Syria to describe pharaohs and kings. The term is frequently used in the late second millennium BCE in Egypt and occasionally in the first millennium BCE for Assyrian and Babylonian kings in regard to their royal function as representatives of the gods on earth (Middleton 108–36). In an old Aramaic inscription from Tell Fakhariyah in Syria both terms are used together to describe King Adad-iti (Wenham 1987:29; Middleton 47, 106–7). The Mesopotamian words sound very much like their Hebrew counterparts. The Hebrew words for "image" and "likeness" are *selem* and *demuth*, and the cognate words in Mesopotamia are *salmu* and *demuti*.

Mesopotamian inscriptions declared that kings were in the "image" and "likeness" of the gods because they exemplified the rule of the gods in the world, they ruled on behalf of the gods, and they had the authority of gods in relationship to their people. In both Egypt and Mesopotamia a particular king was said to be in the "image" of a particular deity. The statues that portrayed these kings were called "images" because they were the visible presence of the kings and stood for their authority, and kings were the symbolic presence of the deity to the people they ruled (Bird 140–41; Middleton 104–8). Kings were seen as being semi-divine or at least the "stewards of the gods" according to the religious political rhetoric of Mesopotamian texts. The Mesopotamian word *salmu* literally means "shadow," which is interchangeable with "image."

An image casts a shadow to provide shade or protection. As the god provides protection for the king with the divine shadow, so the king casts a shadow of protection over the people (Machinist 174–75). Since the word can functionally mean a physical "statue," usually a three-dimensional statue set up in a temple, use of the word implied vividly that kings had a god-like nature in their rule over people (Middleton 45). Kings in the ancient Near East, who were in the "image" of the gods, ruled on behalf of the gods by taming the chaotic wilderness so that it might produce crops. They protected people against flooding, assured that irrigation systems worked, and did whatever necessary to prevent destruction to civilization. In a similar fashion, the images of the gods in the temples of the ancient Near East were the presence of those divine beings among people (Bird 141–44; Löning and Zenger 108–11). Comparing kings to the very statues of the gods in the temples gave tremendous authority and power to such rulers.

The immediate implication is that the biblical man and woman are like gods to the world; they represent God in the world. They have been delegated authority by God to administer the world. They are not only in the "image" of God by virtue of their rule, but they also provide the "image" or "shade" of protection over the world (Machinist 174–75). In the heat of the Middle East the idea of "shade" is a wonderful image of care and comfort.

Our biblical author may be using these terms, in effect, to say that the man and the woman are kings "to the world." This obviously ridicules the ideology of kingship articulated among the foreign kingdoms, which declares that mere mortals are to be subservient to their rulers who are in the divine image of the god. In the Bible all mere mortals are kings and queens by the grace of God. But it also implies that the man and the woman have the responsibility to wisely steward the world. Royal imagery has been democratized; all men and women are kings and queens (Bird 144; Wenham 1987:30–31; Fretheim 345; Löning and Zenger 108; Middleton 204–231; McKeown 279–80; Walton 2009:176–77). The image means that, "dignity and responsibility belong to all human beings without distinction" (Löning and Zenger 108). Only in one literary work of Egyptian wisdom literature in *The Instruction of Merikare* do we find the expression that people are in the "image" of a god, but no connection is made to a ruling function as is the case in the biblical text (Middleton 99–100; Walton 2009:84, 196); otherwise the expression or the concept is not found. Note especially that both the man and the woman are in the divine image and rule the world. Including the woman along with the man in these statements is unique in the ancient world and a radical statement (Lind 124; Walton 2009:176–77).

That this particular interpretation has merit is reinforced by another expression. God says, "Let them have dominion" over the animals of the world. The verb used for dominion is *radah*. Elsewhere the word has the following meanings: 1) Joel 4:13, "to tread the wine press," 2) Lev 26:17; Num 24:19, "to subdue," 3) Lev 25:43, 46; 1 Kgs 5:4; Ps 72:8; 110:2; Isa 14:6; 41:2; Ezek 34:4, "to rule over," or "the dominion of kings." Since the verb is used to describe the role of kings in their rule, this makes the entire passage appear to characterize the man and the woman as king and queen. The expressions "image" and "likeness" are paired once, the word for "image" is used two more times, and the verb for "dominion" is used twice, in order to emphasize this message. Combining the verb "to rule" with "image of God" really presses home the imagery.

A related word is used in verse 8: *kabas*, which means "subdue." Though it can have a negative meaning such as "rape" in Esth 7:8 or the conquest of one's enemies in Num 32:22 and Josh 18:1, here it means a harmonious supremacy, especially when used in conjunction with the royal word *radah*. To "subdue" the earth means to harness its creative and life-giving power; the overall tone of Genesis 1 gives this irenic tone to the interpretation of the word (Brown 1999:46).

Humanity is in the "image of God" because humans "rule" over creation wisely. They are not to use the earth for their own personal needs; they are to steward and to provide for the animals and the plants. It is not the domination of exploitation, an arbitrary rule. Royal imagery is used to emphasize how humanity is to rule the world on God's behalf. They are the agents of God in the world who nurture the world in a care-giving fashion (Vawter 58–59; Westermann 152; Kselman 87; Wenham 1987:30–38; Fretheim 346; Löning and Zenger 107–108; P. Miller 2003:325–27; Middleton 70–74). People are not naturally superior to the animals; the "image" is a gift from God that elevates them (McKeown 282). This is an insight that we badly need today, as we pillage and pollute our modern world, and as global warming threatens to seriously endanger human life. It appears that nature is fighting back at our horrible mismanagement. Nature is rebelling against its "kings" who have become tyrants. We badly need to hear the message "nature" is trying to tell us. Richard Middleton provides the best exposition of how the image of God makes humanity not only equal with each other but also very responsible for the stewardship of the world around us (Middleton passim).

These royal descriptions should be understood as a "commission" or a "responsibility," not just an inherent characteristic or privilege of our nature. We are not to struggle with the earth but to struggle for the earth so that it is a life-giving place (Löning and Zenger 111; P. Miller 2003:325; Cotter 18). If we recall that the Bible forbids making images of God, then the fact that the man and the woman are in the image of God is rather significant, for they alone are the only acceptable symbols of the divine presence in the world. That tells us that we have the responsibility to act wisely, like God, in the world (van Wolde 1997:25–31; Brodie 136).

Royal imagery also is used, in part, to declare that because the man and the woman rule over creation, they do not live in fear of the forces of nature, as so many people did in the ancient world, who offered up sacrifices to avert the destructive natural phenomena they observed all around them. People are free and no longer part of a deterministic process in the cosmos that affects their actions; they are free from fate. In the New Testament Col 1:13–16 speaks of how we are free from the cosmic powers; the biblical rhetoric continues into that later age. But if we are free, we must act responsibly with our freedom and no longer blame the forces around us for what we might do.

As an additional observation, it should be noted that kings in Mesopotamia were responsible for creating gardens and planting exotic and beautiful trees in them. This was a metaphor for mastering the chaos of the desert and the wilderness. In parallel fashion the man and the woman are placed in a garden in Genesis 2–3. Perhaps the garden story is just a coincidence, or perhaps it is meant to reinforce the imagery of kingship associated with the man and the woman.

There are other reasons why the biblical author connects the man and the woman with royal imagery. In Mesopotamian creation stories, people are created from dirt and the blood of an evil, defeated god. Hence, they are slaves of the gods and serve the gods on the divine manor of this world by offering up sacrifice. This was the reason for their creation. Of course, their sacrifices and offerings went to the priests. Mesopotamian temples garnered enough wealth to become the banks and lending institutions of that age. This Mesopotamian mythology is a political-economic legitimation of the power of priests in Mesopotamia (Middleton 167–71). Our biblical author undercuts that propaganda by declaring that the man and the woman, as well as their descendants, are royalty and not slaves of the gods; they are free agents, made in the image of God. Thus people, who are not slaves of the gods, are not slaves of the priests either. If the man and the woman are both royalty, then all men and women are equal with each other as they stand equally before the one God (Middleton 204–31). To declare all people equal with each other and to undercut the authority of kings is radical democratic thought for the first millennium BCE.

If all people are equal, what does that say about the relationship of men and women? Christian preachers have often pontificated that these texts in Genesis underscore the authority of men over women. But this narrative overturns such arguments. According to Gen 1:27, God made "man" or "Adam," and God made "them" into male (*zakar*) and female (*neqebah*). The word for "man" or "Adam" is singular, but the plural reference back to the word "man" considers the word to be plural, so that both the male and the female are part of "man" or "Adam," and both are said to be in the "image" and "likeness" of God and "rule" over creation. In other words, both sexes are created at the same time. The man is not created before the woman. (We shall see that the same is true in Genesis 2, where the "man" does not have "male" identity until after the "woman" is created.) In both Genesis 1 and Genesis 2 the "male" and "female" identities are created at the same time. Genesis 1:27 presses home this notion, when it twice says, "God created them."

Hence, it is best to translate "man" as "humankind," as the New Revised Standard Version does, so as to indicate that both sexes are implied under the word "man." Many Christians unfortunately have difficulty accepting this clear wording of the text. I recall hearing a local Baton Rouge preacher, Jimmy Swaggert, who was televised years ago, quote the text as saying, "God made man, He gave him to rule over the woman." No one in the pews pulled out their pew Bibles to correct Jimmy; they just kept smiling for the cameras. (You would think that pew Bibles would keep fundamentalist preachers from misquoting the text! Oh, the cameras are there to prevent that! Everyone concentrates on smiling.)

The word for "man" or "humankind" is 'adam, a word that too often is understood to mean masculine man, but really means "generic man," both the male and the female. When the woman receives the name Eve in Gen 3:20, the word Adam becomes a real name. But even after that event, the word Adam is used twice by God in Gen 3:22, 24 to refer to both the male and the female.

Thus, man and the woman are equal with each other, being made in the "image" and "likeness" of God and being commissioned to "rule" the world. The American Constitution and the Declaration of Independence speak of the equality of all men in the eighteenth century, so the biblical text anticipates this American political development by over two thousand years (Brodie 130). The founding fathers did not include women in their understanding; however, the biblical text did. The text proclaims an incredibly high view of women for that age. It would not be until the late twentieth century that Christian society would catch up to the values of the biblical text, and some parts of the Christian world have still not caught up to the biblical text. Ellen van Wolde believes that church fathers in the first three centuries understood this notion of equality, but once Christianity became the religion of the Roman empire, the focus on the first three chapters of Genesis was to stress the patriarchal superiority of the man over the woman (van Wolde 1997:67-68).

There is an interesting comparison here with the Greek author Hesiod, who lived in the late seventh and early sixth century BCE. In his writings, *Theogony* 588–607, and *Works and Days* 51–114, women are portrayed negatively. In *Theogony* 585, 593, 599, 603, the woman is described as beautiful but at the same time evil, lazy, and not supportive of men in poverty. In Gen 1:31 she is described as "good," for such is the description given by God to all creation. Hesiod also spoke of marriage negatively, but Gen 2:23-24 portrays marriage positively. It is possible that the biblical author may have been familiar with the abrasive views of Hesiod, especially if the biblical author wrote in the late sixth century BCE (Brodie 141).

The man and the woman are told to be "fruitful" and "multiply." They are to "fill" the earth. This is an imperative that the Israelites and the later Judeans could understand. They always had a shortage of population, unlike the Mesopotamians, whose land was overpopulated. They needed to have as many children as possible for a healthy society, so this command and many commands elsewhere mandated that every married couple should have many children. The command to be fruitful and reproduce, given repeatedly throughout the Old Testament was a necessary commandment given to ancient Israel and especially Judeans who were living in exile in sixth century BCE Babylon. They suffered from too little population; their existence was threatened. Moral imperatives to have children were needed for them, and laws in the book of Leviticus forbade any form of sexuality that did not potentially produce children.

The imperative was given so that the Israelites and later Judeans would have a healthy society with a sufficient population to be a strong, vibrant community. If their need was a shortage of people, are their moral guidelines to be used by us? We live in an overpopulated world and we strain the capacity of our planet to support us. If we were to hear the imperative today, the message might say to us not to keeping multiplying like rabbits, but to restrain the number of children that we have, in order that we have a healthy society. Sometimes in order to keep the spirit of a biblical command today we have to do something other than what the literal words of the biblical text say. The laws in the Bible mandated more children, but if the laws were articulated in the modern era, they might mandate restraint in the generation of children lest we overpopulate and impoverish life on our planet. People are to fill the earth, but when the earth is full, then the human conscience must appropriately reinterpret this command (Fretheim 346).

It is worth noting that God tells the people that "every plant yielding seed" and "every tree with seed in its fruit" has been given to them for food, verse 29. In the next verse, God states that "every green plant" has been given as food to animals. Food from the plants is to be shared by both people and animals in a symbiotic relationship. This bespeaks a harmony that should exist between humans and the animal realm. We should share the resources of our world with the animal kingdom (Brown 1999:45). How often do we destroy the land wherein significant numbers of animals live, driving some of them into extinction. How often do we kill animals simply because they are on our land? In the south farmers killed coyotes to protect their sheep and chicken, but since the coyote was the predator for armadillos, we now are overpopulated with armadillos. We too often disturb the natural harmony life in our world when we should be living symbiotically with it. How many animals exist only in our zoos because they are soon to vanish in the wild?

Nowhere does it say in Genesis 1 that people can eat the animals. People are vegetarians at this point in their existence. The permission to eat meat is given only to Noah and subsequent generations of people. The man and the woman are designed to be vegetarians and live harmoniously with the animal realm. This seems to be overlooked by many preachers. I am always fascinated how preachers do not see this in the text when they squeeze the text in so many other ways.

In the final few verses our text speaks of how God rests on the seventh day. The image of a deity resting is found in ancient texts; the image of a deity resting after seven days is sometimes found in connection with the deity resting in a temple. Furthermore, in Mesopotamia the image of the deity resting in the temple seems to imply that the deity is now ruling from the temple or ruling the universe subsequent to his creation of the cosmos. Such an image would describe Marduk's rest in Esagila Temple after establishing order in the cosmos in the *Enuma Elish*. God does not rest in a temple in this text, but rather rests in a more general and universal sense. The text may imply that the entire world is God's temple, and now God rules the universe as the only deity in the cosmos (Walton 2009:76; 2011:181). Furthermore, if people are made in the image of God and thus are God to the world, the rest of God may imply that people henceforth are to administer the affairs of the world by ruling over it. People are now responsible for the creation of culture, not the gods, because they are God in the world (Middleton 212-19).

John Walton creatively suggests that it is significant that Sabbath rest comes on the seventh day of the creative process. The seven days may refer to a period of time connected to the inauguration of a new temple in the ancient world (as well as Jerusalem). Genesis 1 may describe the creation of the cosmos and also the creation of the Jerusalem Temple. The bronze sea represents the chaotic ocean, the temple columns are the pillars of the earth, the menorah is the sun and the moon, and the holy of holies is the abode of God. Perhaps Genesis 1 was crafted as a liturgy for the dedication of the Temple in Jerusalem in 516 BCE or perhaps it was read at an annual celebration by the priests in the post-exilic era (Walton 2009:78-102; so also Middleton 77-88). William Brown's perception of the text may reinforce this observation. He believes the seven days parallel the shape of the Temple; the first six days symbolize the Temple forecourt and holy area, while the seventh day betokens the holy of holies where God "rests" symbolically above the Ark of the Covenant (Brown 2010:40-41).

This divine rest will have implications for humans; it is not for the sake of God's need to rest physically. The word for rest is *shabbat*, which means to "cease or desist," and it provides the meaning for the word Sabbath. The text says that God rested, and then "blessed" and "hallowed" the seventh day, and this is language that occurs in the version of the Ten Commandments found in Exodus 20 (though the term is not found in the version of the Ten Commandments in Deuteronomy 5). That the Sabbath is a holy day of worship and a day of rest stands in contrast to Mesopotamian beliefs. In the *Enuma Elish*, the warrior Marduk rests after the battle with Tiamat and as he now rules the cosmos. The other gods rest with Marduk because human beings have been created to do their work. Thus, both Genesis 1 and the *Enuma Elish* end with the theme of rest. In the *Atrahasis Epic* humans are created so that the *Igigi*, the lesser gods, may rest, and later the "rest" of Enlil is disturbed by noisy and rebellious people. Divine rest is a symbol of the gods, especially powerful gods who win battles. It seems to be the nature of the gods that they rest and eat food sacrificed to them. The God of the Bible does not really require rest or lunch; instead God makes a statement to creation about the necessity of rest for people. In the *Enuma Elish* and *Atrahasis Epic* people work so that the gods may rest, but in Genesis 1 God creates the Sabbath so that people may rest. Once again the biblical author has debunked Mesopotamian beliefs dramatically (Westermann 167–68; Hamilton 143; Batto 1992:78, 2004:172; Hurowitz 48; McKeown 14; Smith 106). Marduk is role-played by the king in the New Year's festival; consequently the blessing of rest is not for the common people, it is the prerogative of gods and kings. But in the Bible God rests so that people, peasants, slaves, the weak, and the poor may rest, folk who otherwise would get no rest in the cultures outside of Israel. There is liberation theology here in a short and subtle message.

The nature of the Sabbath also stands in distinction to Mesopotamian concepts. The concept of the week was not common in Mesopotamia; the month was a unit of time, established by the cycle of the moon. During the month the Mesopotamians viewed certain days as *limnu* or "unlucky" days—the seventh, fourteenth, nineteenth, twenty-first and twenty-eighth days were days on which to avoid doing important things (Skinner 38). The numeration is close enough to the Jewish week for us to make a comparison. But the Jewish concept is distinct from the Mesopotamian view, for the seventh day is blessed by God and a gift for humanity, not a day of misfortune. The Sabbath is a self-contained unit of time, not certain days within the month. Historically the Sabbath was a new moon festival in Israel (Amos 8:5; Hos 2:13; Isa 1:13; 2 Kgs 4:22–24) and probably a day of rest, but during the sixth century BCE Babylonian Exile it took on fuller religious meaning as a holy day. Genesis 1 provides a great measure of this transformation of the Sabbath rest into a holy day as a reaction against Mesopotamian customs and beliefs to help set Judeans apart from their Mesopotamian neighbors.

The Sabbath language is one of the more important parts of the creation account for the biblical author. Our author crunched eight creative acts of God into six days so as to lead up the Sabbath Rest. The entire creation of the world is told to explain and under-gird the institution of the Sabbath. The Sabbath cycle is the most sacred unit of time, standing in opposition to

Mesopotamian beliefs that envisioned the cosmic year as the most sacred unit of the time.

If this passage comes from the late sixth century or fifth century BCE, when the Judeans languished in the Babylonian Exile, then the affirmation of the Sabbath in opposition to the sacred cosmic year is quite significant. Judeans hear the biblical author saying that they should pay no attention to the Babylonian year and the New Year's ceremonies that extol the power of Marduk. Instead, the more important ceremony is the celebration of Sabbath. Keep the Sabbath and you please God and maintain cosmic order far better than offering up sacrifices to Marduk.

Since the Sabbath was instituted at the beginning of human existence, it is incumbent upon all people to observe it. By keeping the Sabbath, as well as observing kosher food laws, Judeans perform the service of obedience owed by all people. Judeans alone comply with cosmic order (Simpson 498). Their obedience deters the deserved wrath of God upon all humanity. Judeans may be persecuted for their faith and practice, but they ironically save those who persecute them and thus become "suffering servants" for others by their obedience to these universal laws and by suffering for their beliefs. This image is articulated in Isaiah 53 by the contemporary sixth century BCE prophet, Second Isaiah, who probably is also a priest. Of course, Christians would apply this imagery to Jesus, the ultimate "suffering servant."

Furthermore, one could point out that Sabbath is a weekly rest for all people, even the weak and lowly, since everyone is descended from that original man and woman. It gives everyone, including slaves, a rest from their labor. It is a day of justice in that it provides something for even the servants and the slaves. It does not involve great sacrifices, the powerful cultic activity of priestly guilds. Rather, it is a ceremony observed best in the homes of all who worship the true God. Sabbath is democratic institution; it levels society. Sabbath observation is kept by all people, who are now equal with each other, as they worship their God.

When we look at Gen 1:1–2:4a, we see a beautiful hymn to the creation of our majestic universe. Yet, we sense that there is a more powerful message: the affirmation of one God and a denial of the many gods worshipped by the other peoples. But I feel that the most important part of this text is Gen 1:26–2:4a. Here the biblical author speaks of the creation of people and the institution of the Sabbath. Maybe the dramatic talk of the six days of cosmic creation is really meant to set up the more important talk about the creation of men and women. Men and women are created to be "lords" of creation and all men and women are equal with each other. I cannot help but think that this revolutionary statement about human dignity and equality is really the high point of the author's message. In the *Enuma Elish* people were created as an afterthought to assist the gods, but in Genesis 1 people are the pinnacle of creation (Hamilton 140). This was a revolutionary message for that ancient age. Even more astounding is the fact that it comes from a community of people living in exile, living in the land of the Babylonians, whose religion and political beliefs are attacked by this biblical passage. Our biblical author, living in a foreign land, courageously envisions an understanding of humanity which defies his oppressors and sets in motion a vision that has been, in part, the inspiration for the emergence of our modern world's beliefs. If one were to speak of divine inspiration of sacred texts, can this message of Genesis 1 not be the most dramatic testimony to such a charism?

Much of Genesis 1 reacts against the polytheistic creation narratives of the ancient Near East, especially the *Enuma Elish*. A summary of the relationship between the biblical text and those other texts would be most appropriate. The Priestly Editors who created Genesis 1 created an imitation of the *Enuma Elish* that could be called a "parody," or an "echo," or a "mimotext" (Sparks 627). Kenton Sparks speaks of how Genesis 1 is an "elite imitation" of that Mesopotamian text; that is, it reuses the *Enuma Elish* and generates an intellectually "elevated" text (Sparks 627).

Similarities between Genesis 1 and Mesopotamian accounts, particularly *Enuma Elish*, include the following: 1) The narratives begin with a temporal, dependent clause. 2) Reference is made to how things were either barren or chaotic. 3) Allusions are made to the cosmic ocean, a watery chaos, either *tehom* in Genesis or Tiamat in *Enuma Elish*. 4) The separation or splitting of water occurs. 5) Separation of water creates the heavenly and earthly realms. 6) Heavenly bodies are created after the separation of the waters. 7) Light exists before the creation of the heavenly bodies. 8) Categories of space and time are created by heavenly bodies. 9) The sequences of how things were created are fairly similar. 10) Separate created works specifically mentioned include the firmament, earth, luminaries, plants, animals, and people (Skinner 45–47; Sparks 630–31).

Differences between the biblical text and the ancient Near Eastern accounts are significant and include the following: 1) There is only one God, not many, so there is no conflict between the gods (Marduk and Tiamat) or disagreement between the gods on the course of action (Anu, Ea, and Marduk). 2) There is no cosmogony of the gods. 3) The ocean waters are impersonal, not divine. 4) The Mesopotamian firmament is made of out Tiamat's body, but God makes the heavens out of beaten metal. 5) Heavenly bodies are not divine, but rather serve simply to order the seasons. 6) People are created by one God directly, not by a mother goddess. 7) People are not created as an afterthought, but appear to be created by God for their special purpose in the created order. 8) All people have the image of God, not just kings. 9) People are not slaves of the gods, serving the gods through sacrifice, but they are free and made in the divine image and rule the world wisely. 10) If in Mesopotamia people are created to sacrifice to the gods, then the cult existed from the beginning of time, but this is not so in Genesis 1. 11) All people are equal, there is no legitimation of the special privileges of kings and priests. 12) Whereas Marduk is king of the gods, people are kings over creation. 13) With the final section of the biblical narrative focused upon the nobility of human creation, one would have to say the biblical story is about both God and humanity, while the *Enuma Elish* is simply about the glory of the god Marduk (Westermann 12; Wenham 1987:9; Cotter 10; Sparks 631; Hurowitz 43). We concur with Kenton Sparks who characterizes Genesis 1 ultimately as a "mimesis" of the *Enuma Elish* designed to primarily critique the ideology of the ruling empire from the perspective of the conquered Judeans (Sparks 625–48).

4

Creation of the Adam

Genesis 2:4b–7

(4b) In the day that the LORD God made the earth and the heavens, (5) when no plant of the field was yet in the earth and no herb of the field had yet sprung up—for the LORD God had not caused it to rain upon the earth, and there was no one to till the ground; (6) but a stream would rise from the earth, and water the whole face of the ground—(7) then the LORD God formed man from the dust of the ground, and breathed into his nostrils the breath of life; and the man became a living being.

IN MANY CREATION ACCOUNTS a temporal clause begins the narrative and is followed by a main clause. Verses 2–6 effectively constitute a temporal clause that describes what conditions were like before the creative process began, and verse 7 is actually the main clause that describes what the first creative act of God was. Both the *Enuma Elish* and the *Sumerian Flood Story* begin this way (Wallace 67). As mentioned above, though debate exists concerning the form of the first few verses in Genesis 1, most concur that it also begins with a temporal clause. Most creation accounts begin with reference to "heaven" and "earth," and Gen 2:4, like Gen 1:1, is no exception. Genesis 2:4 reverses the expression found in Gen 1:1 to say "earth and heavens," perhaps because this chapter views the process from the perspective of earth rather than the cosmos as in Gen 1:1 (McKeown 30).

The text undertakes a negative way of describing the world, as is the case again in other creation narratives of the ancient world. Genesis 2:5 declares there was a time before pastures and crops. This reminds us of the *Enuma Elish* which speaks of how there was a time before the heavens and the earth were named, and before such things existed as reed huts, marshlands, and other gods. The Genesis account is also comparable to a Sumerian account about the creation of Lahar and Ashan, the cattle and grain deities, wherein a temporal clause is followed by a long list of negative attributes (Wallace 68–69). Even Prov 8:22–31 alludes to the time when Wisdom was created and how this occurred before the beginning of the earth when there were no ocean depths, springs, mountains, hills, earth, fields, or "bits of soil" (human beings). The specific reference to the lack of rain and the plants of the field in verse 5 reminds us of agricultural dry farming in Palestine, as opposed to the irrigation farming of Mesopotamia (Hiebert 36; Brown 1999:136).

This chapter begins in strikingly different fashion than Genesis 1. One gets the impression that there was a pre-existing formless dry wasteland, and God began to create using that desert wasteland. This contrasts with Genesis 1, which implies that the unformed world was made of watery chaos or both watery and desert chaos. Genesis 1 might remind Judeans of how their ancestors passed through the sea in Exodus 14–15 and the dry wasteland of Genesis 2 might recall how the ancestors subsequently traveled through the wilderness in Exodus 16–17 (Kselman 88). It also might remind them of the growing seasons in Palestine: winter rains from the Mediterranean blew hard upon the land while the hot desert wind of summer parched the land.

In both Genesis 1 and 2 there was prior material, so creation by God was not truly "creation out of nothing." However, some commentators believe that the creation of the heavens and the earth had been accomplished and this dry wasteland was part of that initial creation. The point at which the story begins in Genesis 2 is the stage wherein God brings life to the wasteland. So they can still affirm the concept of "creation out of nothing" in Genesis 1.

The expression "for the LORD God had not caused it to rain upon the earth" has led commentators to speculate what this means. Older translations (King James Version, Revised Standard Version, New American Standard, New World Translation, Jewish Publication Society) translated the word "stream" in verse 6 as "mist," providing the image of a green house effect. Scientific creationists who deny the evolutionary theory suggest that before Noah's flood there was no rain, but rather a mist created a greenhouse effect, or that this biblical reference recalls how the ante-diluvian world functioned with the great water canopy overhead. This canopy collapsed to cause the flood that drowned the dinosaurs, and only after the worldwide flood could true rain occur. Scientific creationists take portions of the biblical text extremely literally, but blatantly ignore and contradict other texts. More sensible commentators usually suggest that this reference simply refers to a mist and say nothing more.

Recent translations indicate that the word should be "stream" (New Revised Standard Version, New American Bible, Contemporary English Version, New International Version). Through the years other translations have rendered the word as "flood" (New English Bible and Jerusalem Bible), or "spring" (Rheims-Douay, An American Translation), or "moisture" (Revised English Bible), or simply "water" (Today's English Version, Living Bible).

The Hebrew word is *ed*. Some believe this word is related to the Sumerian word *a.dé.a*, the Akkadian word *'edu*, the Akkadian word *id*, or the north Mesopotamian Eblaite *I-du*, all which mean underground source of water or a significant flow of high water that comes up to the surface (Speiser 1964:19; Vawter 66; Tsumura 1994:40, 2005:85–106; McCarter 446). The water would flow over the whole land and water it, and people are required to harness this water for crop irrigation (Tsumura 2005:107–27). The idea of water rising from the ground is a Mesopotamian image, for they believed that streams and brooks, personified by Enki, were connected to the deep water below the earth, personified by Apsu. Some scholars, however, still prefer "mist" or "dew" on the basis of Egyptian and Arabic parallels (Hasel and Hasel 321–40). It is possible that the biblical word may refer to the Mesopotamian deity, Id, yet another god of the great waters of the deep (like Apsu). If this is so, then this is comparable to how Genesis 1 speaks of *tehom*. The author of Genesis 2 debunks any deity of chaotic waters by reducing that deity to a flow of water up from below the earth (LaCocque 2006:59).

This "stream" may be the river in verse 10. The image of a stream or river from whence all the rivers of the world flow is a common image in the ancient world. It is a stream rooted in the great cosmic oceans believed by the ancients to lie below the earth and surface around all the great landmasses to become the oceans. Some authors translate the word as "flood" for that reason, and view it in supernatural terms, for it is ultimately the source of all water on the earth in mysterious fashion (Skinner 55; Fritsch 28; Simpson 493). It has been suggested these waters are destructive and must be mastered by God, thus hinting at the theme of how God defeats chaotic waters (Benjamin 40). Sometimes this stream flows out of the cosmic mountain and divides to become the great rivers of the world. Ezekiel poetically describes how a stream will flow out of Jerusalem in the final age and wind its course to the Dead Sea, whereupon it will cause the Dead Sea to come to life. However, to apply this image to Genesis 2 is speculative, since we are not sure how to translate the word.

Closer to the imagery of Genesis 2 is the oracle of the lofty cedar in Ezek 31:2–18, which is a political metaphor for the fallen empire of Assyria. In verse 9 Ezekiel explicitly says this tree was in Eden, which should make us ready to draw a comparison with Genesis 2. In verse 4 of his oracle, Ezekiel says that the "waters nourished it, the deep made it grow tall," and in verse 7 we read that "its roots went down to abundant water," implying that the lofty cedar tree's roots went down to the cosmic depths or the great oceans below the earth. The image is of a supernatural tree with its branches up in the divine dwelling and its roots located in the cosmic depths below the earth. This sounds like the source of the waters that come to the surface in Genesis 2. Furthermore, in Canaanite texts the high god El, the creator god, dwells at the source of the two cosmic rivers which nourish the earth, and in Mesopotamian texts the land of Dilmun is the place where the "sweet waters" of the gods Apsu and Enki arise to nourish the world (Wallace 75). Thus, there is the belief that cosmic waters below the earth rise to provide the world with the fresh water it needs for rivers and other bodies of water. The author of Genesis 2 may be alluding to this imagery when we hear of the water that rises up out of the ground.

The text then reads, "the LORD God formed man from the dust of the ground, and breathed into his nostrils the breath of life; and the man became a living being." These are incredibly significant words in the text, especially when we are familiar with the ancient Near Eastern accounts concerning the formation of humanity.

God does the creative work; the task is not assigned to a fertility goddess, such as Nintu-Mami. This, of course, reflects the monotheism of the author, who excludes all deities save God from the creation narrative. That is a difficult task; for even among the Israelites there was a tendency to admit the existence of other gods, even revere them at times. The deity most difficult for people to surrender was the fertility goddess, regardless of her name—Asherah, Anat, Astarte, names all popular in Palestine, Isis in Egypt, Inanna or Ishtar in Mesopotamia and elsewhere, and a host of female deities throughout the ancient world. Even as Christianity arose, it found itself competing against the piety of many female deities of fertility and compassion, Aphrodite among the Greeks, Atargatis in Syria, Cybele and Diana in Asia Minor, and Isis throughout the Roman Empire. People crave a feminine principle in the heavens to balance out the masculine deities. The female deities offer fertility and compassion; the masculine deities are often gods of the state, legal justice, and war. This is why Christians ultimately had to raise the importance of Mary as a saint in the heavens beginning in the fourth century CE, and why she absorbed so many of the attributes of these other goddesses. (Isis was the "Queen of Heaven" and romanticized as the mother of baby Horus—the "pieta"). In the light of this historic urge of humanity to have a divine feminine principle in the heavens, it was a bold act on the part of the biblical author of Genesis 2 to attempt an exclusion of the female goddess from the creation of humanity. Instead, God sits down in the mud alone and makes humanity.

Many cultures believe that the gods created people out of the earth, and this is especially true in the ancient Near East. The most obvious comparison is with the *Atrahasis Epic* where the goddess, the Belet-ili, pinches off fourteen pieces of clay to begin the process of creating people. In the *Gilgamesh Epic* Arura made Enkidu from clay; in Egypt the god Khnum made pharaoh out of clay as the goddess Hathor held an Anhk to the form he created; and in Greece Prometheus made people from soil and water by adding a spark stolen from the gods (Westermann 204–205; Wenham 1987:59–60).

This portrayal of God makes him seem quite close and personal with the created order. Verse 7 states that God "formed" man out of the dust of the ground. The word for "formed," *yazar*, has the nuance of shaping and forming with the hands, as a potter would shape the clay for his pot. It is a physical verb implying the direct presence of the deity in the process. One can almost envision God squatting in the mud to make this new creature, the "dirt-person." One author believes the text seems to portray God like a child playing in the mud, creating a new special creature to place in the newly created garden (Stratton 32). This intimate relationship of God with the world and human beings, in particular, will continue in the biblical author's portrayal of God throughout the ensuing narratives in Genesis, Exodus, and Numbers. It is a symbolic way of speaking; we should not assume that the author has a primitive view of God. During the nineteenth and early twentieth century biblical commentators often stated that these texts, which portrayed God anthropomorphically (having human form) and anthropopathically (having human emotions), reflected the primitive mindset of those ancient Israelites. Over the years, as we learned much about the thought of ancient Near Easterners, we sensed that the Israelites, like their neighbors, did not think in the primitive fashion we imputed to them. Sometimes we attribute primitive thought to the ancients or even to village folk in our Third World today, because we wish to separate ourselves from them and thereby elevate ourselves in our own conceit. We now recognize that the ancients, including the Israelites, thought in ways that were both sophisticated and primitive at times, and we now admit that we also think in ways that are still both sophisticated and primitive. They are closer to us in their thought processes than we would like to admit. When the biblical authors described God as having human body parts or human emotions, they did not do so in a literal fashion, although some folks in that age might have thought this to be the case. Rather, this language was a symbolic way of describing a close, personal relationship between God and the creation (LaCocque 2006:53–56).

To be sure, there were statues of gods throughout the ancient world, and perhaps, as some have suggested, there were statues created by Israelites that portrayed God in human form (sometimes as a bull or a snake). But the author of our text opposed such statuary, and the condemnation of that statuary is found throughout the Hebrew Bible. Biblical authors did not envision God as literally having a human form. They were "aniconic," that is, they rejected icons or images of God, perhaps even portraying God with empty space, such as an empty throne or the empty space above the Ark of the Covenant, for God was said to be enthroned invisibly above the Ark. When God is described as creating humanity out of the ground by hand, the apparent physical attributes that should be attributed to God are not literal but symbolic, and they are part of a testimony found throughout many texts that speak of the personal and intimate relationship between God and the entire created order.

Another significant departure from the ancient Near Eastern accounts, found in Genesis 2, concerns the enlivening force that makes the clay human into a living creature. In Mesopotamian accounts clay is mixed with blood or body parts of a defeated evil god. The Mesopotamian story implies that people are alive because of their creation out of a divine force that is essentially evil, and this is why people are slaves of the gods (LaCocque 49). People are portrayed rather negatively in Mesopotamian accounts.

Because people are slaves of the gods, they serve the gods by offering gifts and sacrifices to the priests of the various temples in the land, especially to the priests of Babylon according to the *Enuma Elish*. Mesopotamian myths justify a political and economic system in which the priests are one of the powerful classes in society. Some priestly Mesopotamian texts characterize all the land of the city and the surrounding countryside as a "Temple Manor," which belongs to the gods (Middleton 167–71). If all land belongs to the gods, then who administers that land in the name of the gods? The priests, of course! We do sense from other texts, however, that apparently many Mesopotamian businessmen and traders did not take this religious propaganda too seriously, for a great amount of private property and trade existed outside the control of the temples.

The priests attempted to create a "Temple State" economic system in which wealth was controlled by them. In many historical periods the great amount of wealth donated to the Mesopotamian temples by sacrifice and temple tax gave tremendous power to the priests. Temples became great banks, loaning money to businessmen and traders. The temples also foreclosed on many loans to peasants, garnering their land and turning the peasant farmers and sometimes middle-class people into debt slaves. The temples had so much economic clout, that at times the temples owned half of the lands around the city and almost up to half of the people as debt slaves. Sometimes the king would intervene and declare a "remission" of debts and debt slaves, and such decrees were called *mishnarum* and *anduraru* in early second millennium BCE Amorite Babylon. Kings had the military clout to force the temples to cough up the tremendous wealth they had garnered. If kings were weak, however, for too many years, the economy of the Mesopotamia cities would stagnate under such priestly monopoly, and this often paved the way for economic collapse in the Mesopotamian cities and permitted the invasion of the land by foreigners. Often in our history books we describe the fall of Mesopotamia cities to foreign invasion as though the Mesopotamians could not resist the overwhelming military might of the invaders, when in reality, the invasion occurred because of economic weakness. If you destroy your middle class, as the Mesopotamians often did, your kingdom will collapse. Those are words well worth heeding today as the gap between our middle class and the rich continues to grow.

All of this is important to realize when we observe the biblical text's account of how people are created. God does not make people out of the blood or body parts of an evil, defeated god. People are quickened or enlivened by the breath of a good deity. People are brought to life by having part of the good deity placed into them. If all people are enlivened by the breath of God, then all people share in the divine essence, not just the kings (LaCocque 2006:62–63). People are equal with each other, not trapped in a class pecking order; people are good, not bad; and people are free, not slaves. People have a different relationship with this deity than is envisioned elsewhere in the ancient world. If people are good and they are not slaves, it also means they are free, and if they are free, they are morally responsible for their actions before this deity. This is revolutionary! The biblical author has created a vision of humanity that characterizes them as free, moral agents. In so doing, the biblical author undercuts royal power, the authority and prerogatives of the king and the priests, as well as the assumptions by which states in that age functioned politically and economically. Move over Karl Marx, the biblical author stated a revolutionary message over two millennia before you! What first appears to us as a primitive image, God making a clay image and blowing into it, really is a powerful metaphor with political, social, and economic implications. But in order for us to sense the symbolic biblical metaphors, we need to know about the myths and religious-political beliefs of the ancient world.

What is that breath of God? Most commentators have made the connection with the "spirit" of God, an enlivening and inspiring force that sometimes seizes people and enables them to do great things. It has also been connected to the life force within people that makes them living beings, and when that spirit leaves, they die. One interesting suggestion is that the breath is simply moisture. All potters create using clay with water. In *Atrahasis Epic* Mami uses blood and clay, in the *Gilgamesh Epic* the goddess Aruru uses saliva, and in the biblical story God uses condensation from breathing (Benjamin 41). At any rate, the breath of God is the force that makes the Adam truly alive and human.

An interesting comparison has been drawn up by Conrad L'Heureux between this biblical account and the narrative about Enkidu in the Gilgamesh Epic. Enkidu is the hero created by the gods to distract Gilgamesh from oppressing the people of Uruk. Enkidu remains a wild man until a temple prostitute makes love to him and thereby brings him from the animal state into a civilized human state. After heroic adventures with Gilgamesh, Enkidu offends the gods and is put to death. His death sends Gilgamesh forth on the quest for immortality until he finds Utnapishtim and learns the story of the flood. L'Heureux sees the following parallels between Enkidu and Adam: 1) Both are created from clay. 2) Both are naked and without shame initially. 3) Both are initiated into civilized life by a woman. 4) Both become "wise." The prostitute and the snake promise wisdom and the ability to be like the gods to their listeners. 5) Both "fall" into civilized life. 6) Both face pain and death. 7) The prostitute clothes Enkidu as God makes leather clothing for the man and the woman. If the biblical author of Genesis 2 is familiar with the tale of Enkidu, the author clearly has suppressed the sexual imagery (L'Heureux 64). The story of Enkidu and the prostitute may be an ancient way of talking about the transition from an early human state to civilized life, represented by the temple prostitute, who really personifies the temple, the pinnacle of organized life in the city.

When we look closely at the words of the biblical text we may observe the clever style of the author. Verse 7 states that God formed the "man," *ha'adam*, out of the "dust," *'aphar*, of the "ground," *ha'adam*, so that the word for "man" or "human being" is the same as the word for "ground." This implies that people come from the earth and are one with the earth. "From dust we come and to dust we shall return," and the biblical author alludes to this old saying by the subtle play on words. The *'aphar* might best be translated as "clay" or "lumps of clay" (Speiser 1964:16; Vawter 66–67), which then connects it closely to *'adam*, which means earth or dirt. Elsewhere humanity is called *'aphar*, and sometimes the *'aphar* is the dust or dirt to which people return when they die (Job 10:9; 17:16; Ps 22:30; Eccl 12:7).

The "Adam" is made from "dust" and comes from the "earth," from whence "he" gets the name "Adam." We are born and when we die, we shall be placed into the earth and become one with the earth once more. For the Israelites, as for many ancient people, the grave was a symbol for the afterlife, which was believed to be in the earth. At death we return to our origin; the "adam" becomes "adam" once more. "Adam" means person, humanity in general, dirt, red clay, and the world. It has a wide range of meaning, and many word plays are possible. "Adam" is related to the name "Edom," the name of a country that bordered Israel to the southeast. "Edom" means red clay or red man, since the red dirt of that country gave a red hue to the skin of the farmers and herders who worked there. For modern people, our connection with the earth, established by that common word "adam," can be seen as a strong affirmation of our oneness with the earth, the world, the environment, and our responsibility to that earth. It reminds us that we must steward wisely our farmlands and avoid turning them wholesale into the sprawling landscape of urban and suburban centers.

It should be noted that the name "Adam" does not necessarily carry the gender nuance of a male "man," rather it means more "mankind" in the generic sense, "humanity." "Adam" is a "poetic personification" of human beings in general (Richardson 59). It is like the German word "Mann," which we translate as "one" or "person" in English. For the Germans have the word "Mensch" to denote someone who is male. "Adam" means person, and theoretically it could mean someone either male or female. The person created by God is called "Adam" until the female is created, and only after that point is the first creature referred to as a "male" by use of the Hebrew word for "male" person (*'ish*). The word for "male" is first used in verse 23, and it is used from that point onward to refer to the male Adam. Hence, this implies that the creature made by God becomes masculine only once the female is created (Bal 112–18). Thus, contrary to what popularly gets said, man was not created before the woman, only "man" in the generic sense existed at this prior time. For that reason it is best to call this being the person, the human, or simply the "adam," and perhaps we might want to call him the "dirt person," since he was made out of earth.

Now that "Dirt-Person" has been created, God must decide what to do with him. Thus, God next will create a garden in which to place this new creature.

5

The Garden

GOD MAKES A GARDEN

Genesis 2:8–9

(8) And the LORD God planted a garden in Eden, in the east; and there he put the man whom he had formed. (9) Out of the ground the LORD God made to grow every tree that is pleasant to the sight and good for food, the tree of life also in the midst of the garden, and the tree of the knowledge of good and evil.

IN MESOPOTAMIA IT WAS believed that the gods created humanity on the island of Dilmun, modern-day Bahrain, an island from whence all fresh water springs flowed. It was the island to which the flood heroes were taken by the gods after being made divine. For a period of time Mesopotamians sought to be buried on the island of Dilmun, if it were financially feasible for them to do so. Thus, some scholars are tempted to place Eden in south Mesopotamia near Dilmun. The Mesopotamian myth *Enki and the World Manor* tells of how Enki creates the world on the island of Dilmun in eight creative acts. Comparing this account with the biblical story we discern that both Mesopotamian Dilmun and Eden were in the east, both had fresh water associated with them, and Enki ate fruit as did the man and the woman. Dilmun is made fertile by Enki as he brings a flowing river through it, just as it appears that God makes the garden fertile by using this flowing stream mentioned in Gen 2:6. Other mythic themes connected with Enki tell how the goddess Nintu or Ninti came from his rib, and one of her titles is the "lady of life" (Tsumura 1994:37). Such interesting parallels make us think the biblical author may have known this story and used its details.

Kings in Mesopotamia often created gardens near their palaces wherein they cultivated fruit trees especially along with many other trees and plants. Rulers of empires took plants from various parts of the empire and put them in their gardens as a statement of how they ruled over such great regions. Assyrian kings of the eighth and seventh centuries BCE took plants from around their empire (Stordalen 94–98) and spread plants from Assyria to distant parts of the empire as a symbolic statement about the unity of their empire. In Babylon the temples often had gardens around them. Some Sumerian texts from the third millennium BCE speak about an herb of life that grows in the temple gardens. In Eridu there supposedly was a *kishkanu* tree that spread its branches over the oceans beneath the world (Jacobs-Hornig 34–35). Our knowledge is limited so we speculate that these gardens may have been viewed as divine gardens and perhaps it was believed that as the king or the priests walked in these gardens, they might encounter the gods.

In Syria the folk at Ugarit around 1400 BCE spoke of the high god El living "at the sources of the two rivers, in the midst of the two oceans," and this has led some scholars to believe that this might be a symbolic location for the West-Semitic paradise (and that it might be on a mountain also) (Wenham 1987:52).

We often think Eden is the name of the garden, but it is interesting to observe that the garden is in Eden according to verse 8. Thus, for some Eden is the name of the garden and for others Eden indicates the location. There also is disagreement over the meaning of the name Eden. Some believe it comes from the Sumerian and Akkadian word *edinu*, which means steppe or plain (Skinner 62; Speiser 1964:16; Hamilton 161; Lim 121; Bertman 313; Tsumura 2005:107–27). Others believe the word means "luxury," "delight," "pleasure," or "paradise." The name of the garden in Hebrew is *'edhen* and the word for delight is *'eden*. An Aramaic text from the ninth century BCE from Tell Fakhariyeh in Syria uses the word *m'dn* with this meaning (Richardson 62; Wallace 84; G. Anderson 1988:195–99; Batto 1992:49). Still others suggest the word comes from the Ugaritic (north Phoenician or Syrian) word *'dn*, which means "place of abundant water supply" (Tsumura 1994:40–41). It is probably not by coincidence that the name of the garden sounds like the name for the stream mentioned in Gen 2:6. The garden of Eden is mentioned in Ezek 28:13; 31:9, 16, 18; 36:35; Isa 51:3; Joel 2:3, references which come from the sixth century BCE or later, indicating to us the lateness of this tradition.

We have tried to guess the location of the garden implied by the biblical author. The expression "in the east" suggests the garden is in Mesopotamia, which is east of Palestine. Some assume Eden refers to an area north of Babylon, where the Euphrates and the Tigris come within 20 miles of each other, located near the modern city of Tikrit in Iraq (famous for being the home of Saddam Hussein). A location on an isthmus south of Babylon has been suggested. Many favor a site in south Mesopotamia, a garden south of the ancient Sumerian city of Eridu, where the various rivers come together in a large marshy area north of the Persian Gulf (Skinner 62–63). But elsewhere in the Bible Eden can be characterized as a "garden of God" existing on the "mountain of God" (Ezek 28:13; 31:9), which has no real literal location. In that case, one could place it anywhere, and the position of the four rivers would indicate the garden's location.

God causes beautiful trees with delicious fruit to grow out of the ground. The graciousness of God is demonstrated in God's efforts to create a food source for the Adam. Perhaps this was a subtle testimony that God should be praised for the fruit trees that later Israelites grew on their land. God is the life-giving source behind the pleasant trees that bear fruit for humanity. Were we to have such a deep awareness of the awesome nature of trees today, perhaps we would not deforest so much of our world.

Two special trees are mentioned: the tree of life in the middle of the garden, and the tree of the knowledge of good and evil. At first it seems vague as to whether the tree of the knowledge of good and evil was in the center of the garden along with the tree of life, but in Gen 3:3 it is implied that the tree of the knowledge of good and evil was also in the middle of the garden. Thus, an interesting question is raised as readers look closely at the biblical text. The tree of life is mentioned only in Gen 2:9 and 3:22. The tree of the knowledge of good and evil is called such only in Gen 2:9 and 2:17. In other passages the tree of the knowledge of good and evil is called the tree in the midst of the garden (Gen 3:3), or even more simply, it is designated merely as "the tree" (twice in Gen 3:6, once each in Gen 3:11, 3:12, and 3:17). Because of those six references in Genesis 3 to "the tree" without characterizing it as the tree of the knowledge of good and evil, some commentators wonder whether the original story in Genesis 2–3 had only one tree, the tree of the knowledge of good and evil. That only two references speak of the tree of life suggests this motif might have been added to the original story. This might explain why the woman is unaware of the tree of life, for she speaks of the tree of knowledge as simply the "tree in the midst of the garden," not knowing that the tree of life is likewise "in the midst of the garden" (Gen 3:3).

Karl Budde first suggested the one-tree theory in 1883 (Mettinger 7) and many commentators have assumed this in subsequent years. The tree of knowledge was given its longer title once the motif of the tree of life was added to the story, prior to that it simply was called "the tree" or "the tree in the midst of the garden" (Gunkel 16, 25; Westermann 212, 223; Wallace 101–41; Dohmen 208–14; Carr 1993:583). It is difficult to say whether that is the best explanation or whether the biblical author simply referred to the tree of the knowledge of good and evil as "the tree" to make the plot flow more smoothly in Genesis 3. Some scholars believe that even though there may have been an account with only one tree, our present account makes good sense with two trees (Steck 27; Barr 57–61; Stordalen 187–97; Schmidt 32). A creative interpretation suggests that the man and the woman only knew about the tree of knowledge, the tree of life was unknown to them and would be given to them as a reward for obedience if they did not eat from the tree of knowledge. This would explain why the woman spoke of the tree of knowledge as though it were the only tree in the "midst of the garden" (Mettinger 36–41). An even more creative suggestion is that the tree of knowledge and the tree of life are the same tree; one side of the tree is life, and the other is knowledge. One tree brings life; the other brings death. The tree is a dialectic, just as people are both good and evil, and as many other ambiguities and poetic tensions are found in Genesis 2–3 (LaCocque 2006:21, 70).

What are these trees? There are vague allusions in Mesopotamian texts to a tree of life in the southern city of Eridu, but there are no references to a tree of the knowledge of good and evil. There are Mesopotamian allusions to how the good king waters the sacred tree, and there seem to be artistic portrayals of such an action. Sometimes kings were metaphored as a great tree that gave shade to people, perhaps a "tree of life." The Sumerian king Shulgi of Ur III around 2000 BCE was described as a cedar tree who gave shade to his people. Around 1800 BCE Ishme-Dagan of the Amorite Babylonian city of Isin declared that he was a "shoot of cedar" and the "tallest of trees which are the flesh of the gods." The royal scepter may be envisioned symbolically as a branch from such a tree. The mythical ruler, Enmeduranki, who ruled before the flood in Mesopotamia, received a scepter of cedar from the gods by which to impart life to subjects who kneeled before him. The Assyrian ruler Esarhaddon (680 BCE) was poetically described as placing the "plant of life" under the noses of his people, who were symbolically dead. Thus, the tree of life may be connected to ideas of divine kingship and immortality in Mesopotamia, if the king is gardener for the tree or even equated with the tree (Stratton 33; Stordalen 29; Fitzpatrick 158–60). But overall, the allusions and pictures are too vague for us to make any serious comparisons with the biblical text. There is also the story of the *huluppu*-tree, perhaps a willow, planted by the goddess Inanna in the city of Uruk so she could someday make a throne and a couch for herself from the wood. A snake built its nest in the base of the tree, which saddened Inanna, until Gilgamesh killed the snake (Kramer 1963:198). This is a tree with a snake "who knows no charm," but there is no reference to immortality or knowledge, so the story may not be too relevant. In general, we suspect that the image of the tree of life was taken from ancient Near Eastern literature, but the image of the tree of the knowledge of good and evil was created by the biblical author.

According to some fragmentary references, a sacred tree grew in the cult city of Eridu, deep in the southern part of Mesopotamia. In one text this tree is said to be rooted between the rivers with two mouths. That could be a poetic reference to the Tigris and Euphrates Rivers, or it could refer to two rivers rooted in the primordial waters beneath the earth, the waters rooted in the god Apsu, which come to the surface and water the earth (Wallace 106). Eridu was the cult site of Enki, a garden of the gods was said to be there, and so the sacred tree could be associated with Enki in some artistic portrayals and on cylinder seals. Enki was the god of fresh or sweet waters, rooted in the waters of Apsu beneath the earth. Other sacred symbols for Enki included the antelope, the fish (especially the goat-fish), and the turtle. Enki is recalled in several Mesopotamian creation narratives, so the sacred tree could be seen as an artistic theme connected to creation.

What truly exercises the minds of biblical commentators is the meaning of the knowledge of good and evil. What do people know when they have the knowledge of good and evil? Different answers have been given. The most common answers are as follows: 1) "Knowledge of good and evil" means moral discernment, the ability to tell good from evil, the ability to know there is a difference between good and evil acts and the moral capacity to consciously choose between those actions (Hamilton 166; Barr 62; Albertz 2003a:28). Moral discernment is what children learn as they grow to become adults. The implication might also be that by knowing what evil was, the human would become more capable of doing evil. The plot line in Genesis 3 seems to favor this definition. When the man and the woman eat of the fruit and gain the knowledge, they also gain shame, which implies the awareness of moral categories and the awareness that nakedness is inappropriate. 2) The "knowledge of good and evil" may mean the knowledge of everything from good to evil, that is, the knowledge of a wide range of things in life (Westermann 243; Batto 1992:59; Cotter 31). 3) Some have suggested that the phrase means knowledge, or in a more particular sense, knowledge and wisdom by which to live everyday life, knowledge of the world which can lead a person to self-sufficiency. Perhaps, it might mean, in particular, the knowledge of sex, pleasure, pain, life, and death. This would be the knowledge that adults have. The shame that the couple feels at being naked is not to be associated with moral categories, if this interpretation is correct. Their shame simply results from the awareness that normal adults are not supposed to run around without any clothing. In the parallel story of the man in the garden on a mountain in Ezekiel 28, the man is said to be "wise," and the impression given is that this is wisdom of a broad range of things. In the *Gilgamesh Epic* the prostitute says to Enkidu, after he has been "civilized" by his sexual encounter, that he has become "wise" like the gods (Westermann 247). 4) The popular understanding that the man and the woman become specifically aware of sex when they receive "knowledge" is wrong. God says that with this knowledge the man and the woman have become "like us," and sexual awareness is not a characteristic of God and divine beings in the mind of the biblical author (Hamilton 164).

Elsewhere wisdom for living a successful life is metaphored as the "tree of life" (Prov 3:18; 11:30; 13:12; 15:4). This muddies the water, for this brings the image of the tree of the knowledge of good and evil very close in meaning to the tree of life. Perhaps they were actually the same tree in the symbolic metaphors used by Israelite authors, and perhaps our biblical author in Genesis 2–3 split them into two separate trees for the sake of the plot (Brown 1999:154–55). All we can do is guess.

Over the years commentators have tried to advocate some very nuanced form of the basic arguments mentioned above. Those who believe that the knowledge refers to the ability to distinguish good from evil suggest several options. The knowledge of good and evil has been equated with moral values taught by society, not just moral awareness in general (Barr 62; van Wolde 1989:216–19). Those who suggest that the knowledge of all things from "good to evil" is a wide range of knowledge also have proposed several variations on this concept. Some believe it is the movement from the child-like innocence of youth to the maturity of adulthood (Speiser 1964:26; York 406–10). Others believe it speaks of the emergence within the individual of a sense of self-determination. Some believe it is practical knowledge necessary for everyday life (Kass 63). Perhaps, it refers to the secrets of nature. Still others suggest that it is general knowledge, to be sure, but it is the knowledge that leads to the advance of civilization. This argument then sees a connection with Genesis 4 that describes the emergence of civilization among the descendants of Cain and states that such activity becomes possible when the primal couple attains knowledge (Skinner 96; Mettinger 62; Wallace 116–18). Conrad L'Heureux says it means to be "successful in the management of one's existence," a more comprehensive definition involving insight and actions (L'Heureux 69). Several scholars provide nicely detailed evaluations of these various views (Skinner 96; Wallace 116–18; Mettinger 62).

The Rivers of the Garden

Genesis 2:10–14

(10) A river flows out of Eden to water the garden, and from there it divides and becomes four branches. (11) The name of the first is Pishon; it is the one that flows around the whole land of Havilah, where there is gold; (12) and the gold of that land is good; bdellium and onyx stone are there. (13) The name of the second river is Gihon; it is the one that flows around the whole land of Cush. (14) The name of the third river is Tigris, which flows east of Assyria. And the fourth river is the Euphrates.

The location of the garden depends upon how we wish to equate the rivers listed in the biblical text with rivers in the ancient world. The Hebrew of the biblical text identifies the Euphrates, but uses the word Hiddekal for the Tigris. Since Dan 10:4 identifies the Hiddekal as the Tigris, we assume the same is true here. Thus, two of the rivers are clearly described, the Tigris and the Euphrates, which define the Mesopotamian valley, but there is some disagreement over what rivers are indicated by the Gihon and the Pishon. Also, one confronts the complicating detail of what the text is actually saying. It is unclear as to whether the four rivers flow into the Garden of Eden, or whether they flow out of the Garden of Eden. In the former instance we should look for an area where four rivers come together (like southern Mesopotamia); in the latter instance we should look for the "headwaters" or the origins of great rivers (which could make the garden cover a very large area). In general, there are several theories concerning the location of these rivers.

1) One theory suggests that the rivers do not locate the garden in a specific place, but rather allude to the great rivers of the ancient world, the Tigris, Euphrates, Nile, and Indus Rivers, for these were the great rivers where the earliest developed civilizations arose. Thus, the Garden of Eden would encompass all the lands of ancient Egypt, Mesopotamia, and western India (modern day Pakistan). That would be a sensible symbolic portrayal by the biblical author of the ancient garden, for it would explain how later peoples came to find fertility and good crop production in those river valley areas—they were remnants of the Garden of Eden.

The peoples located in these four river valleys traded with each other, or at least the Mesopotamians traded both with the Egyptians and the people who lived in the Indus Valley regions during the third and second millennia BCE. Hence, there were trade and cultural connections between all these areas. In the post-exilic period the Persian Empire ruled all four of these river valleys at various times. In this theory the Gihon is the Nile, assuming that the land of Cush refers to Ethiopia or the Sudan, which in the biblical text is often called Cush. Unfortunately, the land of Cush south of Egypt is spelled in a slightly different way than the word Cush here in Genesis 2, even though the words look alike in English. Also, by this theory the Pishon would be the Indus River in western India. In the first century CE Josephus equated the Pishon with the Indus or the Ganges rivers in India (Westermann 217). One particular explanation suggests that Havilah is Saudi Arabia, as it appears to be in Gen 25:18 and 1 Sam 15:7, but the ancients believed Saudi Arabia extended far to the south and then to the east to become the land of India. Hence, a river in Saudi Arabia could be the Indus River in western India. One commentator, however, who follows this argument, suggests that the river is not the Indus, but the Ganges River, which lies to the east of the Indus (Simpson 495). This might make sense, because in the first millennium BCE, the Ganges was a more significant center of population and commerce than was the Indus. Another variation on this model suggests that the Nile is not one of the rivers, but rather the Ganges and Indus, both in India, are the other two rivers besides the Tigris and the Euphrates (Skinner 64).

A totally different model assumes that part of the ancient world is portrayed in the story. It is feasible to say that the garden is in the place where the "headwaters" or origins of these rivers may be found. The origins of the Tigris and Euphrates are found north of Mesopotamia in the Anatolian highlands, or southeastern Turkey. The "headwaters" of the Gihon, if it is the Nile, are to be found in Ethiopia. Maybe the Pishon is another river in Egypt or Ethiopia. Maybe the two rivers are the While Nile and the Blue Nile, which flow together to become the Nile. In that case, Ethiopia is the origin of both rivers. If this model is correct, then the garden extends from Turkey (home of the Hittite Empire in the second millennium BCE) down to Egypt (Hiebert 53, suggests this theory but does not defend it).

2) The second theory suggests that the four rivers are to be found in the Mesopotamian Valley, either in the northern part of the valley where rivers originate, or in the south where the rivers empty into the Persian Gulf. Most commentators prefer either of these two explanations, since the other accounts in the Primeval History seem to have such a close connection to

Mesopotamian stories and themes, as well as allusions to Mesopotamian geographic locations.

The favorite location for most writers is in south Mesopotamia. The Tigris and the Euphrates come together and eventually flow into the Persian Gulf; it simply becomes a matter of identifying the other two rivers (Speiser 1964:20). Since the Tigris and the Euphrates come together into a "river" called the Shatt el-'Arab, that could be identified as the single "river" which flows out of Eden to become the four branches, or the other four rivers (Vawter 69, points out that this area produces many dates, and the forbidden tree in the garden might have been a date tree). If this model is correct, then the land of Cush could refer to the land of the Kassites in north Mesopotamia. The Pishon might be the Karun River in Elam, and the Gihon might be the Choaspes River or the modern Kerkha River (Vawter 70; Hamilton 169–70). A slight variation on this suggests that the "river" which flows out of Eden is really the Persian Gulf (Skinner 63, who identifies the other two rivers with the Pallakopos and the Choaspes).

The location of south Mesopotamia has been given a significant boost in recent years by the discovery of a dry riverbed under the surface of the ground, which used to be a major river in the ancient world. It is called the Kuwait River, and it flows through northern Saudi Arabia from the west and empties into the Persian Gulf near the other rivers. It would possibly be equated with the Pishon River of the biblical text. It was discovered during the Gulf War of 1990–1991 by satellite surveillance. Farouk El-Baz located this riverbed, which ran from the Hijaz in western Saudi Arabia (near the holy city of Medina) to Kuwait. It was a viable river during the years 9000 BCE to 2000 BCE. It began to dry up from 3500 to 2000 BCE, which was also a period of time in Mesopotamia when we suspect there were numerous floods in the river valley (Sauer 373, 382–84). It may be a coincidence, but it is interesting to note that the inspiration for flood stories and one of the four rivers, both recalled in the Primeval History of Genesis 1–11, may date to events in the fourth millennium BCE. Some suggest that the river may not have dried up completely until 2000 BCE, making the contact between the historical experience and the emergence of the biblical memory more likely (Sauer 386). Obviously people moved from region of the dying Kuwait River to southern Mesopotamia. Maybe they became the part of the people called the Sumerians, who brought significant development of civilization to Mesopotamia. If the Kuwait River is the Pishon, then the identification of Havilah with Saudi Arabia is good. There is gold in Havilah according to the biblical text, and gold does exist one hundred miles south of Medina in a place called Mahd edh-Dhahab ("Cradle of God"), and the bdellium and onyx mentioned in the biblical text may correspond to the bdellium and precious stones found in Yemen down in the southwestern part of the Saudi Arabian peninsula (Sauer 387).

Authors who locate the garden in Mesopotamia sometimes look to northern Mesopotamia as the location. They stress that the biblical text seems to say that the four rivers flow off of the one river that comes out of the garden. Thus, it may indicate that we should look for the origins or "headwaters" of great rivers. Certainly the Tigris and the Euphrates originate in the far northern highlands in Mesopotamia, or almost outside of Mesopotamia, in modern day Turkey. The question remains as to how to identify the other two rivers. Again, the area of Cush associated with the Gihon would be equated with the land of the Kassites, but the land of Pishon would be a little more vague. Various rivers in northern Mesopotamia might be suggested for these two vague biblical references. The Zab River in the area of Assyria would be one such suggestion.

3) A third theory, advocated by only a few, suggests the environment around Jerusalem and the southern part of Palestine is the locale for the garden. The subtle implication of the text might be that the Garden of Eden was located where the city of Jerusalem or even the Temple was later built. The starting point for this argument is that Gihon is the name of a spring in Jerusalem that flows through the Kidron Valley, near the city, and this spring functioned as a primary source of water for Jerusalem. With the Gihon spring as one of the four rivers, we might identify rivers or streams in the general vicinity of Jerusalem with the other rivers (Wallace 74; G. Anderson 1988:190–99; Hiebert 53). Furthermore, the reference to the stream that arises out of the ground to become the four rivers may refer to the exilic and post-exilic poetic vision of living waters or the river that comes out of the Temple and goes forth to the Dead Sea and the Mediterranean Sea bringing life to the wilderness areas (Ps 46:4; 65:9; Ezek 47:1–12; Joel 3:18; Zech 14:8).

Perhaps the narrative implies that the Garden of Eden was in the general vicinity of Jerusalem, but more likely located across the Jordan River in the Transjordan. The area of the Transjordan was more fertile prior to the biblical period, and the biblical authors also had that perception. Stories about the cities of the plain (Sodom, Gomorrah, Admah, Zeboiim, and Bela or Zoar), found in Genesis 13–14, 18–19, imply that regions around the Dead Sea, and perhaps in the Transjordan, were fertile until their destruction in the days of Abraham. Recent archaeology indicates that land north and northeast of the Dead Sea in an area called the "kikkar" was fertile and the site of five significant cities, especially one at Tall el-Hammam in modern Jordan, during the Middle Bronze Age (2000–1550 BCE). These settlements were destroyed by fire at the end of the Middle Bronze Age, perhaps giving rise to the biblical memory of the destruction of Sodom and Gomorrah, rather than the destruction of cities located to the southeast of the Dead Sea that scholars have looked to in the past (Collins 30–41, 70–71). The biblical text (Gen 13:10) compares the "well watered" land where these cities were located to the "garden of the LORD." If that "garden of the LORD" is a reference to Eden, then this is a strong hint that Eden was in this area. In later years this land east of the Dead Sea would have oases, and date palms grow there. (Perhaps Eden is to be perceived as an oasis.) This area would be in the east from the perspective of an Israelite or a Jew living in Jerusalem. When Cain fled to the east, he would be moving into the desert, if he left from this Transjordanian area of oases. Also, when the sixth century BCE prophet Ezekiel envisions a restoration of the land in Ezekiel 40–48, he envisions a return of great fertility to the Jordan Valley area. That would be symbolically appropriate if Ezekiel somehow believes that the original Garden of Eden were somewhere in that neighborhood (Hiebert 54–57).

Thus, an interesting argument might be made for the location of the Garden of Eden somewhere in south Palestine. One might suggest the city of Jerusalem, or one might suggest some location in the Transjordan across the Jordan River or across the Dead Sea from Jerusalem. This would be appropriate symbolism and would resonate with imagery from the rest of the biblical text. The only problem with this theory would be in locating four significant rivers. Obviously the Gihon spring in Jerusalem would be one, and the Jordan River would be selected naturally as one of the others. But the difficulty would be picking out two more rivers. We could look at a map and select some of the rivers or wadis in the Transjordan. Wadis are bodies of water that flow with water only part of the year, and the rest of the year they appear as damp riverbeds with water flowing beneath the surface of the ground. Perhaps these wadis were more significant rivers in an age when the climate was moister and there was more water in the Transjordan area. If so, we might select from the following wadis: 1) the Zered, which was the border between the countries of Edom to the south and Moab to the north, and it flows into the south end of the Dead Sea; 2) the Arnon, which was the border between the countries of Moab and Ammon (when either were strong), theoretically it was the southern border for the Israelite tribe of Reuben, and it flows into the central part of the Dead Sea; and 3) the Jabbok, which sometimes was the border between the Israelite tribes of Gad and Manasseh or between the country of Ammon and the tribe of Manasseh (when Ammon was strong), and it flows into the Jordan River, north of the Dead Sea. These bodies of water are variously called rivers, brooks, and wadis in biblical atlases. Perhaps they might have been considered part of the river system for the garden in some loose sense, if the biblical author located the garden in the Transjordan.

4) The fourth major theory suggests Eden is located on a cosmic mountain. The main river then flows up through the cosmic mountain from the great ocean depths beneath the earth, and when it surfaces upon the mountain, it breaks into four rivers that flow to the four corners of the earth. The primeval stream is then the "headwaters" of great rivers. This is obviously a symbolic and mythic view of the garden, and it is an image that can be found in other cultures. In terms of universal mythic imagery the spring would be where the gods live in the depths of the great waters below the earth (Hiebert 52, 58). The Canaanite god El, for example, lived at the source of the great primeval waters below the earth. Since Mesopotamian kings often placed gardens next to their palaces, one could suggest that Eden is God's garden and it is placed next to the divine palace (Kawashima 497). This would imply a symbolic place on a cosmic mountain. It might also draw an analogy to how the Temple in Jerusalem was next to the royal palace, thus implying that the Temple in Jerusalem symbolically was Eden. John Walton poetically sees parallels between Eden and the Temple: in both there are cherubim, a symbolic tree of life, symbolic flowing rivers of life, an imperative not to touch holy things, and the symbolic understanding that this holy place is the center of the world (Walton 2009:185–89). Ancient Jewish literature from 300 BCE to 200 CE also believed that Eden became the later Temple (*Jubilees* 8:19; *Psalms of Solomon* 11:5; *1 Enoch* 25:1–5; *4 Ezra* 8:52–53).

In support of this symbolic theory it could be noted that in the Mesopotamian palace of Zimri-Lim of Mari (1750 BCE) there is a wall fresco in which the goddess Ishtar invests Zimri-Lim with the authority of kingship and in a lower panel of that fresco there is a goddess with a vase out of which flow four streams from a single source to water the entire land (Lind 125; Batto 2004:158; Fitzpatrick 191; Walton 2009:185; Lanfer 40). The image of the four streams of water might have been inspired in this artwork by the myth of four rivers from the sacred mountain. Elsewhere in the Old Testament we find references to this symbolic cosmic mountain with water flowing from it. Psalms 24:1–2 and 46:3–5 speak of it as a refuge. King Ahaz of Judah is told to trust in the cosmic stream that comes from Mount Zion (Isa 8:5–9). Other passages speak generically of a stream of fertility that comes from Zion (Isa 33:21–23; Ezek 47:1–12; Joel 4:18; Zech 14:8; Ps 36:9–10).

For the biblical author the symbolic mountain might be anywhere, or it could specifically be a mount or mountain. Thus, this symbolic mountain theory may dovetail with previous suggestions for locations of the garden. The symbolic mountain might be Sinai in the wilderness south of Israel or

Zion in Jerusalem with four rivers or wadis in the area (Levenson 127-37). Maybe there is a hint that Mount Zion was the place where Eden (Temple) and God's palace (royal palace) might be found. One might suggest that the biblical author envisioned a symbolic mountain in north Mesopotamia, or modern Turkey, and the rivers which flow from there include the Tigris, Euphrates, and two other north Mesopotamian rivers. (South Mesopotamia lacks mountains, so a symbolic mountain would not be there.) One could suggest that the garden was on a sacred mountain in symbolic space and thus cannot be located geographically. Then the four rivers could be four of the great rivers of the entire world, including the Tigris and the Euphrates.

The biblical text in Genesis 2-3 does not clearly say that Eden was on a mountain; rather, it seems to imply that Eden was created on a plain, though it does not say that directly either. However, if Eden were on a mountain, it would explain some details in the text. If four rivers flow out of the garden, it would make sense for them to flow away from the garden, downhill from a mountaintop location. The idea of gods living on a mountaintop is common in ancient mythologies, including the Greek notion of Mt. Olympus in the north of Greece and the Canaanite notion of Mt. Zaphon also in the north. (The Greeks probably obtained this image from the Canaanites or the Phoenicians.) When God walks in the garden and visits humanity, it would make sense to assume that the audience envisioned this as occurring in a mountaintop garden. Furthermore, when God places cherubim to guard the garden against human intrusions, a mountain location would make more sense. It would be easier for cherubim to guard a mountain pass rather than running back and forth across along a border in a garden on a flat plain (otherwise picture panting cherubim dragging their flaming swords for endless years as they patrol the border and build ineffective border fences to stop human immigrants).

The most important piece of evidence to suggest that Eden might have been on top of a mountain comes to us from the prophet Ezekiel, who lived in the sixth century BCE in the Babylonian Exile, which places him at the same time when these Genesis stories might have originated. In Ezek 27:1-36 and 28:1-19 he utters judgment oracles against the king of the Phoenician city of Tyre. In part of his oracles he uses imagery of the primordial man in the garden, and Ezekiel compares the king of Tyre to that primordial man to imply that the king of Tyre will receive punishment, as did the primordial man (Ezek 28:1-19). The language that Ezekiel uses, strikes us as incredibly similar to the Genesis 3 account of the man and woman in the garden. The king of Tyre or the primordial man in the rhetoric of Ezekiel has the following characteristics: 1) his "heart is proud" (v. 2); 2) he says, "I am a god" (v.2); 3) he says, "I sit in the seat of the gods" (v. 2); 4) he was "mortal" (v.

2); 5) he compares his mind "with the mind of a god" (v. 2); 6) he will be "thrust down to the Pit" (v. 8); 7) he is "the signet of perfection" (v. 12); 8) he is "full of wisdom" (v. 12); 9) he is "full of beauty" (v. 12); 10) he is "in Eden, the garden of God" (v. 13); 11) he has a "cherub as guardian" (v. 14); 12) he is on a "holy mountain" (v. 14); 13) he is "blameless" (v. 15); 14) eventually "iniquity is found in" him (v. 15); 15) he "sins" (v. 15); 16) the "guardian cherub drives" him out (v. 16); 17) he is "cast to the ground" (v. 17); and 18) he is turned "to ashes on the earth" (v. 18). The similarity with themes and language in Genesis 3 is great. The sin of the man and the woman is the desire to be like God knowing all things and thus to obtain wisdom--the sin of pride (items #1, #2, #5, and #8). The man and the woman visit with God (item #3). The man and the woman are mortal (item #4). The man and the woman are created perfect (items #7 and #9). Most significantly, they live in a garden called Eden, the garden of God (item #10). A cherub drives the man and woman out to protect the garden (items #11 and #16). The man and the woman presumably do not sin (item #13), until they eat the fruit (#14 and #15). The man and the woman are cast out of the garden (items #6, #16 and #17). The man has to earn a living by working the ground (item #17). Eventually both the man and the woman die and are not able to eat from the tree of life. They become the "dust" from which they were created (item #18). The similarities are numerous. The details worth noting are items #10 and #12. The garden is called Eden, and the couple is driven from the "holy mountain." This detail becomes a significant argument to suggest that in Genesis 2–3 the Garden of Eden is on a mountain. The biblical text does not directly say that the garden is on a mountain, but neither does it say exactly where the garden is.

There are, of course, many images in Ezekiel 28, connected to the royal king, which have no parallel in Genesis 2–3. It may be that Ezekiel's image of the king is disdained and rejected by the author of Genesis 3 in order to make the audience identify with the actions of the man and the woman who are portrayed as average people. The man in Ezekiel appears super-terrestrial, but the man and the woman seem very human. The sin of the man and the woman, pride and rebellion against God, are sins that the prophets and biblical authors often accuse Israelites and Judeans of committing. Ezekiel's king has wisdom and becomes proud enough to claim divinity, but the man and the woman seek wisdom, which is located in a tree, to attain divinity. Wisdom moves from a person to a tree in Genesis 3. Genesis 3 adds the two trees and a woman. The most significant detail is the addition of the woman in Genesis 3, which I believe actually gives dignity to the woman, for it implies that she is capable of making a moral decision, albeit bad.

One can suggest three possibilities to describe the literary relationship of Ezekiel 28 to Genesis 2–3. Ezekiel may paraphrase the Genesis narrative, the author of Genesis may be inspired by the oracle of Ezekiel and simply adds the woman to the story, or both Ezekiel and the author of Genesis draw upon a common narrative, and both authors add their own distinctive themes to make the story relevant for the message they wish to communicate. This debate is very involved and complex, but most commentators seem to favor the third theory. The significance of the details in the biblical narrative that differ from the oracle in Ezekiel 28 shall be discussed later.

To conclude, there is an interesting discussion about the location of the Garden of Eden based on the equation of the rivers. People locate Eden in south Mesopotamia, north Mesopotamia, Jerusalem, over the entire world, or in a symbolic non-geographical location. Most authors like the south Mesopotamian equation, and that is what you see on most maps. I prefer the last argument that suggests that the garden and the rivers are in some symbolic place, a mountain that exists in the center of the world. I am reluctant to equate it with Sinai, Zion, or any other mountain, because I believe it is very much in symbolic space. I am especially prone to suggest this because of the strong thematic and linguistic connection between Genesis 2–3 and Ezekiel 28.

I find it interesting that Ezekiel 28 condemns the king of Tyre, who is described as a tyrant who engages in extensive mercantile activity and has committed an egregious sin. Our biblical author flirts with royal imagery in several ways when speaking about the man and the woman. In the account of Genesis 2–3 the biblical author democratizes the account by making the man and the woman into Mr. Everyman and Mrs. Everywoman. I sense an ongoing anti-royal agenda of the biblical author, even though an explicit condemnation of kingship does not appear.

6

The Adam in the Garden

Genesis 2:15–20

(15) The LORD God took the man and put him in the garden of Eden to till it and keep it. (16) And the LORD God commanded the man, "You may freely eat of every tree of the garden; (17) but of the tree of the knowledge of good and evil you shall not eat, for in the day that you eat of it you shall die. (18) Then the LORD God said, "It is not good that the man should be alone; I will make him a helper as his partner." (19) So out of the ground the LORD God formed every animal of the field and every bird of the air, and brought them to the man to see what he would call them; and whatever the man called every living creature, that was its name. (20) The man gave names to all cattle, and to the birds of the air, and to every animal of the field; but for the man there was not found a helper as his partner.

IN THE ANCIENT WORLD the creation and maintenance of gardens was the work of kings. Numerous inscriptions from the Egyptians and the Assyrians attest to the royal pride in building gardens with exotic plants and animals taken from many lands. Such gardens testified to the far-flung conquests of the empire building pharaohs and kings (Brown 2010:248–52). God's garden is not a testimony to a royal empire; it is a place to put the newly created human, the symbolic ancestor of all humanity. The anti-royal rhetoric of the biblical author is found in the described simplicity of this divine undertaking. Ancient Near Eastern kings created gardens not only for the cultivation of fruit trees and the display of beautiful flowers, but they were also zoos where wild animals could be displayed. Often these zoos became big game hunting preserves for the kings. Assyrian kings displayed their prowess in the hunt with grand wall carvings that showed them shooting lions with the bow and arrow as they gallantly rode in chariots. What is not shown is the great number of armed attendants who accompanied the king on his hunt to make sure that the wild animals did no harm to the king. So essentially the king shot wild animals that were enclosed in a large zoo garden, and the brave king hunted with the assistance of many servants, maybe hundreds of well-armed servants. I am reminded of the expression, "shooting fish in a barrel." Such is the nature of kings or tyrants in any age, who brag of their courage while peasants do the really dangerous work. The Persians, who built beautiful gardens, had a word for such gardens or wild game preserves; it is the word from which comes the English word, "paradise."

The Adam is placed into a "paradise" to maintain it. Kings in the ancient world spoke of how they maintained their gardens, which were assigned to them by the gods. God places Adam in a garden because he is the king who rules over the world in the name of God. Once more we encounter the imagery of Genesis 1: the Adam is a king on the earth, but he is also a simple man, the ancestor of all of us. We are all kings, and we have all been placed in God's garden, the garden that is our world. We are to take care of the world, not ruin and pollute it.

Ancient Near Eastern accounts spoke of how the gods created people to till the ground as their slaves to produce food for sacrifice to the gods, and the biblical text alludes to this role of humanity. Yet it becomes evident throughout the narrative that people are not the slaves of the gods producing food for the gods and the priests who serve the gods. Mesopotamian stories legitimate the power of the priests, their privileges, and their food supply. So the brief reference to human toil on the ground with no corresponding reference to providing food for priests or gods may be the biblical polemic against this entire system of human religious servitude. God made people to till the ground, but they do it for their own food not as menial servitude to hungry gods and their human minions (Westermann 222).

I believe this short reference is a critique of the economic and religious systems of the ancient world because otherwise the image of tilling the ground is somewhat out of place here. The reference to tilling the ground must be made at the original creation of humanity by the biblical author because the image occurs at that point in the Mesopotamian accounts. However, the reference is not needed for the plot in the biblical narrative this early; it should come after the fall.

But once the author places the statement here in verse 15 for a polemical reason, it also gives the impression that something is amiss in the plot. The Adam is to till the garden and keep it. But the man and the woman do not till the garden; they eat fruit from trees. They are not farmers; they are merely fruit pickers. Perhaps, this is in keeping with the imagery of a simple man instead of a king residing in and maintaining the garden. But in the rest of Genesis 2–3 there is no reference to agricultural (growing grain) or serious viticultural activity (growing fruit) undertaken in the garden by the man and the woman, unless they ate the wrong fruit so quickly that God never had a chance to show them how the John Deere tractor worked. One gets the impression that maybe they were not to engage in agricultural or viticultural activity in the garden, but merely live off of the abundant produce provided by the trees. For the judgment upon the man that he would labor in producing food in Gen 3:17–19 gives us the impression that he did not do any farming until he left the garden. We possibly could suggest that the man and the woman did engage in farming in the garden, but it was not labor intensive, and the later divine judgment made agricultural activity an onerous burden. However, I prefer the first interpretation, as have other commentators, because there is no indication that the man and the woman engaged in any agricultural labor. That means the Adam would not do that duly assigned task until after expulsion from the garden.

Does the biblical author imply that Adam has to leave the garden to do what is expected by God at some proper time, when he attains a certain level of development? Or does God know in advance that the Adam will rebel and be cast out of the garden? If God knows the Adam will rebel, is it God's ultimate will that the Adam sin and be exiled to fulfill the human task of agriculture? Christian theologians in the seventeenth century suggested just such a possibility. Dutch Calvinist theologians, who believed firmly in predestination, suggested that God willed human sin (and the grand exit from the garden) so that ultimately God could manifest divine grace in the death and resurrection of Jesus. These theologians were called "supralapsarians" because they believed the "fall" (the "lapse") was willed or predestined by God. The Adam had to sin and leave the garden, for it was the only way that humanity would engage in agriculture and produce human culture. The biblical author certainly was not a Calvinist "supralapsarian," but we might wonder if the author is telling us that God willed the man and the woman to leave the garden to become fully human, to farm, and to produce culture. The other possibility is that the man and the woman did tend the garden, and their exile sent them outside the garden where agricultural activity was much more difficult. But there are some symbolic images in the text that imply the first option is preferable.

The Adam is told that all the trees were there for consumption, except one. There is a special tree in the garden from which the Adam could not eat the fruit—"the tree of the knowledge of good and evil." If the Adam eats of the fruit of the tree of knowledge, God says, "for in the day that you eat of it you shall die." The Hebrew expression, "you shall die," or more literally, "you shall surely die," is a formula found in the law codes of the Hebrew Bible in conjunction with capital crimes in which the guilty party is to be executed immediately by the community. In such laws the crime is stated in the initial clause, followed by the harsh formula, "surely he shall be put to death." Thus, on the very day in which the Adam eats the forbidden fruit, the Adam is to be executed. But that is not what happens. Does God experience a change of heart? We must read through the next chapter and discover this.

Over the years ancient and modern commentators have suggested several answers as to why the man and the woman do not die immediately when they eat the fruit or subsequent to God's interrogation. Most commentators, ancient and modern, suggest that God meant humans would become mortal, which indeed they do become eventually. (However, given their life spans, we should all live so long!) Adam lived nine hundred and thirty years! Is eventual death a threat with this life span? Certainly the biblical audience would not have seen this as a horrid threat. The best answer in this regard is to say that they became aware of their human finitude and the pain of life (LaCocque 2006:182). However, their ultimate longevity undercuts the pain of such an awareness of human finitude.

This answer also implies that the man and the woman are inherently immortal, perhaps, and they lose immortality by eating the fruit (Skinner 88). A number of ancient Jewish and Christian works stated this two thousand years ago. We see this interpretation already in Apocryphal or Deutero-canonical books in the Old Testament—Sirach and the Wisdom of Solomon. (Apocryphal books are those found in the Greek translation of the Hebrew Bible called the Septuagint but not in the Hebrew Bible itself. Roman Catholics place them in their Old Testament; Protestants locate them in a special section called the Apocrypha.) In the second century BCE Sir 25:24 says that because of the woman's sin, we all will die. In the first century BCE Wis 1:13; 2:23–24 says that God originally created humanity immortal. In the first century CE, Pseudo-Philo writes in *Biblical Antiquities* 13:10, "then death was ordained for the generations of men." Jewish Pseudepigraphical literature also makes mention of this immortality. (Pseudepigrapha works are Jewish writings not included in either Roman Catholic or Protestant versions of the Bible, though some Eastern Christians use some of these works.) In the second century BCE work, *Apocalypse of Moses* 14:2, Adam speaks of "death gaining rule over all our race" subsequent to the eating of the fruit. *4 Ezra* 3:7, from the second century CE, states that God "established death for him and his descendants." In the second century CE, *2 Baruch* 17:2–3 states, "Adam sinned, and death was decreed against those who were to be."

Another explanation, which is rather colorful, maintains that indeed the man and the woman did die the "day" that they ate of the fruit. But the "day" was defined by God's sense of time, and God's definition of a "day" was provided by Ps 90:4, which says, "A thousand years in your sight are like yesterday," and 2 Pet 3:8, from the New Testament, which says, "that with the Lord one day is as a thousand years, and a thousand years as one day." Hence, a thousand years are a divine day. According to Gen 5:5 Adam lived to be nine hundred and thirty years old, and thus died within the parameters of a "divine day." In the Pseudepigraphical book *Jubilees* 4:29, it suggests that Adam died seventy years short of a thousand years, and thus according to the interpretation of Psalm 90, Adam fulfilled the command of God by dying on the day that he ate the fruit. The Christian author Justin Martyr in his *Dialogue with Trypho* (81:3) states that Adam died on the very same day because he "did not quite fill up a thousand years." I doubt that modern commentators would buy into this particular explanation.

The problem with all the arguments that assume the man and the woman lose immortality is that the biblical text seems to disagree with them. God says that the couple must leave the garden before they eat of the tree of life and become immortal. This implies that they are not immortal inherently, and so they do not lose immortality by eating the fruit.

Other traditional Christian commentators interpret the passage to mean that once the man and the woman eat the fruit, they die a spiritual death, even though they would remain alive physically. That sounds much more like a later Christian interpretation rather than something in the text, for nothing else in the story seems to back up the notion of a spiritual death separate from a physical death.

I believe the expression that the man and woman would die meant that they would die on that day. In 1 Kgs 2:37 Solomon tells Shimei that if he crosses the Kidron Valley, he will surely die on that day, and the expression is the same as in Gen 2:17 text. Shimei crosses the Kidron and is executed by military commander Benaiah as soon as Solomon discovers what Shimei did (1 Kgs 2:39–46).

I concur with commentators who believe that God truly intends that the man should die on the day he eats the fruit, but the biblical text implies God has a change of heart and does not kill the humans (Westermann 224). The purpose of this plot twist is to emphasize the graciousness of God, a theme that permeates the rest of the Primeval History.

It is odd that God now decides that the man needs a partner. Did not God know that before? Isn't God all-knowing? God should have known ahead of time what would transpire. (At least that more or less makes sense according to traditional philosophical discourse about God.) This portrayal in the biblical text makes it appear as though God is experimenting and does not quite know what is going to happen next, especially when we discover that first God creates the animals, then God creates the woman, and the man says, "at last." It sounds like the man was a little exasperated at the divine tinkering.

When we back up and look at the text as a whole, we should not bring our modern philosophical and theological perspectives into the text. Nor should we use this narrative to craft a systematic image of what God is like. This is Hebrew narrative and it seeks to portray the story of God and humanity in a meaningful religious fashion as well as telling it in an entertaining way (Good 27). The narrator throughout much of Genesis seeks to portray God as a gracious and loving deity, who is deeply involved in the relationship with humanity. The narrative accomplishes that by portraying God almost as if God were human and by portraying God as physically and emotionally involved in the earthly process. Thus, God is down on the earth playing in the mud to make the "earth creature," and now God is making animals as though they are playmates for the man. This is the image of a God who is personal and close to humanity, and it is what the author seeks to accomplish with these narrative details. We should view the narrative as symbolic discourse, which communicates a serious point: God loves the creation and human beings and is with them in everyday life. God is present dynamically present for the "earth creature" and can still be present in the lives of people at a later time.

I like to think that we can interpret this imagery in another way. The text shows God acting one step at a time, experimenting in order to find the right helper for the man. God seems to improvise in the work of creation, acting in a processual sort of way, unlike the dramatic imagery of Genesis 1 where God declares specific things created on a single day. Here God makes things more individually, as a deity involved in the process of life development. This imagery is closer to how we think about the development of life, for we see life emerging, growing, and developing. We do not see animals and plants as absolute forms, we view them as growing and changing entities. We understand the origin of life as an evolutionary process that took an enormous amount of time. We stress gradual growth, development, and evolution when we speak about life, society, history, and even individuals. The language of divine involvement in this chapter resonates more with the way we think in our modern world.

In a contemporary strand of Christian theology called process theology, Christian thinkers stress the close relationship of God to humanity and the world. They especially stress the incarnation of God in the person of Jesus and speak of how God suffers with humanity rather than how pain and suffering result from the will of God. God suffers when people sin; the prophet Hosea implies that. The ultimate image of a suffering God, of course, is God suffering in the person of Jesus. God chooses to become part of the physical world by limiting divine powers and relating intimately with people. God is no longer spoken of as omnipotent by these theologians, but is described as ultimately personal (Hartshorne passim). The language of Genesis 2 reinforces this imagery, because it imagines God being so involved in the process of creation, that God experiments with the created order and discovers, along with the Adam, what the wisest course of action might be (Gnuse 2002:23–41).

Notice how God forms the creatures out of the ground; God creates them the same way that he creates the man. A lot of Bible readers do not seem to notice this! How often do we hear it said that people are special in our world because God took special time to create humanity out of the dust of the ground. When they say that, they obviously did not read this verse, for the animals were created in the same way that we were. One gets the image of God creating each animal one at a time, like little mud pies. The same care that was shown to the human is now shown to the animals. Humanity has common origin with the animals; we are all made out of the dust of the ground.

How often do people act with superiority to the animal world? How often do religionists affirm the special role of human beings in creation, and thus unwittingly justify the subordination of the created order and the environment to the will of people. This then supports our too often indiscriminate destruction of plant and animal life throughout the world as we expand human activity for business and commercial reasons. Often this justification of human superiority is made by an appeal to the concept of the "image of God," which is spoken of in Gen 1:26–28. Well, this is the corollary. We may be special with that "image of God," but we are still made from the same earth as our animal brothers and sisters. We are one with the animal realm, and this text reminds us of that.

I once was asked if I believed that we were descended from monkeys, and I was further asked if the Bible taught that we were descended from monkeys. I responded by saying that according to the Bible we were descended from dirt, which is lower than monkeys, and that the monkeys are not our parents, but our brothers and sisters. I added that the monkeys, if they had more intelligence and self-consciousness, and if they could read papers, would be so very ashamed to be our brothers and sisters. Monkeys did not invent death camps and thermonuclear weapons. They do not burn the jungles down. They should be embarrassed to be kin to us, not we to them. They should be sitting in the jungle with bags on their heads saying, "Humans, no we never heard of humans! Why do you ask?" Maybe it's good for us that monkeys don't read newspapers.

There are statements that religious people make, especially when they are teaching children, which I find rather odd and humorous at times. We teach children Genesis 1 and say that humanity was created last and that is why people are the ultimate and most important thing in creation. But then we seem to ignore Genesis 2, wherein the "Adam" is created first. We also seem to ignore the implication of our statement that "man" is superior because he is created last. In Genesis 2 the female seemingly appears to be created after the male, and no one says that women are superior to men because they were created after them. Actually the biblical author probably was trying to say that humanity was the final grand act of creation in Genesis 1, but in Genesis 2 humanity is created first so as to assist God in the process of naming, which then gives great importance to the role of humanity.

God creates the creatures out of the ground, as God did with the Adam. Then God brings them to the man for the purpose of naming them. Perhaps also God brings them before the Adam to see if the Adam will recognize any of the creatures as a suitable partner. (Dogs probably thought they had the best chance of being a suitable partner; cats thought the Adam had been created to be their pet.)

A serious translation issue emerges with this passage. The animals are referred to with the expression "living creature" in verse 19. The Hebrew expression is *nephesh hayya'*, two words that could be translated as "living soul." In Gen 2:7 the Adam is also called a *nephesh hayya'*, but we translate those two words differently. For example, the King James Version says "living soul" and the New Revised Standard Version says "living being." Our English translations create a significant difference between people and the animals, calling the former a "living soul" and the latter a "living creature" (Hiebert 62). But the Hebrew makes people and animals kindred. We need to recapture that Hebrew original meaning today. We are destroying our world with pollution and industrialization, and species of animals are disappearing and becoming endangered at a frightening rate. We need to be reminded of our oneness with the animal realm and our responsibility for stewardship of the animal realm. It is tragic when our English translations fail to provide us with texts that affirm this divinely created unity and responsibility. We need to realize that we and the animals are together the "living souls" in our world.

Commentators argue over the significance of the naming process. Many have said that it betokens the fact that God was gracious and permitted the Adam to share in the activity of creation. For naming something gives it identity and helps bring it into existence. In Genesis 1 God creates things in the universe by naming them or calling them into existence. So the biblical author may imply that the human being is allowed by God to become a co-creator of the animal kingdom by naming the animals (Stratton 38). Other commentators go farther with this concept and declare that by naming something the Adam is given power or dominion over it (Richardson 67), so that humanity in this passage is granted dominion over the animal realm, parallel to the comparable passages in Genesis 1. It has been stated that not only does naming something define it in the eyes of the person who names it, but it also defines the relationship between namer and the named, effectively declaring what the future will bring for this relationship, and giving the namer access to the thing named (Lim 121). Some commentators suggest that the naming process, in particular, distinguished the wild from the domestic animals (Brown 1999:141). John Walton compared the naming of the animals by the man to the "decreeing of the destinies" undertaken by Marduk in the *Enuma Elish* (Walton 2009:181), a very powerful function indeed.

This story takes us into the greater question of how the biblical author sees the on-going relationship of people and the animal realm. Even more important, it raises questions for Christians and Jews of how we are to act today in regard to the animal realm. How does the biblical author distinguish people and animals? What does it mean that the Adam named the animals? Do people have total authority over the animal realm with the ability to put the animal realm at their disposal? Or is our biblical text really speaking more of a symbiotic harmony between people and the animal realm? All of these are difficult questions to answer.

God created both human beings and animals out of the dust of the ground, which gives them a common kinship and origin (much in the same way that the evolutionary theory tries to teach us today). But at the same time the animals are not created with the "breath of life," whatever that might mean. Some believe that this implies the difference between people and animals lies in the fact that God has a personal relationship with people, but not with animals (Fritsch 28; Richardson 67). All commentators agree that the biblical text assumes a significant difference between the animals and humanity, and that difference may be difficult for us to define completely in our modern worldview. But likewise all commentators agree that humanity has gone too far in developing a domineering control over the animal realm, to the point of being destructive. We have forgotten the reference to our common origin with the animal realm in favor of an attitude of domination. This has been especially true in western European culture in the last few centuries. We need to continue reminding ourselves that we come from the dust of the ground, as do our animal brothers and sisters.

7

Creation of the Woman

THE ANCIENT NEAR EAST does not provide any stories about the creation of women separate from the creation of men. However, there are allusions in the myths that elucidate some of the language and imagery in the biblical account. The Sumerian myth of *Enki and Ninhursag* (2500–2000 BCE) describes the creation of gods. Enki impregnated the goddess Ninhursag, who gave birth to Ninmu; then he impregnated Ninmu, who gave birth to Ninkurra; then he impregnated Ninkurra, who gave birth to Uttu. When Uttu removed Enki's semen, Ninhursag took the semen to generate eight plants. After Enki ate these plants he was in tremendous pain and ready to die, so Ninhursag acted as a midwife to Enki so that he gave birth to eight separate deities who healed each of the eight parts of his body that hurt (skull, jaw, tooth, mouth, throat, arm, rib, etc.) (Pritchard 37–41; Kramer and Maier 22–31). This may be an early myth that reflects the importance of Ninhursag as a creator deity, for in later years Enki became increasingly important as a creator (Sharon 75–76). The deity created or birthed to heal Enki's rib was Nintu or Ninti, whose title, according to other narratives, was "the mother of all living beings." In the *Atrahasis Epic* she was the goddess who makes seven pairs of people out of blood and clay. This is an interesting coincidence, for Eve is created from the rib of Adam, and her name is said to be the "mother of all living beings." Eve's name really means something more like "life," but to call her the mother of all living things is to usurp the role of a female deity and give it to a human woman, the ancestress of the race. Furthermore, the two words *nin* and *tu* or *ti* separately may mean "from the rib" in Sumerian. Some linguists, however, translate *tu* or *ti* as "life," and associate Nintu's name with Eve's name because of the reference to "life" in both. In Sumerian the same symbol was used to mean "life" and "rib" and Sumerians probably told a story with this pun for some significant meaning. Nintu can be called "Lady Life" or "Lady Rib" (Vawter 75; Benjamin 45–46; Lim 127).

This creates a perfect image for the biblical author, so that the woman who is taken from the Adam's rib and will be called, "Mother of all living," is the human version of Nintu. Nintu was associated with Ea or Enki, the god of the sweet waters who was symbolized by flowing water, but sometimes the image of a snake was associated with him. Nintu was portrayed as the patron goddess of pregnant women and sometimes portrayed bare-breasted with outstretched, loving arms that have snakes wrapped around them. Eve encounters the snake and bad things result. This is a classic example of how the biblical authors cleverly assimilate imagery from the ancient Mesopotamians to attack their beliefs (Lim 130). There is no goddess Nintu, but rather she was really a human being named Eve. The sneaky monotheist Eve steals Nintu's identity.

> Genesis 2:21–25
>
> *(21) So the LORD God caused a deep sleep to fall upon the man, and he slept; then he took one of his ribs and closed up its place with flesh. (22) And the rib that the LORD God had taken from the man he made into a woman and brought her to the man. (23) Then the man said,*
> *"This at last is bone of my bones and flesh of my flesh; this one shall be called Woman, for out of Man this one was taken."*
> *(24) Therefore a man leaves his father and his mother and clings to his wife, and they become one flesh. (25) And the man and his wife were both naked, and were not ashamed.*

In Gen 2:18 God declares that the Adam needs an *'ezer*, a helper, so the animals are created. But, alas, none of the animals can function as a true helper, so God has to embark upon a more drastic plan. God creates a woman and the natural corollary: sex between the man and the woman. Inherent in the creation of two genders is the natural emergence of sexual activity. Too often teachers and preachers give us the impression that sex was the result of the sin in Genesis 3, but that is wrong. Sex as an activity is created and blessed as a natural human function in Genesis 2. Again, popular piety foists upon us an interpretation not found in the text.

God creates the animals to find a helper for the man, but none of them fit the bill. After God creates the animals, the Adam still looks pathetic and lonely, and we almost hear God saying, "Well, that didn't work, let me try another idea." This somewhat humorous interpretation of God's actions may not be too far from the biblical author's intent. God experiments until God finally decides to create the woman out of the Adam, for that is the best way to get a closely related being.

Jews and Christians have declared for many years that since the "male" was created first and the "female" was taken from his rib, this is why men are superior to women. Strangely, however, no one has ever stated that because the woman was "taken from" the man and therefore subordinate to him, that likewise man who was "taken from" the earth is therefore subordinate to the earth (Kselman 88; Fretheim 353; Brodie 141). Nor has anyone ever interpreted Genesis 1 to say that since the animals were created first and people on the sixth day, the animals were superior to people. Usually interpreters of Genesis 1 proclaim that humanity was created on the sixth day to be the crown of creation. Why don't they say that woman was created after man in order to be the "crown" of the human race, and thus superior. People too often interpret the biblical text for their own ideological convenience.

The Hebrew in Genesis 2 undercuts the nonsense of all such arguments. The "man" is called 'adam in Hebrew until the woman is created. The 'adam, as noted previously, is a generic word, which can refer to people of both sexes, as it clearly does in Genesis 1. Even in Gen 3:23–34 when the 'adam is expelled from the garden, obviously it refers both to the male and the female (Bal 112–17; van Wolde 1994:24). It is a generic word that can refer to the whole human race. But after the "woman" is taken from Adam's rib, and only from that point onward is the Adam called by a word that clearly implies masculine identity, 'ish or "male." The term occurs in Gen 2:23; 2:24; 3:6. The word for "male" then alternates with the word Adam throughout Genesis 3. Hence, the "Adam" does not become masculine until after the woman is created (Trible 1978:94–105; Swidler 76–78; Bal 112–17). This is a major point to make. Male and female identities arise together; the male did not exist before the female. The same is said in Gen 1:27. Gender identities or sexual identities emerge at the same time. Any argument that speaks of which sex came first or later is not rooted in this biblical text.

God creates the woman to be a "helper" for the Adam. The old King James translation said she was a "helpmeet." Sometimes readers of the Bible and teachers declare that this expression indicates how the woman was created to serve the man as his subordinate. Essentially all women were created by God to "serve" men. However, the text is absolutely not saying this at all. The word usually refers to a person who helps in time of need, and it could imply a degree of superiority, though commentators disagree on whether that is the intention here (Trible 1978:90; Stratton 96; van Wolde 1994:18; Miller 2003:323). Sometimes when the term 'ezer is used, it describes the actions of God in saving a helpless humanity in dramatic fashion (Exod 18:4;

Deut 33:7, 26, 29; Pss 33:20; 70:5; 115:9–11; 121:1–2; 124:8; 146:5). One would certainly not say that God was subordinate to people when such divine deliverance came. At other times the word refers to military assistance (Isa 30:5; Ezek 12:14; Hos 13:9). People who say this passage implies that women were created to serve men obviously have not looked at these other passages. The woman is a helper to the man as God is a helper to humankind (Mullen 102; LaCocque 2006:103). The word *'ezer* comes from the Hebrew word for "strength," *'oz*, and it was used in royal names such as Azariah and Uzziah (2 Kgs 14:21; 2 Chron 26:1), both names mean "strength of Yahweh" (Westermann 32). The word *'ezer* is a powerful word by which to describe the newly created woman. She is an aide to the man, certainly an equal partner, and, as we shall discover in the next chapter, an articulate spokesperson.

To anticipate our discussion a little, we must say something about the woman's role in Genesis 3. She does the talking with the snake. Over the years people have interpreted this to mean that she was the weaker sex and so the serpent came to tempt her. The implication of the text is otherwise. She was an *'ezer*, an intelligent partner for the man. Perhaps we might even say she was a perfect co-conspirator, for they both ultimately connived together to eat the fruit, as we shall see. She did the talking, because she was clever, and perhaps she was the better speaker. She spoke for both of them, because she was an *'ezer*.

It is worth noting that in other comparable ancient Near Eastern accounts of the entrance of suffering or mortality into the world, the dramatic personage who "falls" or "fails" is a man, such as Adapa. The creation of woman is a unique story in the ancient Near East, and as such it places high value on the woman (Westermann 232). The only exception comes from outside the ancient Near East in the Greek story about Pandora opening the box and letting all those bad things out. Otherwise the dramatic personage is a man, because women were simply not considered rational, intelligent beings worthy of being the central personage in an account about the origins of suffering or mortality. By the mere fact that the woman is the central personage in Genesis 3, the biblical text portrays her as rational, intelligent, articulate, and worthy of being the one who is tempted. This story is actually a compliment for women by assuming the woman to be the central persona. Yet preachers and teachers have missed that point and instead dwelt upon the inferior moral fiber (or intelligence) of the woman. Perhaps the point is missed because too often men and not women have interpreted the narrative in authoritative fashion in the past. Only in the modern era with more female biblical scholars have we come to see the text in a different light.

God created the woman by first placing the Adam into a deep sleep. The Hebrew word is *tardemah*, which elsewhere is a word which refers to the deep sleep or an induced sleep (1 Sam 26:12; Isa 29:10) in which a vision is received from God (Gen 15:12; Job 4:13) (Wenham 1987:69). Why the author chose this term rather than a simple word for sleep has never received a good explanation. In this deep sleep God makes a woman out of the man's body. As the man was produced from the earth, so he becomes like the earth to produce the woman, his body is a fertile field to produce new life (Naidoff 6).

The woman is fashioned out of a rib taken from the Adam. The Hebrew word is *tsela*, which generally means "side." In fact, nowhere else in the Old Testament does it mean "rib." We take our cue from the Septuagint, the Greek translation of the Old Testament, which does translate this word as "rib." We also assume that if Adam's "side" is alluded to, it probably means a "rib" from his side. However, a very creative recent suggestion by Ziony Zevit proposes that God took Adam's penis bone, a bone found in other animals, but not man (or the spider monkey). The story would explain why men lack this bone, why the underside of the penis appears to be "stitched," and how the bone returns to the man as he embraces the woman face to face (Sanders 26). But such an interpretation loses completely the allusions to Nintu in this passage, and Nintu is alluded to later in the story when Eve is called the mother of living beings and so steals Nintu's title.

In making the woman God exhibits the same careful craftsmanship demonstrated in the initial creation of the Adam and the subsequent creation of the animals. Again, God is intimately involved in the direct creation of things and people (Trible 2003:96). It is worth noting that woman was made from only one bone taken from the man, the rib, the rest came from God (Lim 128). Why was the rib chosen? A clever statement was made by the old commentator, Matthew Henry in 1710,

> the woman was not made out of the man's head to rule over him, nor out of his feet to be trampled upon by him, but out of his side to be equal with him, under his arm to be protected, and near his heart to be beloved . . . if man is the head, she is the crown, a crown to her husband, the crown of the visible creation. The man was dust refined, but the woman was dust double refined, one removed further from the earth. (Henry 7, quoted in Lim 128).

What is so nice about this quote is that Henry says the woman's creation from the man's rib is not a sign of her subordination or inferiority to the man, but a sign of her equality. This statement comes from a Protestant divine in the early eighteenth century. Truly, Henry's observations are a refreshing change from so much of the rhetoric of female subordination that has come from Christian preachers and teachers over the years. In comparable fashion, Alan Richardson notes that the woman is taken from the rib, for her place is beside the man, not before or after him (Richardson 67). Bruce Vawter and Ellen van Wolde believe that when the man says that the woman is "bone of his bone," he is making a statement about her equality with him (Vawter 75; van Wolde 1997:54).

But seriously, why was the rib chosen? One good observation is that the Adam, subsequently the masculine man, symbolically will have a rib on one side missing. That rib returns to him when he holds the woman in a close embrace. The man will have his rib especially when he holds his wife tightly in the embrace of love and sexual activity. When a man and a woman hold each other in such sexual embrace, the result will be the creation of people. Elsewhere in the biblical text, laws encourage people to engage in sexual activity in order to have children, and the missionary position is the one favored, for it is perceived as the sexual position most likely to produce pregnancy. Thus, our author may use this imagery to explain why this position of embrace between males and females is the natural one for procreation.

As noted above, the Sumerian goddess Nintu or Ninti, whose name can mean "from the rib," is called the "mother of all living," is portrayed with snakes around her arms, and is considered to be the patron of pregnant women. All of these characteristics become attributes of Eve, and it begins with the allusion to her creation "from of the rib." The rib imagery is used by the biblical author to undercut the concept of the goddess Nintu, and comparable deities who perform her same functions, by saying that a human ancestor, Eve, is mistaken for a goddess by those foolish Mesopotamians. Eve is the demythologized version of the Mesopotamian mother goddess (Van Seters 124).

The word play on Nintu's name is lost in translation in the Hebrew, but the biblical author seems to provide another possible word play with the use of the terms for man and woman. The Hebrew word for masculine man is 'aesch, and the word for woman is 'aeschah. The word for man in Hebrew has three consonants: *aleph, yod,* and *shin.* The word for woman has three consonants: *aleph, shin,* and *heh.* Now the two consonants shared by these two words are *aleph* and *shin,* and these two consonants by themselves are the consonants in the word "fire." The consonant unique to the word for man is *yod,* and the consonant unique to the word for woman is *heh. Yod* and *heh* are the first two consonants in the most sacred name for God in Hebrew, Yahweh. These two consonants alone can be an abbreviated form of that sacred name in some of the ancient poetry found in the Hebrew Bible. Thus, one senses that the biblical author might have an interesting but subtle religious message in our narrative. One could say that if you take God out of the marriage relationship, all that will remain is the fire of contention. Or you might say that the fire of sexual passion is what people naturally have in common, but God binds the husband and wife to each other.

When God brought the newly created woman to the man, he responded, "this at last" is my helper. She is "bone of my bones, flesh of my flesh." It was an astute insight on the man's part to observe that the helper for him would be a creature made from his own body. When he speaks of her as being from his bones and his flesh, especially since she was made from his rib, the man is expressing a sense of solidarity with the woman, not a sense of superiority. He calls her woman, but he does not "name" her, as he did with the animals, so he does not have that mark of authority over her as with the animals (Trible 2003:96).

One cannot help but feel that there might be a little petulance in the tone of the man's voice, a little impatience, as if he were saying, "Well, it's about time, God!" God appears to experiment, trying to find an adequate helper for the man. In turn, the man is critical of the divine attempts, some of them not so successful, to find this helper. God is patient with the man's impatience, for God is gracious.

The man has a new creature formed out of his own body. The man has "given birth" in a sense to another creature; he has performed the function of being a mother, and God, of course, was the midwife. This imagery may not really be intended by the biblical author, but if it is, the implications are interesting. It means that the male is the creator of life until the woman is commissioned to become "Eve," the mother of all living beings. Then the right of birthing new life passes to her. In part, this might explain some of the enthusiasm behind Eve's statement in Genesis 4 when she gives birth to Cain. She now has become the creator of life and has taken that role away from her husband. (Poor guy didn't have it very long, did he!)

The biblical narrative then offers an aetiology that explains the institution of marriage. Some commentators suggest that this story does not relate the creation of the institution of marriage but rather explains mutual sexual attraction of men and women, or the establishment of close interpersonal relationships (Gunkel 41; Westermann 232). But a comparison with the *Atrahasis Epic* reinforces the idea that this story is an aetiology for marriage. In that narrative seven pairs of males and females are created out of clay, and they are called husbands and wives. The institution of marriage is clearly affirmed in that story, and the biblical story appears to be parallel to the *Atrahasis Epic* in so many aspects from Genesis 2 onward, that the biblical author probably intends this narrative to relate the institution of marriage (Batto 2000:621–31).

Because the woman was made out of the man, the man is deficient—missing a rib. This deficiency is overcome when the woman is restored in the marriage relationship. Thus, marriage exists because it is necessary to restore the original organic relationship that should exist between men and women. This metaphor has different implications. It conveys the image of intimate sexual relationships between men and women. The man receives back his rib only when he holds the woman in sexual embrace. Furthermore, if the word rib in Hebrew is a double entendre metaphor for the male penis, which we suspect, then the image is even more sexual. The man receives his rib back from the woman at the same time he gives a "rib" to the woman in the act of sex.

The word for "clings" comes from the Hebrew word *dabak*, which also has a strong sexual connotation. It provides us with the imagery of husband and wife clinging tightly to each other both in sexual passion and for mutual protection against the challenges of life. It provides us with the picture of marriage as the tight union of two people, natural and necessary for human existence. When the ancient Judeans heard this story, the image of the creation of the first family spoke to them about human survival. A man and a woman raising children and living on the land was the primary human institution for survival. It took a family, and a large family, to engage in the agricultural struggle to survive in highland Palestine. The creation of the woman for the man puts in place the necessary component for the creation of a family (Hiebert 60–61).

Some commentators wonder whether the passage implies matrilocal marriage, wherein the husband lives with the father of the bride and her family or clan instead of a patrilocal marriage relationship in which the bride comes to live with the groom's family. Most marriage relationships in our world are patrilocal, and that was the usual custom among Israelites. But some of Israel's neighbors, especially the nomadic people who surrounded Israel, practiced matrilocal relationship. It seems that Moses may have married into a clan that practiced matrilocal relationships, and perhaps this is why the deity came to challenge his leaving the tribal territory with his wife and child and even tried to kill him (Exod 4:24–26). At any rate, some commentators believe that a matrilocal relationship might be implied by the reference to how the husband leaves his father and his mother when he gets married. Athalya Brenner creatively suggests that this passage hints at an initial superiority of the woman, but it was later lost with the patriarchy established by the divine judgment in Genesis 3 (Brenner 1984:128). I believe that the reference to leaving the father and the mother simply refers to how the husband leaves his parents' home and sets up a home of his own, and how his primary familial allegiance transfers from commitment to mother and father to a commitment to wife and children (so also LaCocque 2006:132).

This reference to leaving parents in order to enter into a marriage relationship foreshadows Genesis 3. Just as the man must leave his parents when he marries, so the man and the woman must leave the garden. Is this a hint that they should leave the garden at a similarly appropriate time? Should they leave the garden when they become adults? Perhaps their rebellion is part of the process of growing up and challenging parental authority (van Wolde 1997:59–62). If so, then there is an interesting parallel between Genesis 2 and Genesis 3 about the process of human maturation.

If marriage and sexual relationships are established in Genesis 2 and the first reference to procreation does not occur until Genesis 3, then sexual activity existed in the garden as a possibility. Marriage theoretically is established as an institution in Genesis 2 without procreation being the primary purpose. The primary purpose of marriage and sexual relations then would appear to be for the healthy psychological relationship of the man and the woman, especially since God is seeking a partner or a "helper" for the Adam (Batto 2000:621–31; Miller 2003:322). This contrasts with later biblical legislation that lays a heavy emphasis upon having children, and laws that condemn forms of sexual behavior that do not effectively produce offspring.

This passage raises significant questions for theologians in denominations today that stress human reproduction and are critical of birth control. If the man and the woman engage in sex because that is integral to their psychological relationship, then, having children, though important, is not the primary purpose of sex. In some traditions, this interpretation of the passage has caused serious reflection and debate over the ecclesiastical position that condemns birth control by married couples.

That brings us to other significant questions. Did the man and the woman actually have sex in the garden? Some Rabbis felt that they did engage in sex; *Genesis Rabbah* 22:2 states that they had sex on the very day that they were created (Blenkinsopp 2011:71). (Rather eager!) However, most readers get the impression from the narrative that they did not have sex. Perhaps they did not find time because they were quickly expelled in Genesis 3. Perhaps they did not have sex for another reason, which we will discuss shortly. Could they theoretically have engaged in sex? The implication seems to be yes. They were married and the language associated with their relationship is strongly sexual. Too many Christians over the years have assumed that the fall into sin was somehow connected to a sexual act, and only after they sinned, did they have sex. Or they believe that sexual activity could not come into existence until the couple had been exiled from the garden. This is false. Those who believe that sexual activity did not arise until after the couple left the garden imply that sex is sinful. They believe that sex either was part of the sinful rebellion or arose after the rebellion, and therefore sex is evil, though necessary for bearing children. Some Christians have often enjoined other Christians to refrain from sex, because it is an evil act. This biblical text does not teach that. Instead, it teaches that sexual activity in marriage was instituted by God and was part of the created order in the garden.

The man and the woman did not have sex. Why not? The clue may be in the phrase that they were naked and not ashamed. This statement is not saying that sex and shame go together, so that the absence of sex meant the absence of shame. The statement really indicates that the man and the woman are not aware of their respective sexual identities. They have no shame because they have no sexual awareness. They have no sex because they are not mature enough or aware of sexual activity. They have no sex in the garden because they are children. In Genesis 3 it will become clearer that they are children.

Not all commentators agree with me. Bernard Batto believes that describing the man and the woman as naked was an ancient Near Eastern literary convention used to describe people who were not yet civilized. For example, in the *Gilgamesh Epic* Enkidu is naked before he becomes civilized through the help of the sacred prostitute Samhat. Batto also refers to a Sumerian myth *Ewe and Wheat*, as well as another text, both of which describe people in the very distant past as living naked (Batto 1992:55-56). Nonetheless, I believe my interpretation fits more consistently with other imagery in Genesis 3. But we shall determine that by consideration of Genesis 3.

8

The Origin of Evil according to the Ancients

WHY WOULD THE GOOD gods create evil and suffering? The ancients could not attribute the origin of evil as a direct act willed by the good gods. They told stories that implied human mortality, human suffering, and evil came into the world as a mistake or chance happening. If willed by the gods, perhaps it was unintentional or the side effect of another act designed primarily to be good. Mortality, suffering, and evil were tragedies, mistakes, and once these things entered into the universe, they were destined to remain. Throughout the mythic narratives we sense a fated-ness about their presence. Perhaps ancients preserved the goodness of the gods by sacrificing the concept of freedom in the universe. Bad things existed because of fate or "bad luck" on the part of some primal ancestor.

Biblical authors stressed human freedom, disdaining the notion of fate and the fixity of forces in the universe. In return they stressed that the presence of mortality, suffering, and evil resulted from human free will. They had to admit that to some degree these things existed by the will of the one God. Thus, the biblical tradition portrays God somewhat "darkly" at times. But this tension is the price paid to affirm monotheism and human freedom.

In the ancient Mesopotamian creation myths, the first evil actions were committed by rebellious gods who were defeated by the creator deity. People were created from the blood of those rebellious gods and thus inherited their evil and rebellious nature. Evil is thus predetermined, fated, built into the fabric of the universe and people by the events in the divine realm in the primordial age. In the biblical narrative, however, people freely rebel against

God by eating the fruit, and that begins the scenario in which evil will arise. Evil comes from human will, not the cosmos (LaCocque 2006:49).

A number of myths arose in the ancient Near East that spoke of the origin of evil, suffering, and mortality. The greater number came from Mesopotamia where intelligentsia were more interested in such questions. Scholars speak of the more pessimistic view of life held by Mesopotamians, and indeed we have far more of this literature from them than from the Egyptians.

Earlier we spoke of an ancient Sumerian myth (3000–2000 BCE) entitled *Enki and Ninmah*, a myth that describes the creation of people by Enki and Ninmah. The latter half of the story describes how these two deities became drunk and entered into a contest. They created defective human beings and challenged the other to find a place for these people. This myth indicates that the good gods would not have created people with misery and suffering, the gods were drunk when they did it. Though it sounds silly when you first hear the idea, it has merit as an explanation in that it preserves the essential goodness of the gods. A mother of a child with Down's Syndrome told me that she would prefer that explanation over the notion that such evil was the ultimate result of human sin.

A short Akkadian myth from the second millennium tells the story of *Adapa*, whose name can linguistically mean "man." Adapa was a king and priest in the service of Ea or Enki in Eridu, the garden of the gods. He also was a sage with special wisdom and understanding; he was blameless, but he did not possess eternal life. Adapa reminds us very much of Adam in the garden, who ultimately obtained wisdom or knowledge by eating the fruit but lost access to immortality. In other references to Adapa we also learn that Enki created him to be an ideal man and granted power to Adapa to name animals, as did Adam (Lind 125; York 401). In this short story Adapa was fishing and the south wind submerged him, so he cursed the wind, and the result was that it no longer blew over the land. This caused the rain to cease and brought drought and loss of crop yield, thus offending the gods of vegetation. Adapa was called to the heavens to appear before Anu, but before his arrival, Enki advised him not to eat bread or drink water while in the heavens, lest he die. Adapa dressed in mourning garments with ashes in his hair. When the vegetation gods, Dumuzi and Gizzida, saw him, they felt sorry for him and pleaded his case to Anu. Adapa was given new garments and oil by Anu, which he accepted, and then when he was offered the bread and water of life by Anu, he turned it down. Anu laughed at his decision, and Adapa went back to earth, thereby losing eternal life for himself and all humanity (Pritchard 101–3; Hallo and Younger 1:449). Eternal life was lost because of a bad turn of events. But the question that remains is the nature of Enki's advice. Did Enki give Adapa the correct advice not to eat, but then Anu changed his mind after hearing Adapa's speech and provided the bread and water of life? Or did Enki lie so that Adapa and humanity might not become immortal? If the latter is the case, was Enki preventing human immortality out of compassion for humanity, lest they overpopulate the world and thereby suffer? Was Enki preventing Adapa and humanity from encroaching upon the gods by becoming immortal, in addition to being wise? A third possibility might be that Enki did this because Anu wished it (Stordalen 246). The text is difficult to read at the end of this myth, but it seems that Anu released Enki's city Eridu from some obligation perhaps as a reward to Enki. Whatever the answer, immortality was denied to humanity because of fate and bad luck. The Adapa story also tells us that wisdom and immortality combined constitute equality with the gods. Like the man and woman in the garden, Adapa ultimately has wisdom but was denied immortality (Skinner 92; Pritchard 101–3; Mettinger 101).

There are interesting similarities between Adapa and Adam: 1) both underwent a test, 2) both failed the test, 3) both lost the possibility of obtaining immortality, 4) humanity received the consequences of their loss, 5) both are part of the first generation of humanity, 6) both have linguistically equivalent names, and 7) both may have been deceived by the deity about the results of the test (Enki said the food was poison; God said they would die immediately when they ate of the tree of knowledge) (Tsumura 1994:35; Carr 1996:245). Yet there is one truly significant difference. Adapa lost immortality because he obeyed Enki; the man and the woman lost immortality because they disobeyed God (Wenham 1987:1, 53). This betokens the fated nature of life in the Mesopotamian account, while the biblical narrative hinges on the freely chosen decisions of the man and the woman.

A very cute little story, which may speak to the issue of the origin of pain and suffering, is the short Akkadian myth of the *Worm and the Toothache* from the early second millennium BCE. The story is told that after Anu created heaven and earth, the little worm was created by the marsh. The little worm went weeping to Shamash, the sun god, and Ea (or Enki) saying he had no place to live. The worm asked to live in the teeth and gums of people, an obvious allusion to dental problems faced by the ancients. The worm was given places to stay, including the fig, the apricot, and human teeth, because the gods had to order creation (Pritchard 100–101). So again we encounter the idea that the good gods would not create evil, but sometimes in the course of the emergence of world order bad things will happen. Evil once more arises as a result of fate.

The Akkadian *Gilgamesh Epic*, from the late second millennium BCE, relates how Gilgamesh undertook a quest to find the secret of immortality because he was unnerved by the death of his friend Enkidu. He sought the survivor of the flood, Utnapishtim, in a far and distant land to discover the secret of immortality. Gilgamesh learned that Utnapishtim was uniquely granted immortality for surviving the flood, and thus Gilgamesh could not share in this gift. However, Utnapishtim told Gilgamesh of a plant that could rejuvenate his youth when he grew old. Gilgamesh tied rocks to his feet to sink to the bottom of the ocean and find this plant. Upon returning to his home city of Uruk, Gilgamesh took a swim in a pond to refresh himself after his long journey. He left the plant on the bank of the pond where a snake ate it. Obviously the story explains why snakes apparently would not die a natural death, but would regenerate, leaving behind their old bodies (the snake skins we see in the forest). This story may also explain why human beings are mortal: Gilgamesh lost the plant of life or rejuvenation in the ancient time. Bad luck again for human beings. What is striking about this story, however, is the presence of the snake, which we find in Genesis 3 also. Once again we observe another common theme. Gilgamesh has wisdom, but not immortality at the conclusion of the epic, like his counterparts Adapa and the couple in Genesis 3 (Mettinger 101).

Earlier in the Gilgamesh Epic there is an interesting account that may be germane to Genesis 3. When Gilgamesh ruled Uruk with an oppressive hand, he demanded the right to make love to newly wed brides on their wedding night—truly the act of a tyrant in any age. People cried to the gods, and the gods sent Enkidu down to earth to distract Gilgamesh. Enkidu was a wild beast who terrified people in the countryside and cavorted with wild animals. To tame this wild beast Gilgamesh sent a temple priestess or temple prostitute named Samhat to have sex with him. The temple prostitute was really a symbol of great urban civilization. She represented the temple, which was the other important symbol of civilization in the city, in addition to the palace. Priests and kings were the rulers of the cities and they symbolized the gods to the people. So the prostitute represented the authority of the city, as well as the urbane sophistication of the cities and sedentary society. (I guess she was like the modern-day movie star, a similar kind of icon!) Her sexual activity was considered to be an avenue to the divine realm that could obtain fertility for people and the land, and fertility for the land was extremely important for settled river valley agriculturalists. So perhaps she also represented agricultural society. Enkidu, on the other hand, was a wild beast of the highlands. Perhaps, he represented the wild tribes of the mountains or the shepherds of the pastoral regions, both of whom lacked the sophisticated civilization of the river valley from whence the prostitute came. The temple priestess made love to Enkidu for days, and when Enkidu was finished (finally), he went to play with his animal friends, but they ran from him. He had become civilized; he had a "fall" into civilization. The temple priestess had domesticated him and made him part of civilization with an activity that was part of the divine cultus in the temples. Enkidu had no choice but to put on clothing and go into the city where he ultimately became Gilgamesh's friend. Later in the epic when Enkidu died, he cursed the temple priestess for bringing him into the civilized life style that led to his death. Does his curse also imply that by "falling" from his earlier natural state into a civilized state he gave up immortality for wisdom? That is difficult to say. But the story bears strange similarities with Genesis 3, because Genesis 3 also associates "coming into knowledge" with some form of sexual awareness on the part of the man and the woman. In fact, one also notices that as Enkidu puts on clothing, in Genesis 3 God clothes the man and the woman. Hence, one sees the images of knowledge, sexuality, and clothing in both stories. The significant difference, however, is that while Enkidu died, the man and the woman went forth to create a community and ultimately civilization (Westermann 226; Carr 1996:245).

Zoroastrian traditions are interesting for consideration also. The problem is that we do not know how to date Persian accounts. The Zend-Avesta was written in the seventh century CE, but the literature was in oral and fragmentary written form for centuries before that. Persian kings who ruled the Judeans in the late sixth century BCE, Cyrus the Great (perhaps) and Darius I, were Zoroastrians, as were the successor kings in the next two centuries. If the biblical material in Genesis 1–11 arose in the sixth and fifth centuries BCE, the biblical authors might have been aware of some Persian beliefs and stories. In Persian mythology the gods lived on sacred mountains with gold and flashing gems, and where miraculous trees impart immortality. Persians tell of Meshia and Meshiane who lived on fruits but were tempted by Ahriman, and they did wickedness. Also, Yima, who had no illness or death, ruler of the golden age, gave way to pride and fell under dominion of the evil serpent Dahaka (Skinner 92–93; Hinnells 34, 38). Could the biblical author have known these stories, or could biblical narratives have fallen into the hands of later faithful Zoroastrians? Either avenue of contact is possible, since we cannot date Persian traditions very well.

When we turn to Genesis 3 and read the account, it appears that the man and the woman are exiled from the garden because they sinned against God by eating the fruit. The story is then understood by the Christian tradition to be the beginning of human sinfulness, pain, and suffering in the world, as well as the origin of original sin. Christians assume that had the man and the woman not eaten the fruit, we would still be in the garden today.

The narrative, however, is more complex than that simple understanding. When we read it closely, interesting questions arise. What is the relationship between the two trees? Were the man and the woman inherently immortal? Was sex somehow connected symbolically to the sin? (That seems to be a very popular assumption.) Who or what is the snake? (The narrative does not associate the snake with the devil as the later Christian tradition does.) Why does this sin seem to take precedence over the sin of murder in the next account of Cain and Abel? What was the overall message of the story when it was first presented to the ancient Israelite or Jewish audience? For more than a century commentators have realized that there is a sophisticated message in this text, and they have asked these questions of the narrative.

Those trees in the garden produces not only fruit, but also many scholarly responses in the modern era. Hermann Gunkel (1997) believes that the story tells how humans obtained knowledge at the price of getting pain and misery (Gunkel 28-33). Gerhard von Rad (1961) feels that the narrative is about human pride, the desire to be like God, and the self-destruction caused by such *hubris* (von Rad 87). Odil Hannes Steck (1970) states that the message of the text is to describe the alienation between God and people, as well as between people (Steck 66-73, 124-25). Gordon Wenham (1987) states that the story is a parable of what happens whenever people disobey God (Wenham 1987:90). Ellen van Wolde (1989) sees the account as a parable about humanity coming to adulthood (van Wolde 1989:216-19). James Barr (1993) believes the story tells how people almost attained immortality but lost it (Barr 4). Terje Stordalen (2000) opines that the narrative bespeaks how humanity began with little knowledge and access to immortality but moves to a state with more knowledge and no immortality, for humanity cannot have both without being divine (Stordalen 241-42). Mettinger (2003) believes the story describes a test that the man and the woman fail, for had they refrained from eating from the tree of knowledge, they would have freely been given immortality from the tree of life. The account also reflects Deuteronomic theological assumptions (Mettinger 42-64). Presumably scholars will continue to provide creative and insightful interpretations to this narrative. Everyone's opinion may capture part of the meaning of this deep and theologically profound text.

9

Sin in the Garden

Genesis 3:1–7

(1) Now the serpent was more crafty than any other wild animal that the LORD God had made. He said to the woman, "Did God say, 'You shall not eat from any tree in the garden'?" (2) The woman said to the serpent, "We may eat of the fruit of the trees in the garden; (3) but God said, 'You shall not eat of the fruit of the tree that is in the middle of the garden, nor shall you touch it, or you shall die.'" (4) But the serpent said to the woman, "You will not die (5) for God knows that when you eat of it your eyes will be opened, and you will be like God, knowing good and evil." (6) So when the woman saw that the tree was good for food, and that it was a delight to the eyes, and that the tree was to be desired to make one wise, she took of its fruit and ate; and she also gave some to her husband, who was with her, and he ate. (7) Then the eyes of both were opened, and they knew that they were naked; and they sewed fig leaves together and made loincloths for themselves.

The snake asks a simple question, nothing more, a simple question. "Did God say, 'You shall not eat from any tree in the garden?'" At first blush it appears to be a straightforward question seeking information from one of the human inhabitants of the garden. After all, the humans were in charge, weren't they? They had named all the animals, including the serpent. So it seems that the snake is simply asking for clarification. Or perhaps he is simply asking a question to pass the time of day, much the same as when we make mindless observations about the weather to people on the elevator simply to fill the empty silence with human sound. It is a harmless question, or so it might seem, were it not for the first sentence in the narrative, which tells us that the serpent is crafty.

The snake speaks in the plural (the "you" in the text is masculine plural in the Hebrew—masculine is used whenever the audience has at least one male), so he addresses his question and the rest of his dialogue to both the man and the woman (Vawter 79; Fretheim 360; Stratton 260). Some might maintain that the serpent is merely repeating the command that God had spoken to the couple previously, and that is why a masculine plural occurs. However, God gave the command to the Adam in chapter 2, not to both of them. Hence, I assume that with the use of the plural verb here the author intends us to see the snake speaking to both the man and the woman as they stand before him. If the snake is speaking to both, they are equally tempted and tempted together. Too often Christians popularly teach that the woman was tempted first and then the man came on the scene later to be ambushed by the woman giving him an apple. The text implies both are standing there, and later the narrative will more clearly indicate the man was present with the woman throughout.

"Now the serpent was more crafty than any other wild animal that the LORD God had made." So the audience knows that something is afoot. The serpent is crafty, and crafty animals do not engage in conversation simply to pass the time of day. Doves and rabbits might do that, but not crafty serpents. The audience is alerted to the possibility that the serpent is going somewhere with this question. The woman and the man are going to be "set up" or at least "tested" by the crafty serpent.

The audience, however, is alerted to something else about the serpent. He is a wild animal and the God made him. He is smart, but still just an animal. The man and the woman have no business being outwitted by him. The audience is alerted to the realization that if something bad happens, it surely is more the fault of the human creatures than this wild animal, no matter how crafty he may be. The snake is a creature made by God, and since everything made by God is good, we realize that the snake is not an intruder or some alien evil force (Westermann 238).

In the ancient world of Israel snakes were imbued with divine or at least semi-divine power according to popular lore. Ancient folk saw snake skins lying about on the ground and assumed that a living snake had arisen out of a dead snake. Snakes knew the secret of resurrection. A snake would not die by itself, it would simply come to life again. The snake would die only if killed, and that should lead us to realize the importance of the image of how people would crush the heads of snakes according to one of the curses (Gen 3:15). The image of the snake rising anew from its own dead body was transformed in later mythology, in one part of the ancient world, to the symbol of the phoenix bird rising from its own ashes.

If snakes could come alive again, then according to the logic of ancient belief, they must know the secret of immortality. In addition, they must know the secrets of healing, which would enable them to resurrect themselves. Hence, snakes became objects of veneration by people seeking healing, long-life, and immortality. They were associated with healing gods and goddesses.

Throughout the ancient Near East we observe snake symbolism. In Mesopotamia they were associated with goddesses of childbirth and fertility, especially Nintu, the goddess of pregnant women, who was portrayed with coiled snakes around her arms. Nintu's title was "the mother of all living things," which ironically becomes the supposed meaning of Eve's name. The snake image in Egypt was found on the crown of pharaoh in the form of the Wajet or Uraeus, a helping serpent who protects the wearer against his enemies. The serpent swallowing his tail was Egypt's symbol of immortality; the coiled serpent represents the principle of *Ma'at*, which means law, order, wisdom, and the ultimate structure of the universe. Ordinary Egyptians carried snake skins to help them make good decisions (Benjamin 51).

Snakes in the Greek world were also associated with healing deities, the most famous of whom was Asklepios (spelled Asclepius in the Roman world). His cult would be one of the three great rival religions to Christianity for the commitment of people in the third and fourth centuries CE. Asklepios was a human hero in the *Iliad*, later a semi-divine figure, and finally a full-fledged god, a god of healing. Devotees would come to his temples on various Aegean islands (Cos, Lebedae, and Tricca) and in western Turkey. They would offer up sacrifice, purify themselves, undertake rituals, consume special potions, and then sleep in the central temple area on an animal skins. During the night they would have dreams in which the god Asklepios would come to them and touch the afflicted parts of their bodies to heal them. Sometimes the god was accompanied by his faithful assistants, snakes and dogs, and occasionally these animals would lick the afflicted portions of a dreamer's body. (I suppose the god gave them the easy cases!) The experiences of these dreamers are classic "incubation dream" theophanies, that is, dreams deliberately sought by sleeping overnight in a shrine. Such incubation dreams could be for the sake of healing, but others could be for the purpose of obtaining a message from the gods.

In the ancient Near East important people, kings and priests, slept in shrines after undergoing the proper rituals, in order to receive a message from the deity, which could be either a spoken auditory message dream or a visual symbolic dream (Gnuse 1984:11–55, 1996:34–68). Usually common people did not seek such messages, but they would undertake an incubational experience in a shrine for healing, and this, of course, was the custom that spread to Greece and evolved into the Asklepian cult. In the Asklepian shrines many people were healed, or so they thought, over the years, and suppliants left inscriptions of their religious healings in the temple precincts. We have dug up these inscriptions and evaluated them, and we call them the "Testimonies." They "testify" to the many ailments for which people sought remedies from the god, but they also "testify" to the graciousness of the deity in healing human ailments. Actually, there were numerous Greek deities who were sought in incubational dreams for healing, but the most famous and most popular was Asklepios.

What is fascinating about these "testimonies" left in Asklepian shrines is that in some instances the incubants describe experiences in their dreams wherein the priests gather around them and engage in some activity connected to their healing. It makes us think that the priests performed operations. It makes us suspect further that the dream visions were caused by some powerful potion they drank, and this potion may have been a sedative or pain-killer which enabled the priests, who were doctors, to perform simple operations (Gnuse 1996:113–14). It is worth pointing out that Hippocrates, the Greek doctor who gave us the medical oath that bears his name, was a priest in the shrine of Asklepios on the island of Cos. It seems that the dreamers at times may have experienced surgery, which they remembered as a dream or a divine theophany. At other times, however, it seems as though they simply had dreams in which they believed that the god healed them, and no real medical procedures were performed. So we are not absolutely sure of what happened at all times.

One final point is worthy of mention. Hippocrates is credited with giving us the symbol of the caduceus, which modern medical professionals wear. It is the image of a snake wrapped around a pole. (The Army Medical Corps has two snakes wrapped around the pole.) That is interesting, for that clearly is an ancient Near Eastern symbol, which the Greeks probably received from the Phoenicians. Is this snake around the pole a symbol of Asherah in Palestine? Many times in the Bible Asherah is described as being in the form of a "pole." This may be sarcasm on the part of the biblical authors, who reduce the snake image to a mere "pole," or perhaps she was portrayed as a stylized pole with a stylized snake wrapped around it. Was this the symbol that was exported to the Greek world to become a symbol for Asklepios and the later medical profession? Is the snake in the tree in Genesis 3 a parody of that symbol, the symbol of a healing god or goddess in the ancient world? I am tempted to say yes to both questions. Thus, in Genesis 3 the snake could symbolize Asherah, the tree would be the "tree of life," the fruit might be a sacred meal in an Asherah shrine, and all of Eden could be seen as the garden precincts of an Asherah shrine. The biblical author parodies the Asherah cult with these narrative symbols to declare that Asherah worship brings death not healing and immortality (Stordalen 289–90; Lanfer 38).

The relevance of this entire discussion for the consideration of our biblical text is important. The narrative in Genesis 3 reduces the snake to merely a talking animal. The snake is not a god, not a goddess, not a divine force with power to overwhelm the will of the man and the woman. The narrative is a monotheistic attack upon the ancient piety connected with snakes and snake deities. The text, in effect, implies that these gods do not exist, and the snake is just a snake. In a polytheistic age the biblical author had to deny the divinity of the snake to affirm the oneness of God. Only once the battle for monotheism had been won could readers of the text begin to connect the snake with a being such as Satan. Perhaps, Wis 2:24 might be the first text to say that the snake in the garden was the devil, or perhaps this passage may actually refer to another account lost to us. Jack Levison, for example, believes this text actually refers to a "bad" wife, not "Eve" at all (Levison 617–23). The second or first century BCE book of *1 Enoch* says that a being called Gadreel seduced Eve—*1 Enoch* 69:6. Not until several centuries into the Christian era do we actually find concrete references that connect the snake in Genesis 3 with Satan or the devil. But Genesis 3 does not make this equation (Skinner 73–81).

For now, we must return to our talking snake in the tree. The biblical text says that he is "crafty" or "cunning" (according to various English translations). The Hebrew word is *'arum* which sounds strikingly like the word for "naked," *'arummim*, which, of course, is what the man and the woman become after listening to the snake's advice (Vawter 76; van Wolde 1997:50; Cotter 34). The word play is a joke, which denotes that the man and woman listen to the cunning snake, but they do not become cunning or wise, only naked. Or perhaps, the cunning snake leaves the couple naked, but not wise. Or perhaps, the people should have known that if the snake were cunning, it would only lead to their nakedness. Whatever! It's meant to be humorous! The bottom line is that when you try to explain a joke, it never really sounds as funny as it was with the original word play.

After the snake asks his question, the woman responds, "We may eat of the fruit of the trees in the garden; but God said, 'You shall not eat of the fruit of the tree that is in the middle of the garden, nor shall you touch it, or you shall die.'" We immediately notice that the woman expands the command to include the additional imperative, "nor shall you touch it." She also deletes the expression, "for in the day that you eat of it." The latter omission may not be that great since the verb form "you shall die" is a Hebrew verb form used in law codes to mean swift justice, hence, the implication of immediate death might still be included. But that addition, "nor shall you touch it," is a major addition to the divine command, which makes the imperative even more difficult to keep. For centuries commentators have noticed this and they have tried to come up with reasons why the woman added the expression. The theories fall into three categories.

1) The man and the woman simply expanded upon the command somewhat unconsciously, assuming by implication that if you cannot eat the fruit, you really should not be holding it in your hand, since that would be the prelude to eating. This is a nice, logical explanation, rather banal in its perception of the entire plot, however. The real question should be why did the biblical author choose to put these words into the woman's mouth, for it clearly indicates that the command has been expanded, and the author appears to be making some symbolic observation.

2) The woman exaggerated because of her emotional state. Commentators have suggested that she was anxious about the issue of dying, if she were to eat the fruit (Fretheim 360). Perhaps, she says this because she is suddenly confused while talking about this fruit to the snake, or perhaps it is innocent defensiveness, or perhaps she has general anxiety simply in speaking about such matters to a strange talking snake!

I do not like these answers because they try to rationalize what might have in the woman's mind without asking the question of why the narrator tells the story this way. The fact that the woman changes the command of God means something significant, it is banal to assume that the narrator simply wishes to portray her as anxious or confused.

3) The rabbis suggested that perhaps the man expanded upon the command in order to protect the woman. Wasn't that sweet of him? If the man could keep the woman from touching the tree, then certainly she would be less tempted to eat the fruit from the tree. For this reason the snake was able to convince the woman to eat the fruit, because the snake touched the tree and did not die. One rabbinic story (*Abot Nathan*, chap 1) has the snake shaking the tree with his hands and feet so that the fruit fell from the tree, and then he turned to the woman and pointed out that he could touch and eat the fruit without dying, and so could she (Skinner 74; Kugel 77; G. Anderson 2001:77–78). If the man indeed exaggerated the command of God in order to protect the woman, the man was putting a "hedge" around the command, that is, adding laws to the original command to make sure that the original command would be kept. Often the rabbis felt that such expansion upon the Torah's guidelines for living should have such a "hedge" made up of additional logical deductions from the original laws in order

to assure faithful obedience. (Other rabbis dissented and declared that the Torah did not need such a "hedge," the Torah was sufficient in itself for a life of religious obedience.) If the man made an additional guideline or "hedge," it was to protect the woman and insure that she would not eat of the fruit and be lost to him. Of course, the woman was not present when God gave the command to the man in the first place, so the man could have feasibly done such a thing. This is a sweet, romantic explanation. One addendum to this argument came from Rabbi Nathan who said that the man exaggerated the command for lack of trust in Eve, and since this lack of trust led to the fall, it was a greater sin than eating the fruit (Cotter 38–39). (Even though I disagree with Rabbi Nathan overall, I like his suggestion of the man's greater culpability in this regard.)

I do not like the explanation that the man exaggerated the command to protect the woman. There is an assumption here that demeans the woman. It implies that the man has to make additional legislation to protect his sweet, simple-minded, weak-willed wife. Baloney! She was an *'ezer*, a strong helper. She needed no such protection from her husband. Perhaps, you might say he expanded upon the guideline because she was strong-willed and headstrong. That, too, is demeaning, for it implies she had not the good sense to obey, as supposedly the man did. In both instances, it is assumed that the man is capable of not eating the fruit, but that the problem was with the woman. As we shall see, the biblical text implies equal culpability for both, so it is not a question of his superiority in an attempt to restrain her.

I believe that the author of Genesis 3 is trying to say something about the psychological attitudes of both the man and the woman. The addition of the expression, "nor shall you touch it," implies that they both have been thinking about eating the fruit. As Claus Westermann said, "One who defends a command can be on the way to breaking it" (Westermann 239–40). Perhaps, they have even brooded on it, wondering just exactly what would happen if they ate the fruit. Perhaps this is why they have left out the expression, "for in that day that you eat of it." They forgot that supposedly there would be immediate punishment; they can only think about what will happen when they eat of it.

There are some other things that the woman has left out of the original divine statement. God said that they could eat from "all" of the trees, and the woman leaves that out. She is limiting the gift of God and brooding over the one tree that they cannot eat from. She has also left out an infinitive absolute, a word that modifies and strengthens the word "eat" in reference to those other trees. Usually infinitive absolutes in Hebrew are translated as "surely" so as to strengthen the meaning of the main verb. In our text the translation is "freely." The woman has left out that word, once more limiting the graciousness of the divine gift of being able to freely eat of the other trees (Naidoff 8). What she has left out is perhaps more revealing about her mental attitude. She is limiting the nature of the divine gift. Perhaps she believes that if God can take away one tree from the, perhaps more will be taken away in the future. God is made to look irrational and tyrannical. She has turned God from being the Divine Provider into the Divine Withholder (Naidoff 8). Yeah, she's thinking about eating that fruit! Furthermore, she does not name the tree as God did in the initial command. She simply refers to it as the tree in the middle of the garden. Is this a way of implying that the other trees are forgotten as the couple obsesses on this one tree? If so, the theory that at one time the narrative only had the "one tree" and then the "tree of life" was added to the story becomes an unnecessary theory. Are the man and the woman obsessed with "that tree," the tree "in the middle of the garden," to the exclusion of everything else?

They have exaggerated the command of God. They have made the command more difficult to keep, perhaps even impossible to keep. For it may be possible to avoid eating the fruit directly, but if the command includes touching, that is an activity which could occur quite by accident. One of them might inadvertently walk through the garden and touch the tree or the fruit and then be punished. How unfair is that? The man and the woman have exaggerated the command of God to make it appear unfair, almost impossible to keep, a command that will inevitably be broken during a casual stroll in the garden. God must be incredibly unfair, so they reason, to create a command that will be broken by unintended actions. They have already justified in their minds the eating of the fruit. We can hear them reason, "If I'm going to touch the tree by accident someday, I might as well eat the fruit now and get it over with!" We can hear them say, "Yeah, I'll trip over the knobby knees of that cypress tree, roll up against this tree of knowledge and then, 'zap,' God will get me. I might as well eat the fruit now." The man and the woman thought about eating the fruit well before the snake popped the question.

They exaggerate the command of God to rationalize breaking the command. For them the first step to disobedience is redefining the command. Leon Kass cleverly observes this little scene from the legal perspective that "sloppy speech is a corruption of law" (Kass 85). He further notes that their free decision to eat the fruit reflects that already they have reason and judgment; they simply advance further in their autonomy by this act of rebellion. The sin results in "the rise of man to his mature humanity . . . in all its pathos and ambiguity" (Kass 88).

Do you recognize the logic of the man and the woman? I like to ask this of my college students, and they never seem to get the point. If, however, there is an older person in the class, that person always knows the answer. The man and the woman in the garden are children (Gunkel 18; van Wolde 1997:62). Children exaggerate commands that their parents give them, making them impossible to keep because the commands become irrational to the child's mind. I then say to the college kids, wait ten or fifteen years until you have children. If I come back again and ask you the same question, you will know the answer.

If the man and the woman were children, this would explain why they were naked, but not ashamed. They were too young to be embarrassed. It would explain why they did not seem to engage in sexual intercourse even though they were married. It explains why they tried to blame each other; that's what children do. It indicates that the curses proclaimed by God are not a reality that begins because of their sin; rather, they are a painful introduction to the "children" what the adult world is really all about. Leaving the "garden" becomes a symbol for entering into the adult world. Finally, the narrative of the fall becomes also a narrative of "ascent," or "coming of age," as the children now painfully become adults, perhaps a little earlier than God willed. Certainly God then can be envisioned as a parent, and their rebellion is the necessary act of ascent that leads to adulthood and ultimately "culture" and "civilization."

The serpent counters with a more direct approach. He senses that the man and the woman have been thinking about eating this fruit. So he directly states, "You shall not die; for God knows that when you eat of it your eyes will be opened, and you will be like God, knowing good and evil." How cleverly worded the snake's response is! What is said by the serpent is both true and untrue at the same time.

God has said that the people would die on the day on which they ate the fruit. The snake says that this will not happen. Ironically, what the snake says is true, for the couple did not die. God will be merciful and not execute them; the snake apparently knows the merciful nature of God and knows that God will forgive them. The snake is correct in saying that they will not die on the day on which they eat the fruit, but he does not inform them that they will die someday. The serpent tells them what they might gain; he does not tell them what they will lose (Lim 141–42). Some commentators have noted that the snake appears to be more truthful in describing the eventual consequence of eating the fruit than does God. R. W. L. Moberly comments that this unveils the ambiguity of faith in God, which can be difficult when the snake appears more truthful than God and likewise the great mysteries of life seem to be hidden from us (Moberly 78–87). Carr suggests that God directly lied to the humans simply to protect them, just as Enki may have lied to Adapa in the Sumerian myth (Carr 1996:245).

As noted in our discussion in Genesis 2, some Christian commentators have suggested that God meant they would become mortal and die eventually. This implies that they were inherently immortal. I suspect that the man and the woman were not immortal; they were very mortal, otherwise the tree of life would not have been a significant tree for them. If eventual mortality was what the text meant, it was not much of a threat, considering how long they lived. Eventual mortality would not have meant much to the man and the woman at that moment; the threat of death had to be more of an immediate death.

Thus, the snake tells the truth even though his intent is to be deceptive. They will not die that very day. I suspect that to be true because the next statement by the snake is also ironically true. The second statement by the snake is the reference to how their eyes will be opened and they will be like God, or like the gods, knowing good and evil. The Hebrew word for god, *'elohim*, may be either singular or plural, as we saw in Genesis 1. When the man and the woman eat the fruit their eyes are indeed opened. But they do not get what they expected. They do not know what they expect to receive, but they want something that makes them like God. They do not really know what it means to understand "good" and "evil." When their eyes are opened, what they realize is that they are naked. That is not what they expected. They realize shame. Oops. The snake tricked them into eating by promising something that they really did not understand. They were greedy, they wanted this knowledge, whatever it was. Once they got it, they knew they had been tricked. In reality, they deceived themselves by their own greed. After the fateful step had been taken, the man and the woman realize the deception that came with the snake's statements.

As the woman considers eating the fruit, it is interesting to observe the language of the text. The woman: 1) "saw that the tree was good for food," 2) "that it was a delight to the eyes," and 3) "that the tree was to be desired to make one wise." Commentators wax eloquently on how these characteristics indicate the intellectual abilities of the woman. She is able to assess that the fruit can provide physical sustenance, she is able to appreciate the aesthetic beauty of the tree, and she is able to appreciate that eating this fruit will bring her something she wishes to have, wisdom, even though she does not understand completely what that might be. Commentators point out that the woman's ability to discern distinct aspects of the tree, its fruit, and the expected consequences betokens not only intelligence, but even more significantly, free will. She eats from the tree out of her own free will. She cannot say that the "snake" made her do it, as so often modern Christians want to say about their own misdeeds. Genesis 3 strongly suggests this is an act volitionally undertaken by her freely and rationally. The woman sees how the fruit is to be desired; ironically the same word later will be used to describe the "desire" for her husband that would lead to her subordination (Stratton 93, 141; Lim 144–45).

What was the fruit? The biblical text never identifies the fruit. Popularly we like to say it was an apple. In the second century BCE the book of *1 Enoch* described it as a tall tree with leaves like the carob and fruit like grapes (*1 Enoch* 32:4). The association with the apple was made by the Christian Latin poet, Commodianus, who lived in the fourth or fifth century CE, probably because the Latin word for apple (*malum*) was like the adjective for bad (*malus, mala, malum*). They did not have apples in the ancient Near East. The rabbis variously identified the fruit with grapes, figs, wheat, carob, etrog, and nuts, some of which were considered aphrodisiacs. For a number of years there was the popular belief that the fruit was the tomato. That idea was sometimes found in Hispanic cultures in the early modern period.

A truly good guess, however, would be that the tree was a fig tree. Fig trees were fruit trees commonly grown in the ancient Near East. Furthermore, the text immediately says that they sewed fig leaves together to make clothing. It would be logical for them to take the leaves from the tree under which they were standing, especially if they were extremely embarrassed by the realization of their nakedness. (They probably knew not to make clothing out of the poison ivy on the neighboring tree.)

The implied allusion to a fig tree might be a polemic against Mesopotamian beliefs. Dates and figs were symbolic fruit associated with the lovely Inanna, the fertility goddess, and Dumuzi, the sometimes shepherd and sometimes fertility god, who was her lover. In the earliest Sumerian texts of the third millennium BCE, the relationship of Inanna and Dumuzi is associated with the fertilizing process of fig and date trees. Since Nintu appears to be a manifestation of the great high goddess Inanna (or Ishtar according to her Akkadian Semitic name), it seems that there are hints of this goddess throughout the narrative in Genesis 2–3. But in every instance, one gets the impression that the biblical author is debunking the existence of Inanna by attributing so many of the images and themes connected to her with the human woman, Eve, instead. The allusion to the fig might be part of the author's overall theological strategy.

A recent interesting suggestion is that the tree might have been a pomegranate tree, because that was a common religious symbol used in Egyptian artwork and apparently used also in the Temple of Jerusalem. The pomegranate tree was associated with fertility, sometimes it was a symbol connected to the goddess Asherah, and the bright flower of the pomegranate tree was sometimes envisioned as a symbolic representation of the male testicles. Sometimes in the ancient world the pomegranate symbolized the female womb because its many seeds represented the woman's potential for many children (Sanders 61). Since sexual imagery seems to occur obliquely in this text, perhaps the sexual symbolism connected to the pomegranate might make it a tree worth considering as a possibility. However, the fruit of the pomegranate tree is a very hard nut, which would break your teeth, if you bit into it. In that case, if the man and the woman ate a pomegranate nut, they would have gained some wisdom, and the criminal deed would have been its own punishment. Probably, the fig is a better suggestion. Perhaps, the biblical author simply does not wish to identify any particular tree as the special tree, lest the audience place a stigma on that tree and its fruit.

Christians often declare again that woman is inferior to man because the woman was tempted first, ate the fruit, and then tempted the man in return. Once more the biblical text says something else. In Gen 3:6 it states that the woman took the fruit and ate, and "she also gave some to her husband, who was with her, and he ate." Notice that the male was with her through this process of dialogue with the snake. He stood by her silently during her discussion with the snake, and he did not disagree, which implies his agreement with her. The male and the woman were tempted simultaneously.

The woman ate the fruit and she gave some to her husband, who was with her. There is no indication that she became aware of her nakedness and then gave the fruit to him at some later time. It appears that she gave the fruit to him almost immediately. For the text declares that their eyes were opened, and the implication is that the eyes of both were opened immediately. He had to be standing there next to her. That would be the logical sense of the Hebrew expression, "who was with her." This is further reinforced by the fact that when the snake spoke to the woman, he spoke in the second person plural, as though he was speaking to more than one person.

The man stands there the entire time and does not try to stop the woman from eating the fruit. He does not try to respond to the snake. He does not correct the woman when she says that they should not touch the tree. As Terence Fretheim aptly states, he "acts as a silent partner" who neither resists, reflects, or asks any questions (Fretheim 360). What is the matter with this dope? Why doesn't he do anything? The answer is simple. He wants to eat the fruit, too. Why does the woman do all talking? (Don't say he couldn't get a word in edgewise!) Perhaps, that is part of her skill as the *'ezer*, she is the better speaker of the two. The man is simply silent during the dialogue with the snake; his moral behavior is lower than that of the woman (Stratton 86). Johnson Lim points out that the expression "with her" could additionally imply that he supported her in the plan to seize the fruit, and his response to so quickly eat the fruit implies that he is more culpable than she (Lim 138–41).

When I was little and this story was recounted to me, I received the impression that the man was not around when the woman talked to the snake and ate the fruit. He was in the back of the garden, he was playing cards with the penguins, working on the car, strolling in another part of the garden, but he was not with the woman. When he encountered the woman, she then deceitfully gave him the apple to trick him into the fall. She fed him an apple, or apple pie, or apple crisp, or an apple tart, or something, and behold, we got ten thousand years of original sin! But I was left with the impression that she tricked him into eating the apple. One very romantic interpretation of the story suggests that he knew she had eaten the apple, had fallen into sin, and soon would have to leave the garden. So he willingly ate the apple because he loved her and wished to accompany her wherever she went. That's an adorable story! But that is not what the text really says. "He was with her," says the text. He stood beside her the entire time, and they ate the fruit together.

In the east Mediterranean world, from whence this story originates, it is understood that when a woman speaks in the presence of her husband, she speaks on his behalf, or at least she speaks in unison with him. Normally a woman does not speak at all to outsiders in the presence of her husband. But we have been told by the account that she is a remarkable woman, she is an 'ezer. She speaks for him as well as herself; she acts on his behalf. In fact, according to east Mediterranean values, the man would be more culpable than the woman, for theoretically she acts at his behest. This would explain why the curse on the man is as long as the curse on both the snake and the woman combined. One might reply that the subordinate silence of the woman in east Mediterranean culture came into being only after the curse. Nevertheless, we must ask the question as to what the audience would have assumed when they heard the story. Their assumption would be that anything stated by the woman represented the man's views or at least the views of both of them acting together. That is not how I was taught to read the story. I was taught to blame the woman.

That the woman does the speaking is actually a compliment to her skills as an 'ezer, for it implies that she was intelligent enough to speak for the both of them. She was truly the "helper" that God intended her to be for the man. That the story compliments the woman and credits her with being the more articulate speaker is a point we sorely miss in our Sunday School narrations. Instead, we blame the woman inordinately. Other ancient Near Eastern literature did not give women credit for being intelligent, so the other literature did not even put a woman in the story. Elsewhere, the loss of innocence or immortality is blamed on a man, either Adapa or Gilgamesh. The Bible compliments the woman greatly by assuming that she is intelligent enough to engage in the dialogue with the snake and be the focal point of the temptation experience. One creative suggestion proposes that the woman dialogues with the snake because in the ancient world the tree of life was associated with a mother-goddess, so that this narrative is another polemic against polytheism and mother-goddesses (Schüngel-Straumann 89).

In order the blame the woman even more than the man, some translations omit the Hebrew expression "he was with her." This implies that she engaged in dialogue with the snake and ate the fruit when the man was not around. It is amazing how much you can change the nature of the account by leaving out or ignoring that little Hebrew expression, which is only one word in Hebrew. Over the years a number of rather official translations of the Bible into English have left out the expression, "he was with her," and the result was that countless readers were encouraged to believe that the woman sinned on her own part and later suckered the man into eating the fruit. Translations guilty of omitting the expression, "he was with her," include the following: Rheims-Douay Version (1582/1609), the Revised Standard Version (1952) (fortunately the New Revised Standard Version (1993) includes "who was with her"), the New English Bible (1970), the Living Bible (1971), the Good News Bible (1976), the Revised English Bible (1989), and the Bible of the Jewish Publication Society. The New World Translation (1984) is deceptive by saying, "when he was with her," which directly implies that he came along later. The most honest translation is the Contemporary English Version (1995), which says, "Her husband was there with her." One must begin to wonder if some of these translations did not provide the missing expression because the translators were afraid to include it (Parker 729–47). Selling Bibles is big business, and if a translation offends its audience, the Bibles might not sell. Since conservative Protestants are the biggest market for Bibles, this is a crowd that the publishers might be loath to offend.

There is a New Testament passage that affixes blame upon the woman, and this passage often is used to interpret Genesis 3. The author of 1 Tim 2:13–15 says, (13) "For Adam was formed first, then Eve; (14) and Adam was not deceived, but the woman was deceived and became a transgressor. (15) Yet she will be saved through childbearing . . ." This passage states that the male was formed before the female, and that the woman and not the man was deceived. We must painfully admit that this New Testament passage misinterprets Genesis 3. As we have seen, the word male is not even used in Genesis 2 until the word female appears. Adam does not mean male. Furthermore, 1 Tim 2:14 literally says that the male was not deceived but the woman was. A simple reading of Genesis 3 will not permit anyone to say that the man was not deceived, for he admits it before God in Gen 3:12, if only to say that the woman deceived him. The author of 1 Tim 2:13–15 has played freely with the text in Genesis.

We must acknowledge that the author of 1 Timothy had a noble reason for attempting to subordinate women. The later authors of the New Testament after Paul's death attempted to subordinate women and legitimate slavery because they needed to make Christianity more compatible with Graeco-Roman family values in order to enable Christianity to spread throughout the empire. We must view this as a temporary concession made by the writers of those letters in the late first century CE that enabled Christianity to survive in those early difficult years. Their advice is not meant to be used on a long-term basis. Ultimately, when Christianity became the successful religion of the empire, it would have been capable of returning to the more normative rhetoric of Paul in Gal 3:28 wherein he says that the differences between slave and free, male and female, Greek and Jew were abolished in the Christian movement. That is the normative message of Christianity; Gal 3:38 is the major voice, 1 Tim 2:13–15 is minor voice in the biblical testimony. Christian theologians have often said that "scripture interprets scripture" and sometimes scripture corrects scripture. Galatians contains the enduring message that is far more congruent in the Gospel message of divine love for humanity, while 1 Timothy contains the temporary message (like telling Corinthian women to wear hats, but not women of all time). We must wisely see that in the greater message of the Bible, the passage in Galatians is the normative statement for Christian life. First Timothy 2:13–15 clearly misread the text for his own situational needs, but that situation is past. We must have the courage and good sense to make the appropriate interpretation. Unfortunately, I believe, too many have allowed 1 Tim 2:13–15 to interpret Genesis 2–3 against the rather clear message of those latter passages, rather than to let Gal 5:28 interpret 1 Tim 2:13–15.

The Genesis 3 narrative declares, "Their eyes were opened." Opened to what? This introduces the great debate as to what the fruit brought to the human beings in terms of "knowledge." What is that "knowledge" more precisely, and what does it mean that the knowledge encompasses everything from "good to evil" or that the knowledge brings the awareness or discernment of "good and evil." We spoke of this earlier.

Whatever that knowledge entailed, it certainly brought with it the awareness of nakedness, which correspondingly implies the awareness or consciousness of shame. Those who argue for various aspects of moral awareness or discernment have this piece of significant evidence on their side. The awareness of shame at being naked does seem to imply some form of moral awareness, especially the moral awareness that comes with adulthood.

I am inclined to suspect that whatever form of knowledge or awareness that was brought by eating the fruit, a significant aspect of this awareness was that the man and the woman are no longer children but adults. This becomes even more evident to me in the following narrative where the man and the woman, like children, try to pass the blame to someone else, when they should be acting like the adults that they have become. It seems that they may have developed the awareness and the shame of adulthood, but they are still living with the moral responsibility of children, that is, they do not want to take moral responsibility for their own personal behavior. By eating the fruit, they have rebelled against God and they have grown up too soon, sooner than God wished for them to do. This is why they have shame with no corresponding sense of moral responsibility for their actions. If, indeed, they are children, this would explain not only why they were naked, for that so often is the way in which children run around in warm climates. It would explain why they apparently had not engaged in the act of sex, even though they had been married in the previous chapter.

Now that they know that their own nakedness is a condition that they should avoid, they undertake actions to cover themselves. They sew garments of fig leaves together to make loincloths. One can only wonder what they sew these fig leaves together with; the text tells us nothing. So the man and the woman hide in the underbrush, wearing the latest in fig-leaf fashion. One can only wonder what they thought that they were going to do next.

10

Divine Pronouncements

THE HUMAN ENCOUNTER WITH GOD

Genesis 3:8–15

(8) *They heard the sound of the LORD God walking in the garden at the time of the evening breeze, and the man and his wife hid themselves from the presence of the LORD God among the trees of the garden. (9) But the LORD God called to the man, and said to him, "Where are you?" (10) He said, "I heard the sound of you in the garden, and I was afraid, because I was naked; and I hid myself." (11) He said, "Who told you that you were naked? Have you eaten from the tree of which I commanded you not to eat?" (12) The man said, "The woman whom you gave to be with me, she gave me fruit from the tree, and I ate." (13) Then the LORD God said to the woman, "What is this that you have done?" The woman said, "The serpent tricked me, and I ate."*

GOD COMES WALKING IN the garden, perhaps enjoying the beautiful garden, much in the same way that a Mesopotamian king would stroll through one of his artificially created gardens. We sometimes sense that this is one of those royal images that implies God is the king who has created and "stocked" a "paradise," as was the custom of kings. God strolls in the late afternoon or early evening as the heat of the day begins to abate. The man and the woman hear God walking. (One wonders how large was the divine shoe size and how much noise did God make? Yet again our biblical author symbolically portrays God anthropomorphically to emphasize the personal relationship of God to the people.) But the man and the woman, God's favorite pets, are hiding among the trees. God immediately knows that something is wrong. When God calls, the man responds that he was afraid because he knew he was naked. That rather large admission communicates a great deal to God. God immediately asks whether they have eaten from the tree of knowledge.

When the man responds to the question, he is rather disappointing. He says, "the woman whom you gave to be with me, she gave me fruit from the tree, and I ate." Notice how ironically he reverses that little expression, "with me." Previously he was "with" the woman when she talked to the snake and ate, and he was "with" her in his eating of the fruit. But now he says that she is "with" him. Is he trying to regain his own self-perceived role of leader? But overall his response shows a great lack of responsibility for his own personal actions. He seeks to blame the woman for giving him the fruit. But, in reality, he seeks to blame God for making the woman in the first place. Under the rhetorical guise of passing the blame to the woman, he is really passing the blame back to God.

Children pass the blame to each other when they have disobeyed a parental guideline, and ultimately they try to blame the parent. This is what the woman was doing when she (or the man before her) exaggerated the command of God not to eat the fruit. They made the parental command impossible to keep. Now they pass the blame down the line and back to God. That is what children do, as well as adults who fail to grow up and accept responsibility for their own actions. Moral responsibility means accepting the responsibility for your own actions, right or wrong, owning up to your own deeds. The man and the woman in the garden do not do that, and they are portrayed as children. They have eaten the fruit, they have become adults in their knowledge, but they still act like children. Actually the biblical author wishes for the listeners and readers of the story to realize that when they fail to own up to the responsibility for their own actions, they act like children. The biblical author may be calling upon an entire generation to accept their responsibility for their sins, and perhaps for their exile in sixth century BCE Babylon.

Picture, if you will, three small children in the kitchen. Mommy has made wonderful homemade cookies and placed them in a jar high above their reach. The six-year-old places the four-year-old on his shoulders, who then pushes the two-year-old up to the level of the cookie jar. However, the cookie jar comes down with a crash and shatters. Mommy comes into the room to see what happened, and of course, she can figure it out immediately. Mothers have that ability. The six-year-old blames the four-year-old, the four-year-old blames the two-year-old, and then both the six-year-old and the four-year-old blame the two-year-old, because the two-year-old cannot talk well enough to defend himself, and the older two siblings figure mommy won't punish the two-year-old as hard. They also imply that had mommy not made the cookies smell so nice, it never would have happened. That is the scene, more or less, with the man and the woman (though the snake hardly counts as a two-year-old).

The man's response is irresponsible; he blames God immediately. "The woman whom you gave to be with me" is the first sentence out of his mouth, simultaneously blaming her and God. He probably would have continued to blather about how she did all the talking and ate the fruit first, but God turns to the woman. She says more simply, "The serpent tricked me, and I ate." She does not insinuate directly that God is responsible, as the man so crudely did, but perhaps by blaming an animal, she indirectly blames God, for God made the animals. The animal supposedly "tricked" her. That is true in part, but not totally true. She ate of her own free will, she made the decision that the tree was good for food, a delight to the eyes, and to be desired for wisdom. She made all of those decisions on her own; the serpent did not do her thinking for her. Some commentators, however, suspect that when the woman admits that the snake "tricked" her, perhaps she is admitting that she did something for which she should be ashamed (Stratton 54, 90). The text implies that she and the man had been thinking about eating the fruit, it is not true that the serpent tricked her.

God does not even speak to the snake. Why should God do this? God will not address an animal, he is not worthy of a question. God's relationship is with the people, and they have failed. God's children have failed. The snake is not a being with a special relationship to God, the snake is not a child, the snake is not a divine being, certainly not the devil, the snake is just a clever wild animal.

The man and the woman have actually committed two sins, and perhaps the second sin is worse than the first. They rebelled against the command of God by eating the fruit. They failed the test that God had given them by placing the tree of knowledge in the garden. Then they refused to accept responsibility for their actions; they tried to pass the blame down the line, ultimately back to God. They were free; they chose to eat the fruit freely. Then they denied that freedom by refusing to take responsibility for their actions, even after they had become adults by eating the fruit. This was the greater sin. I like to think that theoretically that if the man and woman had fallen to their knees and begged God for forgiveness, they would have been forgiven and allowed to stay in the garden (Brown 2010:288; LaCocque 2006:228, opines they at least would be forgiven). That is the impression that I get from so many other stories in the biblical tradition. But they never repented, never asked for forgiveness, never said that they were sorry. That was their second sin; they denied responsibility for their actions. That, I believe, was the greater sin, the sin that cast them out of the garden. The biblical author may be trying to impress upon the audience the significance of this second sin, which is greater than the first. For it is immediately after this dialogue with the man and the woman that God utters the curses upon all involved in the rebellion.

When we tell the story to small children, we emphasize how the man and the woman ate the fruit, but we never really mention how they behaved so badly in trying to pass the blame to each other. Maybe we don't understand the story because we too often are guilty of the same offense.

The biblical author was speaking to his generation, Israelites and Judeans in the first millennium BCE. In their age, there was a strong belief in fate. The ancients believed that the fated-ness of the events in the universe could be overcome only by offering up powerful sacrifices to appease the gods and bend the cosmic fates. Our monotheistic author, however, assumes one God and a universe in which people are free and responsible. Our author paralleled the actions of the man and the woman with people in his age who viewed themselves as fated, and believed the most important religious response to the universe and the gods was to offer up powerful cultic sacrifices. Such people were living as the man and the woman, not accepting their freedom and the responsibility for moral behavior that came with such freedom. The man and woman sinned by acting as though they were fated, and the biblical author wished for his audience to move beyond their beliefs in a fated universe with its many nature deities to a monotheistic understanding of God that entailed belief in true human freedom and moral responsibility. Such a worldview would maintain that obedience to the law and to moral norms was far more important than cultic ritual activity. If I am correct, the sin of eating the fruit was only the foil for unveiling the deeper sin of the man and the woman—their refusal to accept their own personal freedom and moral responsibility.

The man and the woman ate the fruit and rebelled against God. They failed the test of obedience. Now they await the divine sentence. They were told that they would die on the day that they ate the fruit. Would that happen?

Misunderstood Stories

Pronouncements by God

Genesis 3:14–19

(14) The LORD God said to the serpent, "Because you have done this, cursed are you among all animals and among all wild creatures; upon your belly you shall go, and dust you shall eat all the days of your life. (15) I will put enmity between you and the woman, and between your offspring and hers; he will strike your head, and you will strike his heel." (16) To the woman he said, "I will greatly increase your pangs in childbearing; in pain you shall bring forth children, yet your desire shall be for your husband, and he shall rule over you." (17) And to the man he said, "Because you have listened to the voice of your wife, and have eaten from the tree about which I commanded you, 'You shall not eat of it,' cursed is the ground because of you; in toil you shall eat of it all the days of your life; (18) thorns and thistles it shall bring forth for you; and you shall eat the plants of the field. (19) By the sweat of your face you shall eat bread until you return to the ground, for out of it you were taken; you are dust, and to dust you shall return."

The curses issued by God upon the man and the woman are well-known and oft quoted. Actually, however, only the snake and the ground are cursed, the man and the woman are not cursed, but rather are told the bad things that now await them. The fact that we so often speak of the curses on the man and the woman reflects the fact that we are misinterpreting this narrative to some degree. God is not cursing the man and the woman, but rather informing them of the difficult aspects of life that they will encounter. Perhaps, God is informing them of what awaits them now that they have knowledge, and that these things were awaiting them even before they ate the fruit.

These statements by God explain why human work must be difficult, why women must be subordinate to men, and why there is conflict between snakes and people (or perhaps the entire animal realm may be represented by the snake). At least that's what we were taught as small children. We were also taught that these realities were fixed and would remain such until the end of time.

Is God really declaring that these painful aspects of reality have now begun as a result of human sin, or is God informing the man and the woman of what now lies ahead for them outside the garden? (Blenkinsopp 2011:56, 77) Let us begin with an initial question. Did the snake walk before the curse, or did he always crawl? If the snake is in the tree when he talks to the woman, it implies that his method of locomotion did not really change after the curse, for he never had hands and feet. His curse simply reinforces the existing reality of being a snake. If so, then the information imparted to the man and woman also describes an existing reality awaiting them before they ate the fruit. We so often think that hard labor, female birth pains, and female subordination result from eating the fruit. But the text only says that when they ate the fruit, they would die (either immediately or eventually), but hard labor, birth pangs, and female subordination are not mentioned as threats. Presumably they are part of life, and when the man and the woman gained knowledge, they gained knowledge of what awaited them in real life.

If they are children, eating the fruit means that they will discover the challenges of adult life. As children grow up and assume the roles of adults, they learn about hard labor and the guidelines of life in a patriarchal society. Leaving the garden means growing up and assuming adulthood. In ancient Israel children engaged in the work in the fields at the age of seven or eight and not their early twenties, after graduating from college, as is the case for so many today. Coming of age in ancient Israel or among post-exilic Judeans occurred about the same time as children came to the age of accountability and were expected to know the difference between right and wrong. It all fits together: about the same time in life children realize the difference between right and wrong, they begin to understand the roles of male and female and truly understand the nature of hard work. God is explaining the "curse" of adulthood to the man and the woman now that they have moral accountability gained from the knowledge of "good and evil." The punishment of the "curses" really seems too great for the crime of eating the fruit, unless the "curses" are also about growing up and learning about real life (Westermann 195). Thus, these "curses" should rather be called "pronouncements."

Growing up also means learning the deeper meaning of death, the loss of one's existence or the loss of a loved one. For small children do not truly fear death or become aware of its existence until they become older and experience the death of others. Seven or eight might be the age when the children began to more clearly understand what death means, especially the death of a loved one. This, of course, raises the question discussed previously of whether the man and woman were inherently mortal or immortal once they were created. It seems to me that they were mortal, but they did not understand the nature of mortality, since they did not understand death. Once they left the garden, they lost access to the tree of life, and that ensured their mortality. Only gradually will they appreciate the depths of their mortality, and full realization will come once one of them dies.

The true punishment for eating the fruit is exile from the garden that deprives them of the tree of life and ensures their mortality. The "curses" are not punishment for their rebellion but rather the description of what adult life is like. The man and the woman leave the garden to encounter hard labor, female subordination, awareness of mortality and conflict with the animal world. Metaphorically speaking they leave the garden and never know what they missed by not eating of the tree of life, making this even more a tragic tale.

Another question needs to be asked: Are these "curses" or descriptions of reality meant to be unchangeable aspects of reality until the end of time? Or are they meant to be overcome sometime in the future? Christians often speak of how the "curses" are overcome by the death and resurrection of Jesus, but by this they mean only in a spiritual sense, not in an everyday practical sense. But is that common Christian understanding correct? I think not. I believe the biblical text means that someday, in real life, in real time, these descriptions of reality are meant to be overcome by the grace of God working through human agents. If the New Testament implies that these things have been overcome, perhaps it means that people need to overcome them in everyday human existence.

When Paul says that in Christ there is no distinction between male and female (Gal 3:28), I believe he means that this is to be the reality in the life of the church and in everyday life, not in some ideal spiritual sense or in the future life. Paul also said that the distinction between Greek and Jew, slave and free was to be abolished. In the life of the church those two distinctions were removed in the ancient church. Ethnic identities did not distinguish Christians. Slaves at times became clergy and even bishops. Even if the church could not abolish slavery, it could ignore it within the Christian community. It would seem that this occurred because early Christians took seriously Paul's guidelines that there were no differences in race, class, or gender. If Paul understands that these other distinctions have been abolished in the life of the Christian community, then Paul implies that the Christ event has brought about equality between men and women, and the divine pronouncements in Genesis 3 have been overcome.

Christians have unconsciously sought to overcome the divine pronouncements in some ways. On the issue of hard labor, Christians understand that in the community of faith, people work together in many different ways in order to make life better for all. Since the arrival of the industrial age machines increasingly do the back-breaking labor once performed by people, and with the rise of labor unions in the early part of the twentieth century the old "curse" of labor was lessened by a more just and fair treatment of laborers. In regard to painful childbirth, science in the modern age has lowered the rate of infant mortality and produced medical procedures and painkillers to lessen the trauma of birth for both mothers and infants.

Ironically, however, some Christians still appeal to this account to justify the subordination of women in the church. That interpretation contradicts both Paul and the spirit of what is being said in Genesis 3.

What about for Judeans? Would they see that the three divine pronouncements are overcome in this world in some way? I believe that the Jewish understanding of the Torah, or the Law, suggests that with the coming of the Torah through Moses on Mount Sinai, the divine pronouncements were to be overcome. Within the laws of the Torah, especially in Exodus 21–23 and Deuteronomy 12–26, one may find laws that seek more rights for women, thus elevating the status of women in a patriarchal society. One can also find laws regulating life on the land and even some laws regulating the relationship of people with the animal world. This implies that the Torah portrays itself as a program for human living issued to humanity from God, through the agency of Moses, which not only creates human community, but also helps to overcome, at least in part, the divine pronouncements of Genesis 3.

If this interpretation is correct, then we have an incredible irony. The church and synagogue in the modern era have appealed to these texts in the last few centuries to legitimate the status quo in human society, saying that because of the ancient "curses," this is the way human life and society must remain forever. However, secular society has in the past few centuries attempted to undo the power of the "curses." Modern society, since the eighteenth century Enlightenment, has fought for the equality of all people, especially equality between the sexes. Certain segments of modern society have sought to create in our modern world a greater respect for the environment, thus removing the conflict between humanity and the world, which in the past few centuries has been one in which people violated the natural world order rather than stewarding it. Finally, modern society has made labor easier for many in western European and American society with the advent of machinery and labor saving devices. Ironically, religious leaders have not encouraged many of these breakthroughs; often they have opposed them. Perhaps secular society is fulfilling the gracious mandate of God to overcome those divine pronouncements. Christians claim that Jesus has overcome the divine pronouncements of Genesis 3, but the Christian Church seems to drag its feet in terms of actualizing the victory. The Christian Church has left that for secular society to accomplish.

I am reminded of a parable told by Jesus in which a man had two sons. He told them to work in the field; one said yes and the other said no. However, the one who said yes eventually changed his mind and did nothing. The one who said no eventually changed his mind and worked in the field. Jesus then asked the crowd who did the will of the father. Of course, the answer was the one son who said no at first, but finally did the work. It seems as though the church has said yes but done nothing to overcome these divine pronouncements, and secular society, which symbolically has said no to God, nevertheless seems to have done the will of God.

Though it appears rather abrupt to us, God begins to make pronouncements upon all three individuals involved in this rebellion. One would almost expect God to say something about their responses, especially since they had tried to pass the blame to each other. But instead the narrative moves directly to the divine pronouncements. The first recipient is the snake, perhaps because the last thing mentioned by the woman was the trickery of the snake. We distinguish between judgments and actual curses. God passes judgment or punishes the man and the woman, but the snake and the ground are cursed (Westermann 257; Wenham 1987:81)

The snake is described as the most cursed of the animals. We, in the modern era, immediately respond by saying, "Yes, that is because the snake is one of those animals feared and hated by people, especially since the bite of some snakes is poisonous." We either say that this state of affairs exists because of the divine curse, or we say that the biblical author chose to say that of the snake because that was the relationship between snakes and people for as long as the human mind could recall. But we overlook something very significant.

In the ancient world the snake was seen as the symbol of healing, immortality, and sexual rejuvenation. Goddesses of fertility had snake imagery associated with them; healing deities often had snakes as their symbols or part of their entourage. The ancient religions of the Near East and the later Graeco-Roman world saw the snake as a powerful symbol of healing and fertility. For the biblical author to say that the snake was cursed was to imply that all that hopeful fertility and healing imagery was a lie. It was to say that the ultimate deception of the snake was the deceptive hope that came with religious snake imagery. There was no hope of fertility, immortality, or healing from any of the rituals associated with the snake or the deities associated with snakes. This little expression, "cursed are you among all animals," is a powerful theological statement by our monotheistic author designed to repudiate all cults other than the worship of Yahweh. The snake is cursed and all cults idealizing and idolizing the snake are bogus.

The snake is cursed to crawl upon its belly. Does this mean that the snake had legs before? The account in Genesis 3 never directly states that the snake was coiled in the tree. But the text does not say he was anywhere else. If the woman saw the snake touching the tree, she may have deduced her touching the tree would not bring death, and this may have emboldened her even more to eat the fruit. We might as well assume that the snake was in the tree, since the iconography of the ancient world seemed to portray snakes wrapped around poles, which may be understood as stylized trees. He did not have legs before, so the real curse is not so much crawling as the conflict with the humans.

The curse ordains that the snake would be in conflict with people, in particular, it would be in conflict with the woman and her "seed," that is, her children. When people encounter snakes in the field, they attack the snakes. Remember the old jingle that helps you to identify the difference between the poisonous coral snake and the harmless and even beneficial king snake. In my rather large yard in southern Louisiana we have both coral snakes and king snakes. When I encounter a brightly colored snake, such as the one which fell upon me when I raised my garage door, I do not quickly chant the little poem to decide whether this snake is poisonous or not. I run or I whap it! I ran from my garage door friend and only later concluded he was a king snake. But I have whapped more than a few water moccasins in my back yard. They are exceedingly poisonous, and I do not stop to look at their heads to determine whether they might be the benign black racers. Yes, I have killed a few black racers, too! While sitting in a wooden yard chair, my wife discovered that a six foot long black snake had crawled into the chair behind her lower back. It was either a water moccasin or a black racer. When she looked down and saw it, she jumped up and ran without investigating its identity, and the frightened snake crawled the other way just as swiftly. This is what most people have done for thousands of years. They see a snake and their first impulse is to run or kill the snake.

Contemporary biblical theologians have seen the inherent conflict between people and snakes as symbolic of the conflict between people and the natural order. The biblical authors were not as aware of ecological issues as we are today, but they still had an awareness of how people lived in harmony with the natural order. They saw the natural order as a reflection of the glory and majesty of God. Although they did not see the presence of other deities in the natural forces (or they tried not to see them anymore), they did, however, see the natural world around them as the handiwork of God's creative purposes. Thus, conflict with the snake was a problem in that world order, for at least part of creation was clearly in conflict with humanity. From our perspective the snake symbolizes the conflict that has so often existed between nature and humanity, especially when humanity has abused and destroyed the environment. Our ancient Israelite and Jewish predecessors would not have seen this symbolism in the text as much as we do, but still our interpretation of this image is appropriate for our modern age. The symbol of conflict with the snake represents the reality of conflict between humanity and the natural order, and we must recognize that this is a curse to be overcome. We must learn to live with the created order around us, or surely we shall be destroyed by the created order that we have so badly violated.

Throughout most of Christian history the symbol of the snake was interpreted as the devil, or the arch principle of evil. This was not the intended meaning of the biblical author. The author sought to debunk the snake as a divine personage or representative of some fertility goddess. Since biblical authors fought the battle for emerging monotheism, they did not wish to impute to the snake some divine or semi-divine attribution. To imply that the snake was the devil, or some comparable figure, would be to create yet another god or goddess, and then one would have at the very least, dualism. Dualism was found in the great world religion Zoroastrianism, a religious movement contemporary with post-exilic Judaism, which spoke of both a God of Light (Ahura-Mazda) and a God of Darkness (Ahriman). Judeans, for the most part, disavowed dualism; they were ardent monotheists. The snake could not be a divine figure.

However, once monotheism won the day, it became possible to portray the snake as the symbol for evil, for devils, for Satan, or for whatever figure represents the force of evil that seems to permeate the world and be rooted in human nature. Theologically educated Christians see the devil as having contingent existence, unlike God, who exists outside the universe and enters into the universe, the human process, and human consciousness. God has independent existence. The devil, or Satan, or demons, or evil (whichever metaphor for evil suits you), is a force that has contingent existence. Traditionally we have said that the devil is created, and not pre-existent like God. Perhaps, it might be even better to say that the devil has contingent existence rooted in human existence, in human consciousness. If people were to cease to exist, so would the devil. Evil comes from humanity, not from any other part of creation. Conservative Christians wish to stress the existence of the devil, while liberal Christians wish to stress that evil comes from human beings and that there is no separate semi-divine entity called the devil. Both are correct. Evil, in some fashion, is truly a palpable force in the universe, as say the conservatives. But evil cannot exist in the universe without humanity, for it is rooted in their existence, in their consciousness. Destroy people and you destroy evil, sin, and the devil. Keep people, and you have to somehow redeem them from their own powerful evil. That has been the divine dilemma, the challenge faced by God.

Many early Jewish commentators viewed the snake in Genesis 3 merely as an animal, and this reinforces our tendency not to view the snake as the devil or the arch-principle of evil. The author of *Jubilees* 3:28, Philo (*On the Creation* 156), and Josephus (*Jewish Antiquities* 1:41) all imply this by pointing out that originally all the animals talked, but that this communication ceased when the man and the woman left the garden (Kugel 72–73).

When did religious authors begin to make the equation of the snake and the devil? Some Jewish authors began to equate the snake and the devil, or at the least imply that the snake was being used by the devil, as early as the second century BCE. Most of this literature, however, tended to be the more wild apocalyptic literature of that age. *First Enoch* 69:6 states that the angel Gadreel led Eve astray, and one might conclude that the author is referring to Gadreel's use of the snake, though the author might be aware of a story different from the one in Genesis 3. In the *Apocalypse of Moses* 16:4 the devil says to the snake, "I will speak a word through your mouth by which you will be able to deceive." Again in *Apocalypse of Moses* 17:4 Eve states, "The devil answered me through the mouth of the serpent." *Second Enoch* 31:6 says, "In such form he (the devil) entered paradise and corrupted Eve." *Third Baruch* 9:7 says that Satanel took the serpent as a garment. *Apocalypse of Sedrach* 4:5 says that Adam was deceived by the devil (Kugel 73–74). In the later story, *Life of Adam and Eve* (100 CE), Satan says to Adam that he was in the snake deceiving Eve. All of these are Judean Pseudepigraphical texts, not accepted as sacred literature by either Christians or modern Jews, so they lack religious authority for us. The earlier texts of Philo and Josephus reflect more the attitudes of educated and sophisticated religious authors (maybe), though that is hard for us to assess two thousand years later. At any rate, the equation of the snake and the devil is rather late and comes from idiosyncratic literature.

Thus, the devil is a late entry into the theological interpretations of Genesis 3, a symbolic interpretation to make, once the battle for monotheism has been won. Once the hearts and minds of people are truly monotheistic, the symbol of the devil or Satan, as a metaphor for human evil, can be used without infringing upon the oneness of God. Though sometimes I wonder about fundamentalist Protestant preachers, who enjoy talking a great deal about the devil. I sometimes wonder if they have not turned the image of the devil into a god who truly can rival God. Preaching about a devil can be too much fun for preachers, and such rhetoric can lead Christian theology in a very bad direction.

Once Christians brought the metaphor of the devil into the text, they could creatively metaphor the reference to the "seed" into a different image for their teachings. "Seed" can mean either plants seeds or human descendants. In Genesis 3 the original author probably intended "seed" to refer to human descendants of the woman who would come into conflict with snakes in the field. But later Christians began to sense that "seed" could stand for something else, and Christians have gone in two directions with the understanding of what the "seed" means.

Many see the "seed" stand for Jesus Christ, and the conflict between the snake and the "seed" reached its culmination in the death and resurrection of Jesus. The bruised heel of Jesus refers to his crucifixion; the crushed head of the snake refers to the defeat of sin, death, and evil by the resurrection of Jesus. This interpretation was made possible by the Greek translation of the Hebrew. For in Hebrew the pronoun "he" in the expression "he will crush," refers back to "seed." Thus, the "seed" will crush the snake. In the Hebrew "seed" refers to people in general, who will crush snakes in the field. However, the word "seed" in Hebrew is actually a singular feminine noun in form with a neuter meaning. The Hebrew pronoun "he" probably should be understood as neuter also, since it refers to people in general. "Seed" should be translated as "people," the Hebrew pronoun "he" should be rendered "they." But the Greek translators used a masculine pronoun, and they used the singular "he" since it referred to "seed" which was singular. So Christians who read the Septuagint in Greek saw the "he" in reference to seed, stressed the masculine, and made the equation with Jesus.

Some Christians over the years, however, have seen the word "seed" refer to Mary, the mother of Jesus. This is because some Latin translations rendered the feminine noun "seed" in feminine, as it was in Hebrew, and readers of the text deduced that if the "seed" was feminine, it must refer to someone in the divine realm who was feminine, and Mary was the logical choice. Ultimately, both interpretations are fine, meaningful interpretations that can give hope and strength to people, and both interpretations can become important components of both theological concepts and great artistic portrayals, as they have been for years. But in all fairness to the biblical text, we must admit that the original author probably intended something else. The author intended to say that the "people" would fight snakes and "they" would kill snakes. This does not vitiate the meaning we wish to impart to the text; rather, we must admit that the text over the years developed the possibility of polyvalent meanings, or different interpretations for believers of many different times and places. We need to hold these different interpretations in tension and respect them all. To respect the different interpretations, provided that they fit meaningfully into a Christian theological worldview that is congruent with the greater faith, is but a way of respecting the beliefs of other Christians.

There is a significant difference between the multiple interpretations given to this image of the "seed" by Christians over the years, and some of those pious interpretations of the woman's role that we have dismissed rather rudely in our earlier discussion. Those pious Christian interpretations which said among other things, that women are subordinate to men because they were created later, that the woman is meant to be the "helper" or servant of man, that the woman was tempted by the snake because women are weaker, and that women are subordinate to men because they sinned first, are to be rejected because they are interpretations designed to oppress people. They are interpretations that contradict the close, literal reading of the text. These interpretations subordinate women, and that contradicts much of the biblical text with its proclamation of divine graciousness and human equality. The various understandings of the "seed" were not interpretations designed to subordinate, oppress, or belittle part of the human race, but rather those interpretations were designed to talk about divine love and grace. Even if those "seed" interpretations are little poetic, a little allegorical, and a little too metaphorical, they resonate clearly with the core message of the biblical text about divine love.

As we turn to the next divine pronouncement, we see that it is addressed to the woman. She is told that she will bring forth children in pain. When this text was heard by ancient ears, there was the awareness that women ran an extremely high risk of death in childbirth, especially women who gave birth for the first time. The ancients also recognized that a high rate of infant mortality existed; sometimes half of all births led to the death of the infant. Indeed, death was often associated with childbirth, and this curse reflects that horrible connection. We forget how childbirth was a threat and a fear for women throughout most of human history. Jacques van Ruiten, however, suggests that the text really says that the woman will bring forth many children in the pain of everyday life; the increase will be an increase in pregnancies while continuing to work hard in the home and on the land (van Ruiten 3–26). Most would agree that is a bad curse, too.

Again, we ask whether this divine pronouncement, like the others, was to be understood as beginning at the moment humans rebelled or whether this was the pre-existing reality. More importantly, we ask whether this is destined by God to be an unalterable part of the human condition, or whether this it is to be overcome by human beings as they rule the world wisely.

These divine pronouncements are descriptive, not prescriptive; they describe the way life is, but not the way life should be. These "curses" of birth pangs and hard toil seem contrary to the ideals of human nature and a gracious God elsewhere taught by the biblical text (Skinner 95; Meyers 86–121). Certainly the lessening of the birth pangs for women has been accomplished with the use of anesthesia, and with the aid of medicine infant mortality and death in childbirth for women no longer loom as grave threats. To be sure, there are still Christian fundamentalists who condemn modern medicine and believe that women and their newborns should face these risks without modern medicine in that "God-willed" way. But the vast majority of Jews and Christians believe that medicine is a gift from God and should be used to help and to protect life. Should we not then realize that perhaps we were commissioned by God to overcome the divine pronouncements when we were told to rule the world wisely?

Many modern commentators who reflect upon these texts declare that the biblical text does not portray the subordination of women to men as a natural part of the social order, but rather a perversion of the natural state of things that needs to be overcome (Skinner 83; Simpson 510; Fretheim 363; Miller 2003:324; Schüngel-Straumann 90–91). Bruce Vawter observes that woman's subordination results from "human mismanagement rather than from a divinely decreed ideal" (Vawter 85). Phyllis Trible calls man's rule over the woman a "perversion of creation" (Trible 2003:99).

Christians may point to New Testament texts that speak of how a woman should "submit" to her husband, especially passages in Eph 5:21–22; Col 3:18; Tit 2:5; and 1 Pet 3:1. But several things need to be said about these passages. They were articulated by late first century CE church leaders who were making concessions to the family values of the Graeco-Roman world so that Christianity might effectively spread among the masses. They stand in tension with Gal 3:28, which speaks of the equality of men and women in Christ. The latter is the normative message of the New Testament, the former passages are meant to be temporary advice for the survival of the church. Furthermore, Eph 5:21–22 places the issue in better perspective. In verse 21 Christians are told to "submit" to one another out of reverence for Christ, and in verse 22 women are told to do likewise, but the verb for "submit" is missing in verse 22. Verse 22 is a dependent clause on verse 21; the reader simply knows to repeat the verb in verse 22. But that indicates the meaning in verse 22 is dependent upon 21. Women "submit" to their husbands in the same way that all Christians submit to each other. It is the submission of equality. Women have the freedom to submit to their husbands, because they are equal in Christ and the Christian community. That is not how the Greek world would have said it. Among Greeks, wives were "slaves" to their husbands; they did not have the "freedom" to "submit." The biblical text actually has a much higher view of women's freedom than the contemporary world did. We fail to appreciate this! Christian women had the "freedom" to submit, they were not slaves. The Christian movement, even with its compromise stance in the late first century CE, gave more rights to women than ancient classical world did. We need to see what these statements were saying in the light of their historical context, instead of quoting them in flat and literal fashion. Christianity was still promoting the dignity of women as best it could in the late first century CE, and we should be doing likewise today. But the final word is to be had by Gal 3:28, for that is the lasting message for the church. The other passages are concessive statements for that era when Christians had no power to change society. The final message is that in Christ all are equal.

We then return to the next passage in Genesis 4 where it says the woman shall have "desire" for her husband. Commentators have argued for years over the meaning of this passage. Some have suggested that this refers to "sexual" desire and have proceeded to talk about the strong sexual desires of the weaker sex. That is nonsense. Phyllis Trible suggests that the woman "desires" or wishes to return to her original state of equality (Trible 1978:128). Joel Lohr creatively suggests that she wishes to return to "oneness" with the man from whose body she was taken, just as the man will return to "dust" (Lohr 227–46). Most have suggested that the "desire" is more of a familial type of desire; the woman desires the man because she personally desires to have a family and personal intimacy (Fretheim 363). That more likely describes the biblical author's perception, and most people in the modern era would probably acknowledge that the instinctive desire of women to procreate, mother children, and raise families is a strong inherited desire. The biblical author probably did not intend this part of the statement to be understood as a punishment, but rather it is part of the natural human order and is more good than bad.

More problematic for many readers is the next verse that says that the man shall "rule" over the woman. The word used there in the Hebrew is the same word used to describe what people should do in relation to the universe according to Genesis 1—they should "rule" wisely. That might be the best clue to understanding the passage. In Genesis 1 both the man and the woman are commissioned to "rule," but now the man alone is commissioned to "rule." Does the text imply that now a distortion has occurred in the original fabric of creation? Again, does this not imply that perhaps this distortion is another aspect of the divine pronouncements that must be overcome by humanity working in concert with God?

The man is then told that because he listened to the temptation and ate the fruit, the ground is cursed and agricultural production will be difficult for him. There will be thorns and thistles and sweat involved in agricultural production. The witty old saying, "no pain, no grain," describes what he will experience in farming.

Upon hearing the pronouncement upon the man, we sense a parallel between the woman's destiny and the man's destiny. She will have childbirth pain and subordination in marriage, which shall alienate her to some degree from her husband from whom she was created. He will struggle painfully with the ground from which he was created (Brown 2010:88). Both are alienated from their source of origin. Is not an ultimate form of alienation to be separate from our origins, from that which is most important to us for our existence? Ultimately, the most severe form of alienation is alienation from God, which now both the man and the woman have experienced.

What, of course, is interesting is the return of this theme of alienation from the soil in later stories. Cain is an agriculturalist, and perhaps his sacrifice to God is not accepted because it is produce procured from the cursed ground. When Cain is exiled from farming, the subsequent genealogies of both Cain and Seth seem to imply that no one farmed. Cain's descendants appear to be pastoralists who graze their flocks, and it is difficult to determine what Seth's descendants do. Is the ground cursed because of Adam's "curse" or because of Cain's sin? The text does not say. Noah is born and it is said of him in Gen 5:29 that he receives his name because "out of the ground that the LORD has cursed, this one shall bring us relief from our work and from the toil of our hands." Is the curse that Noah removes the curse of Adam or of Cain? Does this statement imply that the ground cannot be farmed at all, which would imply Cain's punishment, or that the ground is difficult to farm, which would imply Adam's divine pronouncement? Somehow the flood removed the curse by washing it away. In some way, Noah's production of a vineyard after the flood implied that the ground was no longer cursed. But because we cannot answer the two previous questions, we cannot make a clear judgment about the overall meaning of all these passages.

We return to the overarching question. Does this divine pronouncement describe a fixed reality for all time, or is it to be overcome by people and God working together? Ironically, fundamentalists who eschew medicine and say that natural childbirth is to be endured more often are likely to accept agricultural breakthroughs that make the farming easier. Oh yeah, if it involves women and women's pain, then it should never change, but if it involves the work of men, then progress is acceptable!

Many commentators see this divine pronouncement referring to difficult human labor in general. Modern technological progress has made labor for most people much easier. Again, it is the secular world and not believers who have accomplished these changes, while believers simply watch.

In conclusion, these divine pronouncements cover a wide range of issues. But over the years we have missed the important point to be made about the divine pronouncements or the "curses." They are not meant to be permanent; they are meant to be overcome, either by the divinely inspired Torah of Moses given at Sinai, or by Christians in the new age after the death and resurrection of Jesus. We need to affirm the mission to accomplish that.

11

Divine Blessings and Exile from the Garden

Genesis 3:20–24

(20) The man named his wife Eve, because she was the mother of all living. (21) And the LORD God made garments of skins for the man and for his wife, and clothed them. (22) Then the LORD God said, "See, the man has become like one of us, knowing good and evil; and now, he might reach out his hand and take also from the tree of life, and eat, and live forever"—(23) therefore the LORD God sent him forth from the garden of Eden, to till the ground from which he was taken. (24) He drove out the man; and at the east of the garden of Eden he placed the cherubim and a sword flaming and turning to guard the way to the tree of life.

THE MAN NOW TAKES a definite role in creating the order of things. He names his wife. Up until this time she had been referred to as "woman," or "the woman," which is an accurate translation of the generic noun in Hebrew. Of course paired with his Hebrew word for "man," it means that previously throughout Genesis 2 and 3, the text referred to these two people as "the man and the woman." By that generic reference one gets the feeling that the biblical text does not want us to view them as specific historic individuals, but rather as universal types, "Mr. Everyman and Mrs. Everywoman." In this way the readers of the text might more closely identify with these two characters so as to appreciate that their sin and rebellion against God is the sin and rebellion of every human being against God. But once they receive specific names, Adam and Eve, they seem to move into more "real time." That occurs when she is named "Eve," for then "Adam" can be seen as more of a real name. However, even from this point onward we still are provided with symbolic narratives.

The man "named" his wife Eve. Some folk observe that the man named his wife in the same way that he named the animals, thus exhibiting control or power over her. They assume that this is the first example of patriarchy, the first result of the curse put upon the woman concerning her subordination. Others maintain that his naming her Eve simply recognizes that Eve is her name, and this action is different from the naming of the animals (Brodie 141; Trible 2003:96–97). It is difficult to say what the biblical text is telling us. More important is the meaning of her name.

Now that they have names, they are individuals. They have moved from being universal to specific people. This is the appropriate moment for them to take names, for they have eaten of the fruit of knowledge and now understand what awaits them in life. In many cultures, when children undertake the rite of passage from childhood to adulthood, they receive new names—names that symbolize who they are and what they ought to be in life. So it is also with the names received by the man and the woman. Their names make them appear to be real people, but their names are still symbolic. They still remain representatives of all of humanity; they symbolize each of us.

Eve is a name that somehow means "life." Of course, the text wishes to interpret the name as "mother of all living." In a loose sense, a name which means "life" could be broadly interpreted as "one who gives life to others" or "mother of all living." But the biblical author toys with us. The name "mother of all living" is a title for the great fertility goddess, Inanna, Ishtar, or the more specific manifestation of Ninti or Nintu, whose name has been hinted at before. Our biblical author continues the loose allusions to the mother goddess or goddesses of Mesopotamia with the persona of the woman. The biblical author says there is no fertility goddess, it is simply the confusion of the ancient Mesopotamians that they thought our ancient human ancestor, Eve, was a goddess. Our biblical author debunks the gods of Mesopotamia and perhaps also takes aim at a local Palestinian goddess, Asherah. If Inanna/Ishtar falls, so also does Asherah. With the hint of Asherah imagery floating in the text of Genesis 3, we cannot help but suspect that the biblical author denies the existence of this goddess too. There was no goddess, only a little girl, a human being, full of life and subject to temptation, as are we all.

There are commentators who suggest a different meaning for the woman's name. Some suggest that Eve's name is related to the Hebrew word *hawwa'* or the Aramaic word *hwyh*, as well as other Arabic words, all of which mean snake (Stratton 62; Benjamin 53). I suspect, however, that the spoof on Nintu's title is most likely the explanation, for that would connect with the image of the woman's creation from the man's rib. (Remember, Nintu's name is connected to the Sumerian word for rib!)

Once the woman has a name, the man's generic title, Adam, also can be viewed as a name. But lest we too glibly say that this is now a natural name, we must point out that nowhere else in the Hebrew Bible is Adam used as a proper name. Nor is Eve for that matter. One suspects that if these are not really proper names in the Israelite and early Jewish tradition, perhaps we should regard them as symbolic names throughout the rest of Genesis 4 and 5. Thus, we have Mr. Human Being and Mrs. Life presented to us for the duration of their performance on stage.

God made clothing for the two people; their fig leaves were probably not holding up very well. This is the first sign of divine compassion for the man and the woman after their rebellion. So often when we tell this story to children, we do not mention that God made clothing, the first of several acts of kindness by God. It seems we like to end the story with the image of the couple punished by God and exiled from the garden. Notice that in our artistic tradition we often paint the couple as naked when they leave the garden. Those artists need to read the account; God gave them clothing before they left the garden. Famous artists over the years have often committed this *faux pas*, including Michelangelo's portrayal in the Sistine Chapel, Lucas Cranach the Elder's "Expulsion from the Garden," and Masaccio's "Adam and Eve Expelled from Paradise" (fifteenth century) (Sanders 155). But then artists enjoy portraying the human body, and this scene affords them an opportunity.

What we also fail to realize is that the making of clothing reflects the skills of a seamstress. God is a seamstress for the man and woman. In the ancient religions, especially in Mesopotamia, it was believed that the skill of making clothing was given to people by the gods, usually a female deity. Once again our biblical author debunks the realm of the gods. The God of Israel, the God of the man and the woman, is a seamstress deity who has snatched the sewing machine away from yet another female fertility goddess. Those other gods do not exist, our God does it all, says the biblical author. Somewhere a tearful seamstress deity still mourns the loss of her sewing machine.

It may be simply a coincidence, but clothing people is something that kings do to honor people (Gen 41:42; 1 Sam 17:38). God's activity is an act of honoring and blessing the man and the woman. When Anu gave Adapa fresh clothing in the divine realm, it was a way of honoring him. (Notice this is yet another parallel between Adam and Adapa!) In the same way Moses dresses the priests in the wilderness by giving them their vestments (Exod 28:41; 29:8; 40:14; Lev 8:13). This enables them to perform their function. Is this nuance of meaning also found in the action by God toward the man and the woman?

There is perhaps another meaning to the clothing made of animal skins. Animals had to die to make that clothing. The man and woman wear the skins of dead animals, a sign that the breach between the animal and the human realm has begun (Kawashima 487). Thus, in subtle fashion we see the curses having effect on the lives of the people. The man perhaps "names" the woman in patriarchal fashion, and the animals serve humanity by their death.

Now the scene switches dramatically to the divine realm, and we hear God speaking to someone. God says, "See, the man has become like one of us." Who are the "us"? Over the years commentators have said many things, and they have repeated the arguments offered to explain a similarly spoken divine "us" in Genesis 1 (which we discussed earlier): 1) It has been described as a plural of majesty or a deliberative cohortative; God was talking to himself in the plural. 2) God was speaking to the other lesser divine beings or gods in the divine council, a reflection of the movement from polytheism to monotheism. 3) They are angels, the "heavenly host" or the old gods transformed into lesser beings. 4) These are the different persons of the Trinity talking to each other. Of these four arguments most commentators prefer the second or third option. We will observe this same mode of speaking again in the Tower of Babel story. Maybe the answer is to be found in the combination of all three accounts. In all the narratives God must do something to "initiate" or "prevent" activity by people and this is a dramatic form of the divine speech.

God says that man (meaning both the male and the female) might take fruit from the tree of life and live forever. This is the strongest argument for advocating that the man and the woman were inherently mortal when they were created. Immortality would be possible only if they ate from the tree of life. If you wish to dispute this and maintain that the man and the woman were inherently immortal from their creation, then you must argue that they lost immortality once they ate from the tree of the knowledge and good and evil, and only if they ate from the tree of life would they regain it. I would respond that Genesis 3 gives no indication that immortality was lost when they ate the fruit of the tree, nor was the loss of immortality initially stated by God to be a punishment for eating of the tree. Though later Jewish and Christian authors declare that the man and the woman lost immortality for later humanity (2 *Baruch* 23:4; 4 *Ezra* 7:48), I think the sense of the narrative indicates they lost immortality by being cast out of the garden and losing access to the tree of life. Once they ate from the tree of knowledge they "knew" the potential of the tree of life and realized that they needed it also to complement their new-found knowledge. Perhaps, if the tree of life is a plant of rejuvenation, like that of Gilgamesh's plant, they did not require rejuvenation at first, because they were children. But now that they have knowledge, they realize that they will need such reinvigoration someday (Stordalen 292; Blenkinsopp 2011:74).

The man and the woman are exiled from the garden and the possibility of immortality. This reminds us of Adapa, who left the divine realm without eating the food of immortality. Most commentators suggest that by eating the fruit, the man and the woman unconsciously chose knowledge over immortality, adulthood over childhood, and civilization over idyllic life in the garden. If they had eaten from the tree of life, then they would have had both knowledge and immortality, and the line between their human identity and the divine would be blurred. Furthermore, if sexual discernment were combined with immortality, this would cause worldwide overpopulation (van Wolde 1997:48). How interesting—that was the Mesopotamian concern that caused the gods to lessen human numbers with a flood!

By leaving the garden they lost immortality, but civilization would begin as a result of their actions outside the garden. They lost personal immortality, but they would have another immortality in the form of children (LaCocque 2006:122). The ancients regarded children as a form of immortality; your name would be recalled by your children. If all people today had that dynamic sense of how their immortality was carried on through their children, maybe we would have less child abuse in our modern world.

The man or "Adam," meaning both the male and the female, is sent forth from the garden to till the ground (Gen 3:23). Man was created and placed in the garden according to Gen 2:15 to till the ground. Farming appears to have been the primary job function designed by God, but the man does not perform this function until he is cast from the garden. Does this mean that the man could only perform the function for which he was created by being cast from the garden? Some Christian authors have declared that indeed it was the ultimate destiny of man to be cast from the garden, for only then could he do the task for which he was created. That is what the sixteenth century Calvinist "supralapsarians" deduced, as we noted previously. These "supralapsarians" believed that sin had been predestined for humanity in order for divine love to be demonstrated.

The best way to interpret these two passages may be to view the male and the female as children whose destiny was to grow up and undertake the responsibility of adulthood. Their rebellion caused them to grow up, leave the garden of innocence, and assume adult responsibilities sooner than should have been expected. Their rebellion cast a pall over what might have been a later exit from the garden in a more honorable and congenial fashion. (That may push the logic of the story beyond the symbolism of the author, however.) Or perhaps, they were meant to grow up and assume responsibilities for tilling the ground and childbirth in the garden. If their responsibility was to till the soil, at some point they had to do that. Genesis 2:15 states the man was to till the soil. He never got to do that in the garden; instead, he had to do it outside the garden where the soil was harsher. Genesis 3:23 combined with Gen 2:15 tells us that a total state of idyllic bliss and non-work was not their ultimate destiny. At some point they had to till the ground, either in the garden or outside. Eating the fruit may have meant leaving the garden in addition to assuming the eventual responsibilities of adulthood.

Is there another way to support this interpretation? Though it will not be convincing to everyone, I would point out that the divine pronouncements are given to the man and woman before God decides they must be exiled from the garden. Is it possible to read the text and assume that they could have heard the pronouncements and still stayed in the garden? God pontificates to the man and the woman because they have eaten the fruit. God exiles them from the garden so that they do not eat from the tree of life. These are separate rationales. Their eating of the fruit of knowledge led to the need to keep them from partaking of the tree of life. God's process of dealing with them seems to imply that there are separate issues here. It seems they could have remained in the garden, if they could have been kept from the tree of life. Exile from the garden is prevention, not punishment.

Some have suggested their exile from the garden would remind the Jewish audience of their exile from Judah in 586 BCE. The man and the woman were exiled to the east, and Judeans were dragged off to Mesopotamia in the east (Anderson 2001:120–21; LaCocque 2006:64–65, 253). I am sure the Jewish audience made that connection, but it does not mean that punishment is the motivation for God's decision. Authors often work with more than one level of meaning in a story. I think the author intended his audience to see the connection with exile of the human couple and the Jewish exile from Jerusalem. Returning from exile in Babylon after 539 BCE would symbolically be like returning to the garden (LaCocque 2006:65–66).

If exile from the garden is separate from the divine pronouncements, then we must raise the question of how to interpret this chapter altogether. By eating the fruit of the tree of knowledge the humans must be informed of the trials and tribulations that come with adulthood, for their knowledge is now the symbolic awareness of what the loss of childhood innocence entails. Theoretically, they could have raised children and tilled the soil in the garden. But they have shown that they like to eat a wide range of fruit, so they most likely will eat from the tree of life rather soon. Thus, God exiles them from the garden. The fact that the sewing of the clothing intervenes between the divine pronouncements and the exile leads me to believe that the pronouncements and the exile are two separate issues. Once exiled from the garden, they find that the soil outside the garden makes the bitterness of the pronouncements even worse. Growing up in the garden and assuming responsibilities for childbirth and tilling would not have been as bad as doing those things outside the garden. They now see the real harsh consequences of their rebellion.

The man and the woman leave the garden with "knowledge" or maturity, but without immortality. They are above the animals with such knowledge, but below God without immortality. To obtain immortality from the tree of life without the tree of knowledge would mean remaining a child; civilization would never be born. Civilization (arts, crafts, farming, metalwork) arises because of their struggle with the outside world (Westermann 272; Van Seters 126; York 405–9; Kass 94–96; Kawashima 483–86; Lanfer 41). Their story becomes the same as that of Adapa and Gilgamesh—knowledge without immortality. Perhaps obtaining knowledge, growing up, really makes this a story of ascent as well as a story of rebellion. Perhaps in rebellion people leave behind childhood and their parents' home for the reality of adulthood. This is a story of ascent and descent. Anthony York even states there is no fall in this narrative, only a story about the emergence of knowledge and human civilization (York 396). This is not really just a modern interpretation; already in the second century the church father Irenaeus saw the story as one in which the man and the woman move toward adulthood and out of parental rule (Fretheim 368).

To keep them from returning to the garden God places cherubim (plural) at the east. The word cherub is cognate to a Mesopotamian word, the Akkadian *kuribu*, who was a divine being that protected holy things, especially temples. This makes us suspect that Eden may have been perceived as a temple or shrine. Or perhaps Judeans envisioned the Temple in Jerusalem as a new Eden. Cherubim were on the Ark of the Covenant in the holiest part of the Temple, the "holy of holies" (1 Kgs 6:23–28), portraits of cherubim decorated the walls of Temple (1 Kgs 6:29) as well as the supposed earlier form of the Temple, the Tabernacle in the wilderness (Exod 26:31). God walked in the garden and was present in the later sanctuaries (Lev 26:12; Deut 23:15). Trees were said to be in sanctuaries symbolically (or perhaps in physical form), and the Jewish Menorah also may be a stylized tree. Rivers or living waters that bring the desert to life are said to come forth from the divine sanctuary in Jerusalem, as the underground stream and the four rivers come forth from Eden (Ps 46:4; Ezek 47:1–12; Joel 3:18; Zech 14:8). So there is fascinating imagery to connect Eden with sacred sanctuaries, and especially the Temple in Jerusalem (Wenham 1986:19–22; LaCocque 2006:253, 259; Stordalen 307–10; Lanfer 127–57). This would reinforce the imagery of how the expulsion of the man and the woman from the garden paralleled the Jewish exile from Jerusalem and the Temple after 586 BCE. Exile from the garden and exile from the Temple in Jerusalem might both be seen as a form of symbolic death. Finally, cherubim may have been some of the divine beings to whom God spoke when the words "let us" were uttered (Wallace 80).

The text suggests that the man and the woman are driven eastward. If the setting of the garden is Mesopotamia, that direction makes little sense. However, if the garden is envisioned as being in Palestine or even in Jerusalem, the reference makes sense. They are driven into the Transjordan, a land less fertile than the Cisjordan or Palestine. They are driven in the same direction that Cain will go after the murder of Abel, and he, of course, becomes a nomad, which is a logical lifestyle out in the Transjordan. They are driven into the land that later becomes the site of the cities of Sodom, Gomorrah, Admah, and Zeboiim in the days of Abraham. From the perspective of an Israelite or a Jew living in Palestine, the image of being sent into the east, into the Transjordan, would be perceived as grim experience. Of course, the ultimate symbol of being driven eastward from Palestine would be the Babylonian Exile of 586 BCE when thousands of Judeans were forced to trek to the east, to Mesopotamia. That is probably the most significant reason for the allusion.

Finally, cherubim are assigned to guard the way into the garden. How many are there? Later iconography would have two cherubim on the Ark of the Covenant. Perhaps we should assume two likewise guard the garden. What happens if the man and the woman try to sneak back into the garden from the west? Were the cherubim fast enough to keep moving around the entire perimeter of the garden to forever keep nosey people out of the garden? They must be computer-generated cherubim with lightning quick speed. This is the visual problem you have, if you try to envision the garden being on a plain. However, if the garden is on a mountain, then it is much easier for our cherubim to guard the one pass that leads up the mountainside into the garden. Since so many ancient peoples envisioned the special realm of the gods to be on a mountain, this image makes a great deal of sense. The cherubim guard the one accessible mountain pass to the garden.

Let's think out this image some more. If the sacred garden is on a mountain, and if that garden is west of the Jordan, where would that sacred garden be? There is only one possibility—Mount Zion, the location of Jerusalem and in particular, the Temple. Could the Garden of Eden have been envisioned to be where the holy city and the Temple were located? As a matter of fact, some Jewish traditions over the years have suggested that notion. Perhaps, the Ark of the Covenant was supposedly over the spot where the Tree of Life was to be found. I might go even farther and muse that the cherubim guarded the eastern entrance, which would be the eastern gate to the city of Jerusalem. This eastern gate was kept closed in post-exilic times, for it had been the gate through which kings of Judah had passed when they were crowned or when they celebrated their coronation during the New Year festival (if, indeed, they ever celebrated such a festival in the pre-exilic era).

There is a radical implication of this suggestion. If my musings are correct, then the exile from the garden was overcome by the return to the land of the Judeans in the late sixth century BCE and their rebuilding of the Temple. If Genesis 1–11 is dated to a time after 539 BCE, when Judeans are allowed to return home, then the audience who heard this story might realize that the garden is Jerusalem, and they are the man and the woman once more. This could be the period of time from 539–400 BCE.

Eventually Jerusalem was rebuilt and people entered the symbolic garden again. Christians might note that Jesus entered the city of Jerusalem from the east, through the eastern gate (which some of his disciples may have opened secretly), on a donkey (like the old kings of Judah used to do), during the Passover, and it ignited quite a crowd reaction—one that we still celebrate on Palm Sunday every year. Ultimately, Jesus entered the garden again also to accomplish what Christians view as the central tenet of their faith. The garden was re-entered by humanity symbolically by Christians after the death and resurrection of Jesus.

The man and the woman leave the garden . . . the scene is sad. Artists have often portrayed the naked couple (positioned discreetly) leaving the garden with sorrow, while an extremely tall angel (only one?) stands with a large flaming sword behind them. As a small child I vividly recall one such picture. The judgment of God was upon them. But wait! Have we forgotten something? God did not kill them. God gave them clothing. They now have names, and therefore individual identity. Furthermore, they will have children, the greatest blessing from God. The story ends not with judgment but with divine grace. The popular version we learned was wrong; grace is the final word, not judgment. Christians teach the stories to children and leave out the happy ending. We forget that grace is the final word.

To this end there is a wonderful quote by Matthew Henry in 1710:

> He (God) might have chased him out the world (Job 18:18), but he only chased him out of the garden. But man was only sent to till the ground out of which he was taken. He was sent to a place of toil, not to a place of torment. He was sent to the ground, not to the grave—to the workhouse, not to the dungeon, not to the prison-house—to hold the plough, not to drag the chain. (Lim 146)

The final word was divine grace, not divine judgment. We must remember that.

12

Cain and Abel

THE ACCOUNT OF A man who murders his brother and yet retains some degree of the divine presence is a testimony to the graciousness and faithfulness of God. Cain is a symbol for the totality of humankind, in all their brutal ways throughout history. Abel is a symbol for the meek and gentle people crushed by the "Cains" of the world (LaCocque 2008:1–145). Cain should die for the murder of his brother, yet God does not give up on Cain or any of the human creatures. That fratricide is the first truly violent human sin is symbolically appropriate, for it reveals the ultimate fragility of human relationships among people who should be closely knit together (Bremmer 91). It is the human tragedy of brother against brother.

Stories about the conflict between brothers abound. In the Bible we have the tensions between Isaac and Ishmael, the conflict between Jacob and Esau, and the sale of Joseph into slavery by his brothers. Twins even fight in their mother's womb, as Jacob and Esau did (Gen 25:22), and as also Perez and Zerah (Gen 38:27–30). It seems that the authors of Genesis were attracted to traditions about family conflict. In none of these later accounts did one brother actually kill the other. The woman who comes to David with the tragic tale of how one of her sons murdered the other (2 Sam 14:1–20) is our best parallel to the Cain and Abel account. From Egypt comes the myth of how the god Seth killed his brother, the god Osiris, as well as the tale of humans, Anubis and Bata, who fought over a woman. From Philo of Byblos in Phoenicia comes the tale about the sons of Aeon, Ousoos and Hypsouranious, and how the latter killed the former and subsequently founded the city of Tyre (Westermann 315; Blenkinsopp 2011:90). That sounds so much like Cain, who founded a city after he killed his brother. Greek tales recount the brotherly conflict between Pelius and Neleus, Eteokles and Polyneikes, Danaus and Aegyptus, Proetus and Acrisius, and Panopueus and Krisos. The last two pairs were twins who also fought in the womb (Bremmer 88). There are also a number of stories about brothers who founded kingdoms or cities together: Sarpedon and Minos (Crete), Dardanus and Iasius (Troy), Atreus and Thyestes (Mycenae), Lycus and Aegeus (Athens), and Romulus and Remus (Rome) (Blenkinsopp 2011:90). Of course, Romulus also killed Remus. The ancients were fascinated with this theme. One might suggest that the Cain and Abel story as a "founding myth" might have been the narrative of human beginnings before Genesis 3 might have been added to it (Blenkinsopp 2011:90–91).

Among the stories that come to us from the ancient Near East there is a third millennium BCE Mesopotamian myth, written in Sumerian, which bears a somewhat oblique relationship to the biblical story of Cain and Abel. The story of *Dumuzi and Enkimdu* speaks of how the shepherd Dumuzi and the farmer Enkimdu both wooed the lovely Inanna. They proposed a division of territory in which the farmer received the lowlands next to the river, suitable for farming, and the shepherd received the steppe lands which are suitable for grazing, a really good decision on the part of both. This would seem to be a very early myth, for Innana and Dumuzi do not appear to be deities, as they are in other accounts and myths. The story is a "myth of origins," for it explains how world order came into existence, and especially the origin of sedentary farmers and pastoralist shepherds. One also is reminded of the choice of land Abraham offers to Lot in Gen 13:8–13, wherein Lot chooses the valley and sedentary city life, while Abraham remains in the highlands with his flocks. The Mesopotamian story favors the lifestyle of the farmer, which was the lifestyle of the Mesopotamians, and they tended to despise the lifestyle of the pastoralist shepherds in the steppe lands outside the river valley. This, of course, is the opposite of Israelite cultural assumptions, which appear to be reflected in the Cain and Abel story, and which are even more clearly evident in the Genesis 13 account of Abraham and Lot. When Israelites and Judeans heard the tale of Cain and Abel, they were unconsciously inclined to favor the shepherd Abel. They idealized the life of the shepherd, often claiming that the pastoralist life-style was the way of existence their ancestors lived. Israelites often used language reflecting the life setting of semi-nomadic shepherds, they attributed this mode of existence to their great patriarchal ancestors, and they even used the nomadic terminology of "tribes" and "clans" instead of "states" to delineate their political units. A different and clever twist on this interpretation is provided by André LaCocque who believes the Cain refers to northern Israel where farming predominated, while Abel refers to southern Judah where shepherding predominated in the early history of the Israelites. Cain's exile to the east would allude to the exile of northern Israel in 722 BCE by the Assyrians (LaCocque 2008:27–28).

Ironically, throughout their history most Israelites really were farmers, and in actuality the majority of people who lived in late second millennium BCE Palestine were farmers who peacefully and gradually became Israelites after 1200 BCE. Only a very few people came into Palestine out of the wilderness of the Transjordan where they had been wandering pastoralists or nomads. Even those particular few who entered with Joshua around 1200 BCE, bringing the worship of Yahweh into the land, were people not comfortable with the wilderness in which they had wandered. In general, early Israelites and their Canaanite ancestors were farmers who could occasionally engage in herding. That pattern of subsistence would remain for most Israelites throughout their history. They would farm and in dry periods they would depend more upon their flocks than their crops. Some commentators point out that Cain and Abel could be natural brothers in a historical highland Israelite family that engaged in both farming and herding of flocks, and perhaps the author knew that (Brown 1999:164). But more likely in the parable of Genesis 4 the two sons symbolize the two general lifestyles known to the Israelite and Jewish audience. The audience would be prone to identify more with Abel the shepherd. Israelites and later Judeans were farmers who idealized the freedom of the shepherd's way of life, even though they probably would not desire to live as such. But so often people of any age will idealize a past they never had. Americans idealize the existence of their rugged ancestors on the frontier with their strong sense of individualism and independence, when most of us are probably descended from immigrants who got off the boat and proceeded to live and work in urban centers or small towns. Today we live in large metropolitan centers or suburbs, and we sometimes idealize the values of small town America from the mid or early twentieth century, even though we would not consider moving back to the small towns of our origin. In similar fashion the ancient biblical audience might have identified unconsciously with Abel more than Cain.

Genesis 4:1–16

(1) Now the man knew his wife Eve, and she conceived and bore Cain, saying, "I have produced a man with the help of the LORD." (2) Next she bore his brother Abel. Now Abel was a keeper of sheep, and Cain a tiller of the ground. (3) In the course of time Cain brought to the LORD an offering of fruit of the ground, (4) and Abel for his part brought of the firstlings of his flock, their fat portions. And the LORD had regard for Abel and his offering, (5)

> but for Cain and his offering he had no regard. So Cain was very angry, and his countenance fell. (6) The LORD said to Cain, "Why are you angry, and why has your countenance fallen? (7) If you do well, will you not be accepted? And if you do not do well, sin is lurking at the door; its desire is for you, but you must master it."
>
> (8) Cain said to his brother Abel, "Let us go out to the field." And when they were in the field, Cain rose up against his brother Abel, and killed him. (9) Then the LORD said to Cain, "Where is your brother Abel?" He said, "I do not know; am I my brother's keeper?" (10) And the LORD said, "What have you done? Listen, your brother's blood is crying out to me from the ground! (11) And now you are cursed from the ground, which has opened its mouth to receive your brother's blood from your hand. (12) When you till the ground, it will no longer yield to you its strength; you will be a fugitive and a wanderer on the earth." (13) Cain said to the LORD, "My punishment is greater than I can bear! (14) Today you have driven me away from the soil, and I shall be hidden from your face; I shall be a fugitive and a wanderer on the earth, and anyone who meets me may kill me." (15) Then the LORD said to him, "Not so! Whoever kills Cain will suffer a sevenfold vengeance." And the LORD put a mark on Cain, so that no one who came upon him would kill him. (16) Then Cain went away from the presence of the LORD, and settled in the land of Nod, east of Eden.

This narrative speaks of the first true sin of humanity in the real world—murder. This surpasses in violence the first sin in the garden, which was but a metaphor for coming to adulthood. The most common word in Hebrew for sin, *hatta'*, occurs first with this account. Some authors have suggested that in an early version of these ancient stories this tale was the first account in a cycle about the primeval times. Even later Jewish literature, which was not included in the Hebrew Bible (1 *Enoch* 6:1–5; 7:1–6; 15:2–16:1; *Jubilees* 5:1–6; 10:1–9), viewed the first human sin as the activity described in Gen 6:1–4. Perhaps Genesis 3 arose and was partially influenced by the narrative in Genesis 4.

There are in both Genesis 2–3 and Genesis 4 the following elements: 1) origin of the two persona (Gen 2:7, 21–23; 4:1–2), 2) role of the humans in the created order (Gen 2:15; 4:2), 3) divine warning (Gen 2:17; 4:7), 4) anticipation of the "sin" (Gen 3:1–5; 4:5–7), 5) the "sin" (Gen 3:6; 4:8), 6) divine confrontation (Gen 3:9–19; 4:9–15), 7) divine question as to where someone is (Gen 3:9; 4:9), 8) divine questions directed to the guilty party as to what has happened (Gen 3:8–13; 4:9–10), 9) people are told of their sin (Gen 3:11–13; 4:10), 10) punishment (Gen 3:14–19; 4:11–12), 11) alienation from the earth (Gen 3:17–19; 4:11–12), 12) reduction of the punishment

(Gen 3:21; 4:13–15), 13) divine gift of clothing or a mark (Gen 3:21; 4:15), and 14) expulsion toward the east (Gen 3:24; 4:16) (Gunkel 45; Richardson 80). One is tempted by virtue of these similarities to suggest that originally Genesis 4 may have begun the cycle of primeval tales and Genesis 2–3 was added. Perhaps, both stories were meant to remind Judeans of their exile from Jerusalem in 586 BCE. Some commentators also believe that the Cain and Abel account especially was meant to remind the audience of the strife between David's sons, particularly when Absalom killed Amnon (Kselman 87).

The story of Cain and Abel is famous in the popular mind not only for the horrific image of brother murdering brother, but also because it has inspired so many to ask the question, "Where did Cain get his wife, if these were the only people in the world?" Actually there are six comparable questions that can be asked of this narrative and the subsequent account of Cain's descendants. 1) If there are only four people in the world how can farming and shepherding be so clearly delineated in the persons of Cain and Abel? 2) When Cain took Abel to the open field, obviously to avoid being seen by others, who were those other people? 3) Who were the people who would hunt Cain for the murder of his brother? 4) Who does Cain marry? 5) Who lives in the city built by Cain? 6) Cain's descendants create musical instruments, forging, and other aspects of human culture. But since these descendants die in the flood, and other people reinvent them after the flood, why are Cain's descendants given credit for their invention? Christians in the past who have taken these stories to be literal history have tried to answer these questions by suggesting Cain was hunted by other brothers and nephews, that he married his sister, and that his own descendants lived in his city, but these are forced explanations. Further, no good answers can be given for questions #1, #2, and #6.

The stories are obviously not literal historical memories, but one still might ask about the lack of logic in the overall narrative plot in Genesis 1–11. Two answers might be given. The stories of Cain in Genesis 4 might have been separate accounts that spoke of life in a later era with a normal population rather than being located at the beginning of human existence. They were then crafted into this Primeval History as paradigms for human existence from the beginning of time, thus creating incongruities in the greater plot. Or the stories were crafted by the biblical narrator who was not worried about the greater plot in Genesis 1–11, but simply wished to offer a brilliant tale about human existence with all the attendant symbolism found in this narrative. I prefer the second option and maintain that we should not weary our biblical author with our modern pedantic issues of logic and historicity. The details in the narrative make theological sense in the greater Primeval History, the incongruity of some of the details is irrelevant.

The familial setting of Gen 4:1–2 implies a state of goodness, a state of grace. New life and hope came with the birth of Cain. Cain would carry the expectations of his parents for a better future. How tragic would be the contrast between the joy of the parents with their first birth and the future horror of discovery that one son has murdered the other. Readers who know that ending must wince at the sound of Eve's statements, the satisfaction of a young woman giving birth to her first child.

Eve's statement, "I have produced a man with the help of the LORD," is a proclamation of a woman's success in giving birth to a son for the household, which was a source of pride for Israelite women in a culture that suffered from having too few people. In patriarchal society especially, being able to bear sons for one's husband garnered for women recognition and honor. Eve's cry may even have been an ancient formula used by women to introduce the newborn baby into the household. The child would have been presented to the father, or patriarchal leader of the clan, for acceptance. In theory the patriarchal father could reject the baby, and thus condemn it to be exposed to the elements and die.

Some have suggested significant symbolism in Eve's statement. Perhaps she rejoices in that she has produced life. For previously life had been made out of her husband's body—she was formed from his rib. But now life comes out of her body; she claims the right of childbearing from Adam (Stratton 220; Kass 126). (We hear no comment from Adam on this point!) She perhaps claims the right to make life from God, who made her life out of Adam's body. Her cry reminds us of the exultation of the goddess Nintu-Mami in the *Atrahasis Epic*, who rejoices in her creation of human couples, and perhaps our biblical author draws that parallel to reject the existence of foreign gods once more (Batto 1992:63). Some interpreters see this negatively, however. If she is crying as the mother goddess, perhaps she usurps the creative power of God in her rhetoric, and her refusal to accept her humanity leads to the destructive pride found in Cain and his later descendants (Eslinger 68).

Cain's name comes from a generic root word (*qayin*) found in languages related to Hebrew and is connected to manufacturing, metal work, or forging, a theme that will surface again in the list of Cain's children wherein we find Tubal-cain, the father of metalworkers (Speiser 1964:30; Westermann 289; Wenham 1987:101). Some have even suggested that the name Qayn may have been a patron deity for metalworkers (Becking 180). Cain's name (*qayin*) in Hebrew also sounds like a word (*qanah*) that means either "acquisition" or "create" or "strong," which thus has a wide range of possible meanings. When Eve says I have "produced" a man, and other translations read, "I have gotten" or "I have acquired," our English translations attempt to indicate that there is a word play in the Hebrew text. The word "acquired" or *qanah* is used eighty-two times in the Old Testament (Simpson 517; Hamilton 220; Lim 153). This is called a "false etymology," that is, the text hints that the words "Cain" and "acquired" are related, but they really are not, they simply sound alike. False etymologies often are used to communicate a religious message, and often they are meant to provide a little humor too. Such biblical humor, unfortunately, gets lost in translation.

There are commentators, however, who believe that Cain's name really does mean, "create" or "acquire." If Cain's name has the particular nuanced meaning of "create," it implies that Eve has created a man with God's help. This could be reminiscent not only of the Mesopotamian goddess Nintu-Mami, but also the Canaanite goddess Asherah, for it is said of Asherah that she was the "creatress of men and gods" (Wallace 158). As noted previously, Eve's persona and name seems to hint at connections with fertility goddesses like Nintu and Asherah, if only to refute their existence. The foreign kingdoms have confused fertility goddesses with our human mother according to the biblical author. If Cain's name means "acquired," we have a word play on the entire expression in the biblical text, for Eve states that she has "acquired" a man from God and his name is "acquire." Even if that is not the exact meaning of the word, Cain's name still sounds like the word "acquire" which Eve used to describe "getting" a man from God.

On the other hand, Cain's brother is named Abel (from the root *hbl*), which means "breath," "vapor," "puff of smoke," "vanity" (as in the expression "vanity of vanities" found in Eccl 1:2), "morning mist," or "passing shadow" (a term used to describe humanity in Ps 144:4) (Wenham 1987:102; Lim 153). The early morning mist evaporates with the first rays of the sun after the dawn. One senses that Abel is not going last too long in this story (van Wolde 1994:52). Cain truly is the dramatic figure in this narrative, Abel is a "stage extra" who is fated to play his "bit role" and leave the theater for the evening while the performance continues.

The text may portray the boys as brothers born years apart or perhaps as twins born only a few minutes apart. In verse 2, when the text says, "next she bore," it may imply they are twins (Simpson 517). Since there is no reference to Eve's separate conception of Abel, one is even more likely to assume they are twins (Moberly 92; van Ruiten 7). Given how frequently the motif of twins is found among the patriarchal narratives, especially twins who struggle with each other, one would suggest that Cain and Abel are twins. Jacob and Esau in Gen 25:22–26, and Perez and Zerah in Gen 38:27–30, all struggle with each other in their mothers' wombs, and the struggle between Jacob and Esau will span their lifetimes.

Were the boys the first two births for Eve? A minority of scholars suggest that perhaps there were other children born prior to Cain and Abel. Perhaps there are other families besides the family of Adam and Eve. This would explain where Cain ultimately obtained his wife. Also, it would explain why the farming practice of Cain and the shepherding efforts of Abel exist in such a well-developed form for them; other people have developed it prior to Cain and Abel. Cain kills Abel in an open field implying that they were out of sight of other witnesses. If Cain has to constantly flee blood revenge, there must have been a significant number of people to hunt him. When Cain builds a city, the implication is that there must be a goodly number of people to inhabit it. Thus, there may have been people other than Adam and Eve, or they had a lot of children (Vawter 95; Van Seters 136; Moberly 24–25). On the other hand, these details are not the intent of this story. Eve's dramatic announcement of birth seems to suggest these are the first natural born babies in the world. Nor would the author think it irregular that Cain and Abel engaged in their respective economic life styles without a prior evolution of those patterns of subsistence. The ancient authors would have assumed that someone had to be the first farmer and the first shepherd. Nor would the ancients have assumed that there was an evolution of these economic life-styles, for the concept of evolutionary development is distinctly a modern way of thinking. When we posit the existence of other people to make the story more logical, as noted above, we forget that these tales are symbolic, more like parables, and we should not be too logical with the portrayal of the characters and plot.

Cain became a farmer, and as such he appeared destined to fulfill God's hope for an agriculturalist to till the soil, expressed already in Gen 1:15. The Adam and his wife were placed in the garden with this expectation, but they did not engage in this activity—they were merely "fruit-pickers." More seriously, though, they were but children according to the story line in Genesis 2–3, and only upon leaving the garden could they have undertaken the adult responsibility of tilling the soil. Now with the birth of their first-born son, that hope and responsibility will be fulfilled. How great their hopes must have been, and how drastically those hopes would be shattered. God's hopes, too, are raised by the possibility of a creature who will do the job intended for humanity. God's hopes will be dashed to pieces also, and then a terrible decision will confront the divine creator.

Both sons offer up sacrifice, but the sacrifice of one is accepted and the other sacrifice is not. How does he know if his sacrifice is accepted or not? Does the smoke blow in his face, as one movie had it many years ago?

Cain and Abel

Pious traditions suggest that perhaps fire came from heaven to ignite Abel's sacrifice, or that the smoke of his sacrifice ascended, while these things did not happen for Cain (Skinner 104–5). The biblical text simply does not tell us. But the reason for this rejection has exercised the imagination of commentators and theologians over the years.

Jewish and Christian thinkers have offered many reasons for the rejection of Cain's sacrifice: 1) Most suggest that Cain did not offer the best of his produce, whereas Abel did (Wenham 1987:104). Genesis 4:3 merely says that Cain "brought to the LORD an offering," whereas verse 4 says that Abel "brought of the firstlings of his flock, their fat portions." Abel acted ideally whereas Cain seemed content merely to fulfill his religious obligation with no excess effort (Craig 111). Clearly Abel brought the best, the "choicest," "the firstlings," and indeed the fat of an animal was considered the best part of the animal to sacrifice. Fat was connected to the blood in their minds, and blood belonged to God alone. Abel abided by the laws in Exod 22:19 about firstlings and Lev 3:3–17 about fat portions. Yes, the biblical author had no trouble being anachronistic by having Abel conform to the later laws of Moses. (Today we might not see the fat as such a good portion, since we are, as a society, rather overweight and calorie conscious, and we avoid the fat in our meat, even cutting it off in the butcher shop before sale. But in a subsistence economy, when people live on the edge of starvation, the fat of an animal gives that extra energy necessary for the labor of daily life. To give fat to God was truly a "sacrifice.") Early Rabbinic and Christian commentators often believed that Cain's sacrifice was perhaps from the "leftovers" of the harvest, or food substances that he casually collected. He brought "some" of his produce, not the best. This, however, might not be the explanation, if the biblical text is simply stating neutrally that he brought sacrifice. We have to read into the text that the sacrifice Cain brought was not the best.

2) Perhaps Cain's attitude with the sacrificial offering was not as positive as Abel's (Richardson 82; McKeown 40–41). Genesis 3:3 states that Cain brought his offering "in the course of time" (the Hebrew literally reads, "after some days"). Some commentators have read that to mean that he dallied in bringing his offering, perhaps with the begrudging attitude of a small child ordered to do something by his parents. This may be correct, or we may be reading a temporal reference designed to refer to the sacrifices of both Cain and Abel, and the expression "in the course of time" simply implies that when it was time for both of them to sacrifice. Another variation of this argument is inspired by Heb 11:4 in the New Testament wherein it says that Abel provided a more acceptable offering by faith than did Cain. Thus, an attitude known only to God was the difference. But the text in Genesis

4 does not say this directly. Also, the very reference to Abel's "faith" could imply a number of possibilities.

3) Some ancient commentators assumed that prior to their sacrifices there was a moral difference between the two brothers: Cain was systemically evil while Abel was a righteous person. In the ancient Jewish *Targum Neophyti*, written in Aramaic, the commentary on Gen 4:8 recalls how Abel points this out to Cain very explicitly—"it was because my deeds have been better than yours that my sacrifice was accepted with favor and your sacrifice was not." (No wonder Cain bopped him! I would have done the same—the little twit!) But this is probably a poor reading of the biblical text, for there is nothing to indicate a moral difference between the two youths prior to the sacrifice. At any rate, many ancient Judeans and Christians commonly referred to Abel as the righteous person (Philo, *Questions in Genesis* 1:59; Josephus, *Jewish Antiquities* 1:53; Matt 23:35; Heb 11:4; 1 John 3:12; Augustine, *City of God* 15:7), implying perhaps by inference that Cain might have been intrinsically evil. Heb 11:4, in particular, states that Abel had more faith, which is to say not that Cain was less moral than Abel, but that he had less faith.

4) Some have suggested that perhaps God simply preferred a meat sacrifice to a grain or fruit sacrifice, since it was a more significant offering. Some have even stated that perhaps God prefers sacrifices with blood in them. That, however, overlooks the fact that the majority of sacrifices undertaken by Israelites and Judeans were grain and fruit sacrifices, and only less frequently were animal sacrifices provided for more dramatic circumstances. The biblical author would not want the audience to assume that God was displeased with those sacrifices most frequently offered (Wenham 1987:104).

5) It has been proposed the story implies that God prefers shepherds to farmers (Gunkel 41). This would be rhetoric which one might expect from Israelites who always idealized the shepherd or the pastoralist, even though most of them were farmers throughout their existence. But if this is the case, the implication is that God prefers the shepherd's animal sacrifice rather than the farmer's grain sacrifice. This brings us back to the previous argument and the weaknesses connected to it.

6) A modern suggestion proposes that the curse upon the ground given to Adam by God in Gen 3:17–19 might be the reason for the inadequacy of sacrifices produced from the fruit of the harvest. Hence, livestock would be better intrinsically. Though this logically flows with the thought of the stories, one must acknowledge that the goal of the God was to have people till the ground (Gen 2:15), which is exactly what Cain did, so one should not expect the crops thus produced to be tainted. It has been suggested that if

at one time the Cain and Abel story was told separately from the narratives in Genesis 2–3, then this story also tells why the ground was cursed and duplicates the aetiology in Genesis 3.

7) The first explanation mentioned above may be the best, if an explanation is to be squeezed out of the text. Perhaps, a different kind of answer to be offered is the one which suggests that the biblical author is seeking not to give any reason whatsoever why Cain's offering was rejected. The rejection is a divine mystery that human beings cannot understand. Many Christians, who believe in a strong concept of predestination, affirm this by saying that the inscrutable will of God pre-determined that the sacrifice of Abel would be accepted and that the sacrifice of Cain would be rejected. In comparable fashion, some Jewish commentators, who do not believe in predestination, say we should not attribute anything to divinely pre-determined will, but merely maintain the rejection of Cain's sacrifice is a mystery (von Rad 104–5; Vawter 95).

"So Cain was very angry, and his countenance fell" (Gen 4:5) in response to his rejection. Though popular commentators invent some form of dialogue between Cain and Abel, the biblical plot line has God address Cain initially. God warns him that the sin of envy will devour him, it "is lurking at the door," and Cain must master it. Perhaps, in the light of this statement we might suggest that Cain's rejection was a test to see how he would respond. If so, he failed. Cain's envy led to murder. This reflects the Jewish awareness that inner desire can be the source of radically evil actions. As Jesus rightly said years later, "Whoever hates his brother is a murderer." Christians are mistaken if they think that Jesus was the first religious intellectual to view human emotions and desires as sinful and equally culpable as actions.

Some have noted that the extremely unusual Hebrew verb form for "lurking" or "crouching" is similar to a word in Akkadian that is the name for a threshold demon, Rabisu or Rabisum, who seizes people with illness after lying in wait for them. If so, God would be saying that the demon of temptation is waiting to seize Cain. However, Rabisu is never portrayed as tempting people in Mesopotamia (Barre 682–83; Blenkinsopp 2011:94). But it would be a colorful image.

In dramatic, short fashion the biblical text tells us that Cain invited his brother into the field, perhaps the very field from which Cain drew his sacrificial offering, and there killed him. Abel provided sacrifice by killing his perfect animals, now Cain kills his "perfect" brother. The blood of sacrificial animals had to be properly drained from animals according to later Israelite law, but the blood of Abel drains into the ground where God can hear it. Some have wondered whether Cain had the idea that if God liked meat sacrifice, then he would offer up as a sacrifice the ultimate meat sacrifice, a human sacrifice (Westermann 283; Kass 141). I think the biblical text would provide more hints if this were the understanding we were supposed to derive from the story, but it is an ironic interpretative possibility.

Yes, "hear it" is the verb that is used in the text of Gen 4:10. God hears the "voice" of Abel's blood "crying" from the ground. Cain has usurped the role of God by taking life. The biblical author uses an expression that elsewhere in the Bible describes the "voice" of the poor and oppressed who "cry" to God for justice. The blood of Abel cries for justice to God, and justice requires that one who murders an innocent victim in cold-blooded fashion must be put to death by the community. Later biblical authors stress that victims of economic injustice also cry out to God for justice against their rich oppressors, and God may punish those oppressors in the same way that murderers are treated by village courts.

The imagery of innocent blood shed on the ground was very powerful. Israelites and Judeans believed that the blood of innocent people would pollute the ground so that crops could not grow, unless the community brought about justice and avenged the death of such wrongfully slain innocent folk. (Metaphorically the prophets spoke of the economic oppression of the poor as a form of shedding innocent blood on the ground.) In Deut 21:1–9 guidelines are given to village leaders for purification rites that they would undertake in the event of their discovering a murdered corpse near their village. Furthermore, that village possibly would undertake the responsibility of sending someone to find the murderer in order to kill him or bring him back for trial. Such a person would be called a *go'el*, or a redeemer, because he would redeem the village from the curse of the shed blood and bring about justice and harmony in the universe once more. Hence, the image of Abel's blood shed on the ground and crying to God for justice was an ominous image that implied that the ground would be polluted horribly. It clearly implied that the perpetrator, Cain, could never again farm, for the ground had been explicitly polluted by him. Cain would be forever exiled from the precious earth so dear to him.

With the death of Abel God immediately comes to Cain and asks, "Where is your brother Abel?" Cain's response is that he does not know, and then Cain utters abrasive and impudent words, "Am I my brother's keeper?" The word "keeper" implies ownership or the control that a human being exercises over an animal, which means constantly watching his brother. People do not "keep" other people; only God "keeps" people (Hamilton 231). Cain is sarcastically saying, "Should I shepherd the shepherd?" No one would be expected to exhibit that form of exaggerated control. Cain is probably overstating his responsibility for Abel by using language that extreme so that he can get out of any responsibility for Abel. He is dodging God's question with the common subterfuge of people caught in a trap, he asks a counter-question, an absurd counter-question (Craig 124). But ultimately Cain is saying that he does not see why he should be responsible for his brother's welfare. The Israelite and Jewish audience would have expected lightning to strike Cain from above at that very moment. What an impudent ass Cain was to utter such words! Of course, he was responsible for his brother's well being; all Israelites and Judeans knew that. Cain's response indicates that he is much more "hardened" than his parents in the previous chapter (von Rad 106; Wenham 1987:107). It is possible that Cain is saying that God has failed to "keep" Abel, for elsewhere "keeping" is a divine task (Num 6:24; Ps 121:3–8) (Fretheim 374; LaCocque 2008:70–71). This sounds like his parents who blamed God in the garden for their actions.

Theirs was a kinship society, that is, a society which defined itself by familial and clan language. Everyone was part of a greater "family" called Israel. Your neighbors were your brothers and sisters, and you indeed were responsible for them. Everyone was responsible for everyone else in a kinship familial society. You as an individual belonged to a nuclear family and that family was part of a larger family, "the house of the father," with whom you might actually live. Often, grown sons with their wives and children might still live in the house of their father, the patriarchal leader of this greater family. The "house of the father" was part of the clan; the clan was part of the "large clan" (we lack a word for this in English), which in turn was part of the tribe, which in turn was part of the people of Israel. Society was seen in familial terms, and corporate solidarity and responsibility for each other was the order of the day. Even when this system of inter-relationships began to break down in the late eighth century BCE, Israelites and later Judeans still idealized this form of life.

In our modern western society, the value of the individual is so great that we have lost this sense of corporate solidarity. We are, at times, as a people, mired in self-interest, greed, and narcissism. Institutions, such as the church and synagogue, attempt to recover a sense of corporate solidarity for us and so seek to create a sense of living community among people in the congregations of worship and a sense of moral concern for other people in society. But it is not an easy task for us to recover this sense. We could so very easily say, "Am I my brother's keeper?" and actually mean it in all sincerity. But those very words would have been like the sound of scratching fingernails on a chalkboard for the ancient Israelite and Jewish audience.

In immediate response to Cain's impudent statement God says, "What have you done? Listen, your brother's blood is crying out to me from the ground!" (Gen 4:10). To our modern minds the logic of the story-line might move too quickly when immediately thereafter God says, "And now you are cursed from the ground, which has opened its mouth to receive your brother's blood from your hand" (Gen 4:11). But as mentioned previously the image of innocent blood on the ground was a powerful one for the ancient biblical audience. Thus, the statement of punishment which follows makes sense: Cain will till the ground, but nothing will grow, and he will be forced to wander the earth (Gen 4:12). As will become evident later, the curse on Cain is a curse upon all humanity until the time of Noah. Cain's curse upon the ground appears to intensify the curse that came with Adam (Fretheim 374), unless of course, the Cain and Abel story once stood separately from the story of the man and the woman (Westermann 311). Only with Noah, after the flood, will the ground offer produce to humanity and the curse of Cain be removed. (Adam's curse about hard work will remain).

Ultimately, Cain is cursed "from" the ground, and that is a double-entendre. Cain is cursed and is thus to be taken away from farming, he is removed "from" the ground. But also the ground "curses" him with the presence of Abel's blood in it; the ground bears testimony against him (Brown 1999:168). Does the ground bear testimony against us today? Does it bear testimony for abusive farming and rise up to create a dustbowl as it did in the Midwest during the 1930s? Does it desiccate and no longer bear crops due to global warming? Does it cry out under urban sprawl that destroys so much good farmland? Does it cry out under so much human mismanagement in our modern age? I'm afraid it does. When it does, it withholds the bounty of its crop yield and food from us, and we will suffer.

Cain's punishment is to be banished from the presence of God, to be a perpetual exile from the land, a severe curse for a farmer, and to be hunted as a murderer. As a murderer, he introduced bloodshed, murder, and war into the world. This story is an aetiology that tells of the origin of violence. This is truly a serious sin he has committed, which stands in stark contrast to the sin of his parents (who simply picked the wrong fruit with a bad attitude). If, indeed, the story of Cain and Abel once stood apart from Genesis 2–3, it would have been more properly the first true sin of humanity. This sin parallels the violence mentioned in Gen 6:5, which was in part responsible for the flood and the destruction of humanity.

We do not sense this in our initial reading, but Cain is the ancestor of all humanity. Cain will have descendants, and another son of Adam and Eve, named Seth, will have descendants also. Cain's children are bad; Seth's children are good, and Noah will come from the line of Seth. Christians have been too quick to then say that we are descended from the good Sethites and not the bad Cainites. But we are not reading the text closely enough. As we shall see below, the names of the sons of Cain and the names of the sons of Seth are the same names. They are the same people. The biblical author has made a powerful symbolic statement: we are descended from both the good guys and the bad guys, for we all are both good and evil by nature, or we freely choose between good and evil. (Christians would make the former statement; Jews would make the latter statement.) As we look at the actions and the fate of Cain, we realize that the biblical author symbolically portrays him as the ancestor of all later humanity.

Cain has invented murder, violence, and war (no patent necessary). In order to stop war and murder, to avenge Abel's murder, to bring about harmony in the universe once more, Cain must be killed. This is why Cain responds to God that his punishment is too great. Not only is he exiled from his beloved farmland, he will be hunted mercilessly by many people for years. He must be killed in order to take away what he has introduced into the created order. He will be hunted for centuries; he will be hunted forever. Yes, forever! He is the symbolic ancestor of all humanity; all his later descendants are an extension of him. He is an "eponym," a symbolic ancestor in whom his later descendants live, and he symbolizes their totality. He will live symbolically as long as people exist. Therein lies the problem! In order to end murder, violence, and war, we must kill Cain, our symbolic ancestor. But if we kill Cain, our eponymous ancestor, we will cease to exist.

An ironic dilemma confronts God. If God wishes to end violence, war, and murder, he must kill Cain, who introduced it, or have a *goel* do this task. But if Cain disappears symbolically, so will all humanity. But then, that is the solution, isn't it? If humanity disappears, so will war. Cain is us, we are Cain. Kill Cain, kill us, and God has a solution. But then God has lost the creature once created to live in communion with the divine. God will have to begin anew with another creature. Who will it be? God ponders: "Will it be penguins, they're cute? Will it be porpoises, they're smart?" God makes a fateful decision and decides to keep humanity. Cain is standing below in the mud of the earth, from whence his father came. Cain is standing in mud stained deep with the blood of his brother, deserving death. But God keeps him. So Cain gets a mark to protect him from those who would assail him. The eponymous ancestor of humanity lives, humanity endures upon the planet, and God undertakes a great gamble with the created order. God now must decide how to salvage this humanity and make human beings worthy of communion with the divine. God will select certain individuals (Abraham) and peoples (Israel, the Judeans), and God eventually will send the Law through Moses to inform people how to live a life harmoniously with each other and in communion with God. Christians will build upon the metaphor and say that ultimately God sent Jesus with a message of love and a radical statement of hope for the human condition with the experience of Jesus' resurrection. But all of this theologizing only makes sense if we see the irony of the story that the biblical author has imparted to it. Cain is each of us.

Cain receives a mark to protect him from blood vengeance, and thereby God continues the family of Cain. This mark of protection, as we shall discover later, indicates to anyone who encounters Cain, that if they kill Cain, seven of their clan members will be slain by Cain's family (Gen 4:24). It is possible that this mark reminds the audience of a tribal tattoo, perhaps once associated with a tribal group called the Kenites (we shall discuss that below). I believe this mark is a tattoo, probably on the forehead, for it would be most visible there, and later marks of protection are said to be on the forehead. Some commentators do not believe it was a tribal mark but simply a unique mark for Cain, and the rabbis (*Berakhot Rabba* 22:12) felt that the mark was a dog that accompanied Cain (Westermann 312–14). Yes, a dog!

Do not ask who will slay Cain and who will avenge him, if he is the only person alive in the world other than his parents. Nor should we ask where he found his wife, a question that persistently plagues people. The story is in symbolic time, and the personages are symbolic of realities in human existence. Suffice it to say, the mark is a protection, and hence a blessing. How often do people refer to the "mark of Cain" as though it were a curse or a sign of punishment? In the story it is a blessing, but as is too often the case, popular piety twists a biblical story and inevitably a positive message comes up with a negative connotation. Popular piety is dangerous. We overlook the blessings and remember only the curses.

Cain goes forth and dwells in the east, in the land of Nod, and there he finds a wife. Where is Nod? The biblical author may be pointing to the Transjordan as a steppe land where crops were not grown, but animal husbandry was possible. It was also the symbolic land of origin where the ancestors came out of the wilderness under Joshua to enter the land of Palestine. The word "Nod" may mean, "wandering," a state of existence that describes what Cain will do henceforth. Exiled from the ground and forever disdained by people, he will wander, and his descendants will be nomads. One author described it as "a completely cultureless existence from which Cain's descendants began to rise again only some generations later" (Simpson 520). Thus, our story ends with Cain trudging away from his family to a nomadic existence, just as his parents had to leave the garden and enter into the real world of pain and work.

The biblical author may be pointing even further east, to the land of Mesopotamia, where the ancients lived (including those who built the tower of Babel). Mesopotamia would be a good candidate, because there were indeed cities in the river valley, and the text later speaks of how Cain founded a city. Are we to perceive that Cain built a city to defy God and end his nomadic existence (McKeown 44)? Did he build a city for protection against those who hunted him? We are not told. Our biblical author elsewhere hints that the earliest cities were in Mesopotamia or Shinar. If the reference to the east does hint at Mesopotamia and the land of cities, we may observe the sarcasm of the biblical author. How ironic that our biblical author is correct, for the earliest large cities were in Mesopotamia. Uruk had several thousand people by 5000 BCE. The first murderer goes to Mesopotamia to build the first city, the land that sent murderous armies from Assyria and Chaldean Babylon to destroy the people of Israel. Cain "invents" cities, which are the source of human pride, greed, and oppression. Perhaps we also sense the biblical author's antipathy toward cities, with their kings and their priests, who rule in tyrannical fashion. The tyranny of the cities in Mesopotamia is a theme that will return in the story about the tower of Babel. Being driven eastward by God is an image that would remind the Jewish audience of their exile to Mesopotamia in 586 BCE, when they were driven east by their Babylonian captors. Abraham reverses this direction by coming to the west (Canaan) from Ur of the Chaldees in Mesopotamia (Gen 12:1–3), from the land of exile back perhaps to Canaan, the implied "Eden" (Lacocque 31).

13

The Family of Cain

Genesis 4:17–24

(17) Cain knew his wife; and she conceived and bore Enoch; and he built a city, and named it Enoch after his son Enoch. (18) To Enoch was born Irad; and Irad was the father of Mehujael, and Mehujael the father of Methushael, and Methushael the father of Lamech. (19) Lamech took two wives; the name of the one was Adah, and the name of the other Zillah. (20) Adah bore Jabal; he was the ancestor of those who live in tents and have livestock. (21) His brother's name was Jubal; he was the ancestor of all those who play the lyre and pipe. (22) Zillah bore Tubal-cain, who made all kinds of bronze and iron tools. The sister of Tubal-cain was Naamah. (23) Lamech said to his wives:

"Adah and Zillah hear my voice;
you wives of Lamech, listen to what I say:
I have killed a man for wounding me,
a young man for striking me.
(24) If Cain is avenged sevenfold,
truly Lamech seventy-seven fold."

WHERE DID CAIN GET his wife? That is a favorite and famous question often asked. Supposedly Clarence Darrow asked it of William Jennings Bryant at the Scopes Monkey Trial in Dayton, Tennessee, when the famous defense lawyer actually cross-examined the prosecuting attorney. Bryant responded, "I do not know, I do not think about things that I do not think about!" Darrow then queried, "Do you think about things that you do think about?"

The answer usually given to this question is that we do not know where Cain got his wife. It is commonly suggested that he married one of his sisters many years after he killed Abel. Pious Jewish tradition in the second century BCE tells us that she was 'Awan, his sister. We are told this in a Jewish pseudepigraphical work, *Book of Jubilees* 4:1, 9. Some scholars suspect that the reference to Cain's wife indicates that the story assumes the existence of other people in the world in addition to Cain and Abel, but that overlooks the simple and symbolic nature of the storyteller's style.

We sense a tension between the Cain in the previous story and the Cain of the genealogies. Cain in the story is a farmer who became a nomad and a fugitive. Cain in the genealogies is city builder, he apparently is an eponym or symbolic ancestor for the Kenites, and he and his family become the great architects of human civilization and the arts (Gunkel 41; Skinner 100; M. Miller 164–73). Maybe the two traditions came together from separate sources for the biblical author. However, Gordon Wenham suggests that the two sets of tradition actually belong together by appealing to a Sumerian tradition that speaks of how the deity Nintur ended human nomadic existence by settling people in cities, just as Cain the nomad created cities (Wenham 1987:98). I suspect that the story of Cain the farmer turned nomad might recall the collapse of urban culture in the valleys of Palestine and the peaceful withdrawal of Canaanites into the highlands around 1200 BCE where they evolved into Israelites, and the second set of traditions might recall the re-emergence of well-developed culture and the organized state after 850 BCE in Israel and Judah.

More important than observing tensions in the Cain traditions is asking why the biblical author placed these traditions together. I do not believe the biblical author is merely recording odd pieces of "historical like" information. Perhaps the biblical author casts a critical comment upon cities by saying that they were founded by a fugitive and the first murderer. Or perhaps the biblical author inherited a common ancient tradition. The Phoenician Hypsouranios killed his brother Ousoos and then founded the city of Tyre (Blenkinsopp 2011:90), thus another city founded by a murderer. Perhaps the biblical author knows this Phoenician tradition. Israelites idealized pastoral existence and they were critical of large cities, because from such cities kings and powerful leaders extended their rule over other surrounding areas, such as the highlands where pastoralists lived. In later years the large cities of Mesopotamia were bases for the military expansion of the Assyrians and Chaldean Babylonians, who brutalized and exiled Israelites.

The critique of cities may be the critique of Mesopotamian empires and the tyrants who ruled them.

The genealogy of Cain's family provides interesting information about the Cainites. Cain builds the first city in the east. Genesis 4:17 appears to say that Cain's son was named Enoch, and Cain named the first city after him. The Hebrew text reads strangely here, however, for the reference to the person who built the city might imply that Enoch built the city. So some biblical scholars think that originally the story read that Enoch built the first city and named it after his son, Irad. If so, the reference might be the ancient city of Eridu in south Mesopotamia (Hallo 57–67; Van Seters 141; P. Miller 2003:241), which Mesopotamians regarded not only as a holy city, but one of their most ancient cities. Also, the word *'ir* means "city" in Hebrew, and that might be the reason for the attribution (Blenkinsopp 2011:85). It has been similarly suggested that Enoch's name is from the Sumerian word *unu* or *unug*, which is the Sumerian word for the city of Uruk, the oldest Sumerian city to have a large population and extensive trade connections (Hess 143). If so, maybe the author really does say that the city was named after Enoch.

There is an interesting similarity between the names of Lamech's sons, Jabal and Tubal-cain, and the names of Abel and Cain (Gunkel 49; Skinner 115; Van Seters 135). The J sound on Jabal is actually rather soft in Hebrew, and if dropped, it produces the name Abel. Of course, drop Tubal and you get the name of Cain. Jabal, like Abel, was a herder; and Tubal-cain was a metalworker, which is a characteristic that could be attributed to Cain in his role as a symbolic eponymous ancestor. Some scholars think that the Cainites are to be equated with the Kenites, who have been hypothesized as metalworkers (Gunkel 51). Otherwise scholars who note the similarities of names do not know what to say, though some suggest that the names for Cain and Abel in the story of Genesis 4 may have been inspired by the existence of these names in the genealogy. Another interesting observation is that Ezek 27:13 says that Javan, Tubal, and Meshech were merchant countries or cities, and two of their names sound like the first two of Lamech's sons. Our biblical author may simply be alluding to such regions, implying that they were descended from Lamech. Thus, there may be geographic and political symbolism in this genealogy.

Cain's family generates both sedentarism (cities) and pastoralism (tents). Cain or Enoch build a city, Jabal creates pastoralism (tents and livestock), Jubal creates music and musical instruments, and Tubal-cain creates metallurgy, a great breakthrough for human civilization and a function that serves both urbanites and pastoralists (Hiebert 41–44). Hermann Gunkel suspects that the original list of the Cainites, before the Sethite list was added, included Noah as a son of Lamech. That would mean that viticulture, wine and fermentation, invented by Noah, are also accomplishments of the Cainites. That would make them the creators of the truly significant aspects of civilization (Gunkel 462–65; Wenham 1987:111). Between them the Cainites cover urban and nomadic existence. They were quite a flexible family; in modern terms we would call them "dimorphic," that is, engaging in both sedentary and pastoralist economic pursuits. However, if they were sedentary, did they engage in agriculture? The curse on Cain implies that they did not. If so, what did they do in the cities?

If we look for a historical explanation, we might find a location for the so-called Cainites in the greater Palestinian region. In the Transjordan there were cities and minimal agriculture occurred there; such cities were centers for animal husbandry, mining, and they were located on the trade routes. One significant trade route was called the "King's Highway," and it saw trade caravans going back and forth between Egypt and Mesopotamia, and the folk in these cities probably thrived by engaging in trade. Perhaps, these pursuits are what the biblical author hints at in reference to the Cainites. Some suggest that the Cainite genealogy reflects particularly ancient memories about forges in the Transjordan, especially in Edom, to the southeast of the Dead Sea. Copper mining occurred in this area from the fourth millennium BCE until about 1200 BCE. The Cainite or Kenite copper working industry seems to have been located in Edom to the southeast of the Dead Sea. The people may have worshipped Yahweh there before the name was brought to Palestine with the Joshua people. Perhaps displaced forgers after 1200 BCE wandered about among early Israelites plying their trade and imparting these ancient memories. Adah and Zillah, the wives of Lamech, have Edomite names, and Edom is in the area where this ancient smelting occurred (Sawyer 155–66; Amzallag 393).

The Cainites of the biblical genealogy invented musical instruments and metal tools, both bronze and iron, which hints that they worked with the forge. If musical instruments are seen as being made out of metal, then the Cainites made both metal instruments and tools, and even more are we inclined to suggest that they are portrayed as metal workers. The root for Cain's name might mean "fit together," "fabricate," "forge," or "worker in iron" in addition to the meanings discussed earlier, and this could refer to the crafting of both tools and instruments. Thus, we are not surprised at the connection drawn between the sons of Cain and activities having to do with metal and metal work.

The attributes given to the Cainites by the biblical author imply that these people should be credited with the creation of human culture. That is significant. Elsewhere in the ancient Near East, myths often attributed the origin of human culture to the gods, often female goddesses, and at best people stole some of these skills from the gods. Enki and the goddess Inanna were in charge of the principle of *me* or *mes*, which was foundational for wisdom and culture. Individual Sumerian tales tell of how the gods created the pickaxe, the basket, and baked bricks, and then gave them to humanity (Westermann 269). Etana of Mesopotamia stole kingship from the gods; a fertility goddess *taught* women how to sew; and Prometheus in Greece stole fire from the gods (and had to serve detention by being chained to a rock while birds pecked out his liver for all eternity). In the ancient world the gods received full credit for inventing aspects of culture and teaching the skills of civilization to people. Female goddesses were responsible for sewing, weaving, food storage in pottery, music, songs, wisdom, lamentation hymns, and sometimes wisdom. In a late Babylonian text the god Enki or Ea created a series of deities to teach farming, arts, and religion to people. However, in the biblical account such developments are attributed to people. These are human accomplishments, not great trophies stolen from the divine realm. These are genealogical entries provided by the Yahwist Historian, and throughout the Yahwist History culture is a human endeavor, whereas in the *Atrahasis Epic*, against which the Yahwist reacts, culture comes from the gods. God grants people divine creativity to survive and to create civilization. This implies a positive future for humans and human culture, despite the sin and divine punishment that often follows. The Yahwist stresses human cultural development in contrast to the Priestly narratives, which are more concerned with increasing human population (another theme in contrast to the *Atrahasis Epic*) (Westermann 343; Albertz 2003a:3–21; Kawashima 483–501).

The story is also told of how the seven *apkallu*, the "wise ones," the ancient Mesopotamian sages, were primordial beings before the flood and arose from the sea to teach the cultural arts to humanity. They administered the *usuratu* or the "patterns" of heaven and earth, which were the arts and sciences, as well as the institutions by which people live. These seven venerable sages were: U-An, U-An-dugga, Enmedugga, Enmegalamma, Enmebulugga, An-Enlilda, and Utuabzu. There are similarities between the Cainites and the *apkalu* in terms of cultural contributions. But even those legendary Mesopotamian figures were given their knowledge from the gods (Westermann 325, 350; Vawter 98; Wenham 1987:99, 111; Batto 1992:24; Van Seters 145; Frymer-Kensky 110–15; Kawashima 492). Interestingly, there were seven *apkallu*, just as there were seven persons in the Cain genealogy—probably not a coincidence. Sometimes Mesopotamian traditions attribute the great cultural achievements to kings, but the Cainites are simply normal people (Gunkel 51; Westermann 330). In Mesopotamian traditions cities are founded by gods or by kings, but the biblical author says that Cain, a mere mortal, founded the first city (P. Miller 2003:239–40). This genealogy truly represents an example of demythologization by the biblical author—stories of gods and kings have been turned into stories of people (Fretheim 375).

Tikva Frymer-Kensky notices activities that were linked to goddesses in Mesopotamia are attributed to human efforts in Genesis 4, including food storage, administration, lamentations, songs, weaving, and wisdom. Elements of culture attributed to male gods in Mesopotamia are seen as coming from Yahweh in Israel, including royal rule, laws, the Temple, and the priesthood (Frymer-Kensky 115).

We see in the biblical narratives a greater interest in the value of human existence and human autonomy. This emphasis upon the value of human beings and their accomplishments will increase in later years among Greek thinkers and in Greek culture. The Greek author, Philo Biblius, who lived in Syria, indeed told of how cultural inventions were made by people through several generations. He even spoke of the brothers, Hypsouranious and Ousoos, who were inventors, who argued with each other, and this reminds us of Cain and Abel. His narrative is very close to the assumptions of Genesis 4. Perhaps Philo Biblius and the biblical author shared a common source of tradition, and perhaps the Cainite genealogy is Israel's cultural history comparable to the work of Philo Biblius (Gunkel 51; Van Seters 140, 145; Lowery 97–110). Both Jewish and Greek thought gave tremendous importance to the value of human contributions, thus laying the foundation for the way we in the west think about ourselves and the world.

Furthermore, these significant cultural accomplishments are made by the Cainites, supposedly the bad guys in the story. Perhaps, our biblical author does not see them as bad as we have been wont to assume. Maybe at one point the Cainites in Genesis 4 were seen as the good guys, but with the addition of the genealogy of the Sethites in Genesis 5 by the later Priestly Editors they became seen as the bad guys (Gunkel 54). The Cainites are the authors of human culture; they are people that Yahweh could be proud of in terms of their autonomy and creativeness. But this really gives rise to a question: Who are the Cainites and who is Cain?

On one level of meaning Cain symbolizes all of humanity, as we have observed above. But does he symbolize anyone or anything else? Since the nineteenth century scholars have speculated that the name Cain in Hebrew may hint that he is the eponymous ancestor of the Kenites (Skinner 111, who lists the names of all these scholars). Kenites were a tribal group closely allied with Israel for many years, but they never seem to have merged into the Israelite tribal configuration, although they might have had close connections with the tribe of Judah. What we know about them is tantalizing enough to begin a process of creative speculation about Cain and the Kenites.

Concerning the family of Cain we learn some interesting details. If killing Cain brings seven-fold revenge, his descendant Lamech brings seventy-fold revenge (Gen 4:24). Lamech brags that he will kill a man or a young boy for an injury. Some believe that the young boy reference means a young warrior at peak strength; others believe that the young boy reference implies that Lamech is so brutal that he will kill a small child (Hamilton 241). One interesting theory suggests that since he brags to his wives, he boasts of killing one of his own sons. Rabbinic traditions speak of how he killed both Cain and his son, Tubal-cain (Brown 1999:173). That would be gruesome, and I think the text would mention more, if that were the case. I am inclined to parallel "man" and "young man" as a poetic pair of references, and conclude that both are adults, thus implying that "young man" is a healthy warrior. Cain's children live in tents and develop animal husbandry (Gen 4:20), so they "invent" pastoralism. They also invent musical instruments, and both bronze and iron tools (Gen 4:21).

A sister of Tubal-cain is Naamah, and this item is mentioned with no elaboration. Biblical authors do not mention things casually; the audience probably knew who Naamah was. The only other Naamah in the Bible is an Ammonite princess married to Solomon and mother of King Rehoboam of Judah (1 Kgs 14:21) who reigned for seventeen years beginning around 931 or 922 BCE. Are we to make a connection with this Naamah and the Kenite girl in Gen 4:22? Some suggest that Genesis 4 took shape in the days of Solomon and that a connection should be drawn between the two women, because the biblical author is making positive observations about the role of Kenites in the United Monarchy. If Cain went to the "east," or the Transjordan, and Ammon was a country in the Transjordan, it is tempting to make this connection with Naamah. Furthermore, Kenites can be associated with the Transjordan, and the smelting of copper occurred in the Transjordan, in Edom, south of Ammon.

In various texts we learn more about the Kenites. In Num 24:22 Balaam refers to Kenites by the name of their eponymous ancestor, Kain (except for a shorter "a" vowel, the name is the same as in Genesis 4). In Judg 1:16 we are told that Moses' father, Jethro, is also called Hobab the Kenite, and that he took people into the land of Judah and settled there, and then later settled with the Amalekites. In Judg 4:17–22, general Sisera, an enemy of Israel defeated in battle by Deborah and Barak, is killed by Jael the Kenite. He comes to her assuming she will give him sanctuary, and he may unaware of the Kenite connection to Israel. Because he rudely demands sanctuary and food from her instead asking it of her husband, she kills him in his sleep by driving a tent peg through his head. (Never forget your manners when visiting Kenites.) Both of these accounts imply that Kenites lived among Israelites. The first account implies some connection between Kenites and the family of Moses, which is even more significant. Since Jethro is called a "priest of Midian" in Exod 4:16 and 18:1, we assume that Kenites were a sub-group of Midianites. In 1 Sam 15:6 Saul tells the Kenites to separate themselves from the Amalekites before Saul attacks the Amalekites, for the Kenites had shown kindness to Israel during the exodus. David shares spoil with the Kenites according to 1 Sam 30:29. In 1 Chron 2:55 Kenites are equated with the Rechabites, which implies that they are traditional Yahweh devotees who live among Israelites and preserve a simple lifestyle. They still existed in the seventh century BCE according to Jeremiah (Jer 35:1–18). At any rate, we have some interesting information to weave together as look at the biblical texts. From this point we begin to speculate.

It has been speculated that Moses learns the sacred name of Yahweh from Jethro, and the burning bush experience in Exodus 3–4 is one in which Jethro's tribal deity becomes the patron deity of Moses and the Israelites. When Jethro encounters Moses and the Israelites after the exodus (Exodus 18) he is called a priest, and he is very clearly a Yahweh devotee. Some ancient commentators believed that Jethro converts to Yahweh worship after hearing about the great signs and wonders in Egypt, but modern scholars believe that Jethro is really portrayed as being a Yahweh devotee and priest before he ever met Moses. In many poetic texts throughout the Hebrew Bible Israelites recall that Yahweh came up out of the desert south of Palestine, and they may imply that other people in those regions worshipped Yahweh before they did, especially the Kenites. If this is correct, it would make sense out of the reference in Gen 4:26 that people began to call upon the name of Yahweh at that time of the earliest ancestors.

Since the family history in Genesis 4 attributes metalwork to the Kenites, perhaps they were metal smiths who worked with forges. This might explain why they apparently lived among the Israelites but never merged into any one tribe. Frequently a "guest people" or a "sojourning people" who live among a "host people" maintain their independence because of some specialized trade, and often metalwork is just such a trade. Metalwork would have enabled Kenites to move around among the Israelites, serving their hosts with forging skills in trade relationships. This special skill, plus the mobility that went with it for the sake of trade, kept them from being amalgamated into the tribal system.

If Kenites were a "guest people" living among the Israelites, they were certainly in the minority compared to their "hosts." In such a setting, "guest peoples" often protect themselves by having a principle of multiple revenge, in case one of their members is hurt or killed. Hence, if you kill a Kenite, more than one of your clan members will be killed. This would then explain the references to multiple retribution for the killing of either Cain or Lamech. This makes sense, but we have no real evidence for this idea. Other authors have claimed that such multiple killings, done in revenge, are not really typical for nomadic peoples, but the Kenites may have fallen on hard times with a population decline, and such multiple revenge was necessary for their survival. When Lamech states that he killed a young man (Gen 4:23–24), perhaps he is not describing the death of a child, but rather a young warrior. The implication is that he opposes a formidable enemy, perhaps someone who threatens his clan (Gervitz 25–34). This memory would make sense for a people who need to defend themselves against great odds and whose numbers are dangerously reduced. However, it has been suggested that if the Kenites were part of the Amalekites, a people hated by the Israelites, perhaps the author denigrates both Kenites and Amalekites by attributing the coarse practice of multiple revenge to them (Simpson 520). Most scholars, however, believe the biblical author views Kenites as allies of Israel, and this attribution is not negative.

It has been speculated that Moses learned the concept of Sabbath rest from Kenites (a theory created by H. H. Rowley in the early twentieth century). Archaeologists observed that forgers kept their forges lit with a small fire overnight, so they could readily begin work in the morning. But if the small forge fire is kept lit too long, it will degrade the quality of the clay or stone forge. Thus, it is best to quench the fire and let the forge cool on occasion. Some tests with modern recreations of old forges suggest that cooling was most effective when done every seven days. Hence, the hypothesis was put forward that Kenite forgers rested every seventh day in order to let their forges cool, and Moses got the idea for Sabbath rest from them. This so-called "Kenite hypothesis" is quite interesting, but it is speculation of the highest sort.

This brings us to the suggested possibilities for what the mark of Cain might be. Many commentators suggest that the mark upon Cain was a tattoo, for that was the most logical mark on a person's body in the ancient world. It is also suggested that the mark was on his face, perhaps his forehead, since that was the most common place in the ancient world to put a distinguishing mark. It was visible to a stranger, especially if the Kenite were garbed in such a way as to protect his body against the wind and sand of the wilderness. Elsewhere (Ezek 9:4) there are references to a protective mark placed upon the forehead. In later years such a protective mark was the letter *tau*, the last letter of the Hebrew alphabet. Some authors suggest that the mark on Cain's forehead was the *tau* (Vischer 74–75; Richardson 85). In the two or three centuries before Jesus, the Hebrew letter *tau* was placed upon important religious manuscripts or in the margins of manuscripts next to especially significant verses, such as those which might contain the sacred name for God. The letter appears to protect something or highlight it as sacred. This would be true of both people and written manuscripts. The form of the *tau* that was used was written in an old Paleo-Hebrew script, not the *tau* used in the script of the Hebrew Bible (and learned dutifully by Jews and Christian seminarians when they study Hebrew).

Over the years the Israelites used two different alphabet scripts: prior to the Babylonian Exile (586 BCE) they used the Paleo-Hebrew script, and after the exile they began to use the Aramaic square script, which all biblical texts have been written in ever since. This Aramaic script is what we would call the Hebrew script nowadays, and Jews have used it for over two thousand years. Aramaic was a language spoken by people in Syria (Arameans) and it was very close to Hebrew. Aramaic ultimately became the everyday language spoken by Judeans during and after the sixth century BCE Babylonian Exile. It was the common language spoken in the streets during the days of Jesus, while classical Hebrew was used in worship and in the synagogue (and maybe in pious Judean homes). Part of the Jewish Talmud (200–600 CE) was written in Aramaic. Aramaic was the official language of the Assyrian, Chaldean Babylonian, and Persian empires, all of which had tremendous influence upon Israelite and Jewish culture from 750 to 330 BCE, and that is the reason why Judeans adopted the Aramaic script for their Hebrew texts and even spoke Aramaic as an everyday language. (However, the mark of blessing placed in manuscripts was the old Paleo-Hebrew *tau*.) The fact that the Hebrew Bible is written in an Aramaic script adopted by Judeans after the exile implies the bulk of the Hebrew Bible was not fixed in written form until the sixth century BCE and thereafter. Otherwise Judeans would have retained the old Paleo-Hebrew script.

Let us return to the mark of Cain. Perhaps, the biblical author spoke of the mark, and the audience perceived it as a tattoo upon the forehead. Perhaps, they perceived it as being in the shape of the old Paleo-Hebrew letter *tau*. Perhaps, the historical Kenites had such a tattoo on their foreheads in the shape of the *tau*, and the biblical author's audience recognized that the mark on Cain's forehead was recalled because it was the traditional tattoo Kenites placed on their foreheads to warn other people. Perhaps the Israelites in later years got the idea of using the old *tau* mark as a sign of protection and sacredness from that old Kenite practice.

The old Paleo-Hebrew *tau* looks like the Christian image of the cross, only it leans to one side at a forty-five degree angle to the ground. What did the actual cross of Jesus look like? Roman crosses for crucifixion were beams in the ground, and the prisoner brought the crossbar, which was placed on top of the beam. The Roman cross often appeared to be a capital letter T. But when Christians made the sign of the cross, they lowered the crossbar to make the cross look like a lower case letter t (without the curl at the bottom). Since the earliest Christians were Jewish, it was logical for them to portray the cross of Jesus' crucifixion in a manner reminiscent of the sacred symbol used on manuscripts, the Paleo-Hebrew *tau* (simply straightened up a little). How ironic this is, if our conjectures are correct. The mark of Cain, or the Kenite tattoo, became eventually the Christian sign of the cross. One final little piece of information can be added to this. Nomadic metal workers in the Sudan were distinguished by cross-shaped marks on their foreheads even into the twentieth century (Gaster 56; Vawter 97). Is this the Kenite tattoo in some form, which moved down into Africa? Before we laud the speculative ability of modern scholars, it is worth observing that in the pre-modern era some Christian commentators suggested that the mark of Cain was indeed the sign of the Christian cross, including Martin Luther. Was this just an intuitive blind guess on their part, or were they privy to knowledge in the Middle Ages and early modern era that has been lost to us?

After all of this creative speculation about the Cainites and the Kenites, is there any rebuttal that might be offered against these theories? Critics have responded by pointing out that the Kenites had a close relationship to Israel; it is difficult to imagine a biblical author telling a story in which their symbolic eponymous ancestor stood under a curse. Nor is the concept of seven-fold revenge something that is found elsewhere in the Semitic world. If such a thing did exist, it would be the actions of a desperate, dying tribal group trying to survive against overwhelming odds, which does not seem to describe the Kenites (Skinner 112–14). So the verdict may still be out on this great debate.

These are the kinds of speculative observations biblical scholars make of the biblical text at many points, not just with the narratives of Cain. Biblical studies are like a jigsaw puzzle with most of the pieces missing, because the Bible comes from an age long past. Scholars place the remaining pieces in many different positions to get the total picture, and the result is that different modern authors will get different pictures. As long as we remember that biblical scholarship is an art, not a science, we can appreciate the many suggestive ideas that scholars offer us. Some observations, like those offered above can be profound, exciting, and inspirational. At any rate, we know that the biblical authors were clever and creative, and recovering the deeper levels of meaning can sometimes be exciting.

The family of Cain makes its impression upon the world. But there is another family, the family of Seth. Who are they, and how will they differ from the family of Cain?

14

The Family of Seth

Genesis 4:25–26, 5:1–32

(25) Adam knew his wife again, and she bore a son and named him Seth, for she said, "God has appointed for me another child instead of Abel, because Cain killed him." (26) To Seth also a son was born, and he named him Enosh. At that time people began to invoke the name of the LORD.

(5:1) This is the list of the descendants of Adam. When God created humankind, he made them in the likeness of God. (2) Male and female he created them "Humankind" when they were created. (3) When Adam had lived one hundred thirty years, he became the father of a son in his likeness, according to his image, and named him Seth. (4) The days of Adam after he became the father of Seth were eight hundred years; and he had other sons and daughters. (5) Thus all the days that Adam lived were nine hundred thirty years; and he died. (6) When Seth had lived one hundred five years, he became the father of Enosh. (7) Seth lived after the birth of Enosh eight hundred seven years, and had other sons and daughters. (8) Thus all the days of Seth were nine hundred twelve years; and he died. (9) When Enosh had lived ninety years, he became the father of Kenan. (10) Enosh lived after the birth of Kenan eight hundred fifteen years, and had other sons and daughters. (11) Thus all the days of Enosh were nine hundred five years; and he died.

(12) When Kenan had lived seventy years, he became the father of Mahalalel. (13) Kenan lived after the birth of Mahalalel eight hundred and forty years, and had other sons and daughters.

(14) Thus all the days of Kenan were nine hundred and ten years; and he died.

(15) When Mahalalel had lived sixty-five years, he became the father of Jared. (16) Mahalalel lived after the birth of Jared eight hundred thirty years, and had other sons and daughters. (17) Thus all the days of Mahalalel were eight hundred ninety-five years; and he died. (18) When Jared had lived one hundred sixty-two years be became the father of Enoch. (19) Jared lived after the birth of Enoch eight hundred years, and had other sons and daughters. (20) Thus all the days of Jared were nine hundred sixty-two years; and he died. (21) When Enoch had lived sixty-five years, he became the father of Methuselah. (22) Enoch walked with God after the birth of Methuselah three hundred years, and had other sons and daughters. (23) Thus all the days of Enoch were three hundred sixty-five years. (24) Enoch walked with God; then he was no more, because God took him. (25) When Methuselah had lived one hundred eighty-seven years, he became the father of Lamech. (26) Methuselah lived after the birth of Lamech seven hundred eighty-two years, and had other sons and daughters. (27) Thus all the days of Methuselah were nine hundred sixty-nine years; and he died. (28) When Lamech had lived one hundred eighty-two years, he became the father of a son; (29) he named him Noah, saying, "Out of the ground that the LORD has cursed this one shall bring us relief from our work and from the toil of our hands." (30) Lamech lived after the birth of Noah five hundred ninety-five years, and had other sons and daughters. (31) Thus all the days of Lamech were seven hundred seventy-seven years; and he died. (32) After Noah was five hundred years old, Noah became the father of Shem, Ham, and Japheth.

What an impressive genealogy! Readers have been fascinated by the longevity of these ancient patriarchal figures. Christian fundamentalists, who take the Bible literally, feel compelled to explain why people before the flood lived so long. (They usually say something about the flood destroying the healthy climate of the world.) Why did they live so long? If these are not literal years, is there something symbolic in the numbers? The answer may be found by looking at comparable ancient Near Eastern literature.

The *Sumerian King List* is an ancient Mesopotamian record of one hundred and forty kings who ruled over the land from various cities from the beginning of time down until about 2000 BCE. The list may come from the time of Utuhegal, a ruler during the Ur III Dynasty (2000 BCE) in Mesopotamia. It was designed most likely to be political propaganda to praise the leadership of Sumerian kings, since the Ur III Dynasty witnessed the revival of Sumerian rule after several centuries of Akkadian rule and subsequent chaos. In the *Sumerian King List* kings who lived before the flood had extremely long life-spans, but kings who lived after the great "Mesopotamian flood" had shorter, though still long, life-spans. The similarity with the biblical text is striking in this regard. The biblical author had to be familiar with this Sumerian narrative. The earliest kings are obviously fictitious, but the later kings include true historical personages, Sumerian kings from the third millennium BCE. The first part of that king list reads as follows:

> (1–10) When the kingship came down from heaven, the kingship was in Eridu. In Eridu Alulim became king and reigned for 28,800 years. Alalgar reigned for 36,000 years. Thus two kings reigned for 64, 800 years. I (thus) leave Eridu on one side; its kingship was brought to Bad-tibira.
>
> (11–19) In Bad-tibira Enmenluanna reigned for 43,200 years. Enmengalanna reigned for 28,800 years. The divine Dumuzi, a shepherd, reigned for 36,000 years. (Thus) three kings reigned for 108,000 years. I (thus) leave Bad-tibira on one side; its kingship was brought to Larak.
>
> (20–25) In Larak, Ensipazianna reigned for 28,800 years. (Thus) one king reigned for 28,800 years. I (thus) leave Larak on one side; its kingship was brought to Sippar.
>
> (26–35) In Sippar Enmeduranna became king and reigned for 21,000 years. (Thus) one king reigned for 21,000 years. I (thus) leave Sippar on one side; its kingship was brought to Shuruppak. In Shuruppak, Urbatutu became king and reigned for 18,600 years. (Thus) one king reigned for 18,600 years.
>
> (36–40) These are five cities; eight kings reigned for 241,000 years. (Then) the flood streamed over (the earth)(Beyerlin 88–89).

There is also another version of the *Sumerian King List*, which is more fragmentary, and it has ten names. It adds one name that we cannot read clearly and another name, Ziusudra of Shuruppak, who is the equivalent of the Babylonian Noah (Vawter 105). This is incredibly fascinating, because Noah's name is on the Sethite list, but not on the Kenite list in the biblical accounts. The list of ten names, of course, compares to the Sethite list of ten names.

Furthermore, a Babylonian priest named Berossos, who lived in the third century BCE and wrote in Greek, also listed ten kings who lived before the flood. His list is as follows: 1) Aloros of Babylon (36,000 years), 2) Alaparos of Babylon (10,800 years), 3) Amelon of Pautibibla (46,800 years), 4) Ammenon of Pautibibla (43,200 years), 5) Megalaros of Pautibibla (64,800 years), 6) Daonos, a shepherd of Pautibibla (36,000 years), 7) Evedoranchos of Pautibibla (64,800 years), 8) Amempsinos of Laracha (36,000 years), 9) Otiartes of Laracha (28,800 years), and 10) Xisouthros (64,800 years) (Vawter, 104). Xisouthros is the Babylonian Noah in this list. Also, of interest is Daonos, the shepherd, because Dumuzi in the earlier lists is also a shepherd. Clearly this Greek list is derived from the earlier lists.

In the *Sumerian King List* the pre-diluvian monarchs rule for superhuman periods of time, just as do the biblical personages. There are eight or ten Mesopotamian kings compared to ten biblical figures, and they stand as the chief personages between the beginning of the world and the great flood in both cultural traditions. But the real differences lie in two other details: 1) The biblical personages are not kings; they are probably shepherds (if the ground is cursed for farming). 2) The biblical personages do not live as long. In fact, none of the biblical characters lives more than one thousand years, and that may be significant. The notion of one thousand years has symbolic meaning. If a person lives more than a thousand years, he or she must be divine or semi-divine.

The biblical author is making a political and religious statement against Mesopotamian traditions about the ante-diluvian kings. Mesopotamians claim these great personages were ancient kings of semi-divine origin or sons of the gods. This gives added authority to the power of the contemporary Mesopotamian king, who claims descent (physically or symbolically) from those ancient figures. The biblical author maintains that the pre-flood personages are not kings, but simple shepherds. Their life spans show they are not divine or semi-divine; they are simply humans who live a long time. None of the biblical figures live more than one thousand years; Methuselah tries his best, but even he falls short of the magic number. So the biblical author gives the biblical personages "short" life spans to deny their divinity. Perhaps an awareness of Ps 90:4, which speaks of how a thousand years in the life of God is like a day, leads the biblical author to keep all the numbers under one thousand. When modern readers of the Bible ask why did these people live so long, the answer is that they really lived "short" lives because they were mortal, not divine. This text is a classic example of a biblical passage that makes little sense unless we understand the ancient Near Eastern concepts and narratives against which the biblical author reacts. The text is really a polemic against the royal propaganda of the Mesopotamian kings or any kings with pretentious rhetoric of claimed self-divinity.

When Seth is born the biblical text says that he is in the "likeness of Adam." The previous instance in which this was stated was when the man and the woman were created in the "likeness of God." This, of course, is because both of these texts come from the Priestly Editors who stress how people hold a high position in the created order. But in its final form the entire narrative leaves us with a distinct message: the Sethites are in the divine image and such is not true of the Cainites. This reinforces the impression that the Cainites are bad guys and the Sethites are good guys. We also receive the impression that Adam has the creative power of God to make someone in his "likeness" just as God did, so Adam continues the creative process of God (Kselman 89). This gives sacred importance to the act of sex, for this process of procreation creates someone in the "image" of his or her parent. Too often, this message in the biblical text is missed by interpreters and preachers in the Christian tradition, especially those who have disparaged sex as evil.

Genesis 4:26 speaks of Seth and his son Enosh saying, "at that time people began to invoke the name of the LORD." Specifically, the Hebrew uses the sacred name, Yahweh, in reference to God. The later biblical narratives imply that this most sacred of all names for God was revealed only at the time of Moses and given to him during his encounter with the burning bush (Exod 3:14). So why does it say it here? There is also the question of whether the reference to the use of the sacred name pertains to all the Cainites and the Sethites, or whether it refers specifically to Enosh. Most commentators assume that it refers to Enosh. If so, that is interesting, because the name Enosh means "man," and it sounds as though Enosh could be characterized as the first man (Gunkel 41; Van Seters 142). His name would make him more appropriately a first ancestor, like his grandfather Adam. Some have suggested that perhaps originally the stories were told and Enosh was the first name in the list, but with the addition of Genesis 2–3 and the account about Adam, Adam's name was placed first and Enosh was pushed to third place (Westermann 339). Perhaps, the Primeval History once began with this genealogy. The reference to primeval personages calling upon the deity by the name, Yahweh, which would be the formal name of God, has its parallel in other ancient literature. Philo refers to Genos and Genea, the first human couple after Aeon and Protogonos, who were the first to worship Baalsamen, the high god of many Syrians in the late first millennium BCE. So this has a parallel with later Greek historiography, and some scholars maintain that we need to bring this later Greek material into comparison with biblical texts, especially if the biblical literature was put down in its final written form after the Babylonian Exile (Van Seters 142 et passim).

Another person of interest in the list is Enoch, the seventh patriarchal figure, who walks with God and is taken by God, or translated to heaven. This reminds us of Elijah, who also is taken to heaven alive in a whirlwind alongside a fiery chariot (2 Kgs 2:1–10). The usual interpretation is that

The Family of Seth

Enoch is taken alive into the heavenly realm without dying, though there are some references to his death. This assumption into heaven, of course, gave rise to great speculation in the later Jewish tradition, so that by the second century BCE Enoch was envisioned as a great seer and wise sage who was drawn up into the heavenly realm and permitted to see the future. His visions of the future emerge in several writings most of which were drawn together in the book of *Enoch* (we call it *1 Enoch*). Other literature also bears his name that has developed out of a complex set of traditions about this heavenly seer. Enoch is mentioned in documents from Qumran from the second century BCE, including some fragments of *1 Enoch*. In the Old Testament book of Sirach (which is in the Apocrypha for Protestants) Enoch's perfection is mentioned (Sir 44:16; 49:14), and in the Wisdom of Solomon (another Apocryphal book) Enoch is the example of a righteous man in whom the wisdom of the age came to fruition during his youth. In the New Testament Enoch is seen as a man of faith who did not die (Heb 11:5–6) and was a prophet (Jude 14–15).

Enoch lives for three hundred and sixty five years before God takes him, according to Gen 5:22–24, and that is the number of days in a solar year. This has prompted modern scholars to compare him to Enmeduranna or Enmeduranki who was listed above in the *Sumerian King List*. Both personages are seventh in their succession of ante-diluvian heroes. The Sumerian Enmeduranna was from Sippar, the city of the sun god, Shamash. Enmeduranna was taught divinatory rites by the sun god in the divine realm, which enabled him to found a guild of *baru*-priests, who were the masters of divination for Mesopotamians in later years. His adviser, Utuabzu (who was seventh on a list of antediluvian sages) was said to have ascended to heaven (Gunkel 138; Wenham 1987:28). This is too much similarity to be a coincidence. Enoch seems to combine characteristics of both Mesopotamia figures. However, later Greek and Roman heroes, such as Ganymeade, Aeneas, and Romulus also ascended, and our biblical author might have been familiar with some of these traditions, too (Blenkinsopp 2011:119)

Clearly our biblical author uses the figure of Enoch to spoof the Mesopotamian king Enmeduranna somehow and for some specific reason. Enmeduranna was a sage king with great wisdom obtained from the sun God; Enoch was a wise sage (at least according to later Jewish literature), who had a prominent place in heaven (also according to later Jewish tradition), but he was not a king. Perhaps this is another critique of kingship. It is likely that there is more biblical critique of Mesopotamian belief involved here, but we have to guess at what it is. Perhaps, because Israelites had been prone to worship the sun as a deity, and both Israelites and even later Judeans were tempted to equate Yahweh with the sun, this story is meant to critique sun veneration in some way. At any rate, it seems that the biblical author is trying to equate Enoch and Enmeduranna.

When the reader of the biblical text looks closely at the two genealogies in Genesis 4 and 5, a striking similarity between the two lists appears. The names are the same in both lists. In Genesis 4 there are seven generations of Cainites: 1) Cain, 2) Enoch, 3) Irad, 4) Mehujael, 5) Methushael, 6) Lamech, and 7) Jabal, Jubal, Tubal-cain, and Naamah. In Genesis 5 there are ten generations: 1) Adam, 2) Seth, 3) Enosh, 4) Kenan, 5) Mahalalel, 6) Jared, 7) Enoch, 8) Methuselah, 9) Lamech, and 10) Noah. One can equate the following Cainites with corresponding Sethites: Cain equals Kenan (in Hebrew the names are closer), Enoch equals Enoch, Irad equals Jared (again, in Hebrew the names are closer), Mehujael equals Mahalalel (more or less), Methushael equals Methusaleh (more or less), and Lamech equals Lamech. Jabal, Jubal, Tubal-cain, and Naamah are unique on the Cainite list, while Adam, Seth, Enosh, and Noah are unique on the Sethite list. Enosh may sound like Enoch, but in Hebrew they are quite distinct. Interestingly, Adam and Enosh are both generic words for "man." As Lamech has three sons on the Cainite list, so also Noah has three sons on the Sethite list. The bottom line is that these two lists really contain the same names, and the author writing in Hebrew would notice this very clearly, even though English speaking readers to miss it frequently.

Some scholars suggest that originally both lists come from the same source, which had ten names. The biblical author created the genealogy of Cain, whose name was Kenan on the other list, and simply dropped Seth and Enosh in order to move the plot line along to Cain (and then dropped Noah at the end of the list) (Vawter 103). The biblical author tinkered with the Sethite genealogical list by switching Enoch and Mahalalel around in order to make Enoch the seventh name on the list, because he was so important symbolically. This would make sense, because one of the Sumerian lists and the Greek list mentioned above had ten names.

Some scholars suggest that the lists were once shorter. Hermann Gunkel believes that the list originally was Adam, Seth, Enosh, and Noah (Gunkel 54). Claus Westermann believes that Enosh, which means man, originally began the list of seven names, and then Adam was a doublet for Enosh once the list was expanded to ten names. When finally there were ten names, the list then paralleled the *Sumerian King List*, which likewise had ten names with the flood hero as the tenth king (Westermann 339, 343).

Why is there this similarity? Clearly biblical genealogies are used frequently for symbolic purposes. The Cainite list has seven names, like the days of the week, and the Sethite list appears to focus on ten names, like the number of commandments. Maybe Adam's name was added to the Sethite list to get ten names. One can point out, however, that Noah's sons are mentioned in the second list—Shem, Ham, and Japheth. Perhaps we should say there are eleven generations of Sethites, or perhaps there were ten generations and Adam was added to the first list to indicate the true succession went through the Sethites, or perhaps the sons of Noah were added to the list. At any rate, it seems as though there might be a comparison with one list of seven names with another list of ten names, and ironically they are the same people. This is why earlier we could say that Cain was the ancestor of all humanity. Initially the narratives may have had only the Cainite genealogy, and he truly was the ancestor of humanity. But even when the Sethite genealogy was added, because of the similarity of names, we are still tempted to call Cain the symbolic ancestor of humanity.

I believe the biblical author who added the Sethite genealogy made a powerful religious statement. The greater biblical narrative implies that the Cainites were bad, since they were descended from the first murderer. Although the genealogy narrative of the Cainites itself does not imply that, the context into which this genealogy has been placed gives that impression. The present biblical narrative implies that the Sethites were good people. Hence, there were two races, the bad guys and the good guys, but the bad guys and the good guys are really the same people. We are descended from both the bad guys and the good guys. We, like our ancestors, are a combination of the bad and the good. In Christian terms it would be said that we are both "sinners" and "saints" in the eyes of God, and we have the capacity for doing both horrendous evil and saintly good actions. In Jewish terms it would be said that as our ancestors were pulled between the inclination for bad (the Cainite ancestry) and the inclination for good (the Sethite ancestry), so also we today are pulled between those same two inclinations and must freely choose every day of our life whether we are "descended" from our Cainite ancestors or our Sethite ancestors. It is fascinating how a biblical author or a later editor can preach a powerful religious message simply by the arrangement of a literary text. Those who read these biblical texts too literally, miss a great sermon.

A puzzle to scholars is the difference in the numbers found in early translations of the Bible. The Septuagint was a Greek translation made of the Hebrew Old Testament over the years from 200 BCE to 100 CE. The Samaritan Pentateuch was a variant Hebrew version of our Old Testament used by the Samaritans who lived in central Palestine in Jesus' day. When we look at those two editions, we see that the numbers of these antediluvian figures are different. The changes are not usually in the lengths of time the personages lived, but rather how old they were when their sons were born. The Septuagint, for example, makes each person one hundred years older when his son was born. Of course, that adds years to the overall chronology. In particular, Adam, Seth, Enosh, Kenan, Mahalalel, and Enoch have the hundred years added to their ages prior to the birth of their sons. Jared is not changed, Methuselah has twenty years subtracted, and Lamech has six years added. In addition, twenty-four years are subtracted from Lamech's overall life (Hamilton 247). Why these differences exist, we do not know. But the Septuagint, in particular, was made from Hebrew manuscripts of the Old Testament that are far older than anything we have today. So we take these numbers seriously. This is why our Hebrew Old Testament chronology implies that there were four thousand years of history before Jesus, while the Greek Septuagint implies there were about five thousand years.

Finally, there is the comment made concerning Noah upon his birth, "Out of the ground that the LORD has cursed this one shall bring us relief from our work and from the toil of our hands" (Gen 5:29). It seems that the relief refers to the fertility brought back to the land by Noah upon his successful cultivation of a vineyard after the flood. But which curse is being alleviated here? If it is the curse upon the soil that came with Adam, then the meaning is that the difficulty in working the soil was made easier with Noah after the flood. That would imply that Cainites were nomads, pastoralists, or city-dwellers who did not farm (perhaps traders and miners), while the Sethites were farmers who toiled under Adam's curse. On the other hand, if the rest brought by Noah is from the curse upon the land resulting from Cain's actions, then all ante-diluvian people were nomads, but farming emerged after the flood. It is possible that the overall meaning in these stories might have changed over the years as the narratives were expanded, so we have to engage in guesswork. I am tempted to think that the curse removed by Noah is the curse of Cain that prevented any farming until after the flood. I am also tempted to think that this motif might have been a connecting link between the stories of Cain and Noah before material in Genesis 2–3 about the man and woman in the garden was added. Then it would clearly be Cain's curse that was removed by Noah. At that point in the history of the narratives, it also would be logical to view all the people as being descended from Cain. The addition of the curse in Genesis 3 makes the freeing actions of Noah ambiguous. However, the story in the form we have can still make good sense. Noah frees up the land from the curse of Cain and makes it possible to farm, though not without hard work brought about by the curse of Adam.

Would there have been a time when Israelites looked back and said that Noah eased the curse and made farming and agriculture easier than it once was? Perhaps there was a romantic memory among Israelites that farming became easier when their ancestors came out of the wilderness, where they were nomads, and into the land of Canaan, where they could farm. If that was their romantic image, then the key is the image of Noah's vineyard. Grapes (and olives as well) were cash crops for Israelites in the land of Palestine, and the long-term commitment to tending olive tree and grape vines was the sign of a person seriously dedicated to sedentary agricultural pursuits. Such crops historically were not grown in the Transjordan or the wilderness. Notice how I say "romantic memory" in reference to the entrance into the land by the Israelites. In actuality, very few Israelites came into the land under Joshua around 1200 BCE, most Israelites were Canaanites who evolved into Israelites.

If there really is a historical memory, it may be that period of time in Iron Age I (1200–1050 BCE) when people withdrew into the highlands to have their own new villages and farms more distant from life in the Palestinian lowlands where war and foreign invasions by Egyptians and Sea Peoples could wreak havoc. There in the highlands, as these people evolved into Israelites, they gradually introduced new agricultural techniques over the next four centuries (highland terracing for crop growing on sloped hills, lime-coated cisterns for deeper wells in the highlands, and iron plows to furrow more deeply into rocky highland soil). These developments made highland agriculture (grain growing) and viticulture (grape and olive cultivation) easier in the once agriculturally foreboding highlands. Maybe this is the memory they attributed to the curse that passed away with the efforts of Noah. The curse was overcome by the gradual emergence of productive Israelites in the highlands of Palestine.

The two genealogies are powerful political statements. While the Mesopotamian lists recorded semi-divine kings who lived for thousands of years, the two biblical genealogies list human beings. There are no semi-divine kings, and ultimately the common folk are as important to God as any king. All stand equally before God. The genealogy of Seth ends with Noah. But with the introduction of Noah the ancient tales begin a new story line, the narrative of the great flood that destroyed the old ante-diluvian world. With the flood begins a new chapter in human history.

15

Ancient Flood Accounts

UNDERSTANDING THE SOPHISTICATED MESSAGE of the biblical flood narrative is made possible by knowing ancient Near Eastern accounts more so than any of the other accounts in the Primeval History. It appears that with the flood narrative our biblical author closely used ancient flood narratives, especially those from Mesopotamia, so that there would be a great similarity between those accounts and the biblical story. Hence, the differences that occur stand out for the listeners or the readers and are truly significant. The biblical author uses a brilliant literary strategy in the creation of the flood narrative.

MESOPOTAMIAN ACCOUNTS

The earliest Mesopotamian flood story comes to us in the Sumerian language and in fragmentary form; we call it the *Sumerian Flood Story*. The actual text we possess dates to about 1600 BCE, though the story is older than that. It is part of a longer tale we call *The Eridu Genesis*. It tells of a hero named Ziusudra, who receives divine revelation about the coming flood from Enki or Ea, the god whom he serves in his role as priest and king in the city of Shuruppak. Enki speaks to him beside a wall and tells how Anu and Enlil have decreed a flood to destroy humanity. Ziusudra builds a boat and collects supplies for his family. The storm lasts for seven days and nights. When the sun appears, he opens a window, worships the sun god, and offers sacrifice of oxen and sheep. In return, Ziusudra is granted eternal life by Anu and Enlil, and he is settled on the island of Dilmun. The story is too fragmentary for us to tell what was the reason for the flood (Pritchard 42–44; Beyerlin 89–90; Bailey 11–16; Van Seters 56–58; Hallo and Younger 1:513–15).

The second significant flood narrative is the *Atrahasis Epic*, which as we mentioned previously, is a narrative that covers both the creation of humanity and the flood. It appears to depend upon the earlier Sumerian account of Ziusudra (Lambert and Millard 10–13; Beyerlin 90–93; Bailey 14–16; Van Seters 50–54; Matthews and Benjamin 35–40; Hallo and Younger 1:450–52).

We summarized the story about the creation of people from the *Atrahasis Epic* earlier, but let us turn to the flood narrative. After the junior gods complain that they are overworked, people are made to serve the gods. The goddess, Nintu-Mami mixes clay with the blood of a rebellious god and molds seven pairs of humans. After they become alive, people multiply greatly and generate much noise during their labors. This noise prevents Enlil from sleeping (wrong god to anger!). Perhaps the noise might be viewed as a form of human rebellion. People rebel as did the lesser gods, for they were made from the blood of a rebellious god. One interpreter, however, believes that neither overpopulation nor noise angers Enlil to bring the flood, but rather it is the inscrutable will of Enlil (Moran 54–55, 68, 71). Enlil summons the gods to inform them that he will limit human population. First, he decides to inflict a plague upon people. But Enki, always sympathetic to humanity, gives advice to the hero Atrahasis to offer sacrifice to the god Namtara, who is responsible for the plague. The plague stops. Enlil sends a famine to diminish human population, but Enki's advice to Atrahasis is to offer sacrifice to Adad, the god of rain and fertility. The famine stops. The third attempt by Enlil involves some disaster, perhaps drought (which we cannot translate clearly), but it also fails when Atrahasis responds with correct sacrifice to the appropriate deity. Finally, Enlil decides to use a flood to thin out humanity.

Enlil orders Enki not to warn Atrahasis about the flood, so that this last attempt will work. But Enki speaks to the reed hut in which Atrahasis is sitting, so as not to speak directly to any human being, and Enki not only warns Atrahasis of the flood, but he gives him directions for building a boat out of the reeds of his house in which he and his family can be saved. Atrahasis tells his neighbors that the conflict between Enlil and Enki has caused him to leave the city in this boat. He caulks the boat with pitch and puts a large roof over the barge or boat, building the boat takes seven days. It has no windows (unlike Noah's ark). The boat takes animals and birds in it as well. Before going into the ark Atrahasis celebrates with a banquet. The flood arrives seven days later, and for seven days and nights the rains pour down. The gods are terrified by the destructive power of the flood, especially the mother goddess, and they question their wisdom in voting for the flood. When the flood is over, the gods discover that Atrahasis is still alive. When Atrahasis offers sacrifice, the gods swarm like hungry flies to the sacrifice.

Enlil is enraged that Enki has defied his orders, but he relents in his desire to punish him. The mother goddess takes lapis lazuli flies from Anu to make a necklace so as to recall the time when people floated on the water like flies. (This necklace is equivalent to the biblical rainbow.) Enki and Nintu-Mami create humanity again, implying that Atrahasis and his family are not the ancestors of later humanity, as is the case with Noah and his sons. Enki and Mami create normal males and females, but they also create childless women to help control human population growth. In addition, they create disease demons responsible for infant mortality. One interpretation suggests that people before the flood actually were immortal and mortality is introduced after the flood (Batto 1992:29).

One senses that a significant social and economic problem for the Mesopotamians was overpopulation, for this theme figures so prominently in the account of the flood and the recreation of humanity. This stands in contrast to biblical narratives and legislation that encouraged people to be fertile and to have as many children as possible. Israel so often faced the problem of under-population in the highlands of Palestine and especially in the years after the destruction of Jerusalem and the Babylonian Exile. Their leaders encouraged people to have children to keep the ethnic group and the Judean identity alive.

The third major flood account is contained within the late second millennium BCE Akkadian narrative entitled *Gilgamesh*. The name of the flood hero is Utnapishtim, which appears to be the Akkadian translation of Ziusudra.

In the *Gilgamesh Epic* the hero, Gilgamesh, is king of Uruk and his tyrannical rule over its inhabitants causes the gods to send the wild man, Enkidu, to the city to distract Gilgamesh. His destructive rampages cause the city leaders to send out a temple prostitute to stop him. After Enkidu is seduced by the temple prostitute, thereby becoming a "civilized" man rather than a wild man who cavorts with the animals, Enkidu goes into the city and meets Gilgamesh, wrestles with him, gains his respect, and becomes his friend. Together the two of them go on journeys and have adventures, including a battle with Humbaba, the beast of the cedar forest in Lebanon, and a fight with the bull of heaven. By killing the bull of heaven, they anger the goddess Ishtar who subsequently demands Enkidu's death from her father Anu, and perhaps Gilgamesh's insult of Ishtar's seductive advances did not help the heroes' cause either. When Enkidu dies, Gilgamesh realizes that he, too, will die, even though he was two-thirds divine (a marvel of genetic engineering). The second half of the epic recounts Gilgamesh's lonely travels in search of the secret of immortality. Finally, Gilgamesh comes to the island where Utnapishtim of Shuruppak lives. Utnapishtim was granted immortality because he survived the flood, and so he tells Gilgamesh the story of the flood and explains that his immortality was a gift and that Gilgamesh cannot receive the same gift. He has Gilgamesh undergo a test to overcome sleep, for if Gilgamesh can conquer sleep, he can conquer death. Gilgamesh fails and sleeps for seven days; each day Utnapishtim's wife bakes a loaf of bread and leaves it beside Gilgamesh, so that when Gilgamesh awakes, he will see how long he slept. When Gilgamesh is about to leave dejected, Utnapishtim tells him where the plant of life or rejuvenation might be found. (Why didn't he mention this sooner?) Gilgamesh retrieves the plant from the bottom of the ocean and returns to Uruk, intending to eat the plant when he becomes old. Gilgamesh takes a swim in a pond near Uruk, and while he swims, a snake eats the plant and that is why snakes know the secret of healing, immortality, and rejuvenation. Gilgamesh, broken-hearted, returns to Uruk, but he learns to affirm the good things he has in life and not to fear death (Pritchard 72–99; Matthews and Benjamin 19–30). That is the ultimate message of the epic.

This epic contains within it many separate stories woven together at some point. For example, the plant of life account obviously was added almost as an afterthought. The flood story told by Utnapishtim is a separate narrative of sizeable proportion, which has been inserted into the greater narrative. But overall the resultant work is a masterpiece of literature from the ancient world.

The flood account told by Utnapishtim appears to be dependent upon the earlier versions of the *Sumerian Flood Story* and *Atrahasis Epic*, especially the latter. Enlil and Ninurta convene the divine assembly and decide to flood the earth, but Ea opposes Enlil. Utnapishtim is told by Ea to build a ship, as Ea speaks to a reed hut in which Utnapishtim is sleeping. Utnapishtim is to tell his neighbors that he must sail away from the city because of the hostility of Enlil toward him. Utnapishtim builds the boat in seven days with six decks, each deck having nine compartments (much larger than Noah's boat). He caulks the boat with asphalt and oil. Each day he sacrifices sheep and provides ample food and wine for the workmen. The boat is loaded with Utnapishtim's family, the craftsmen, wild and domestic animals, and Utnapishtim's gold and silver. Utnapishtim boards the ship, closes the door (unlike Noah, who has God close the door for him). The rains come, last for seven days, and are so violent that even the gods are terrified, and they flee into the highest heavens and "cowered like dogs, crouching outside." Ishtar, the mother goddess, especially laments the flood, and she "screamed like a woman in childbirth." Utnapishtim observes how bodies float on the water like dead fish. After seven days the sea grows quiet and the boat comes to a halt on Mount Nimush or Nisir in Urartu (Armenia). After seven days Utnapishtim releases a dove, which comes back, then a swallow, which comes back, for neither bird could find a place to land. But when Utnapishtim releases a raven and it does not return, he knows that the waters have diminished and they can leave the boat. Utnapishtim releases the animals, leaves the boat, and offers up sacrifice to which the gods come. The gods "smelled the sweet savor" and "crowded like flies about the sacrificer." Enlil comes and is angry that people are alive. Ninurta blames Ea, but Ea or Enki defends his decision to save some of humanity. Enlil relents, takes Utnapishtim aboard the ship with his wife and makes them both immortal, after which they are taken to live at the "source of the rivers." At this point Utnapishtim ends his account and Gilgamesh falls asleep. (At one point Utnapishtim is given the title, "Atrahasis," which means the "exceedingly wise one," thus indicating to us the relationship of these accounts to each other.) (Pritchard 93–95; Beyerlin 93–97; Matthews and Benjamin 25–28; Hallo and Younger 1:458–60)

Interesting differences between the early story of *Atrahasis Epic* and the later account of Utnapishtim may be observed. Directions provided by Enki to Utnapishtim explicitly include the command to take animals aboard. A lament by the mother goddess over the destruction of humanity is omitted. Every mention of divine anger has been edited out, so that the reason for the flood is vague. Nor are the gods described as being hungry or thirsty during the flood. We receive the impression that the Utnapishtim account is biased toward male deities and wishes to portray the deities in more exalted fashion (Pleins 108).

In another literary piece there is a short reference to a flood narrative. From the Assyrian work *Erra Epic*, which comes from eighth century BCE Assyria, there is a speech by Marduk, the god of Babylon, who declares that he flooded the world but saved a small remnant of humanity. This might simply be an Assyrian allusion to one of the major accounts listed above.

A flood narrative which comes to us from a much later era is the account provided by the Babylonian priest, Berossus, who lived in the third century BCE and wrote his work, *Babylonaica*, in Greek. It was an attempt to write a Babylonian history in the style of Greek historiography in an age when Hellenistic rulers and Greek culture dominated Asia. His narrative was recalled by the Jewish historian Josephus in *Jewish Antiquities* I.3.6, written in the late first century CE, and by the Christian historian Eusebius in the early fourth century CE. What makes his work worth consideration is that he used very old sources, and some of his sources may have been known to the biblical author in the sixth or fifth centuries BCE. He speaks of an ancient sage, who appears in fish form, named Oannes, who instructs people in the art of civilization. The Sumerian name behind Oannes appears to be Adapa, whose story we encountered earlier. In his account of the flood the hero is Xisouthros, which appears to come from the name, Ziusudra, and so Berossus may know the *Sumerian Flood Story*. Xisouthros is warned in a dream by the god Kronos about the flood and also is directed to write a history and bury it in Sippar before he builds the boat. He loads the boat with family, friends, and animals. He tells his neighbors that he is going to visit the gods to pray for the welfare of humanity. The boat is huge, one thousand by four hundred yards. At the end of the flood he releases birds, disembarks in Armenia (which would be Urartu), sacrifices to the gods, becomes immortal, and ultimately lives with the gods. His friends from the boat remain on earth, discover the buried writings, and return to rebuild Babylon. The narrative declares that the ark still resides in Armenia (Bailey 11–13; Van Seters 67–70; Pleins 109).

If we compare the biblical account with these Mesopotamian accounts, we notice a tremendous number of similarities in the plot. It appears as if the biblical author wanted the audience to see the similarity in the story so that any differences provided by the author would stand out dramatically.

Similarities include the following: 1) The flood comes because of divine displeasure. 2) A hero is warned by divine message spoken by a god. 3) The hero builds an ark. 4) The dimensions of the ark are described in the divine message. 4) The hero's family is saved in that ark. 5) Animals are brought to the ark by the divine will. 6) The boat is built in seven days after the divine warning is issued. 7) The ark is caulked with asphalt or pitch. 8) An ark door must be closed by a human or divine hand. 9) Rainfall brings the destructive waters. 10) Everything outside the ark drowns. 11) The entire world is covered with water. 12) The boat floats around in the water and comes to rest on a mountain in Armenia (Urartu or Ararat). 13) A window is opened in the ark to see what happened to the floodwaters. 14) Birds are released to see what happened to the floodwaters. 15) The hero offers sacrifice. 16) God or the gods smell the sacrifice. 17) The hero receives a blessing. And 18) the world is repopulated (Bailey 14–18). The number of these plot similarities is overwhelming, especially when we consider flood stories from other cultures and note their differences. Clearly the biblical author chose to use a well-known Mesopotamian story line.

What then becomes truly significant are the differences that the biblical author introduces into the narrative. They convey the crucial messages the biblical author wishes to communicate. Various authors have highlighted these differences well (Skinner 178; Wenham 1987:164–65; Bailey 18–20; Van Seters 165; Kass 166–67).

There is moral purpose behind the reason for the flood in the biblical account. In the Mesopotamian accounts the reason for the flood is human overpopulation that leads to the excessive noise that disturbs the gods. However, in the biblical account God brings the flood because of sin, both in the divine realm where the gods have mated with human women, and on the earth where violence is excessive.

There is one god; monotheistic assumptions permeate the biblical account. In the Mesopotamian accounts there are many gods and thus there are many divine wills. Some of the gods will to destroy humanity, but Ea or Enki wishes to save humanity. There is divine conflict that drives the plot line of the Mesopotamian stories. Even at the conclusion of the flood there is initial disagreement as to what to do with the human survivors. The biblical account by contrast shows a unity of the divine will. Divine will decrees the flood. God brings the flood, directs the events of the flood, saves the people, and is in total control of the entire process.

There is direct revelation by God to the hero in the biblical account. Directions for building the ark are directly decreed. This, of course, flows from the monotheistic assumptions, but it is worth mentioning separately. There is a close relationship between the biblical God and Noah, which leads to more meaningful statements about Noah's faith and his relationship to God. Ea or Enki must be sneaky and speak indirectly to the Mesopotamian flood hero through the hut in which the hero lives. Ea or Enki cannot be forthright in his dealings with the human being.

Noah is distinctly different from the Mesopotamian heroes. He is a commoner; they are kings or priests. This is an extremely important difference. Noah will remain mortal after the flood; the others become immortal. Noah will preserve human and animal life primarily; the other flood heroes are portrayed as saving civilization. Noah is totally obedient to divine directions; Mesopotamians exert self-initiative. Utnapishtim closes the door of the boat, but God does that for Noah. The Mesopotamian heroes have navigational assistance; Utnapishtim has a helmsman. But God steadies and directs the ark for Noah. Noah does not tell his neighbors what is happening; Atrahasis and Utnapishtim deceive people. Most important of all, Noah is explicitly described as righteous; this is not said of the Mesopotamian heroes. Perhaps Noah's righteousness is the equivalent to how the Mesopotamian heroes are made immortal by the gods (Skinner 159).

The age of Noah contrasts with that of the Babylonian personages. Ziusudra reigned for thirty-six thousand years before the flood came, while Noah was only six hundred years old. The age of pre-flood personages is measured in the thousands, while biblical personages only age by the hundreds. The implication is that the Mesopotamian personage is a semi-divine being who can live for countless years. Noah is only a human being, who cannot live for more than one thousand years. Even Methuselah did not make it to one thousand years. This continues the observation made above, that Noah was not a person of special privilege and rank. Babylonians viewed their ancient founders as semi-divine, ruling and living for thousands of years, thus implying that the institutions of the priesthood and kingship were eternally established. To portray your ancient ancestors as less than a one thousand years old is to declare them mortal and to denigrate those special institutions of priesthood and kingship. Notice that thirty-six thousand and six hundred are numbers based on the Mesopotamian numerical system of twelve, a sexagesimal system. This tells us again that the biblical story has its roots in Mesopotamian culture, for Israelites otherwise counted with a decimal system.

Noah says nothing to his friends about why he builds the ark, whereas the Mesopotamian figures deceive their observers with explanations that speak of how they have to move because of conflict between the gods. Their answer is a double-entendre, because there is indeed a conflict among the gods, a conflict between Enki and the rest of the gods who decreed a flood. Noah is portrayed as more honest in this fashion. This is a good example of the moral piety found in the biblical text.

The significant differences in how the hero of the flood is portrayed reflect the religious and political agenda of the biblical author. The Babylonian personages are kings or priests, whereas Noah is simply an average person. This continues the critique of class-consciousness that we find in many texts. The biblical text is critical of those people who have tremendous wealth and power in ancient society, especially kings and priests.

The biblical God is portrayed as being much more powerful. The Mesopotamian gods fight among themselves, they are terrified by the power of the floodwaters and regret having unleashed it, they even bicker at the end of the flood about disposal of the human beings. In the biblical account God brings the flood, closes the door to the ark, steadies the boat in the water, does not hide from the ferocity of the waters, brings the ark to the mountain, and speaks simply and directly with Noah after the flood. While the Mesopotamian gods hide in the heavens, afraid to get their feet wet, God is in the storm and the water with the ark and Noah. (God has hip boots.) References by Utnapishtim to closing the door and steering the boat himself may have been known to the biblical author, which he directly addresses with the otherwise incidental references to door closure and ship guidance by God. The biblical God is directly present for the human beings in the flood process.

In the flood accounts of Ziusudra, Atrahasis, Utnapishtim, Deukalion, Demarius (Phoenicia), and Manu (India) there are references to subsequent sacrifices; the motif seems extremely important. In particular, the Mesopotamian accounts speak of how the gods were hungry for sacrifice after the flood and gratefully received the sacrifice offered up by the hero. In fact, there is the allusion to how they swarmed around the sacrifice hungrily like flies. We are not sure if this is an insult to the gods or not. Clearly the biblical God does not need sacrifice, but merely accepts it as a form of human gratitude. God is not dependent upon sacrifice. Sometimes in Mesopotamia priests would withhold food from the gods in order to get a divine response. That is, they would not place the food offerings before the statues of the divine beings in the temples. They might even place the statues of the gods in a dark room to provoke them to act. (I guess that's like sending child to his room with no supper or television.) The biblical author obviously would not see these actions as having any effect upon the God of Israel, especially since Israelites and Judeans did not even have images or statues of God that they could manipulate. This might be a major reason why such images were outlawed in Israel—no one could even try to manipulate God or have any power over God.

After the flood the Mesopotamian gods provide a blessing to the heroes, Ziusudra and Utnapishtim, by making them immortal. Utnapishtim, in particular, is taken to the island of Dilmun, where later Gilgamesh will encounter him and hear the story of the flood. In the biblical account God provides a blessing to all of humanity, a far more democratic move. God promises the regularity of the seasons and additional promises never to bring a global flood again.

There are implications for the whole human race. In the biblical text all people are descended from Noah, but in the Mesopotamian accounts the gods make a new human race. This implies a greater distance between later people and the great antediluvian kings. This, of course, puts people in a lower status in relationship to kings and priests in their own age. The biblical text declares that the antediluvians were not kings and priests, but were average people. Of course, we are descended from them.

In Mesopotamian accounts the gods create new conditions for human beings. In the *Atrahasis Epic* story the gods create sterility, stillbirth, and celibacy to impede overpopulation. In the biblical account people are told to be fruitful and reproduce. Mesopotamia had too many people, while the highlanders of Palestine had too few, and after the 586 BCE destruction of Judah and exile of the Judeans, it was imperative for them to reproduce lest they be lost among the foreign kingdoms. God provides guidelines concerning the shedding of blood, both for protecting human life and preparing animals that are eaten and sacrificed. This is done to enhance the quality of life. Benefits for human beings in the biblical account are more positive than in the Mesopotamian stories.

There are incidental differences in details between the accounts, and although there might be significant reasons for these differences, we have not yet discerned their purpose. In Genesis it rains for forty days; in Mesopotamian accounts it rains for seven. Noah's boat is made of gopher wood; Atrahasis' is made of reeds. Mesopotamian boats take on more people (including workers) than the small number of eight persons found on Noah's boat. Noah's boat lands on a mountain in Ararat; in Mesopotamian accounts it lands on Mt. Nisir in Urartu (which is Ararat). Noah sends out a raven and a dove; but Utnapishtim sends out a dove, a swallow, and a raven (Bailey 18–20). Why does the biblical author omit the swallow? (Did Noah lose him?)

Noah takes on board seven pairs of "clean" animals in addition to the single pair of other kinds of animals; the Mesopotamian accounts mention nothing like this. This refers to Israelite sacrificial animals, hence implying that the additional animals are taken aboard for sacrifice. But why is this important? Are these the animals to be sacrificed after the ark has landed?

Finally, there are size differences in the arks. Noah's boat is three hundred cubits long, fifty cubits wide, and thirty cubits high. If an Israelite cubit is eighteen inches, then the total volume is 56,250 cubic yards. Utnapishtim's boat is a cube, one hundred and twenty cubits per side. If a Babylonian cubit is 19.7 inches, then his boat has 283,162 cubic yards. Noah's boat has three decks, but Utnapishtim's boat has six decks (Bailey 19). Both boats are sized on the sexagesimal system, but what is the significance of the different volumes and shapes? (Maybe Mesopotamian boats squeezed in the dinosaurs?)

In general one has to admit that the biblical author drew upon Mesopotamian accounts to craft the biblical narratives. This enabled the biblical author to make clear theological and social statements. Most of the differences mentioned above are connected to some significant religious and ideological differences found in the Israelite or Jewish worldview, which the biblical author was able to promote in the flood story. These differences stand out in an otherwise similar plot line. Even the minor differences might have some significance to them that we simply have not discerned.

The most productive avenue for research remains a comparison between the biblical narratives and the Mesopotamian accounts. This is probably due to the fact that the biblical narratives took their final written form in sixth century BCE or thereafter while Judeans were living in exile in Babylon (the exile for most Judeans continued well after 539 BCE). Educated Judeans, especially scribes who could write, would have been familiar with Mesopotamian literature, and would have crafted many of the biblical accounts with an eye to criticizing Mesopotamian beliefs from their monotheistic perspective.

It is possible, however, that the educated Jewish scribes might have been familiar with flood narratives from other cultures outside Mesopotamia. We have noticed that the author of the Primeval History seems to show some awareness of the writings of Hesiod. Thus, Greek literature merits our attention. In addition, Judeans were ruled by Persians after 540 BCE, and post-exilic Judah and Jerusalem were rebuilt under Persian patronage. Persian literature, though it is extremely difficult to date, also merits our attention.

Other Flood Narratives

As with creation accounts, so also with flood accounts, there are not many texts from ancient Egypt for our consideration. An Egyptian story of the flood is recounted in the second millennium BCE *Book of the Dead*. The god Atum floods wicked humanity with the waters from the primeval ocean (the god Nun). The flood begins in Upper Egypt at the shrine of Herankleopolis and covers all of Egypt. A few survivors escape in the "boat of millions of years," the boat of the sun-god. The boat is guided by a person named Temu, who sails to the Island of Flame. The text is partial, so we do not know the ending (Gaster 84).

An interesting parallel to the biblical text is the Persian Zoroastrian account found in the sacred text, the *Vendidad* (chapter 1). A primeval personage named Yima lives in a world that knows no death, and Yima is the overseer for that world. After three hundred years the world is saturated with people. Yima receives tools from Ahura Mazda to enlarge the world every three hundred years, and this is done three times. Then the heavenly beings decide to freeze the world to stop overpopulation, and Ahura Mazda, the great high god, informs Yima of this decision. Yima makes a Vara, an underground cavern or enclosure with three levels with nine streets on every level. There are one thousand humans in the upper part, six hundred humans in the middle part, and three hundred humans in the lower part. The Vara is lit by its own light. Yima is directed to take perfect specimens of animals and plants with him. There is also a window and a door to the world above ground. After the freeze Yima re-emerges to repopulate the world by releasing the animals and spreading the seeds that he had taken with him (Bailey 25-27). Since the *Vendidad* arose in the first century CE, some scholars have suggested the possibility that these Persian traditions were influenced by the biblical narrative (Hinnells 34).

There are a number of similarities with Mesopotamian and biblical flood accounts. 1) There is human overpopulation. 2) A single human is warned of the coming destruction. 3) There is reference to twelve hundred years, as with the *Atrahasis Epic*. 4) The deity speaks directly to Yima, as with the biblical account. 5) Vara is a square or cube, like Utnapishtim's ark. 6) Vara has three levels, like Noah's ark. 7) Vara has nine streets, like the nine parts of Utnapishtim's ark. 8) There is a window and a door, as with Noah's ark. 9) There are pairs of animals, as with Noah's menagerie, while the Mesopotamian sources simply mention animals in general. 10) There is reference to a bird, the Karshipta, which may be a raven, a motif in both biblical and Mesopotamian sources. It appears that this Persian story is familiar with both Mesopotamian and biblical accounts, but has adapted the catastrophe to the cold winter conditions of north Persia (Bailey 26-27).

The Greek version of the flood narrative is worthy of consideration, since it may have been influenced by accounts coming out of the Near East. Our present form dates to the second century BCE, but it was older than that, for references to the tale were told by the poet Pindar and the historian Hellanicus in the fifth century BCE. The story is told of how Zeus sent rain to destroy humanity. Prometheus tells his son Deukalion to prepare a chest with provisions and bring his wife Pyrrha along with him in order to survive. They float for nine days until they land on Parnassus. Thereupon, Deukalion sacrifices to Zeus. They pray to Zeus for new people to repopulate the world. These people are created from stones that Deukalion and Pyrrha throw over their shoulders. They create the first city at Opus in Greece. A slightly different version recounted by Hecataeus of Miletus from the fifth century BCE tells us that Deukalion had three sons, who respectively became the fathers of the Aeolians, Ionians, and Dorians of classical Greece. This immediately reminds us of Noah's three sons who were the ancestors of all the folk in the ancient Near East. In fact, both the biblical narrative and Hecataeus' account follow the flood narrative with description of the beginning of human history (Blenkinsopp 2011:14, 155, 175). One might suggest the biblical author was familiar with Hecataeus, who might have been a contemporary. At a much later date Plutarch tells a version of the flood which adds the detail of how Deukalion lets loose a dove from the ark, and one suspects greater Semitic influence in this version (Skinner 179; Gaster 85, 87).

A version of the flood account from Syria in the Hellenistic period shows Greek influence, but also appears to have some biblical themes. We find it recalled in Lucian's *The Syrian Goddess*. People are drowned in a great flood due to their sin and lawlessness. The flood hero, Deukalion-Sisuthros, is saved due to his great piety. He survives in a great chest along with paired animals that he takes along. Once the water retreats, the hero opens the ark, erects altars for sacrifice, and thus creates sanctuaries at Derketo and Hierapolis. He ultimately becomes the founder of a new race (Skinner 180; Van Seters 167). One sees similarities with the biblical account in several ways that the story does not share with Mesopotamian accounts: 1) sin brings destruction, 2) the hero is pious, 3) animals explicitly are taken in pairs, and 4) the hero gives birth to a new race. One suspects biblical influence (Van Seters 167, 177).

A story from India may have some relevance for the biblical narrative (Skinner 179). It comes from *Catapatha Brahmana* i.8.1–10, perhaps dated to the sixth century BCE. Manu finds a fish, cares for it, and the fish warns him of an impending flood and gives him directions for building a boat. The flood comes, the fish returns, and the ship's cable is attached to the fish's horn so that the fish can tow the ship to the mountain of the north. After the ship settles on the mountain, a woman comes to the ship and says that she is the daughter produced from offerings that were cast into the water. Manu marries her and they become the first couple. It is suggested that this tale reflects influence from the Mesopotamian accounts (Skinner 179; Gaster 94–95).

We have interesting ancient parallels to consider when we read the biblical text. It appears that especially with the flood account we must be familiar with the ancient Near Eastern parallel stories to appreciate the theological message of the biblical author.

16

The Giants

Genesis 6:1–4

(1) When people began to multiply on the face of the ground, and daughters were born to them, (2) the sons of God saw that they were fair; and they took wives for themselves of all that they chose. (3) Then the LORD said, "My spirit shall not abide in mortals forever, for they are flesh; their days shall be one hundred twenty years." (4) The Nephilim were on the earth in those days—and also afterward—when the sons of God went in to the daughters of humans, who bore children to them. These were the heroes that were of old, warriors of renown.

THIS RATHER BIZARRE SHORT account has elicited many different interpretations by commentators over the years. It tells how the "sons of God" or "sons of the gods" came down and had sex with the "daughters of men" (Gen 6:2). The text says that *nephilim* were on the earth when the "sons of God" had children by the "daughters of men" and these were the heroes of renown (Gen 6:4). Now these "heroes of renown" may refer to the *nephilim* or it may refer to the children birthed by the "daughters of men," or the text most likely may be saying that the *nephilim* were the children who were born to the "daughters of men" and they were the also the "heroes of renown." The implication of the ensuing narrative about the flood is that the birth of these individuals was one of the reasons for the flood. This breeding between divine beings and humans offends God who then limits human beings to a one hundred and twenty year life span (Day 428, 437, 441). In Genesis human age is limited; in the *Atrahasis Epic* population is limited. Ironically, a bilingual Sumerian and Akkadian text speaks of how one hundred and twenty years is the upper limit for human beings (Batto 1992:65; Day 442). Beyond this basic plot there are a number of interesting issues that arise.

Commentators have noted that this short account appears to refer to the same plot we find in the second century BCE narrative in *1 Enoch* 6–11, the story of the "watchers." This narrative about divine beings who come down and impregnate women is told in greater detail than Gen 6:1–4, and Gen 6:1–4 is so brief that it does not make sense unless you know the story in *1 Enoch* 6–11. That has led many to suggest that indeed Gen 6:1–4 is a shortened version of *1 Enoch* 6–11 (Blenkinsopp 2011:122–23). There is a chronological problem here, unless the traditions behind *1 Enoch* 6–11 are much older than the overall book of *1 Enoch* (Day 434–35), or unless Gen 6:1–4 is inserted into the biblical narrative much later than we have suspected in the past.

Who are these "sons of God" or "sons of the gods" who come down to have sex with women? Biblical interpreters have suggested three opinions.

1) Some believe the "sons of God" are the descendants of Seth, while the "daughters of men" are the descendants of Cain (Gunkel 57; Kass 158). This would be a story about the good people intermarrying with bad people. But that would not be dramatic enough to anger God. Other scholars reverse the identification, and say that the Cainites are the "sons of God," in that their arrogant pride makes them believe they are semi-divine, while the Sethites are the "sons of men" who have accepted their humanity (Eslinger 65–73). This is more plausible, especially if the Cainites are connected to tyrants, as another theory has it.

2) Some believe that the "sons of God" or the "sons of the gods" are kings in the ancient Near East who claimed to be divine. In particular, they might be great Mesopotamian rulers, like the epic figure Gilgamesh, who claimed the right to have initial sex with any women recently married (hence the reference to sex with the "daughters of men"). Since Gilgamesh was said to be two-thirds divine, he would be a "son of the gods." Kings in Mesopotamia often claimed divine status, using the expression *dinger* in their titles, which implied divinity. Thus, says our biblical author, such kings brought the destruction of the flood upon us. Furthermore, Gen 6:4 refers to the heroes of "renown," or men of great name. This reminds us of Genesis 11 wherein the builders of the tower seek to make a name for themselves (Gen 11:4). Even though kings are not mentioned in Genesis 11, the hint of royal authority is there. "Making a name for oneself" is what Mesopotamian kings did by their wars and their building projects. The allusion to "renown" and "making a name" in these two stories seems to hint strongly at the

activities of kings, especially when combined with the themes of the royal right of sex with any women in Genesis 6 and the building project in Genesis 11 (Kline 187–210; Clines 1976:495, 1978:69–70, 1979:33–46; Wenham 1987:140; McKeown 49; Carr 1996:238). If this is a correct interpretation, then Gen 6:1–4 and Gen 11:1–9 are both about the arrogant overweening pride of kings, who claim to be divine and attempt to usurp the prerogatives of God. In both stories God strikes them down for their pride.

The flood story declares that God destroys the world because of the sin of kings and the sin of people in general, who commit violence throughout the world. The text speaks of this general human violence in Gen 6:5–6, and then in verse 7 God declares that the world must be flooded. The flood is brought about by sin among people from the highest position in society to the lowest. Bernard Batto sees a parallel between the noisy and rebellious humanity prior to the flood in the *Atrahasis Epic* and these giants of the biblical narrative, for they both are long-lived and seek to challenge the divine by their own semi-divine status (Batto 1992:65–68).

3) A majority of commentators believe that these are heavenly beings or members of the divine council who serve God (Day 427–28). These divine beings, the lesser gods and messengers of God could mate with human beings to produce children of mixed divine and human heritage, like the Babylonian epic hero Gilgamesh. Such heroes were praised in the myths by ancient Near Easterners and often claimed as ancestors by kings in order to engage in self-glorification. In the Greek world the author Hesiod spoke of how gods and mortal women mated to produce the great heroes of the past (*Theogony* 963–1022 and *Catalogue of Women*). It is fascinating how often the Primeval History parallels the writings of Hesiod, especially with the interest in genealogies. Hecateus of Miletus (520 BCE) also displayed an interest in divine-human genealogies in recalling world history. Probably the biblical author was familiar with the early Greek traditions as well as the Mesopotamian (Van Seters 156–57; Brodie 158, 177, 186; Day 445–46).

If the mating occurs between gods and humans, the sexual activity might be described by the biblical text as either rape or consensual sex—commentators disagree. Ultimately, our biblical author probably does not believe that such activities occur, but rather our author ridicules the stories of contemporaries in the ancient world who praise such individuals as heroes and the ancestors of their kingdoms. The biblical author disdains the idea of such a union between the divine and the earthly realms (Wenham 1987:146; McKeown 49). The critique comes with the biblical author's implication that the birth of such heroes was evil and caused the flood. "So much for your ancestors, they caused only destruction!," says the biblical author. The image of divine beings or gods and human beings mating is found throughout ancient Near Eastern and classical Greek and Roman mythology. Usually such beings, who had at least one divine parent, were people of exceptional ability and often had great strength, like the Greek hero Herakles (Hercules in Latin). Some scholars believe that the biblical story additionally ridicules the rite of the "sacred marriage" practiced in many Mesopotamian cities at the New Year Festival, wherein the king of the city had sex with the high priestess in the temple precincts in an *eninnu* tent in order to assure fertility for the land in the coming year. In that ceremony the king encountered the divine realm, the mother goddess, in the person of the high priestess. The "sons of God" would be the kings or the priests, and the "daughters of men" would refer to the priestesses (Wenham 1987:xlix; McKeown 49). This, of course, gave prestige and even more authority to the king, a common theme in Mesopotamian mythology.

Often such beings live for a great length of time, which might explain why the motif of limiting the age of humankind to one hundred and twenty years is mentioned in this passage. It is God's attempt to limit their age lest their divine nature enables them to live for many centuries. Since the *Atrahasis Epic* attributes the flood to overpopulation, this interpretation views the story in Gen 6:1–4 as an ironic parallel, for limiting the age of the semi-divine offspring would be a form of population control. Also, the biblical narrative here implies that God undertakes a form of population control before the flood, thus undermining the rationale given in the *Atrahasis Epic* (van Wolde 1997:115; Day 428).

Of similar ilk is the traditional Jewish and Christian argument that these divine beings are evil, perhaps demons, who defy God by coming down to earth to have sex with human women. If the divine beings are evil, then even more is the rationale for the flood justified. God attempts to stem the tide of evil created by such evil divine beings. This sounds like a theme found in contemporary horror cinema.

At any rate, God is angry with these heaven-to-earth sexual unions, and it becomes a reason for the flood. God then destroys the earth because of two different sins—bad behavior in the divine realm when gods have sex with human women and bad behavior in the human realm when people engage in violence. Thus, God must wipe the slate clean with the flood. If the flood removes these sins, the flood must destroy not only evil human beings but also evil gods who have sex with humans. Does our author really believe that? Probably not! But for the sake of advocating monotheism the author may imply that once upon a time God had to destroy lesser deities for their sin, and the flood was the means by which God did that. The God of Israel drowned the ill-behaved lesser gods, the gods of the foreign kingdoms. That's truly monotheistic humor. Our biblical author is saying that no other gods exist besides Yahweh, the God of Israel, because in the distant past Yahweh killed the other gods. That's truly hard nosed monotheistic rhetoric designed to get Judeans to stop worshipping those other gods.

Our biblical author may be familiar with the lines in the Mesopotamian flood accounts that speak of how the gods became afraid when the flood was unleashed and how they retreated into the heavens. Maybe our biblical author wishes us to believe that when those Mesopotamian gods retreated, they really were not successful. They were drowned. That's a truly sarcastic response to the Mesopotamians who tell their flood stories to Judeans in exile.

This understanding of the passage is reinforced by another biblical text that likewise implies that the God of Israel kills the gods of the other kingdoms. In Psalm 82 God stands in judgment over the other gods. Ps 82:1 states, "God has taken his place in the divine council; in the midst of the gods he holds judgment." In verse 2 God condemns the other gods by saying, "How long will you judge unjustly and show partiality to the wicked?" In verse 5 the other gods are described as follows, "They have neither knowledge nor understanding, they walk around in darkness." Finally, in verses 6–7 it God declares, "I say, 'You are gods, children of the Most High, all of you; nevertheless, you shall die like mortals, and fall like any prince.'" You cannot get clearer than that. God condemns the other deities to death. Does Psalm 82 know the story in Gen 6:1–4 and assume that Israel's God drowned the other deities in the flood? Or is Psalm 82 older, and Gen 6:1–4 explains how those other gods were killed?

Either way, the Bible offers at least two texts in which it declares that the true God killed other deities because of their evil. This rhetoric speaks to polytheists ready to make a radical leap to monotheism by providing a transition for their beliefs. He tacitly admits the existence of other gods by saying that they existed once. But they exist no more, for our God killed them. For a person who once was a polytheist, it is difficult to acknowledge that there was no reality behind those other divine beings. But if you say that once they existed, but they no longer exist now, the convert from polytheism finds it easier to accept a new radical monotheistic commitment.

But the story has another punch in its message. The beings who are half human and half divine, the *nephilim*, are also critiqued. Our monotheistic author does not believe in the existence of such beings. However, many people in the surrounding world did believe in such creatures, regarding such beings as great heroes or warriors. The word *nephilim*, or giants, may have been a term used in Syria and Palestine by the neighbors of the Israelites to refer to their eponymous semi-divine ancestors, and the word actually may be a loan word taken from a cognate language. Our author ridicules those beliefs by implying that such beings were so evil, God had to destroy them with their divine parents. These beings crossed the line between the divine realm and the human realm, and for that they had to be punished. So God drowned them with a flood; their evil caused the flood.

A further sarcastic motif is thrown into this imagery of the great *nephilim* of yore when the biblical author indicates their limited life span. One would expect that beings who were half human and half divine would share some of the immortality inherited from their fathers' side. But the biblical author says that these great giants of yore were still men, still mortal, and rather limited. God decrees that the age of humanity will be limited to one hundred and twenty years. Since this verse comes before the story of the giants, one should assume that the giants, too, were limited by the one hundred and twenty year life span. That means that they did not live as long as the human beings listed in the genealogies of Cain and Seth, for they were still men (van Wolde 1994:71). This debunks the great warriors, giants, and heroes of the past and especially kings who claim descent from them.

Even though the author of the flood narrative implies that the flood destroyed the *nephilim*, they will come back again. In Num 13:33 invading Israelites are afraid to enter the land of Palestine because the inhabitants are *nephilim*, or giants. These probably are the figures called the "mighty men of old" in Ezek 32:27.

An interesting image, for which no one has a good explanation, is the characterization of the women as "good." The gods saw that the women were good, so they took them as wives. The text does not say beautiful or sexy. It says "good," which in any context is a compliment. The word often denotes moral virtue when used to describe people. The gods appreciated the goodness of these women. It is an interesting way for the text to describe why the gods were attracted to these women (van Wolde 1994:73). Does it mean that the gods wished to destroy the goodness of the women by taking them? If that were the meaning of the text, the author would make that much clearer in order to further justify the coming flood. We simply do not know what the author's point was in using this characterization.

Often kingdoms claimed descent from a particular personage, a symbolic ancestor, whom we call an "eponymous ancestor." This symbolic ancestor was viewed as being half human and half divine. A group of people might claim their right to conquer and rule other peoples because that mythical ancestor was a great warrior. Frequently kings would claim to be descended from some half divine, half human being, and this gave them the right to sit upon the throne, they and their sons after them. Often the deity of a particular group was claimed by the king as an ancestor. Kings and tyrants usually claimed that the same particular deity adopted them at some point to further provide divine support for their rule. But the biblical text attacks this form of political propaganda. When gods generate beings that are half human and half divine, these are not great and wonderful folk, but rather they bring divine judgment. Our biblical author engages in counter propaganda, criticizing beliefs used by kings to legitimate their rule. Those who are "descended" from the gods are not good people, they are evil. Thus, all tyrannical kings are evil and worthy of destruction.

How people in any age talk about their ancestors really reflects how they talk about themselves. When people speak of the ancestor from whom they are descended, they attribute characteristics to that individual that they wish to attribute to themselves. So if they envision themselves as great warriors, their symbolic ancestor was the greatest of all warriors in his age. If they fancy themselves as wise or as good merchants, their ancestor is described as a brilliant sage or merchant. Such a symbolic ancestor, or eponym, may have been a historical person, or sometimes several historical persons become gradually merged into one eponym. Sometimes there actually are people descended from that symbolic person, if he was a historical personage, but it is only an infinitesimal percentage of all the people who claim descent. Actions attributed to the symbolic ancestor often are things done by the later corporate group, or at least things the later corporate group wishes to accomplish in their own era.

When we see a mythical ancestor described as half human and half divine, it really means that the people, who claim that he was their ancestor or their founder, make grandiose claims for themselves. They declare that what they do is totally justified because they are descended from a demi-god, including the conquest of other peoples. Sometimes when a society claims descent from a divine or semi-divine ancestor, they are saying that this ancestor created their society and all their social institutions, and therefore their political, economic, and social structures are perfect and need no reform. An appeal to semi-divine ancestors becomes justification for maintaining the political-social status quo, opposing any change or reform in society. Thus, the rich and the powerful keep themselves in place by appealing to ancestors who created a perfect society that continues to this present age and needs no reform. Totalitarian societies in any age appeal to symbolic divine ancestors and thus freeze the structures of the existing regime by implying that no change needs to be made. Think of how the Soviet Union created a cult of Lenin and Stalin, obviously under-girding the ideology of a regime that resisted change. When the society collapsed, the cult of their leaders was quickly terminated.

When kings claim descent from a mythical semi-divine figure, they arrogate authoritarian power. Pharaohs in Egypt claimed to be the living god Horus on earth as they ruled, and then they ultimately became the god Osiris in the underworld once they died. Kings in Mesopotamia usually claimed to be "stewards of the gods," but occasionally they claimed divine status in their inscriptions.

If Americans speak of their eighteenth century founding fathers as though they were perfect, it implies that they created a perfect political system that requires no political change or reform. However, if we speak of them as normal human beings who made mistakes, we are saying that they initiated a political system destined to undergo constant change and evolution, as it moves toward an increasingly better democracy.

Our biblical text enters into this debate with these few short verses. The original audience recognized that political rhetoric of their age, for it was used by all the other political regimes around them. The biblical author throws the ultimate curve ball by saying these ancient semi-divine beings were not good, but evil and worthy of destruction. This is an ultimate insult to the other kingdoms, and saying that the gods they worship do not exist is an even worse insult. So the biblical author tells his Jewish audience to say to the people all around them, "Your eponymous ancestors were evil, and so were your gods who sired them. Once in the distant past our God had to drown them all. You are stupid—you worship nothing and your justification for your social and political institutions is groundless."

In a few short verses we discover flaming religious and political rhetoric against the cultures round about. The biblical author assaults the rationale for kings' divine right to rule and their justification of imperial conquest. In that ancient age when mythological rhetoric justified empires, it is amazing to see the biblical author stand forth with a different kind of rhetoric. The biblical author opposes talk about mixing the divine and human realms, or talk about beings who might be human and divine. Monotheists often make a clean distinction between the divine and human realm. But I believe the assault on mythical half human and half divine beings is an attack on rhetoric used to justify political regimes and the oppression of people, especially the activities of the Assyrians and Chaldean Babylonians. This little story prepares us for the flood, God's response to tyranny.

17

The Flood

THE STORY OF THE flood appears to be two narratives woven together: a Yahwist narrative (J) and a Priestly narrative (P), both from the late sixth or fifth centuries BCE. Most scholars assume that Priestly narrative was added to the Yahwist narrative; however, some sense that the Priestly narrative appears more complete in its plot line than the Yahwist narrative, so that the Yahwist narrative was added later (Bailey 150; Blenkinsopp 1992:77–87 et passim). This is problematic since most scholars believe that the Priestly Editors reworked the Yahwist narratives elsewhere in Genesis, Exodus, and Numbers. This debate will continue for years.

The reason for positing two narratives are the presence of numerous duplications in the overall story: 1) People are said to be sinful: 6:5 (J), 6:12 (P). 2) The coming of the flood is announced: 7:4 (J), 6:13, 17 (P). 3) Noah is ordered into the ark: 7:1–3 (J), 6:18–20 (P). 4) Noah obeys this directive: 7:5 (J), 6:22 (P). 5) Noah enters the ark: 7:7 (J), 7:13 (P). 6) The flood begins: 7:12 (J), 7:11 (P). 7) The floodwaters increase: 7:17 (J), 7:20–21 (P). 8) The floodwaters abate: 8:3a (J), 8:1 (P). 9) Promise of no more flood is given: 8:20–22 (J), 9:11–17 (P).

In addition, there are details that portray events differently, although in their final narrative synthesis they do not appear contradictory. These include: 1) Animals come in pairs, 6:19–20; 7:15–16 (P); clean animals come in seven pairs, 7:2 (J). 2) The flood is caused by rain, 7:4, 12; 8:2b (J); the flood is caused by the breaking of the "fountains of the deep" and the "firmament," a reversal of creation on day two of Genesis 1 and a return to the chaos that existed before God created the world, 7:11; 8:2a (P). 3) The flood lasts forty days, 7:4, 12 (J); the flood lasts one year 8:13 (P). 4) According to

8:5 the mountains appear (P), but later according to 8:9 the waters still cover the earth (J). 5) Noah discovers the flood is ended from the response of the birds in 8:6, 12, 13b (J), but in 8:14-16 God informs him (P). 6) According to J, after forty days of rain (7:4, 12) the waters endure upon the earth for sixty-one days (7:10; 8:8-12); according the P the flood lasts for one hundred and fifty days (7:24; 8:2a, 3b) and the waters do not recede until after one year (8:13a). 7) J texts in 6:5-7; 7:2; 8:21 allude to language in Genesis 2-3, such as the words for "dirt" and "form," which are Yahwist in origin; P texts in 6:12, 20-21; 7:11, 17-21; 8:1-2; 9:1-3, 6-7 allude to words such as "seeing," "divine wind, "image of God," "rule" (over the animals), and "be fruitful and multiply" from Genesis 1, which is Priestly in origin. 8) In 6:18 P alludes to the covenant, but J has no such reference. 9) Generally J uses Yahweh (English translation is LORD) for the name of God; P uses Elohim (English translation is God). 10) P often uses language from Genesis 1 to describe the animals (6:20; 7:14, 16, 21; 8:17, 19) and refers to provisioning the animals (6:21; 9:2-3) (Skinner 164; Vawter 115; Bailey 149-50; Carr 64-65). Obviously the biblical author who created the final text respected both accounts and wove them together rather well.

Thus, the J narrative is reconstructed as follows: Gen 6:5-8; 7:1-5, 7-10, 12, 16b-17, 22-22; 8:2b-3a, 6-12, 13b, 20-22. The P narrative is reconstructed as follows: Gen 6:9-22; 7:6, 11, 13-16a, 18-21, 24; 8:1, 2a, 3b-5, 13a, 14-19; 9:1-17. We shall make occasional references to these divisions when it is theologically significant.

PREPARATION FOR THE FLOOD

Genesis 6:5-8

(5) The LORD saw that the wickedness of humankind was great in the earth, and that every inclination of the thoughts of their hearts was only evil continually. (6) And the LORD was sorry that he had made humankind on the earth, and it grieved him to his heart. (7) So the LORD said, "I will blot out from the earth the human beings I have created—people together with animals and creeping things and birds of the air, for I am sorry that I have made them. (8) But Noah found favor in the sight of the LORD.

Our text then adds that there was violence upon the earth. The word in Hebrew used for violence usually describes violent crime, such as murder, rape, and robbery. Such actions undermine social order, as we see happening even now in our own modern age. The biblical audience knows that God must destroy the world, for everything is out of order, evil prevails in both the divine and the human realm. It must be flushed clean with water, so that God can begin anew. Whereas Mesopotamian stories told of how the flood came due to human overpopulation and human noise, the biblical account focuses upon morally reprehensible causes, human and divine.

There then occurs one of those amazing statements in the biblical text. God "repents" of having made humanity. Poetically Claus Westermann says that the dissension in the Mesopotamian flood accounts among the gods has become dissension in the mind of God (Westermann 408). Several times in the Bible it will say that God "repents." At one point God "repents" of having brought Israel out of slavery in Egypt because they are so rebellious in the wilderness. This is not the way we speak of God, because in our modern era we think of God in more abstract and absolute ways. God is perfect, omnipotent, omniscience, omnipresent, and absolute in just about every way imaginable. Saying that God repents is not our language, but it is the language of the Bible.

Years ago commentators attributed such language to the primitive ways of thinking among the biblical authors. However, in the past century we have discerned that biblical authors are rather sophisticated, not primitive. They speak of God in particular ways for effect. When they talk about God "repenting," they attribute human emotions to God. They are speaking anthropopathically, that is, they ascribe human (Greek, "anthropos") passions (Greek, "pathos") to God for dramatic effect and theological meaning. They imply that when God enters into dialogue or a relationship with humanity, God takes on human characteristics or human emotions to make the relationship possible. Now we know that people throughout the ancient world by this time had a rather sophisticated view of their gods (or at least the intelligentsia did). The biblical author's choice of language was noticeable to the audience because of its earthy nature. Such language captured the attention of the audience and communicated the personal nature of God's presence.

Christians speak of Jesus being God, and this, for them, is the ultimate form of divine identification with the human condition. So also, the same language occurs in the Old Testament. Some Old Testament authors speak of God in intensely personal terms, and even speak of God getting "angry" and "repenting" in order to describe God's relationship with the world in such personal fashion. At any rate, God is sorry that humanity was created, and so now the solution is to destroy them and start anew. The prelude for the flood story has been laid. It is all about human sin and not divine fickleness as in Mesopotamian accounts.

Misunderstood Stories

Divine Directions for the Ark

Genesis 6:9–22

> (9) These are the descendants of Noah. Noah was a righteous man, blameless in his generation; Noah walked with God. (10) And Noah had three sons, Shem, Ham, and Japheth.
>
> (11) Now the earth was corrupt in God's sight, and the earth was filled with violence. (12) And God saw that the earth was corrupt; for all flesh had corrupted its ways upon the earth. (13) And God said to Noah, "I have determined to make an end of all flesh, for the earth is filled with violence because of them; now I am going to destroy them along with the earth. (14) Make yourself an ark of cypress wood; make rooms in the ark, and cover it inside and out with pitch. (15) This is how you are to make it: the length of the ark three hundred cubits, its width fifty cubits, and its height thirty cubits. (16) Make a roof for the ark, and finish it to a cubit above; and put the door of the ark in its side; make it with lower, second, and third decks. (17) For my part, I am going to bring a flood of waters on the earth, to destroy from under heaven all flesh in which is the breath of life; everything that is on the earth shall die. (18) But I will establish my covenant with you; and you shall come into the ark, you, your sons, your wife, and your sons' wives with you. (19) And of every living thing, of all flesh, you shall bring two of every kind into the ark, to keep them alive with you; they shall be male and female. (20) Of the birds according to their kinds, and of the animals according to their kinds, of every creeping thing of the ground according to its kind, two of every kind shall come in to you, to keep them alive. (21) Also take with you every kind of food that is eaten, and store it up; and it shall serve as food for you and for them." (22) Noah did this; he did all that God commanded him.

God had decided to destroy humanity. Twice before God faced such a decision, once with the man and the woman in the garden, the other time with Cain. Should the man and the woman die on the very day in which they ate the fruit or should they live? God decided on the latter option. Should Cain die for his crime of murder or live? God chose the latter. In both instances God continued the experiment with humanity. It now appears that God is still experimenting with this newly created humanity. But this third time God finally decides to significantly alter the experiment and destroy them.

God appears to have over-reacted. Not only humanity, but the beasts, the creeping things, and the fowl of the air are to be destroyed. The words for animal life hearken back to the very words used in Genesis 1 on the fifth and sixth days of creation. In fact, the words for beasts, creeping things, and fowl are in reverse order as they were created in Genesis 1. Symbolically God truly is reversing creation and undoing or destroying what had been done in Genesis 1. (By way of interest, one should note that Gen 6:7 is a Yahwist text which uses the name, LORD, while Genesis 1 is a Priestly text. If the Yahwist knows the Priestly text, this is a good argument for the priority of the Priestly tradition over the Yahwist tradition.)

The final word in verse 8 is that Noah finds grace with God. God chooses yet again not to destroy humanity completely. This time, however, many will die and God will begin anew with one family. God takes a radical new direction with the human experiment by focusing upon one part of humanity, Noah's clan. This may not impress us as very gracious, but it was perceived by the biblical audience as a sign of grace. Biblical people lived in extremely harsh times. If this account in its final form dates to the late sixth or fifth century BCE, the audience includes people who lived after the time when their kingdom was destroyed by Babylonian armies. They would see God's decision as gracious, because it was a decision in which a few were snatched from the jaws of death, and that was their historical experience. They could identify with Noah's family because they were Noah's family, survivors once more trying to repopulate and rebuild. Eventually a great people would emerge out of them, as it had out of Noah's family.

Theologians sometimes observe that the scope of the flood and the destruction it causes raises a question of theodicy, that is, how can we justify the actions of God in the face of such a human holocaust. I am tempted to say that the real question is why did the biblical author choose to include the story of the flood and thus risk such a negative portrayal of God. I personally feel that the biblical author may have felt it necessary to include this account as a response to Mesopotamian accounts of the flood. Perhaps Judeans in exile were pressured by their Babylonian neighbors to worship Marduk at the New Year Festival to help avoid another flood caused by Tiamat that would bring world destruction. Perhaps our biblical author felt constrained to tell a different version of the Babylonian flood account to indicate that such a flood would never come because God was gracious and promised that no flood would occur again. I suspect that the biblical author had to have a flood account in his narrative of the primordial times, even if it appeared to somewhat compromise the gracious nature of God who otherwise had previously forgiven the man and the woman, as well as Cain, and would subsequently scatter but not destroy the builders of the tower of Babel.

Who is Noah? The name appears to come from the root *n.w.ch*, which means rest, for it was said of him at birth by his father Lamech that he would bring rest (Gen 5:29). The rest that Noah brings may be one or all of the following: 1) The curse of Cain is taken off of the ground after the flood, so that farming may begin again. 2) The development of viticulture by Noah, grape production, brings a cash crop, which is more profitable than grain production for people living in Palestine. People can make and sell wine for profit (along with olive oil). This would make farming easier and perhaps take off the curse of hard labor on the land that was consigned to Adam. 3) Wine brings pleasure to people to ease the difficult challenges of life. It will be a sign of blessing in the future age brought by God (Hos 9:10; Amos 9:13–15; Matt 26:26–29) (Westermann 360; Kselman 92).

Noah's name may be connected with word plays. If you reverse the consonants of Noah's name (*n.ch*), you get the word for grace. If you add a final mem sound to Noah's name (*n.ch.m*) you have the word for "repent" (*nacham*), the verb used to describe how God repented of making humanity. It appears our author is playing word games with us. However, the name seems to appear in other ancient Near Eastern flood narratives. A people called the Hurrians, who lived in Syria and north Mesopotamia in the middle of the second millennium BCE, called their flood hero Na-ah-ma-su-le-el, a word that sounds similar to Noah (Speiser 42; Bertman 315). If there is a connection with this ancient figure, then the name was not simply created for symbolic wordplays.

Beginning with verse 9 we have what almost appears to be another introduction, and with the switch from the word LORD to the word God, commentators suggest that there was a seam or division between verses 8 and 9—the division between the Yahwist and the Priestly sources. But with the use of the name, God, previously in verse 5, this theory is rendered tenuous, because verse 5 flows logically into verses 6–8. Thus, verse 5 should go with verses 9 onward due to the use of the divine name, but it fits with the plot in verses 6–8. Perhaps the editorial process for this narrative is more complex than we can reconstruct by simply observing the final product. Biblical authors are artists, not just brick masons, laying sources next to each other mechanically. The sources used by the biblical authors are created, changed, and woven together. At any rate, the narrative continues with the name, "God," and the plot appears somewhat to be a parallel version to what was recounted in verses 5–8, yet the division is not clean enough to be convincing to all commentators.

In verse 9 we hear that Noah is "perfect" (Hebrew word is *tam*), a word often used to describe the perfect sacrificial animal victims. Is Noah destined to be a sacrifice? Not that we can tell, unless our author is clever in someway that we have not yet discerned. Such is often the case with many biblical narratives.

In verses 11–13 God observes that the earth is corrupt and filled with violence. Violence refers to social crimes such as murder, adultery, and theft, the works of human hands. But then verse 12 implies that not only humans are to blame. "All flesh" is corrupted and thus worthy of death. To what does this refer? Animals do not commit murder, adultery, and theft, except in cartoons. Does it refer to nature "red in tooth and claw"—that is, does it refer to the pecking order of "eat and be eaten" found in the animal realm, which the ancients could observe as well as Charles Darwin and us? How can animals be held responsible for what comes most naturally to them? After the flood Noah and humanity would be given permission to eat meat, as long as they drained the blood. Could it be that carnivores in the animal realm only then would receive the permission to hunt? But if so, animals do not drain the blood out of their prey, so how could they receive proper permission to hunt after the flood? We are not inclined to suggest that before the flood carnivore animals were held morally responsible for eating meat. Hence, the animal realm is corrupt for another reason. Traditionally Christian theologians believe that the animal realm was rendered corrupt because of human sin, but that does not seem fair to the animals. In addition, the text speaks of the corruption in the animal realm separately from the corruption in the human realm, so one would have to conclude that there is a separate issue of corruption in the animal realm assumed by our text. We cannot say for sure what the text refers to. Verses 12–13 declare that all humanity and all flesh are corrupt, and thus worthy of destruction. This observation stands somewhat in contrast to (or perhaps it complements) the observation back in verse 5, which imputes evil only to humanity. Hence, we have the ambiguity of whether those two verses belong to separate sources or whether the latter simply elaborates on the former.

In verse 13 God communicates to Noah the divine conclusions about the state of the world and the divine intent to destroy humanity. Noah must have been a little nervous until he began to receive the directions for building the ark. One may observe how this account differs dramatically from other ancient Near Eastern accounts, for God talks directly to Noah, not through a wall.

The directions for building the ark and the inclusion of the people and animals are described in verses 14–22. The word for ark in Hebrew is *teba* and the same word is used to describe the basket into which Moses was placed in Exod 2:3, 5. So the *teba* is responsible for saving God's people on two occasions. The ark is made of gopher wood with pitch in a manner that reminds us of Mesopotamian boats that ply the marshes of that region. Some translate the cypress wood as "reeds" which means that the construction of the ark out of reeds and pitch would make the ark identical to the construction material of the Mesopotamian arks (Blenkinsopp 2011:137). Its shape is three hundred by fifty by thirty cubits—numbers that commentators have played with for years to find some symbolic meaning, but to no avail. Claus Westermann observes that if the floodwaters were fifteen cubits over the highest mound, and the ark was thirty cubits in height, and if it drew fifteen cubits of water, then it would land smoothly on the mountain where it came to rest (Westermann 442). That might simply be a coincidence, however. The ark has three levels, perhaps for the three levels of life—fowl, creeping things, and beasts. Perhaps the three levels symbolize the three levels of the universe: sky, earth, and underworld (Cotter 55). Overall, the dimensions of the ark are smaller than the Mesopotamian counterparts in the other flood narratives. Since the author knew of the Mesopotamian accounts, we can only wonder why the dimensions are smaller. Finally, the ark and the Tabernacle of Moses in the wilderness are the only objects whose measurements are provided by the biblical text. Both are symbols of God's protection for faithful people (Westermann 421). Perhaps, both were symbols of God's protection of exiles in Babylon, who "floated" in the "wilderness" of exile.

The language again reminds us of Genesis 1–2. Verse 17 refers to the "breath of life," an expression in Gen 2:7 given to humanity, but here it is an attribute of all creatures. Verse 20 repeats the reference to cattle and creeping things of day six in Genesis 1. Verse 21 refers to the food to be taken on board for people and animals, and we receive the impression that it is grain. So does this imply that the animals are vegetarian? It is difficult to say! Verse 18 foreshadows the Priestly covenant that God will make with Noah after the flood.

The Flood

Genesis 7:1–24

(1) Then the LORD said to Noah, "Go into the ark, you and all your household, for I have seen that you alone are righteous before me in this generation. (2) Take with you seven pairs of all clean animals, the male and its mate; and a pair of the animals that are not clean, the male and its mate; (3) and seven pairs of the birds of the air also, male and female, to keep their kind alive on the face of all the earth. (4) For in seven days I will send rain on the earth for forty days and forty nights; and every living thing that I have made I will blot out from the face of the ground." (5) And Noah did all that the LORD had commanded him.

(6) Noah was six hundred years old when the flood of waters came on the earth. (7) And Noah with his sons and his wife and his sons' wives went into the ark to escape the waters of the flood. (8) Of clean animals, and of animals that are not clean, and of birds, and of everything that creeps on the ground, (9) two and two, male and female, went into the ark with Noah, as God had commanded Noah. (10) And after seven days the waters of the flood came on the earth.

(11) In the six hundredth year of Noah's life, in the second month, on the seventeenth day of the month, on that day all the fountains of the great deep burst forth, and windows of the heavens were opened. (12) The rain fell on the earth forty days and forty nights. (13) On the very same day Noah with his sons, Shem and Ham and Japheth, and Noah's wife and the three wives of his sons entered the ark, (14) they and every wild animal of every kind, and all domestic animals of every kind, and every creeping thing that creeps on the earth, and every bird of every kind—every bird, every winged creature. (15) They went into the ark with Noah, two and two of all flesh in which there was the breath of life. (16) And those that entered, male and female of all flesh, went in as God had commanded him; and the LORD shut him in.

(17) The flood continued forty days on the earth; and the waters increased, and bore up the ark, and it rose high above the earth. (18) The waters swelled and increased greatly on the earth; and the ark floated on the face of the waters. (19) The waters swelled so mightily on the earth that all the high mountains under the whole heaven were covered; (20) the waters swelled above the mountains, covering them fifteen cubits deep. (21) And all flesh died that moved on the earth, birds, domestic animals, wild animals, all swarming creatures that swarm on the earth, and all human beings; (22) everything on dry land in whose nostrils was breath of life died. (23) He blotted out every living thing that was on the face of the ground, human beings and animals and creeping things and birds of the air; they were blotted out from the earth. Only Noah was left, and those that were with him in the ark. (24) And the waters swelled on the earth for one hundred fifty days.

God gives Noah directions in verses 1–4 that parallel the directions given in chapter 6. Commentators have been tempted to call these passages part of the Yahwist tradition, especially since the reference is now to the LORD rather than to God, as was the case with Gen 6:14–22.

What really stand out are the directions for the animals. Now Noah is commanded to take seven pair of clean animals and one pair of unclean animals. We assume that there were seven pairs of clean animals for food consumption by the humans and the other animals. The reference to seven pairs of every clean animal tempts us into making source divisions of the narrative. Since Priestly traditions attribute the categories of clean and unclean animals to Mosaic legislation, they would not introduce the concept here in the flood narrative. Hence, scholars have suggested that these are Yahwist texts (and the name LORD occurs here). However, one wonders why the Yahwist would have this theme in the flood narrative, when the concept of clean and unclean animals occurs nowhere else in Yahwist texts. Nevertheless, commentators assume these are Yahwist texts. They also point out that since the post flood Priestly narratives speak of God giving permission for meat consumption to people, the residents on the ark would not have been able to eat meat, if, indeed, that was the purpose of the extra animals. Thus, in an overall assessment commentators suspect that the directions given to Noah in Gen 6:14-22 are Priestly and the directions in Gen 7:1-4 are Yahwist. Was our final editor of these narratives so inept as to put in both sets of directions, which appear to contradict each other? No! This editor may have respected both sets of tradition and felt that they could be viewed as complementary, not contradictory. The directions given by God at first in chapter 6 were to be seen as simply undergoing further clarification by the later directions in chapter 7.

In verse 4 we are told that the Lord would cause it to rain for forty days. This Yahwist text will be complemented by Priestly information of a symbolic nature in later verses.

In verses 5-10 we are informed that Noah did as he was commanded by the Lord and took in the clean and unclean animals.

In verse 4 Noah was told that it would rain, but in verse 11 the flood is described in a more destructive manner. This latter verse, which appears to be Priestly in origin, describes how the foundations of the deep broke apart and the waters below the earth came up and met the waters falling down from the heavens. We are reminded of Genesis 1 where God separated the waters above the firmament from the waters below the firmament. In effect, creation was undone and the world returned to its primordial state. Thus, this Priestly text refers back to the Priestly text in Genesis 1.

Verse 13 mentions Noah's three sons by name. It is the second such reference to them. Previously they were mentioned in Gen 6:10, another Priestly text. It is interesting to observe that they parallel Lamech's three sons, a narrative from the Yahwist tradition. Lamech's three sons provide the world with civilization; Noah's three sons provide the world with its people. Does the contrast of interest between civilization and propagation somehow reflect the difference between the Yahwist Historian and the Priestly Editors?

Verse 16 mentions that after Noah and the animals went into the ark that the "LORD shut him in" (either a strange interruption of the Priestly narrative by the Yahwist, or the beginning of Yahwist material). What an interesting observation—God closed the door on the ark! Did Noah forget to put a door handle on the inside of the ark, so God had to close it for him? We suspect that this is one of those images provided by the Yahwist tradition to speak God being intimately involved in the process with the human creation. It also contrasts vividly with the Mesopotamian flood narratives wherein the gods become terrified of the tremendous power of the flood they unleashed. In the biblical narrative God is in control of the flood and the ark throughout the entire experience, closing the ark's door and guiding the ark until it comes to rest on the mountain.

Further testimony to the divine guidance provided for Noah and the ark is the lack of navigational personnel with Noah. Both Atrahasis and Utnapishtim took professional navigators and sailors on board. Noah did not. The guidance of the boat is left entirely to God (Hamilton 296, 303). God does the driving. The reference to how God steadies the boat in the water is probably meant to give us this insight and alert us to the contrast with Mesopotamian accounts.

Verses 19–20 mention that the waters submerged the highest mountain by fifteen cubits. Some scholars, however, believe that the text says that the highest "tell" was submerged. If it is a "tell" of which our text speaks, this may recall some ancient historical memory of actual Mesopotamian floods, or perhaps even one ancient flood in particular. A "tell" is the earthen foundation upon which a major city is built in the Mesopotamian floodplain. It is created over many centuries by the deposition of debris within the city, including knocking down old buildings to rebuild new ones on top of the rubble. The higher the tell, the older the city. A massive flood could sweep over the level of the tell, which is the foundation upon which the city's buildings are constructed, though not necessarily over the top of the highest buildings on the tell. It almost sounds like a realistic description of some actual flood—if, indeed, the biblical text is using a word which has the concept of the "tell" behind it. Some ancient massive flood might be recalled from Mesopotamian experience. Some scholars have looked to the devastating flood that left such a large flood layer in the city Ur early in the third millennium BCE.

Verses 21–23 describe in dramatic terms the total destruction of life on the earth. Creation Scientists, who cobble their theory with the idea of fish surviving the flood outside the ark, have difficulty with these passages, even though they claim to take the Bible literally.

The Flood Subsides

Genesis 8:1–22

(1) But God remembered Noah and all the wild animals and all the domestic animals that were with him in the ark. And God made a wind blow over the earth, and the waters subsided; (2) the fountains of the deep and the windows of the heavens were closed, the rain from the heavens was restrained, (3) and the waters gradually receded from the earth. At the end of one hundred fifty days the waters had abated; (4) and in the seventh month, on the seventeenth day of the month, the ark came to rest on the mountains of Ararat. (5) The waters continued to abate until the tenth month; in the tenth month, on the first day of the month, the tops of the mountains appeared.(6) At the end of forty days Noah opened the window of the ark that he had made (7) and sent out the raven; and it went to and fro until the waters were dried up from the earth. (8) Then he sent out the dove from him, to see if the waters had subsided from the face of the ground; (9) but the dove found no place to set its foot; and it returned to him to the ark, for the waters were still on the face of the whole earth. So he put out his hand and took it and brought it into the ark with him. (10) He waited another seven days, and again he sent out the dove from the ark; (11) and the dove came back to him in the evening, and there in its beak was a freshly plucked olive leaf; so Noah knew that the waters had subsided from the earth. (12) Then he waited another seven days, and sent out the dove; and it did not return to him any more.

(13) In the six hundred first year, in the first month, the first day of the month, the waters dried up from the earth; and Noah removed the covering of the ark, and looked, and saw that the face of the ground was drying. (14) In the second month, on the twenty-seventh day of the month, the earth was dry. (15) Then God said to Noah, (16) "Go out of the ark, you and your wife, and your sons and your sons' wives with you. (17) Bring out with you every living thing that is with you of all flesh—birds and animals and every creeping thing that creeps on the earth—so that they may abound on the earth, and be fruitful and multiply on the earth." (18) So Noah went out with his sons and his wife and his sons' wives. (19) And every animal, every creeping thing, and

every bird, everything that moves on the earth, went out of the ark by families.

(20) The Noah built an altar to the LORD, and took of every clean animal and of every clean bird, and offered burnt offerings on the altar. (21) And when the LORD smelled the pleasing odor, the LORD said in his heart, "I will never again curse the ground because of humankind, for the inclination of the human heart is evil from youth; nor will I ever again destroy every living creature as I have done.

(22) As long as the earth endures,
    seedtime and harvest, cold and heat,
    summer and winter, day and night,
    shall not cease."

It is fascinating to observe the similarities between the creation account and the flood account, especially with the addition of material from the Priestly Editors, who sought to portray the flood as the direct undoing of the creation according to Genesis 1. In both narratives we have chaotic waters and references to the firmament and the fountains of the deep. As the flood comes to a closure, the divine wind moves upon the face of the water, the water and land separate, mountains appear, fresh growth arises on trees, and eventually animals leave the ark and appear on the land (Wenham 1987:207). It is another classic example of how biblical authors loved to make their various narratives appear like other narratives (inter-textuality).

The divine wind dries up the water and the flood subsides. If we wish to view this symbolically as though the "divine wind" defeated the waters, we could return to Gen 1:3 and observe that the divine wind moving over the face of the waters was the biblical author's way of replacing the notion of divine combat with chaotic waters. Is that a coincidence, or does our biblical author wish us to notice the ironic similarities? In the flood account of Ziusudra the sun dries up the floodwaters. In the biblical account the "wind" of God dries up the waters, not the sun god, Shamash.

In the first five verses we are introduced to new aspects of the flood timetable. Scholars have assumed that the Yahwist chronology is one of forty days of rain, while the Priestly chronology is one of a yearlong chaotic flood. The final author or editor of these narratives reconciles these chronologies with the scenario that it rained for forty days and floodwaters endured on the earth for a year.

After forty days in the boat (v. 6) Noah sends out a raven and a dove, but he forgets his Mesopotamian sparrow. Why the biblical text omits one of the three birds, we do not know. It was the custom for ancient mariners, as well as sailors up until the nineteenth century to release birds to discover whether land was near. Releasing the raven first was logical, for the raven could find carrion in high places, but the dove was a bird of the valley. The dove could be released only when the waters were much lower. When the dove returns with an olive leaf, it is a sign that the water level is low, because olives do not grow at high altitudes (Simpson 546; Hamilton 304). Noah reverses the sequence of the Mesopotamian heroes, who let the dove go before the raven, which is not logical. Maybe the biblical author simply decided to "clean up" the story a bit here. Also note that the dove returns with an olive branch. Did olive trees have time to grow back after the devastation of the flood? Do not bother the biblical author with such details. The author is crafting a brilliant and symbolic theological narrative.

The reference to forty days in verse 6 is odd, since by this time the ark had been afloat for over half a year. One good suggestion is that in the original Yahwist narrative it meant after the forty days of rain had stopped. Once Priestly material was added to the Yahwist narrative, then this became simply another period of time in the year long flood chronology to be seen as different from the initial forty days of rain. If so, this is evidence that the Yahwist tradition is prior to the Priestly tradition.

In verse 4 we read that the ark landed on Ararat. Ararat is Hebrew for Urartu, or Armenia. Elsewhere Ararat refers to the region of Urartu (2 Kgs 19:37; Isa 37:38; Jer 51:27). The name is obtained by a vowel shift that occurs when you go from northeastern Semitic to southwestern Semitic, which includes Hebrew. Ararat is really the name for the region in which the mountain is found; it is not the name of the mountain. It thus is "a mountain in Ararat," not "Mount Ararat." This is why our present translation speaks of the "mountains" (plural) of Ararat (v. 4). Later pious Jewish and Christian traditions did their best to identify the particular mountain. For example, the third century BCE Jewish work, *Book of Jubilees*, suggested that the mountain was Mt. Lubar in Armenia (*Jubilees* 5:28; 7:1).

God tells Noah to disembark from the ark. All of the animals come out; there is no reference to the seven pairs of clean animals. In verse 20 the name of the deity changes to the LORD and the reference to the clean animals occurs again, evidence for some readers that this is a Yahwist text.

Noah offers sacrifice of the clean animals and God "smells" the sweet odor. God smells the odor and finds it pleasing. The text contrasts with Mesopotamian texts wherein hungry gods swarm for the sacrifice of Atrahasis or Utnapishtim (ill behaved deities that they are). Furthermore, the Mesopotamia gods are limited in other ways. Enlil, who is responsible for bringing the flood in Mesopotamian accounts, is amazed to discover that Utnapishtim is still alive. God in the Bible is not surprised by anything. The biblical author portrays God with greater respect. God does not require the sacrifice; rather, it pleases God. God accepts the sacrifice. The biblical author may have drawn the idea of God smelling the sacrifice from the Mesopotamian accounts, since elsewhere in the Old Testament God does not smell sacrifice (Vawter 131; Wenham 1987:205; Fretheim 393). The biblical author again contrasts God and the deities of Mesopotamia.

In verse 22 the Yahwist account of the flood ends with a little poem in which God promises the stability of the seasons. This complements verse 21 in which God promises never to flood the earth again. Such a promise flies in the face of Mesopotamian beliefs that fear the possibility of a chaotic flood in the spring of every year, which necessitates devotion and sacrifice to Marduk. This is a powerful polemic with which to conclude the flood story. However, the Priestly Editors will provide a grand conclusion to the flood narrative, a covenant between God and Noah (and the rest of humanity, too) in Genesis 9.

Verse 21 also provides an interesting statement for our reflection. God says that the inclination of the human heart is evil from youth. This is an extremely negative statement about human beings and their sinfulness. Combining this statement with the promise never again to destroy the world with a flood presents us with a powerful theological affirmation. God admits that people are evil, but God will accept them with their limitations. People are evil, but they are still loved by God. This is a powerful statement of grace. This theological observation continues a dialectic found throughout the Primeval History. The narratives often laud the value and dignity of human beings, yet at the same time describe them as finite sinful human beings. People are made from dirt, yet they have the breath of God. They are in the image of God, yet capable of violence and evil. The ultimate symbolic person is Cain, drenched in the blood of his brother. They are sinful, yet loved and kept by God. They are both saints and sinners (*simul justus et peccator*). The Protestant Reformers of the sixteenth century did not invent that concept; they found it in narratives such as these.

In retrospect the biblical account of the flood presents God as totally in charge, and the whole affair is much more organized as a result. God sends the flood for a moral purpose, clearly speaks to Noah, keeps him appraised of the timetable, shuts him up in the ark, "remembers" Noah during the flood, steadies the ark in the water, brings it to rest on a mountain, acts with respect in regard to the sacrifice (better table manners than the Babylonian gods), and honorably promises no more floods in the future. Enki acts in sneaky fashion and the rest of the Babylonian gods argue with each other, fear the waters (they had no swimming lessons), act surprised at human survivors, swarm like flies for sacrificial food, and argue at the very end.

Their flood experience was chaotic (Wenham 1987:205; McKeown 61). The biblical author did a good job in writing a stunning narrative of contrast.

18

Covenant with Noah

Genesis 9:1–17

(1) God blessed Noah and his sons, and said to them, "Be fruitful and multiply, and fill the earth. (2) The fear and dread of you shall rest on every animal of the earth, and on every bird of the air, on everything that creeps on the ground, and on all the fish of the sea; into your hand they are delivered. (3) Every moving thing that lives shall be food for you; and just as I gave you the green plants, I give you everything. (4) Only, you shall not eat flesh with its life, that is, its blood. (5) For your own lifeblood I will surely require a reckoning: from every animal I will require it and from human beings, each one for the blood of another, I will require a reckoning for human life.

(6) Whoever sheds the blood of a human,
by a human shall that person's blood be shed;
    for in his own image
    God made humankind.

(7) And you, be fruitful and multiply, abound on the earth and multiply in it."

(8) Then God said to Noah and to his sons with him, (9) "As for me, I am establishing my covenant with you and your descendants after you, (10) and with every living creature that is with you, the birds, the domestic animals, and every animal of the earth with you, as many as came out of the ark. (11) I establish my covenant with you, that never again shall all flesh be cut off by the waters of a flood, and never again shall there be a flood to destroy the earth." (12) God said, "This is the sign of the covenant

> that I make between me and you and every living creature that is with you, for all future generations: (13) I have set my bow in the clouds, and it shall be a sign of the covenant between me and the earth. (14) When I bring clouds over the earth and the bow is seen in the clouds, (15) I will remember my covenant that is between me and you and every living creature of all flesh; and the waters shall never again become a flood to destroy all flesh. (16) When the bow is in the clouds, I will see it and remember the everlasting covenant between God and every living creature of all flesh that is on the earth." (17) God said to Noah, "This is the sign of the covenant that I have established between me and all flesh that is on the earth."

Genesis 9 is a Priestly text in which a covenant is created between Noah and God as was promised in Gen 6:18. It is worth noting that unlike his Mesopotamian counterparts, Noah does not receive a blessing of immortality. Rather, the truly important blessing of no more worldwide flooding is given to all of humanity. Furthermore, the covenant likewise is given to all humanity.

As Noah and his sons come out of the ark they are told immediately that the prime imperative is for them to have many children and fill the earth. The command is given twice in Genesis 9, once here (v. 1) and again after the statements concerning murder (v. 7). This completely contradicts the message of Mesopotamian accounts. In the *Atrahasis Epic* the concern throughout was human overpopulation, and this was the reason for the flood. When the human survivors come out of the ark, a decision was made by Nintu, the birth goddess, and Enki that there would be mechanisms to limit human population. There would be infertile women, infant mortality caused by the *Pasittu* demon, and classes of women who would be taboo (presumably religious and dedicated to the gods) and thus not have children. Genesis 9:1, 7 appear to be a conscious rejection of the Mesopotamian values (Hamilton 313; Moran 73).

Christians sometimes appeal to this passage and the similar imperative in Genesis 1 to affirm that every sexual encounter has to be one in which procreation is the primary goal. As we noted in our discussion of Genesis 1, if Judeans needed to have many children for the sake of a healthy human community, maybe the spirit of their laws would say to us that we should limit our procreation for the sake of a healthy human community and sustainable environment.

In verse 2 God places the authority of ruling the world and animal life into the hands of people, just as this mandate had been given in Gen 1:29–30. But there is something new now. The passage declares that every animal will now fear humanity. In verse 3 God says that people may now eat animals, just as formerly they had been given permission to eat plants. Apparently people before the flood were vegetarians. Similarly Hesiod spoke of four world ages, and meat eating came after an age of vegetarian diet (Westermann 462). Again, we suspect our biblical author was familiar with Hesiod.

Did people before the flood have any power over the animals? The man and the woman in Genesis 1 were told that they were to rule the earth, and presumably that included the animal realm. So it is difficult to determine what additional power over the animals is bequeathed to humanity with this covenant, other than now human beings have the right to eat them.

People can eat meat, but they must drain the blood out of whatever meat they choose to eat. Hence, Judeans drain blood out of animal meat that they intend to eat, and this becomes one of the chief rules of kosher food guidelines, most of which are listed in the book of Leviticus. The Priestly text here in Genesis 9 elevates this kosher guideline by making it a pre-Mosaic law. Since all people are descended from Noah, then all people ought to observe this guideline of draining blood. God gives Noah part of the kosher food guidelines and the rest will come with Moses and the law on Mount Sinai. Whereas the bulk of kosher food guidelines are meant only for Judeans, the rule to eat meat without blood is to be obeyed by all humanity. The ancients, and the Judeans in particular, believed that there was a life force in the blood of people and animals. When blood left a person or an animal, that being died. Blood was also perceived as the place where the soul dwelt; for the word for "soul" or "spirit" in Hebrew can sometimes be translated as blood. Thus, shedding blood on the ground was tantamount to pouring out a person's soul on the ground.

Judeans maintain that all people should keep this kosher guideline, or this Noahic law. If people throughout the world fail to do this, they offend God, and perhaps God might wish to destroy them for their sin. But God will refrain from destroying humanity if some people somewhere keep this law. (Like finding a few righteous people in the city of Sodom would save Sodom from destruction, Gen 18:32.) God refrains from destroying humanity for their failure not to refrain from blood, because a few faithful Judeans in the world keep the law. Judeans stay the destructive power of God by their obedience to this law and Sabbath observance, keeping the service owed by others and becoming the faithful leaven in a world full of humanity. But the world does not appreciate their saving actions, instead persecutes them for being Judeans. Judeans know their obedience saves all Gentiles, even those who persecute them, so they suffer patiently in their obedience to the Law. They are a corporate "suffering servant," suffering that others might be saved, even when those others persecute them.

The image of the suffering servant as both an individual prophet and the corporate Judeans in exile emerged in the oracles of the sixth century BCE prophet, whom we call Second Isaiah, and whose oracles are found in Isaiah 40–55. This prophet most likely was a priest, so the images resonate with Priestly texts in Genesis 1–11. The suffering servant in Isaiah 40–55 is someone who is obedient, suffers because of this obedience, and suffers knowing that his obedience will save others vicariously. Second Isaiah even declares Israel or the Judeans to be the Suffering Servant in Isa 44:1, but in other passages he describes the Suffering Servant as an individual, especially Isaiah 53. I believe the prophet implies that the Suffering Servant is both the corporate Judeans in exile and any individual who suffers for the Jewish faith. Since Genesis 9 comes from the same era as that prophetic image of the suffering servant, the imagery of the suffering servant subtly permeates the text.

Though Judeans could not make all the people in the world keep this law, they definitely encouraged converts to Judaism to observe this kosher food law. This explains why the question of eating kosher food was a hot topic of debate in the first century CE in the emerging Christian churches. Throughout his ministry Paul argued that newly converted Gentile Christians should not have to keep kosher food guidelines. Many Judeans, who were disciples of the more conservative James, the brother of Jesus, president of the church in Jerusalem, believed that converts to Christianity should still keep this one universal guideline of draining blood from meat, since it was commanded to all humanity and issued before Moses. Acts 15 tells of a council in Jerusalem where Peter, Paul, and James, as well as many others, discussed this issue. In Acts 15:19–20 it was decided that Gentiles did not have to be circumcised, since that guideline was introduced with Abraham, who was later than Noah but still before Moses. However, Gentile converts should abstain from idols, fornication, and from animal meat with blood in it. For the blood guidelines came from Noah, ancestor of all people. This guideline was considered extremely important, and even Gentiles should keep it upon converting to Christianity. Paul agreed to this at the convention, but when he went back to the mission field he refused to encourage Gentiles to keep this guideline. Paul was a snit, fortunately for us. He created a form of Christianity that became incredibly successful in the mission field, especially because of its total freedom from Jewish laws, and all forms of Christianity today are the result of his theological position. Thus, we do not worry about blood in the meat we cook. Next time you eat your steak rare, thank Paul.

Jews today still speak of these universal covenants that God made with people other than the Jews. They regard the covenants with Noah in Genesis 9 and Abraham in Genesis 17 as covenants that demonstrate God's concern for all the peoples of the world. But Jews still view their obedience to the covenant stipulations of Genesis 9 as something they do on behalf of all humanity, since all people are descended from Noah.

The idea that Judeans were keeping some divine mandate to divert God's wrath on humanity may have had special significance in the sixth and fifth centuries BCE. In that age many Judeans, perhaps including the final editor or author of Genesis 1–11, still lived in Babylon, for only a few had returned to Jerusalem. They were surrounded by Babylonians who encouraged them to worship Marduk in the *Akitu* New Year's Festival to save the world from the destructive force of Tiamat. Babylonians may have considered the Judeans to be subversive for not participating in the official religion of the state, just as later Christians were viewed as atheists by the Romans for not recognizing the state deities and the divinity of the Roman emperor. This covenant is recorded in the biblical text right after the story of the destructive flood, and now this covenant implies that obedience to the Law, especially avoidance of blood, averts a future destruction of the world. So Judeans could respond to their Babylonian neighbors, "It is not sacrifice to Marduk but our obedience to Yahweh's Law that saves us all." They probably did not convince many people, but it may have quieted their Babylonian neighbors for a while. Most importantly this explanation encouraged Judeans to maintain their religious identity and not disappear into Babylonian society.

In verses 5–6 the guideline for not shedding blood is extended into the social realm to become a prohibition against murder. The text ties the command not to kill to the reference that people are made in the "image of God," a Priestly theme taken from Genesis 1. This law about human bloodshed is a powerful message about the respect for human life, an imperative that needs to be heard in our modern age. It also implies human equality. For it demands that the life of every human being must be respected. Often in the ancient world, and throughout history for that matter, kings and tyrants had the power of life and death over their subjects, especially the weaker ones. This law abolishes that distinction between people.

This text is often quoted today by Christians to justify the death penalty. If someone spills someone else's blood, that person should be put to death. Unfortunately, they overlook the teachings of the New Testament, and Paul in particular, who declare that the laws of the old covenant have passed away and are no longer binding on Christians. Any discussion of the ethical implications of capital punishment for Christians must work primarily with the appropriate New Testament texts.

In Israelite law there were guidelines for when it was appropriate for society to execute someone. The death penalty was to be used when premeditated murder occurred, or when an individual committed an act of sacrilege that was so offensive that it could bring the punishment of God upon the entire community. The shedding of blood was also considered an act of sacrilege, because the life force of God existed in blood. When someone killed another human being, they usurped the authority of God, thus committing a grave blasphemous or sacrilegious act. This passage occurs in our text because it reinforces the language that will be found later in those texts of Exodus, Leviticus, and Deuteronomy that speak about capital punishment.

Before we quote this text to justify our modern institution of capital punishment, however, we need to be alert to some crucial insights. The ancient Israelites and Judeans executed people because they did so in the name of God, for they saw themselves as a theocracy, a people ruled by God. In our modern age we do not make that claim. We consider ourselves to be a secular society in which religion and the affairs of state are separated. If we do not make that claim to be a theocracy, we should not be appealing to these specific Old Testament laws. If we wish to justify modern capital punishment, we need to do so for other reasons. Furthermore, it must not be forgotten that ancient Israelites and Judeans at the time when this literature was created did not have prisons. When you punished guilty persons, you either fined them, inflicted corporal punishment, or executed them. Imprisonment or incarceration was not an option. It is for us. Thus, it is inappropriate for us to appeal to their custom of capital punishment when we have the option of incarceration, which they did not have.

In verse 9 the actual word "covenant" is used. With this reference it is clear that a specific covenant is being made between God and Noah and his descendants. In the form that we read Genesis 9, the language is reversed. The stipulations of the covenant, that is, eating meat with blood drained from it and avoiding murder, have been told to Noah already. Usually one would read a text and hear that a covenant was being made before the listing of guidelines and stipulations for covenant obedience would be mentioned. Why this is so in this text is not really clear to us.

In verse 11 we hear God's side of the agreement. God gives the promise that there will never again be a flood to destroy people and animals. So the covenant promise goes out to people and animals together. (Can we hear a small cheer come from the contingent of animals gathered around the ark?) At this point we should compare this covenant with the covenants made

Covenant with Noah

with the Babylonian Noah figures, Ziusudra, Atrahasis, and Utnapishtim. When they came out of the ark, they received the blessing of immortality and they were able to live on the special island of Dilmun or in the heavenly realm. But in the biblical narrative the blessing goes forth to all people and all animals, not just one person. This, in part, is because the biblical text does not believe in semi-divine, immortal personages, like the Babylonian Noahs. But more importantly it reflects the democratic spirit of the biblical text. The great blessing goes to all people.

This covenant is not only made between God and humanity; it also involves the animal realm according to verse 11. This important point too often is forgotten: human beings are creatures along with the animals, both created by God from the dust of the ground according to Genesis 2. People and animals both share in the rights of the covenant made with Noah. Yes, people have dominion over the animals according to verse 2, but we must balance this with the realization that we are partners in the covenant according to verse 10. We rule the animals, but we must rule wisely and not destructively, as we have so often done in the past. In verse 7 God again tells people to be fertile, and when combined with the command to rule the animal realm, we have the reiteration of the command given to the first couple in Gen 1:28, who were also told to be fertile and exercise dominion over the world.

In verses 11 and 15 God clearly states "never again" will floodwaters destroy the earth, undercutting the beliefs of the Babylonians, and providing comfort to all those who might fear cosmic destruction by water. Related to this in verses 13, 14, and 16 God speaks of the sign of this covenant, "the bow in the clouds," the rainbow. The ancients knew that when it stopped raining, they could see a rainbow in the sky, and this beautiful image amazed them. In Phoenicia and Palestine it was called the "bow of Aqhat," and the story was told of how the goddess Anat had Aqhat killed in order that she might steal his bow. She failed. The bow ultimately was placed into the sky and Aqhat, the hunter, eventually became the constellation Orion. (Orion was associated with the god Osiris in Egypt.) Thus, the rainbow had significant mythological connotations in the ancient world, some of which we have not yet figured out. Commentators have opined that the rainbow was the bow of war, and its presence in sky would be testimony that God would never make war against the world with a flood again. The weapon of war became the sign of peace (Brueggemann 1982:84; Hamilton 317). Elsewhere God is described as having a bow that shoots arrows (Ps 7:12; Hab 3:9), and the arrows are bolts of lightning (Ps 7:13; 18:14; Hab 3:11).

This rainbow imagery is found in various cultures. In India the rainbow is the battle bow of Indra after he has defeated the evil demon, Tvaster, personified as the monsoon rains. For pre-Islamic Arabs it was the bow of Kuzah, who shot arrows before hanging it in the clouds. For Homer it was the goddess, Iris, and it portended war. Marduk hung up his bow after his victory to become a constellation in the night sky (reminiscent of Aqhat), but not the rainbow. However, the concept is similar (Skinner 173; Vawter 136).

This image might also appeal to ancient Near Eastern imagery of how God fights against water. Marduk "hangs up" his bow after defeating the last of his enemies, including Tiamat, the goddess of chaotic water. Rainbows appear after clouds, and clouds are the vehicles of the warrior storm gods in the ancient Near East. When God blows back the waters with a divine wind in Gen 8:2 after releasing them in Gen 7:11, both Priestly texts, we may have poetic allusions to the image of divine combat with chaotic water. God is finished fighting the waters, if this interpretation is correct, and the rainbow becomes the symbol of peace, for the last battle with chaotic waters has been fought (Batto 2004:168–72). I am not totally convinced by this imagery, but I suspect that the Priestly author might be using this combat language of the ancient world to indicate that there was no real fight between God and another divine being, rather God did everything while being in complete control.

Our biblical author demythologizes the symbol and makes it the sign of the covenant that a major flood will never happen again. It is a clever connection to make, since the rainbow appears after a rainstorm has ended, and it would frequently remind Judeans of God's great covenant with them. Perhaps the rainbow is also a reminder to God not to destroy the earth again, if we wish to see the biblical author once more portraying God with human emotions (Löning and Zenger 125–26).

Our biblical author has made a major issue out of the promise by God not to flood the world in verses 8–17. The Priestly author who added this section significantly expands upon the promise in Gen 8:21–22, wherein God promised never again to destroy the world with a flood. The Priestly author has a powerful message for exilic Judeans with this fuller exposition of a covenant experience.

19

Noah and His Sons

Genesis 9:18–28

(18) The sons of Noah who went out of the ark were Shem, Ham, and Japheth. Ham was the father of Canaan. (19) These three were the sons of Noah; and from these the whole earth was peopled. (20) Noah, a man of the soil, was the first to plant a vineyard. (21) He drank some of the wine and became drunk, and he lay uncovered in his tent. (22) And Ham, the father of Canaan, saw the nakedness of his father, and told his two brothers outside. (23) Then Shem and Japheth took a garment, laid it on both their shoulders, and walked backward and covered the nakedness of their father; their faces were turned away, and they did not see their father's nakedness. (24) When Noah awoke from his wine and knew what his youngest son had done to him, (25) he said,

"Cursed be Canaan; lowest of slaves shall he be to his brothers."
(26) He also said,
"Blessed by the LORD my God be Shem;
and let Canaan be his slave
(27) May God make space for Japheth,
and let him live in the tents of Shem;
and let Canaan be his slave."
(28) After the flood Noah lived three hundred fifty years. (29) All the days of Noah were nine hundred fifty years; and he died.

As the narrative concerning Noah and his sons unfolds, the reader senses that this account is unconnected to the flood story. In the account of the flood, Noah's sons were married, but in this story they appear to be younger and unmarried, for they still live with their father. Commentators often suggest these stories in the Primeval History may have existed separately, perhaps as oral tales, before the biblical author brought them together in their present written form. In this narrative Noah is the first farmer or vine grower. His personality is different from Noah the sailor, zookeeper, and hero of the flood. Perhaps the biblical author combined the two images of Noah the farmer and Noah the sailor, after deciding where to place this account (Gunkel 79; Bailey 158–59). If Noah's sons were younger and unmarried, it would be more logical to place the account before the flood. On the other hand, Noah's invention of agriculture and vineyards makes more sense after the flood to indicate that the world has become fertile once more. So the biblical author choose the latter theme and accepted the incongruity that Noah's sons seem younger in this account (Skinner 182; Simpson 555; Vawter 138).

Noah plants a vineyard, which ultimately produces wine. The curse on the fertility of the ground has been removed in a big way, for vineyards were a major cash crop in ancient Palestine, requiring serious care but providing a big yield. Throughout the ancient Near East and Greece wine was usually seen as the gift of the gods to humanity to make life more bearable (Westermann 487; Hamilton 321). So again the Bible attributes something to humanity that normally was attributed to the gods.

Lamech said that Noah, his son, would bring "rest" or "relief" from work and toil from the ground that God had cursed (Gen 5:29). Perhaps this story describes the "rest" he brings. Noah brings rest by inventing agriculture or a sedentary farming lifestyle, just as the Cainites invented nomadism. That would be a neat contrast of human social historical development by biblical author (Simpson 554). If the biblical author implies that Noah invented agriculture, perhaps a better translation for the word "rest" might be "settle down." Noah invented agriculture thus enabling people to settle in one place (Simpson 531). I think modern farmers might agree that agriculture enables you to "settle down," I doubt that they would admit it gives you "rest." Noah's name might mean, "rest," but the Hebrew word for rest also sounds like the word for "comfort" (*nachem*) (Richardson 92). We might have a word play, a false etymology, so that the audience would think of both words, "rest" and "comfort," and associate them with Noah's name. "Comfort" is what vineyards can bring to people in general with the economic profit and the pleasure of wine.

Productive vineyards result from long-term agricultural effort, and they must be tended by agriculturalists, or more properly speaking, viticulturalists (people who grow the produce of the vine—grapes and olives). After years of careful attention, vineyards produce a significant yield, which makes their owners into more than simple farmers. Grapes and olives are cash crops exported to other countries. Vineyards produce wine for common consumption at meals by Palestinian families, and their value for trade betokens well-established agricultural activity among the community. Along with olive production, another product of the vine that requires careful attention, grapes and wine were the most important cash crops in ancient Palestine long before the Israelites, and they still are today. Noah's invention symbolically was seen as a breakthrough development by our biblical author. As Israelite society evolved in the highlands of Palestine after 1200 BCE, after the collapse of late Bronze Age society, viticulture enabled them to rise above mere subsistence farming. Grape and olive production was sometimes seriously sponsored by a strong central government in the region. Tragically, in war enemy armies would cut down grape and olive vines upon invading Judah or Israel in order to break the backbone of their economy even if they were not successful in besieging the cities.

In Mesopotamian accounts wine existed before the flood, for Utnapishtim paid the workers who built the ark with wine (Wenham 198). Biblical authors projected the domestication of wine later in time. Ironically, the biblical scenario might be closer to the actual historical development. Cain was a farmer, Cain's sons developed pastoralism, and Noah brought viticulture. In the actual historical development in the ancient Near East, farming emerged around 8000 BCE, domestication of flocks arose after 5000 BCE, and viticulture developed more extensively after 3000 BCE, even though the first wines were produced in Armenia around 5400 BCE (Wilson 179; Hiebert 48–49). This, of course, may simply be coincidence.

As the biblical author envisions the history of his own people, he would suppose that once they were pastoralists who did no farming, then they became simple farmers as they came into the land of Palestine, but when they became viticulturalists, producing olives and grapes, they achieved real success. Noah is portrayed as a man who made a great breakthrough for all of humanity, and he brought "rest" to people by developing a crop that could provide financial security, especially for later Israelites. Of course, the actual historical reality was that most Israelites had been Canaanites prior to 1200 BCE who peacefully withdrew to the Palestinian highlands for economic and social reasons. They simply redeveloped the agricultural sophistication in the highlands that they had in the lowlands.

Perhaps what Noah brought is the "rest" or pleasure that comes from the fruit of the vine, wine (Skinner 185). The ancient Israelite did not share the belief of some modern conservative Christians who consider alcohol to be evil and commend its avoidance. Some modern preachers even claim that biblical "wine" was really non-alcoholic "grape juice" and what the

Bible calls "strong drink" was the only true alcohol. This, of course, obviously overlooks the fact that the Bible indicates both "wine" and "strong drink" were intoxicating. The ancient Israelite viewed wine as one of the blessings God had given humanity to make life more enjoyable. Noah's gift of "wine" was the source of joy for people, provided they did not use it excessively. It has been suggested that the figure of Noah was once a Canaanite god who was the patron of wine, who brought wine to humanity for their pleasure and for orgiastic celebrations in the cult. It also has been observed that grape vines may have been domesticated in the Neolithic period (5400 BCE) in the region of Armenia eastward to Pontus (north central Turkey), which is quite close to where the biblical author posits the location of the ark's landing (Ararat essentially is the land of Armenia). Perhaps, this is not a coincidence, and maybe the memory of the origin of grape cultivation was connected to Noah's name (Skinner 183). The hero of the flood narrative in Greece, Deukalion, was connected to Dionysius, the Greek god of wine. Such traditions of Deukalion and Dionysius may have their origin in Turkey, which is close to Armenia. All of these are tantalizing hints for historical reconstruction.

Noah grew his grapes, created wine, drank the wine, and got drunk. Many readers of the biblical text assume that Noah sinned, and that this is the sin being recounted in the tale. That is patently false. Biblical authors did not consider drinking alcohol to be a sin. In Israel getting drunk was neither a sin nor a crime, but it was a "social *gaffe*" which could get you in trouble, as it did with Noah (Vawter 139). Biblical authors warned against the abuse of wine, which could lead to dulled senses, which is turn could lead to such a serious social *gaffe*. Perhaps the most colorful warning against over-imbibing comes from Prov 23:29–35,

> (29) Who has woe? Who has sorrow? Who has strife? Who has complaining? Who has wounds without cause? Who has redness of eyes? (30) Those who linger late over wine, those who keep trying mixed wines. (31) Do not look at wine when it is red, when it sparkles in the cup and goes down smoothly. (32) At the last it bites like a serpent, and stings like an adder. (33) Your eyes will see strange things, and your mind utter perverse things. (34) You will be like one who lies down in the midst of the sea, like one who lies on the top of a mast. (35) "They struck me," you will say, "but I was not hurt; they beat me, but I did not feel it. When shall I awake? I will seek another drink."

It seems as if the biblical author of this saying in Proverbs may speak from experience. The wine is "red" and "sparkles" when it is drunk straight and not mixed with water, which most people would do for ordinary consumption at meals. The wine indeed "bites" after too much consumption, and when a person is really drunk, he or she will have the "spins" and will feel tossed about on a ship at sea. Finally, the morning after brings a hangover, which can be alleviated by having another drink, the so-called "hair of the dog that bit you." Our biblical sage may have been down this road as a young man.

Noah got drunk. If he drank in his hot nomad's tent, he got drunk even faster, for quick inebriation occurs when a person drinks in a hot, tightly enclosed airspace (a piece of information I suppose everyone needs to have at his or her disposal). Apparently the man who "invented wine" also had to discover the first serious "drunk." So Noah drank in his tent, got drunk sooner, because he did not know better. This may be biblical humor, poking fun at the ancestor who invented wine. It may be Israelite humor to poke fun at their ancestors in general, who were perceived as having been nomads before they entered the land, and who were unaware of the powerful intoxicating effects of wine (the "fire-water" of ancient Palestine) because they lived in the wilderness and tended livestock. Generally, wine was drunk more frequently by farmers and settled folk, for whom vineyards were accessible. Nomads did not have that kind of familiarity and may have been more likely to drink wine straight, without cutting it by the addition of water. Hence, the story may be satire on such folk.

There may be another interesting aspect to this story, however. Noah was an old man who got drunk. In the ancient world, and even in medieval and early modern European society, it was socially acceptable for old people to get drunk (instead of today's college student crowd). They had spent a lifetime of hard work, they had raised children, they had served their village and their clan, and thus they deserved an occasional good "drunk." Noah, after all, did more than his fair share of work with the ark, including shoveling out the bottom of the ark for all those animals during the flood. In the Aqhat Epic from Ugarit in Syria (1400 BCE) it is said that a son must take care of his drunken father—"who takes him by the hand when he is drunk, carries him when he is sated with wine" (*Aqhat* 1,32–33) (Pritchard 150; Westermann 485, 488; Blenkinsopp 2011:152). This is an old Near Eastern proverb that speaks of the responsibility of the youth to lead old parents by the hand as they come home from the alehouse at night, lest the old ones fall into a ditch (quite the image). Clearly Noah's drunkenness was not seen as a sin, despite what some modern fundamentalist preachers have said over the years, but rather it was one of the "perks" of old age.

The proverb mentioned above, however, throws into better relief the evilness of what Ham did to Noah. Noah was drunk, and it was the responsibility of sons to care for the old man. Ham certainly failed on this score; Ham perpetrated a great evil upon his father.

As we read the story, the question immediately arises as to the real identity of the person who committed this sin. Two anomalies in the account raise the question of who did this deed to Noah. First, Ham commits the sin, but Canaan receives the curse. Why is this? Some have assumed that this is indeed fair, for in the ancient world the sins of the fathers could be visited upon the children, and this reflects familial solidarity (Westermann 484, 489; Wenham 1987:201). (Biblical law even says that such will occur down unto the fourth generation in Exod 20:6 and Deut 5:10.) Other readers have said that this is not fair. Perhaps there was an old account in which it was told that Canaan committed this sin and was punished. Ham then replaced Canaan as the perpetrator at the beginning of the account by the addition of his name, which requires that only two words in Hebrew be added both to Gen 9:18 and 9:22, "Ham, the father of . . ." before Canaan's name (Gunkel 79; Skinner 182, 195; Speiser 1964:62; Bailey 160–61; Fretheim 403; Blenkinsopp 2011:152).

The second anomaly is that Ham is called the youngest son by Noah in verse 24, when the text reads that Noah "knew what his youngest son had done to him." But elsewhere in the biblical narratives the three sons are listed as Shem, Ham, and Japheth (Gen 5:32; 6:10; 7:13; 9:18; 10:1), which implies that Japheth is the youngest. Some interpreters maintain that it makes no difference; Ham may still be the youngest even though he is normally listed second in the sequence. Other interpreters declare the repeated listing of the sons as Shem, Ham, and Japheth must indicate that Ham is the middle son, not the youngest (Speiser 1964:62).

Those readers who believe that Ham was the second son, not the youngest, suggest that originally in the narrative Canaan perpetrated the deed, and he was the youngest son who was punished subsequently (Skinner 195; Speiser 1964:62; Bailey 160; Fretheim 403). Another theory suggests that originally this story had only two sons in the narrative plot, Eber and Canaan, the symbolic ancestors of the Israelites and the Canaanites. Both of these personages are listed as later descendants of Noah in the genealogies of Genesis 10. When Shem, Ham, and Japheth were placed into the account and the names of Eber and Canaan were taken out, the story was transformed from being a regional account to a universal account of human origins (Van Seters 179).

If the story originally spoke of two sons, and Canaan was then the youngest, why did the biblical author introduce Shem, Ham, and Japheth into the narrative, including the blessing upon Shem and Japheth, but he did not completely displace Canaan? Why did he retain the curse of Canaan?

Perhaps the stories of the flood, Noah's sons, and the genealogies once were separate accounts, and perhaps there were far more accounts that we presently possess. When the biblical author wove them together in written form, smooth transitions had to be created for the sake of a plot that ran throughout the Primeval History. Shem, Ham, and Japheth were placed into the story so that it would follow after the flood account in which Shem, Ham, and Japheth were the direct, actual sons of Noah rather than Eber and Canaan, who may have been the sons of Noah in the vineyard account. But Canaan's name needed to be kept in this account, for the use of his name prepared the readers for narrative plot lines in the books of Numbers and Joshua, wherein the Canaanites are the enemies who must be displaced by the Israelites. (This implies the Primeval History emerged as narrative literature in conjunction with a larger narrative that included the Pentateuch and the historical books.) Also, "Canaanites" may have symbolized people who lived in the land of Palestine who opposed the return of Judeans from the Babylonian Exile in the sixth and fifth centuries BCE. It is for this audience that the Primeval History took its final narrative form. If this theory is correct, it means the biblical author was willing to live with some odd tensions in the story for the sake of a symbolic message. In light of this understanding, yet another theory suggests that originally Ham was the person cursed and only later with a Deuteronomic revision of the narrative was Canaan made the object of the curse. This, of course, was done to justify the aforementioned return of Judeans from exile (Carr 1996:161–62, 311). So we can never be sure whose name originally received the brunt of Noah's wrath.

What was Ham's sin? Ham looks in and sees his father drunk and naked. I guess Noah was overheated from drinking all that wine in a hot, enclosed tent, so he ripped off his clothing (Israelite humor). Ham laughs at the old man and then tells his brothers about it. Though the text does not clearly say it, one gets the impression that Ham ridicules the old man in front of his brothers. However, the expression "to see" someone can be a euphemism for having sex with that person, and so it often has been suggested that Ham took sexual advantage of Noah. Over the years other speculative theories have been suggested by pious rabbis and Christians that Ham "castrated" Noah, or that Ham had sex with Noah's wife (a possible meaning of uncovering the nakedness of someone means having sex with their spouse) (Brueggemann 1982:90), or that Ham saw his parents having sex. But the argument that Ham "saw" Noah visually is reinforced by the actions of the other two brothers who go into the tent very carefully so as not to see their father (Wenham 1987:200). Also, if sex were involved, the biblical author would have mentioned it (Fretheim 404). Ilona Rashkow creatively suggests that perhaps the inebriated and thus uninhibited Noah disrobed before Ham and thus seduced him, and Noah's anger with Ham reflects his own guilt (Rashkow 82–98). The terse nature of the narrative makes this also a possible reading, but it does assume modern psychoanalytic understandings of guilt and shame.

Ham's sin involves at least the sin of social impropriety, for Ham fails to help Noah. There was familial responsibility for sons to take care of their parents when their parents were inebriated. Ham certainly fails to do that. Shem and Ham keep the social guidelines by going in, covering Noah, and helping him to sober up.

There is also a Levitical sin involved in Ham's activity. According to Lev 18:7, it is wrong to see or "uncover" the nakedness of your father. This imperative is in a list of prohibitions that declare it sinful to see the "nakedness" of many of your relatives (Lev 18:6–18). The reason for these prohibitions is that if you see the nakedness of relatives, you may want to have sex with them or marry them, and that would break the taboo of consanguineous marriages that were so often forbidden in ancient society. The ancients did not understand genetics, but they did sense that there were problems with children born to people who were closely related. This is why nomadic societies often required their men to marry women from outside their tribe and why it was important to have alliances with other nomadic tribes for the sake of such marriages. (Marriages outside of one's tribal group are called exogamous). If viewing his father in a naked condition is the sin; then certainly Shem and Japheth avoid that sin by going into Noah's tent backward to avert their eyes.

This reading of those Levitical laws may not be correct, however. Most commentators suspect that "seeing" the nakedness or "uncovering" the nakedness of a relative means having sex. This becomes more apparent with Lev 18:19, which prohibits uncovering the nakedness of a woman (apparently including one's wife) during her menstruation. This law only makes sense if it refers to sex. This interpretation of "seeing" nakedness makes more sense, because it is hard to believe that such a strong prohibition in Leviticus would be directed against an action (seeing nakedness) because it might lead to marriage or sex. It is more likely that the command would prohibit the act of sex itself. This tempts us again to think that Ham has sex with Noah. However, the one reservation that we have arises from the actions of Shem and Japheth, who avoid looking at Noah, as if the command actually meant simply seeing a person naked.

If the interpretation of the laws in Leviticus 18 as sexual activity is correct, that would shed light on Ham's actions. If Ham saw the nakedness of his father, it meant that he had sex with a helpless Noah—he raped him.

Some commentators assume that this is indeed the point of the story. If so, Ham's sin is an egregious sin indeed. I, however, believe the story is a double-entendre. The narrative indicates that Ham only saw with his eyes, but the author wants to hint at the possibility of actual sex.

Why does the biblical author recount such a tale, or hint at such sexual activity? The question really becomes who does Ham symbolize, or who do Ham and Canaan together symbolize? They represent the Canaanites, and by attributing such an action to the ancestor of the Canaanites, the biblical author infers that Canaanites still do such things. Perhaps the biblical author is condemning the sexual practices that took place in Canaanite religious rituals, sex with male and female sacred prostitutes and sometimes even with animals, acts which were done for the sake of crop, animal, and human fertility. Modern scholars have argued hotly over the extent of such ritual sexual activity in the Canaanite cult, or whether it really existed at all. But certainly the Israelites imputed such behavior to the Canaanites in Israelite religious rhetoric, and recounting the sin and the curse upon Canaan was part of that rhetoric.

Upon obtaining sobriety, Noah blesses Shem and Japheth, and he curses Canaan. We sense these are symbolic foreshadowings of later historical and political events. Noah's blessings on the three sons should be separated from the list of the descendants of these three sons in the following chapter. For example, Shem is blessed by Noah, but the descendants of Shem in Genesis 10 include the Arameans, folk whom the biblical author would not bless otherwise. Our biblical author has separate traditions in these two chapters, and they connect to some degree, but there are discontinuities. Thus, we can question who Shem, Japheth, and Canaan refer to in this chapter without assuming the same equations need to be made in Genesis 10.

The blessing of Shem refers to the fortunes of Israelites. In particular, the allusion to "expanding the tent" is a reference in Mesopotamian archival reports to expanding an empire. Commentators suspected for years that Noah's blessing refers to the rise of the Davidic–Solomonic empire in the tenth century BCE, for David was credited with subjugating the remaining Canaanites in Palestine. Consequently for years many biblical historians attributed the literary creation of Genesis 1–11 to the time of Solomon's rule. More recently we attribute Genesis 1–11 to the sixth century BCE Babylonian Exile or later. The blessing of Noah still is seen to refer to David and Solomon initially, but in the sixth and fifth centuries BCE the promises fulfilled once by David may have been viewed as promises to be fulfilled once more by a new David after the return of Judeans from exile. Thus, the blessing, including the hope of an "expanded tent," was a vision of hope that told returning exiles that they would be successful in re-establishing their Jewish state in Palestine.

The identification of Japheth is a little more difficult. Commentators once made a connection with people allied with the Israelites during the time of David and Solomon. The idea of military alliance, suggested by the allusion to Japheth dwelling in the "tent of Shem," then implies that Japheth somehow benefits from an alliance with Shem. If Shem's ascendancy is connected to the Davidic and Solomonic state, then an economic ally to Israel in that period must be sought. Since Japheth is connected to Indo-European peoples in the genealogies of Genesis 10, commentators in years past looked for an Indo-European people in the Solomonic era. The leading suggestion were the small kingdoms in Syria, north of Israel, who were absorbed militarily into Israel's empire or bound by economic alliance to Israel. Some of these Syrian states were Neo-Hittite in origin, that is, they were established by Hittites after the fall of the original Hittite empire in central Turkey around 1200 BCE. Since the Hittites were created, in part, by Indo-European migrations into Turkey after 2000 BCE, the Hittites and Neo-Hittites could be considered Japhethites (if the biblical author really knew all of that history). In the genealogies of Genesis 10 these peoples are included in the descendants of Japheth.

A few commentators in past generations suggested a different Indo-European people, or at least a people with some Indo-European blood, the Philistines (Gunkel 84; Fritsch 47; Vawter 140; Bailey 160). The Philistines, in part, had their origins in the migrations of people out of the Aegean area as well as the Hittite empire after the collapse of societies in those areas around 1200 BCE. These folk were called the Sea Peoples, and on several occasions they were beaten back from Egypt by pharaohs, who commemorated their victories over these folk as significant accomplishments. The Philistines may have arisen out of some population elements forcibly settled by the Egyptians after their defeat in Egypt around 1200 BCE and again around 1100 BCE. In later years Israelites referred to the Philistines with two separate terms, perhaps recalling those two settlements of slightly different population elements. Many Philistines may have been Sea Peoples who chose to settle along the coast in southwest Palestine without ever having attacked Egypt. Although subsequently the Philistines became Semitic in culture, and perhaps in blood lines also, when they settled in southwest Palestine, they retained some of the characteristics of early Greek culture in those early years. Thus, our biblical author may be referring to Philistines, who historically had some Indo-European connections.

Most commentators now suspect that the biblical author did not know enough history to be aware of the Indo-European origins of Hittites or

Philistines. For the biblical author Japhethites were people who lived north of Israel and the Fertile Crescent and had strong political and economic connections with Israel. The text could refer to the Aramean states of Syria to the north of the Davidic and Solomonic kingdom that were militarily and economically connected to the Israelite state, or perhaps the Phoenicians who had close connections to Solomon (Westermann 491–93).

Finally, contemporary commentators, who believe in a sixth or fifth century BCE exilic origin for the Primeval History, suggest the Persians. I prefer this theory. Persians were an Indo-European people also. In the post-exilic era they ruled the Judeans, and they were responsible for allowing the Judeans to return to Palestine. They actively sponsored the creation of a Jewish state from the fifth century BCE onward as a buffer against Greek economic and political expansion along the east Mediterranean coastline. If the Judeans were in a province of the great Persian Empire, it might be that the biblical author envisions a grand reversal of roles in which the future empire of the Judeans would include Persians as grateful vassals instead of overlords. Biblical authors often had a great sense of irony. Thus, when the discussion is over, there are a number of possible equations for Japheth in Genesis 9. Finally, if the curse is later than the sixth or fifth century BCE, it could refer to Greeks, some of whom converted to Judaism after the time of Alexander the Great (Wenham 1987:203).

The curse on Canaan raises issues for discussion, because it may be the most important part of Noah's oracle. As noted above, the allusion to Canaan might refer to the success of the empire of David and Solomon, but it could refer additionally to a sixth and fifth centuries BCE hope of a new Davidic "empire" to be re-established in Palestine. Thus, Canaan could represent the peoples subjugated by David in the tenth century BCE, or the people in fifth century BCE Palestine who opposed the efforts of returning Jewish exiles to re-establish themselves in the land and rebuild Jerusalem and the Temple. I prefer the latter option. In 445–444 BCE Nehemiah rebuilt the city walls of Jerusalem, and his actions were opposed by folks in neighboring Persian provinces, even though Nehemiah had permission from the Persians to rebuild. From the perspective of returning Judeans, the blessing on Shem might have been their mandate to return and the curse on Canaan was a curse on anyone who opposed them. Genesis 9 would have been heard as a blessing that came true once in the past with David, but which was going to come true again in the post-exilic period. A final possibility is that the name "Canaan" might include a wide range of people. In Genesis 10 the descendants of Ham/Canaan include Israel's enemies and oppressors: Egypt, Babylon, and Assyria, who will be punished in the coming golden age for Judeans (Brodie 194). That would be a dramatic re-fulfillment of an oracle that first came true with David. At any rate, it seems that the oracle of Noah is one that may come true dramatically for exilic and post-exilic Judeans.

Biblical authors and their audiences believed that oracles of blessing could come true more than once, and especially great oracles of hope from the past would come true for them again. This is why they recorded them in written form and why we have the Hebrew Bible today. Judeans who followed Christ in the first century CE readily saw these same oracles of hope fulfilled in an ultimate and dramatic way by Jesus.

Many pious Christians, especially in America, teach that the Bible speaks of a "curse of Ham." Often they apparently do not bother to read the text closely to see that Canaan is cursed. But sometimes they have even printed Bibles in which Canaan's name has been replaced with Ham's name. Ham is directly associated with people from Africa and this so-called "curse on Ham" has led to two things according to such Christians. The curse turned Africans' skin black or dark, and it ensured that they would be slaves. Historically the curse was quoted to justify the enslavement of Africans in America. This is absurd, of course, because the descendants of Ham according to Genesis 10 include many people who are not dark-skinned Africans. This last observation was simply ignored by slavery advocates prior to the American War between the States, and it continues to be ignored by modern Americans who believe that the curse explains why Africans should be considered inferior to the white races. This interpretation ignores the text in verse 26, which speaks of how Ham will be a slave primarily to Shem, or modern-day Semitic peoples and the Jews especially. Advocates of slavery years ago and modern spokespersons who affirm the racial inferiority of black people point to the generic reference in verse 25 that says Canaan (read Ham instead) shall be a slave "to his brothers." Sometimes fundamentalist preachers declare that Shem was meant to be the master of Ham, but with the rise of Christianity that right passed from Shem (Jews) to Japheth or the white races (Christians). Thus, modern apologists for white racial superiority justify the suppression of the Hamitic or black races by some additional interpretations of the text.

This way of interpreting the text was extremely popular among southern pro-slavery preachers in the south prior to the Civil War, but this interpretation did not die with the end of the war in 1865. In subsequent years it was used to justify the inferior status held by black people in American society as well as the institution of segregation. When I was a teenager and young adult in the 1960s I heard this interpretation seriously advocated by conservative Protestants. Again, why did no one look in the text and see that the curse was on Canaan and not Ham? They could have concluded logically from the word Canaan that perhaps Canaanites were the people truly targeted by the curse and not modern-day African Americans.

The belief that the curse is on Ham, not Canaan, is a belief that will not die. In 1980 while teaching at a progressive denominational college in eastern North Carolina, I mentioned that a course in Old Testament could clear up misunderstandings. I mentioned the so-called curse on Ham, which was really a curse on Canaan. At that point a young woman in her mid-twenties stood up and said, "That's a lie. The curse really was on Ham. My preacher taught me that. My preacher warned about liberal teachers like you who would try to distort the teachings of the Bible." Since I was holding a Bible in my hand, I walked toward the student and said, "Here, you can read the text for yourself. It clearly says Canaan, not Ham." She responded, "Is that one of those liberal Bibles? They have all kinds of misinterpretations in them." By that she obviously meant the Revised Standard Version, the New English Bible, the Jerusalem Bible, and New American Bible, and Today's English Version (Good News Bible), which were the classic translations available in 1980 that conservative Protestants despised. I had meant to bring my Revised Standard Version, but by accident I had grabbed the King James Version instead. So I thought to myself, "Thank you God, for delivering her into my hand," and thank you Thomas Huxley for that clever statement from the nineteenth century. I said to her, "No, this is a King James Version text, you can read it for yourself." To that she responded, "You've bewitched that Bible," and she ran out of the classroom. I was much younger in those days, so I chased her holding the Bible in my hand, down the hallway, all the time shouting, "You can read the text for yourself. It says the curse was on Canaan, not Ham." She shouted back, "Even devils can quote scripture better than believers." (Teaching college is so much fun.) So here I was chasing a student down a very long hallway calling for her to read the Bible in my hand. I remember that as we passed the history professor, who was standing in his office door, he shouted, "Admirable teaching style, Gnuse, we all do what we can!" (It was sometimes very hard to get students to read their textbooks.) Ultimately she ran out into the parking lot and I lost her; I think she hid under a car. When I returned to the classroom, the other students said, "We get the point; we know why we need to take this course. We are surrounded by people like her." Old beliefs do indeed die hard, especially when they are used to put other people down.

As we come to the end of the stories about Noah there are some interesting observations to be made about this narrative. Literary critics have observed remarkable similarities between Noah and his family and the family of Adam and Eve.

Motifs which have been highlighted include the following: 1) Both Adam and Noah were primeval ancestors of all humanity (Gen 2:7; 9:20). 2) Adam was created from the ground (Gen 2:7–8), Cain farmed the ground (Gen 4:2), and Noah brought relief from the curse on the ground (Gen 5:29) and was removed from the ground by flood. 3) Animals were in Eden and the ark "according to their kind." 4) Animals and people lived first in a garden and later in an ark where they experienced safety. 5) Adam lived with animals, Noah was permitted to eat them (Gen 9:2). 6) Adam ate fruit in the garden (Gen 2:17), Cain produced grain (Gen 4:2), and Noah partook of wine produced from his vineyard (Gen 9:20–21). 7) The consumption of fruit by Adam and grapes/wine by Noah led to difficulties for both. 8) Adam and Noah experienced how their "eyes were opened" (Gen 3:7, 9:22) and their nakedness seen (Gen 3:7; 9:22). 9) Adam and Eve gained knowledge (Gen 3:7), Cain denied knowledge of his brother (Gen 4:9), and Noah lost knowledge while drunk (Gen 9:21). 10) After the human sin, God "came down" both in Eden and at Babel (Gen 3:8; 11:5). 11) As a result of the experiences in Eden (Gen 3:14–19), with the first brothers (Gen 4:11–12), and at Babel there were curses (Gen 9:25–27). 12) Whereas Adam and Cain were cursed by God, Canaan was cursed by a human, Noah, which implies the rise of human autonomy and the withdrawal of God. 13) Both ancestors, Adam and Noah, were told to increase in population as they respectively left the garden and the ark. 14) Both ancestors had children with symbolic eponymous names (Gen 4:1–2; 9:18). 15) Both ancestors had three children, one of whom was cursed. 16) Farming was an occupation of their children (Gen 4:3; 9:20). 17) The children fought each other (Gen 4:4–8; 9:21–23). 18) A curse fell upon one of the children, a brother (Gen 4:11–12; 9:25–26). 19) The one cursed was exiled from the family (Gen 4:16; 9:27). 20) Adam's family gave rise to city culture (through Cain) (Gen 4:17–24), and Noah's family gave rise to kingdoms (Genesis 10). 21) The first world was destroyed by flood, but the second world was allowed to continue to after Babel's sin because God had accepted human sinfulness (Gen 8:21–22). And 22) God feared the line between human and divine would be blurred (Gen 3:22–24; 11:6). In fact, this divine concern arose three times: God feared "they will be like us" in knowledge and immortality (Gen 3:22), God feared the semi-divine beings (Gen 6:1–4), and God feared "nothing will be impossible for them" (Gen 11:6). So respectively God exiled them from the garden (setting a boundary) (Gen 3:23–24), limited their age to one hundred and twenty years (setting a temporal limit) (Gen 6:3), and confused their tongues (preventing a united humanity) (Gen 11:7–9). Whereas the second time God destroyed them all with a flood, the third time God tolerated them and allowed them to build separate civilizations. Throughout these accounts God appears to become more distant and people become morally autonomous. Adam and Eve denied their sin before God, Cain accepted that he sinned, and finally Noah took the place of God in the confrontation with Ham and Canaan and uttered the curse in God's place. (Gros Louis 37–52; Sasson 211–19; R. Cohn 4–6; Niditch 11–69; Steinmetz 193–207, who works with the tri-partite division of Adam, Cain, and Noah; Carr 1996:234–40; Brown 1999:175. Cf. Friedman 7–140 et passim, who traces the theme of the gradual disappearance of God throughout the entire Hebrew Bible.)

As the biblical text moves from the accounts of Noah and his family, we next encounter narratives and genealogies that address group and ethnic concerns. The Tower of Babel speaks of Mesopotamian empires and their imperial concerns. The genealogies address in very symbolic fashion the political and socio-economic scenarios of the ancient Near East and surrounding lands. This ethnic perspective will prepare the audience for God's ultimate choice of Abraham, ancestor of the Hebrews, and the beginning of a new age in human history.

20

Genealogies

Genesis 10:1–32

(1) These are the descendants of Noah's sons, Shem, Ham, and Japheth; children were born to them after the flood. (2) The descendants of Japheth: Gomer, Magog, Madai, Javan, Tubal, Meshech, and Tiras. (3) The descendants of Gomer: Ashkenaz, Riphath, and Togarmah. (4) The descendants of Javan: Elishah, Tarshish, Kittim, and Rodanim. (5) From these the coastland peoples spread. There are the descendants of Japheth in their lands, with their own language, by their families, in their nations. (6) The descendants of Ham: Cush, Egypt, Put, and Canaan. (7) The descendants of Cush: Seba, Havilah, Sabtah, Raamah, and Sabteca. The descendants of Raamah: Sheba and Dedan. (8) Cush became the father of Nimrod; he was the first on earth to become a mighty warrior. (9) He was a mighty hunter before the LORD; therefore it is said, "Like Nimrod a mighty hunter before the LORD." (10) The beginning of his kingdom was Babel, Erech, and Accad, all of them in the land of Shinar. (11) From that land he went into Assyria and built Nineveh, Rehoboth-ir, Calah, and (12) Resen between Nineveh and Calah; that is the great city. (13) Egypt became the father of Ludim, Anamim, Lehabim, Naphtuhim, (14) Pathrusim, Casluhim, and Caphtorim, from which the Philistines come. (15) Canaan became the father of Sidon his firstborn, and Heth, (16) and the Jebusites, the Amorites, the Girgashites, (17) the Hivites, the Arkites, the Sinites, (18) the Arvadites, the Zemarites, and the Hamathites. Afterward the families of the Canaanites spread abroad. (19) And the territory of the Canaanites extended from

Sidon, in the direction of Gerar, as far as Gaza, and in the direction of Sodom, Gomorrah, Admah, and Zeboiim, as far as Lasha. (20) These are the descendants of Ham, by their families, their languages, their lands, and their nations. (21) To Shem also, the father of all the children of Eber, the elder brother of Japheth, children were born. (22) The descendants of Shem: Elam, Asshur, Arpachshad, Lud, and Aram. (23) The descendants of Aram: Uz, Hul, Gether, and Mash. (24) Arpachshad became the father of Shelah; and Shelah became the father of Eber. (25) To Eber were born two sons: the name of the one was Peleg, for in his days the earth was divided, and his brother's name was Joktan. (26) Joktan became the father of Almodad, Sheleph, Hazarmaveth, Jerah, (27) Hadoram, Uzal, Diklah, (28) Obal, Abimael, Sheba, (29) Ophir, Havilah, and Jobab; all these were the descendants of Joktan. (30) The territory in which they lived extended from Mesha in the direction of Sephar, the hill country of the east. (31) These are the descendants of Shem, by their families, their languages, their lands, and their nations. (32) These are the families of Noah's sons, according to their genealogies, in their nations; and from these nations spread abroad on the earth after the flood.

THIS GRAND LIST OF names is often skipped by casual readers of the Bible because it appears boring, full of strange sounding names. But actually genealogies contain fascinating symbolism that communicates sharp political and religious commentary. We cannot appreciate all the hidden messages found therein, for we do not know all the equations for the names. The genealogy mixes names of countries, cities, and individuals in clever fashion. It appears to describe the social, political, and economic world of the sixth century BCE, when the Yahwist Historian wrote. Furthermore, this ethnography of the peoples of the world was undertaken by contemporary Greek historians, including Hecataeus of Miletus in the sixth century BCE and Herodotus in the fifth century BCE, which also impels us to place the Yahwist in this same era. Comparable biblical texts that share names with Genesis 10 include Isa 11:11 (possibly dating from the sixth century BCE), which shares six names, and Isa 66:19 (possibly dating from the fourth century BCE), which shares eight names (Blenkinsopp 2011:156–57).

Critical scholars suppose that the account is composed of two sources. A Yahwist account may be found in verses 8–19, 21, 24–30, and a later Priestly supplement may be found in verses 1–7, 20, 22–23, 31–32. I do not believe this division is really important, for the genealogy is laden with symbolic messages regardless of how we might divide it, and the divisions do not really affect interpretation.

Dividing the peoples of the world into three groups is not a concept unique to this chapter. Such triadic divisions may be found elsewhere. In the genealogy of Cain there are the three sons: Jabal, Jubal, and Tubal-cain. Of greater similarity are the three sons of the Greek flood survivor Deukalion who fathered the three ethnic groups in Greece: Dorians, Ionians, and Aeolians (Blenkinsopp 2011:155).

Various equations of the names may be made. Japheth sounds like Iapetus, the Greek father of Atlas. The descendants of Japheth include: 1) Gomer is Gimirrai in Mesopotamian inscriptions, who are the Cimmerians who lived in Cappadocia, southeastern Turkey. They conquered Urartu (Armenia) in 714 BCE, warred with Esarhaddon of Assyria (681–668 BCE) and lost, then conquered Gugu of Luddi (Gyges of Lydia), and finally settled in Cappadocia. 2) Magog is Gyges of Lydia (central Turkey), a sixth century BCE ruler who was conquered by Cyrus the Great of Persia (c. 550 BCE). 3) Madai are Medes from Persia, who were a major power in the late seventh and early sixth centuries BCE, and they were internally conquered by one of their provinces, Anshan or Persia, and became the Persian Empire under Cyrus. 4) Javan is Ionia, the Greek portion of western Turkey, conquered by Cyrus the Great in the mid sixth century BCE. 5) Tubal may be Cilicia in southeastern Turkey or Tabali in eastern Turkey, or it may refer to the Tibarenians who lived in northern Turkey on the Black Sea. 6) Meshech may be the Moschians who later became Phrygia in central Turkey. 7) Tiras may be the Etruscans in north Italy. The descendants of Gomer include: 1) Ashkenaz, mentioned in Jer 51:27, may refer to south Europe, north of the Black Sea, or it may be an area in the north Euphrates. 2) Riphath is a mystery to us. 3) Togarmah is attested in Hittite texts as area in central Turkey; Assyrians called it Til-garimu. The descendants of Javan include: 1) Elishah is Alashiah or Cyprus or the coast of Asia Minor. 2) Tarshish is Spain in the minds of most, however, the Assyrian king Esarhaddon (680–669 BCE) claims to have conquered as far as Tarshish, which implies it is a city in the Near East. 1 Kgs 10:22 refers to Solomon's fleet that went to Tarshish from Ezion-geber in the Sinai, implying that the site was in the Red Sea. 3) Kittim refers to the city of Kition in Cyprus. 4) Rodanim is the Aegean island of Rhodes (Westermann 504–8; Wenham 1987:218; Hamilton 330–35; Wilson 177, 236).

The descendants of Ham include: 1) Cush is the area south of Egypt, either the Sudan or Ethiopia. 2) Egypt is Egypt, of course. 3) Put has been equated with Somalia or Libya. 4) Canaan is Canaan. Why is Canaan not a descendent of Shem, especially since they are closely connected to the Israelites? Perhaps our biblical author connects Canaan and Egypt because of their trade connections, or because they are both sedentary people living in walled cities, or because of simple geographic proximity, or because the biblical author simply wished to insult the Canaanites by making them descendants of Ham. The descendants of Cush include: 1) Seba is Meroe, a kingdom south of Egypt in the territory of Cush. 2) Havilah is probably Arabia. 3) Sabtah is Sabatah in the Hadramaut, part of south Arabia. 4) Raamah is Ragmat in south Arabia, perhaps. 5) Sabteca may be another name for Sabtah. It could be that Sabtah and Sabteca refer to Ethiopian pharaohs in Egypt from the Twenty-fifth Dynasty, named Sabaka (712–700 BCE) and Sabataka (700–688 BCE). The descendants of Raamah include: 1) Sheba is the area of southwest Arabia. 2) Dedan is a people on the border of Edom according to Jer 25:23; 49:8; Ezek 25:13; 27:5. The descendants of Cush include Nimrod, who has been associated with various kings and deities. He ruled the cities of Babel (Babylon), Erech (Uruk), and Akkad (Akkad) in the land of Shinar (Sumer, which was a title for south Mesopotamia), and then he built cities in Assyria, including Nineveh (Nineveh), Rehoboth-ir (perhaps Nineveh again, for it may refer to undeveloped areas of Nineveh), Calah (Calah), and Resen (perhaps a small city near Nineveh). The descendants of Egypt include: 1) Ludim (Lydians in central Turkey), 2) Anamim (Cyrene on the coast of Libya), 3) Lehabim (Libyans), 4) Naphtuhim (perhaps people from Memphis in Egypt), 5) Pathrusim (perhaps people from Pathros in southern Egypt), 6) Casluhim (perhaps the Delta region in northern Egypt), and 7) Caphtorim (Cyprus). The descendants of Canaan include: 1) Sidon (a chief Phoenician city), 2) Heth (a name for Hittites from Turkey, but Hittites were also in Canaan), 3) Amorites, Girgashites, and Hivites (groups mentioned frequently in the Pentateuch as old inhabitants of Palestine, though Hivites may be Hurrians, an old second millennium BCE population group from north Mesopotamia), 4) Arkites, Sinites, and Zemarites (possibly citizens of small Phoenician cities by those names), 5) Arvadites (citizens of Arvad, a Phoenician city), and 8) Hamathites (residents of Hamath, a Syrian city). Canaanites spread from Sidon on the Phoenician coast to Gerar and Gaza on the southern coast of Palestine. They spread to the east to the cities of the plain south of the Dead Sea, Sodom, Gomorrah, Admah, and Zeboiim, while Lasha may be the tip of a Dead Sea peninsula (Westermann 509–11; Hamilton 335–43). The descendants of Canaan are interesting, because the Jebusites, Amorites, Girgashites, and Hivites are listed elsewhere in the biblical text as ethnic groups that Israel must drive out of Canaan. It has been suggested that these names were added secondarily by Deuteronomic redaction of this text, and perhaps simultaneously the curse on Ham in Genesis 9 was turned into the curse on Canaan, thus justifying a return to the land of Canaan by the sixth century BCE exiled Judeans in Babylon (Carr 1996:161–62, 311).

Nimrod deserves special attention; he has fascinated scholars for years. The image of Nimrod as a hunter is a royal image, since pictorial portrayals of ancient Near Eastern kings often portray them as hunters, protecting the civilized realm from wild animals of the wilderness (Brueggemann 1982:92; Westermann 516). Hermann Gunkel believes that Nimrod was the Sumerian epic hero Gilgamesh of Uruk (Gunkel 90). Some suggest that Nimrod could have been Amenhotep III of Egypt (1416–1379 BCE) who is called Nimmuri in the Amarna tablets (official clay tablet letters sent from Canaanite cities to Egypt in the fourteenth century BCE). Egypt ruled as far north as the Euphrates River under him, and he built massive temples at Luxor and Karnak (van Wolde 156). Ephraim Speiser equates Nimrod with Tulkulti-Ninurta I of Assyria (1246–1206 BCE), who inspired a famous epic and in real life conquered the city of Babylon, which previously was ruled by the Kassites. He was the first Assyrian to conquer Babylon, and he took its king, Kashtiliash IV prisoner. Cush, the father of Nimrod, can be translated as Kas and equated with the Kassites. Furthermore, the city of Calah was built by his father, Shalmaneser I (1272–1243 BCE), and Gen 10:11 says that Nimrod ruled Calah (Speiser 1967:41–52; Hamilton 337). Perhaps Nimrod is Sargon II (721–705 BCE) of Assyria, who made an impression upon Israelites by his conquests and his building of the Assyrian city of Dur-Sharrukin, which he never finished because of his death in battle (shades of the Tower of Babel). Perhaps Ashurbanipal (668–627 BCE), who was closer in time to the biblical author, captured the author's attention by virtue of conquests and cultural achievements (Blenkinsopp 2011:161–62). Josef Scharbert suggests that Nimrod may be the builder of the Tower of Babel, as the Jewish historian Josephus suggested in the first century CE in *Ant* 1:113–119 (Scharbert 112). Otherwise Nimrod is also equated variously with the gods like Marduk of Babylon and Ninurta, a war god, worshipped in both Babylon and Assyria, or with Mesopotamian rulers like Lugalbanda of Sumer (2600 BCE), Sargon I of Akkad (2400 BCE), and Ben-Hadad of Syria (800 BCE) (Speiser 1967:41–52; Wenham 1987:222). Speculation like this is fun for scholars. Generally Nimrod is viewed as a negative persona, but Robert Kawashima views Nimrod positively as a "warrior hunter before the Lord" who is good and thus contrasts with Lamech the Cainite (Kawashima 494). Perhaps it is a coincidence, but Nimrod is connected to both Shinar and Babylon, and both words occur in Genesis 11, thus creating a literary link between these two chapters, not to mention creating the suspicion again that Nimrod was the builder of the Tower in Genesis 11 (Blenkinsopp 2011:169).

The descendants of Shem were important, since Israel belonged to this group. Shem's descendants include: 1) Elam (Elam), 2) Asshur (Assyria), 3)

Arpachshad (probably Babylon or perhaps city of Kirkuk in north Mesopotamia), 4) Lud (who knows!), 5) and Aram (Syria). The descendants of Aram include: 1) Uz (perhaps is a place in Edom), and 2) Hul, Gether, and Mash (Aramean tribes in Syria). Arpachshad fathered Shelah (a family who ruled in Moab according to 1 Chron 4:21–23), who fathered Eber (a name for Hebrews), who fathered Peleg and Joktan. Joktan fathered a list of apparent desert tribes south and east of Israel in Saudi Arabia, including Almodad (a south Arabian people), Sheleph (an area in Yemen), Hazarmaveth (a people in the Wadi Hadramaut of Saudi Arabia), Jerah (another group in the Wadi Hadramaut), Hadoram (possibly Yemen), Uzal (old name of Sanaa, a city in Yemen, or Azalla, a city near Medina), Diklah (which means "date palm grove," an oasis), Obal (perhaps Obal in Yemen), Abimael (who knows!), Sheba (southwest Arabia again), Ophir (perhaps a city in Arabia or Somalia), Havilah (Arabia again), and Jobab (a city near Mecca) (Westermann 511–12, 527; Hamilton 343–48).

This list appears to be a sixth century BCE list, because Israel only knew most of these peoples from the seventh century BCE onward. Many of these regions would have significance for Israel as part of the Persian Empire in the early sixth century BCE, especially the coast of Ionia and the Aegean islands (Westermann 509). This entire list is also reminiscent of the *Theogony* of Hesiod from the sixth century BCE (Gunkel 87–88).

This grand list of descendants sired by Noah's three sons encompasses the peoples of the ancient Near East and parts of the Aegean world. Over the years many people commonly assumed that the three sons were fathers of the three great races. Japheth is father of the Indo-European peoples, Ham is father of the African peoples, and Shem is father of the Semitic peoples. In this regard, the *Historia Brittonum* and Isidore of Seville in the seventh century equated the three sons of Noah with Europe, Africa, and the Middle East (von Woude 151). Those equations, however, are rendered inaccurate with a close and careful reading of the text.

Japheth's descendants appear to have connections to the Indo-Europeans who migrated into the Middle East in the second millennium BCE, and Shem's descendants appear to be part of the southwest Semitic groups of peoples, but Ham's descendants are an unusual mixture. The descendants of Ham include the inhabitants of Egypt, Arabia, and Phoenicia. To be sure, Egyptians have Hamitic or African blood. Modern scholars assess ancient Egyptians to have been 70 percent African, 20 percent Semitic, and 10 percent Berber on the basis of DNA analysis of mummies. (In fact, that is the same mixture that we would find among modern day Egyptians, for they are pretty much the same people who have lived in Egypt for thousands of years.) However, the list of Ham's descendants includes Arabs, who are clearly Semitic. Furthermore, special attention is paid to the descendants of Canaan, which includes the Canaanites and the Phoenicians, who are also clearly Semitic. Thus, the genealogical list is not ethnic or racial; it rather appears to be very geographic. Japheth's descendants live in the north and the Aegean region; Ham's descendants live throughout the fertile-crescent; and Shem's descendants are Israelites and their immediate neighbors. Some commentators have interpreted the three races as economic life-styles: the Japhethites are sea-going peoples mostly, the Hamites are sedentary dwelling in significant urban centers of the fertile-crescent, and the Shemites appear to be nomadic, pastoralist, or settled in simple villages.

The list appears to me to be very political and it reflects the political map of the mid-sixth century BCE. The descendants of Japheth appear to live in areas controlled by the Persian Empire under Cyrus the Great around 550 BCE after he conquered Lydia and controlled Asia Minor to the Aegean. The descendants of Ham and Shem appear to be the areas controlled by the Chaldean Babylonian Empire before that empire was conquered by Cyrus in 540 BCE. Ham also appears to be Egypt and those folk economically connected to Egypt. Thus, loosely speaking Japheth might be Persia in the north, Shem might be Babylon in the center, and Ham might be Egypt in the south. It looks like a child's primer for politics and geography of that age. Of course, the descendants of Shem particularly include Israelites and related folk who have been conquered by Babylon.

The latter part of the sixth century BCE is the time when scholars suggest the Yahwist Historian may have written the Primeval History. If so, this list may have been a source used by that historian, and it reflects a very narrow window of time between when Cyrus the Great conquered Asia Minor and before he took the city of Babylon and absorbed the Chaldean Empire in 540 BCE. A political and economic interpretation makes sense to me, as does the possibility that this list might have been a teaching tool for young scribal students who used it as a writing exercise. Its style reminds me of a learning experience on *Sesame Street*.

Did this list have an ideological message in its formulation before the Yahwist Historian adopted it? Did the Yahwist Historian add some significant editorial comments? The one editorial comment that stands out is the reference to Nimrod, the mighty hunter. It is stated that he was the father of Babel. The story of Babel follows this genealogy in the ensuing chapter, wherein we sense that Babel is the symbol for over-weaning and tyrannical Mesopotamian empires, especially the Chaldean Empire of the sixth century BCE. This is a veiled commentary on rulers and tyrants, of which Nimrod was the first. Erech or Uruk was a venerable old Sumerian city, and archaeologists indicate that it was already a prominent city of wealth and authority as early as pre-Sumerian times around 5000 BCE. Akkad was the first true empire in Mesopotamia under the leadership of Sargon the Great around 2400 BCE. Our biblical sources know some ancient history of Mesopotamia (which would have been available to educated scribes in the sixth century BCE). This little section may have been added by the Yahwist as veiled political commentary on the tyrannical powers that ruled in Mesopotamia.

21

History Behind Babel

THERE ARE FEW ANCIENT Near Eastern literary parallels to this account. A fragmentary myth tells of how Enki will restore unity of language to all people in the future, and the tale concludes, ". . . endowed with wisdom, the Lord of Eridu, will change all existing languages in their mouth, and then the language of mankind will be one" (Beyerlin 87). It may not be a good parallel, since the story describes the reverse of what happens in the biblical text. Some commentators read this myth differently and suggest that the story line reads that once all people used the same language to worship Enlil, but Enki's rivalry with Enlil led Enki to confuse the tongues of people. Enlil wished to destroy humanity, but Enki saved people by the proposal to confuse their language instead. It is worth noting there is no reference to a building (Kramer 1968:108–11; Vawter 152; Watermann 539; Uehlinger 409–26; Van Seters 183). This reminds us of the plot line in the Babylonian flood narrative, *Atrahasis Epic*, wherein Enlil proposes ways to limit human population, but Enki saves people. If their reading is correct, then the story more closely corresponds to the biblical flood narrative. However, it is probably the first reading that is more accurate.

The Sumerian tale, *Enmerkar and the Lord of Aratta*, makes allusions to the one language that all of humanity someday might be able to speak, which originally was created by Enlil (lines 145–46, 154–55), "Yea, the whole world of well ruled people, Will be able to speak to Enlil in one language! . . . Change the tongues in their mouth, as many as he once placed there, And the speech of mankind shall be truly one!" (Vanstiphout 65). This reinforces the first interpretation of the Enki myth previously discussed, for the hope is expressed in both for a future unity of all languages.

In Mesopotamia the diversity of languages is seen as a problem that must be overcome. The myth about Enlil envisions everyone speaking Sumerian someday so that all people may worship Enlil. In the biblical text, diversity of language was necessary as an antidote to human pride and the necessary corollary to spreading people across the world to reproduce (Wenham 1987:231, 237). The Mesopotamians envisioned the ideal as one unified language spoken by all people after they were amalgamated into one great empire. The little country of Israel and the later Judeans did not desire to be absorbed into one empire, so they envisioned everyone having their own language, and by implication, their own independent state. Diversity may really be about human freedom from tyrannical empires. Diversity may still be connected to human freedom today.

A somewhat related story comes from India. In the Vedas the story is recounted how the storm god Indra pulls out a brick from a building to cause that building to collapse so as to overthrow the rulers (Westermann 538). Ironically, this account has the building motif that the Mesopotamian accounts lack.

In general, the story of Babel has much in common with social and political events of the ancient Near East. Mesopotamian kings often built great ziggurats and temples, and they used slave labor, debt slaves, and frequently prisoners of war, in these construction projects. Prisoners of war and foreign exiles, forcibly marched to Mesopotamia from distant lands after successful military campaigns, could provide the labor pool for such monumental building projects. One could expect to hear a cacophony of languages spoken at one of these major building projects. An inscription by Nebuchadnezzar II emphasizes this clearly,

> I called unto me the far dwelling peoples over whom Marduk my Lord had appointed me and whose care was given unto me by Shamash the hero, from all lands and of every inhabited place from the upper sea to the lower sea from distant lands the people of far away habitations kings of distant mountains and remote regions who dwell at the upper and the nether seas with whose strength Marduk the Lord has filled my hands that they should bear his yoke and also the subjects of Shamash and Marduk I summoned to build Eteminanki. (Smith-Christopher 67)

This quote is extremely significant, since Nebuchadnezzar II destroyed Jerusalem in 586 BCE and dragged off many Judeans into the Babylonian Exile (586–539 BCE). His references to foreign peoples most certainly included the Judeans. The Eteminanki or Etemenanki was the great temple ziggurat in Babylon; in Sumerian its name means "house of the foundations of heaven and earth" (Skinner 228; Bertman 13). One begins to wonder if the Etemenanki was the so-called "Tower of Babel" in Genesis 11 (Van Seters 183; Blenkinsopp 2011:166). When Babylon fell to the Persians, and subsequently the Persians allowed exiled people to return home, the allusion in Genesis 11 to the scattered peoples might refer to the return of so many exiles, including Judeans, to their homes.

Nebuchadnezzar II wished to rebuild Babylon after the devastation the city received in the previous century from the Assyrian king Sennacherib in 689 B.C.E. Nebuchadnezzar II restored both the Etemenanki ziggurat and the Esagila temple, which was next to the ziggurat. Esagila means "the house that lifts its head," and this may be spoofed by the biblical text's reference to how the tower had "its top in the heavens" (Gen 11:4). Esagila was just south of the great ziggurat. The massive ziggurat was three hundred feet square and three hundred feet high with seven levels, which represented the five plants, the sun, and the moon (Bertman 13, 197, 316). Nebuchadnezzar also restored the Ezida temple, which was dedicated to the god Nebo and located at the city of Borsippa across the river from Babylon, and the memory of these two projects could have merged in the minds of people and the biblical author.

The ziggurat was the symbol of a stairway to the heavens and it represented the cosmic mountain, the place where the priests could ascend and meet the gods. This sacred mountain may have been seen to rise above the symbolic floodwaters of chaos to the heavens as it visibly rose up from the flood plain of the Tigris and Euphrates Rivers. Genesis 11 alludes to this with the reference to the tower's top in the heavens. Though Mesopotamians would never speak of "storming the heavens" with their ziggurat, Israelites and Judeans might speak with rhetorical sarcasm about a ziggurat being an attempt to get into the divine realm, thus "storming the heavens" (Skinner 226; Bertman 197).

Mesopotamians believed that the gods dwelt on a great cosmic mountain somewhere, and their ziggurat symbolized that cosmic mountain within the confines of their own city. Ziggurats functioned as temples, and some famous ziggurats were built in powerful cities. Mesopotamian rulers considered it one of their chief responsibilities to build and refurbish temple ziggurats in their cities, especially in the capitals of empires.

We have discovered over thirty ziggurats in Mesopotamia. The earliest ziggurats were built by the Sumerian king Ur-Nammu of Ur (2000 BCE) in Eridu, Nippur, Uruk, and most importantly, in Ur (Bertman 21, 109, 194). The Amorite king Hammurabi of Babylon (1750 BCE) built one in his capital, and the later king Nebuchadnezzar I of the Second Sealand Dynasty of Isin (1100 BC) likewise built one in Babylon. All three of these kings built

History Behind Babel 251

their great ziggurats in the capital of their empires, thus implying that their capital city was the abode of the gods, who were present on these symbolic cosmic mountains. Their capital city, Babylon, was the center or the "navel" of the earth, and the ziggurat was built upon that exact center. As mentioned above, Nebuchadnezzar II of Chaldean Babylon repaired the Etemenanki ziggurat that initially was built by Hammurabi and later Nebuchadnezzar I. Also, Nabonidus of Chaldean Babylon repaired this and other ziggurats, as well as undertaking the building of temples and other religious structures in Ur, Babylon, and Haran (550 BCE).

When we look at historical parallels, commentators over the years have been tempted to associate the so-called Tower of Babel with various kings in Mesopotamian history who built significant ziggurats, as well as other settings. An old theory suggests that the story recalls some particular ruined ziggurat observed by Semitic nomads in their wanderings, and they wove a tale to explain its ruined condition (Simpson 563). Paul Seely suggests the account describes a ziggurat and an event between 3500 and 2400 BCE, and the scattering refers to the disruption of Sumerian culture by the Akkadian empire under Sargon (Seely 15–38). Years ago when commentators did a literal chronology of the biblical patriarchs and placed Abraham around 1800 BCE, they suspected that the ziggurat of Ur-Nammu in the southern city of Ur (2000 BCE) inspired the story. More recently Dale De-Witt believes the account recalls the ziggurat of Ur-Nammu and the collapse of the Sumerian Dynasty of Ur III around 1950 BCE, for this was the time when Sumerian culture deteriorated and Sumerians were scattered by the entrance into Mesopotamia of the Amorites (DeWitt 15–26). If scholars place Abraham's dates a little later, they point to Hammurabi's ziggurat (1750 BCE). A generation ago scholars believed that the stories in Genesis 2–11 were written down sometime during the reign of king Solomon (950 BCE), so they pointed to the ziggurat of Nebuchadnezzar I (1100 BCE). Currently biblical scholars suspect that the stories in Genesis 2–11 may have been written down during the time of the Babylonian Exile, so they point to the work of the Chaldean Babylonian kings, Nabopolasar (626–605 BCE), Nebuchadnezzar II (605–562 BCE), or Nabonidus (556–539 BCE). Ulrich Berges believes that Genesis 11 refers in general to various Assyrian and Chaldean ziggurats in the eighth through the sixth centuries BCE (Berges 37–56). As mentioned above, Nebuchadnezzar II conquered Jerusalem and took the Judeans into exile. As he refurbished the great Etemenanki ziggurat in Babylon with slave labor, Jewish exiles would have worked on it. Some authors suggest that the older Esagila temple may have inspired the story, if they date Genesis 11 to a slightly earlier time than Nebuchadnezzar, or the Ezida temple ziggurat in the city of Borsippa, which is near Babylon, because that ziggurat was exceedingly large and dramatic in appearance (Skinner 228; Vawter 157). Many authors simply believe the story is more a negative theological commentary on the building of ziggurats in general, and the ideology behind their creation.

I developed arguments in favor of late sixth-century-BCE Chaldean Babylon as the setting for this story, and the work of Nabonidus in particular. This chapter is an expansion of part of that article (Gnuse 2010:229–44). Several scholars share my ideas by likewise dating the story to the late sixth century BCE. José Croatto thinks it is a sixth century BCE judgment oracle against Babylon (Croatto 65–80). Gershon Hepner believes the tower parodies the destroyed Temple in Jerusalem during the sixth-century-BCE Babylonian Exile of the Judeans (Hepner 85–131). Alberto Soggin suggests that the story is a post-exilic satire on the fall of Babylon in 539 BCE (Soggin 371–75).

Christoph Uehlinger provides the most detailed analysis of this passage, suggesting that the account evolved over the years and spoke to four different historical situations. The primary inspiration for the account was the building effort of Sargon II of Assyria in the late eighth century BCE at the new city of Dur-Sharrukin. Uehlinger points out that Genesis 11 speaks both of a "city" and a "tower," so that if we focus exclusively on the tower, we think of a ziggurat, when instead we should look for an entire newly built city—Dur-Sharrukin. The city bears the name of Sargon II, thus adding meaning to the biblical expression "making a name." Mesopotamian kings, especially neo-Assyrian rulers, undertook naming cities after themselves as a way of immortalizing themselves—the immortality hinted at in the biblical text. Dur-Sharrukin was built by slaves and deportees, and they were to be the people who would inhabit this city. The city was never finished because Sargon II died in battle, and his body was lost. His death may have inspired prophetic oracles in Isaiah 14 and Ezekiel 28, which speak of the king who defied God and was thrown down (and thus his body was lost). Isaiah 14, in turn, may have inspired the creation of Genesis 11. Assyrian inscriptions speak of how when people speak "one language," it is the sign of a strong ruler who has brought all people together in peace and unity. Assyrians tried to make all their subjects speak the common language of Aramaic. Inscriptions by Sargon II indicate that this concept of common language and a united people was part of his agenda and connected with the construction of his new city, Dur-Sharrukin. Thus, Uehlinger emphasizes that behind Genesis 11 is the political propaganda of the eighth century BCE neo-Assyrian empire and Sargon II especially (Uehlinger 419–546).

Uehlinger also recognizes that the chapter has a later history. He notes that references to "brick" and "bitumen" in verse 3 and the reference to

Babel and scattering in verse 9 allude to later times. In the mid-seventh century BCE the Assyrian king Esarhaddon rebuilt Babylon and built the Etemenanki. In a second stage the story could refer to Esarhaddon, or perhaps later kings like the Assyrian king Ashurbanipal, the Chaldean king Nabopolasar, or the Chaldean king Nebuchadnezzar II, all who refurbished the Etemenanki. Nebuchadnezzar II especially sought to make a name for himself with building projects. At a third stage the story becomes part of a pre-Priestly Primeval History, in which Genesis 11 is connected to Genesis 2–3 and 6:1–4 as stories about the timeless experience of human sin and punishment. In a fourth and final stage the narrative, as used by the Priestly author, alludes to the Persian Empire of the fifth century BCE, especially with the addition of the "table of nations" in Genesis 10, which has allusions that fit that era (Uehlinger 546–84).

I like Uehlinger's conclusions, but I believe he underestimates the importance of the sixth century BCE Chaldean Babylonian setting, and Nabonidus in particular (whom he ignores in favor of discussing Nabopolasar and Nebuchadnezzar). I believe Nabonidus is the target of criticism by the "final" version of the narrative, even if there were earlier editions as Uehlinger suggests. Uehlinger too easily dismisses the Chaldean setting, in general, by saying that Genesis 11 refers to a "city," and the Chaldeans built and refurbished ziggurats, the Etemenanki in particular, but not a city. I would respond by saying Chaldeans indeed refurbished cities. I believe the Etemenanki, as the tower, could also symbolize the entire city of Babylon in the mind of the biblical author. Besides, there is the clear reference to Babylon in Genesis 11. Uehlinger may be correct about the initial connection to Sargon II, but the final connection to Nabonidus deserves closer attention.

I believe the historical background behind Genesis 11 in its final form is the sixth century BCE Chaldean Babylonian Empire, the building projects of Nabonidus—the last king of Chaldean Babylon, and the experience of the Judeans in exile (586–539 BCE). If so, the underlying message of Genesis 11 is more political than we have suspected. The text has a strong polemic not only against Babylonian religious and political beliefs, but also against the role of Babylonian kings, and kings in general. The tower represents imperial building projects, the symbolic expression of pride and a manifest physical symbol of the religious and political ideology that under-girded the empire.

In recent years, however, some scholars propose that the story does not condemn great building projects or human accomplishments. Kawashima believes Genesis 11 recalls the once "limitless potential that went strangely unrealized" in Mesopotamia where there was "seamless cooperation underlying the most impressive undertaking" (a ziggurat), which "suggests a moral order" (Kawashima 493). The account may affirm human accomplishments and the generation of human culture, for Genesis 4 likewise seems to do this (Westermann 56-62, 330-44; Kawashima 491-92). But if so, I believe the narrative is in a dialectic mode, so that human accomplishments are praiseworthy, but when humanity exhibits a pride that defies God, then the projects are worthy of condemnation (von Rad 148-49; Westermann 554-55). One almost can sense in this narrative the historical experience of Mesopotamians in the fourth millennium BCE. With the rise of the organized state or city-state, monumental building projects were created, kingship emerged (though exercised by priests at first), and writing appeared. The account hints that monumental building projects were a reflection of the early stages of state formation in the river valleys. Even if the Israelite author knew this old memory; nonetheless, the story is cast in order to criticize the arrogance of Mesopotamians. If the account comes from the Babylonian Exile of the sixth century BCE, our biblical author has a negative view of these Mesopotamians.

Nabonidus engaged in many building projects not only in Babylon, but he repaired temples and sanctuaries throughout Mesopotamia, paying special attention to his patron deity, the moon-god Sin. He refurbished the Etemenanki, after Nebuchadnezzar's extensive work. This edifice had been rebuilt partially by the Assyrian king Esarhaddon in the early seventh century BCE, after the earlier Assyrian king Sennacherib destroyed the venerable Esagila temple and its complex when he razed Babylon. Etemenanki was a new name for the rebuilt temple complex from this time onward. Our oldest reference to the name, Etemenanki, is in an Assyrian literary work called the *Erra Epic* (765 BCE). The Assyrian king Ashurbanipal destroyed the temple complex yet again in the mid seventh century BCE. With the fall of Assyria to Chaldean Babylon in 612 BCE, Nabopolasar began rebuilding the temple complex in the late seventh century BCE, and both Nebuchadnezzar and Nabonidus more seriously refurbished it in the sixth century BCE. With such a dramatic history, one might suspect the Etemenanki inspired the Tower of Babel story (Skinner 228; Van Seters 182-83; Gnuse 2010:238-39), and Nabonidus was the last king to work on this edifice. Herodotus (*Histories* 1:181-82) describes the ruins of the edifice in the fifth century BCE. So passes the glory of the world.

Nabonidus engaged in building renovations because he believed that the gods were still angry with the revenge visited upon the Assyrians in the previous century for their destruction of sacred sites. He believed the gods desired more temple rebuilding. In addition to his work on the Etemenanki, Nabonidus repaired the Eanna sanctuary in Uruk, the Ebabbara temple in Sippar, the Egipar temple in Ur (which refurbished the old ziggurat temple site of Ur-Nammu dedicated to the moon god, Sin), and most importantly for him, the Ehulhul Temple of Sin in Haran (Gnuse 2010:238-39).

He was particularly concerned with reconstruction of temples outside of Babylon, sometime on the periphery of his empire, such as Haran and Ur. This alienated his support in the city of Babylon itself, and may have paved the way for his ultimate demise before the onslaught of Cyrus of Persia. Rebuilding temples in Haran and Ur to the moon god, Sin, caused so much consternation in Babylon, that a revolt occurred among his subjects in 553-552 BCE, which led to a temporary suspension of building projects. However, in 546 BCE and thereafter, he resumed building projects at Larsa and Haran. He even attempted to introduce the worship of Sin in the Marduk temple in Babylon, which obviously alienated the powerful priestly families (Albertz 2003b:59-68; Gnuse 2010:238-39). This may provide the background to the story of the unfinished tower in Genesis 11.

Nabonidus was king when the Chaldean Babylonian Empire fell to the Persians under Cyrus the Great in 540 BCE. Because Cyrus subsequently allowed exiled peoples to return to their homes, including the Judeans in 539 BCE, one could say that with the demise of Nabonidus, workers on the "Tower of Babel" symbolically were scattered across the earth when they returned to their original homes.

We notice also how Abraham moved through three cities in which Nabonidus did construction—Ur, Babylon (by inference), and Haran (Gen 11:31-12:5), which is quite a coincidence. In those cities Nabonidus built to the honor of Sin, the moon god, and the names in Abraham's extended family indicate they were worshippers of the moon god. Thus, Abraham is connected to two cities famous for devotion to the moon god, Ur and Haran, which seems to be more than a coincidence (Skinner 238-39; Gnuse 2010:240). Nabonidus was a Chaldean, and Abraham came from Ur of the Chaldees. The biblical text clearly says "Chaldees" twice in reference to Abraham's home city (Gen 11:28, 31), and that name would have been connected to Ur or Babylon only during a short period of history in the age of the Chaldean Babylonian empire (625-540 BCE). One final detail, which may be a coincidence, is an interesting word play. In Gen 11:3 the people say, "let us burn bricks," an unusual way of describing the preparation of bricks. The word for Ur can also mean "fire" or "flame," so perhaps, Gen 11:3 subtly alludes to Ur of the Chaldees (Kugel and Greer 88; Gnuse 2010:240-41). Abraham accounts might parody the times of Nabonidus, ruler during the Babylonian Exile, so that Abraham became a symbol of returning exiles after 539 BCE.

In later literature, Nebuchadnezzar (Daniel 4) and Nabonidus (Dead Sea Scrolls document, *The Prayer of Nabonidus*) are portrayed as kings who went insane. Originally this attribution belonged to Nabonidus, who was seen as insane because he fled Babylon and stayed in the Arabian desert city of Tema during the Persian attack, and because he ignored the cult of Marduk of Babylon for his patron deity, Sin. Both Babylonians and subsequently Persians portrayed him as insane and disrespectful of tradition. Nebuchadnezzar in Daniel 4 is really the Nabonidus of history. Nebuchadnezzar's name was used at that later date, since he was the king who destroyed Jerusalem and the Temple in 586 BCE, and his name was more known in later years. However, since negative traditions continued to exist about Nabonidus in later years in Jewish literature, perhaps the Tower of Babel story originally might have been a parody on the times and actions of Nabonidus (Gnuse 2010:242–43).

22

The Tower of Babel and Beyond

THE TOWER

Genesis 11:1–9

(1) Now the whole earth had one language and the same words. (2) And as they migrated from the east, they came upon a plain in the land of Shinar and settled there. (3) And they said to one another, "Come let us make bricks, and burn them thoroughly." And they had brick for stone, and bitumen for mortar. (4) Then they said, "Come, let us build ourselves a city, and a tower with its top in the heavens, and let us make a name for ourselves; otherwise we shall be scattered abroad upon the face of the whole earth." (5) The LORD came down to see the city and the tower, which mortals had built. (6) And the LORD said, "Look, they are one people, and they have all one language; and this is only the beginning of what they will do; nothing that they propose to do will now be impossible for them. (7) Come, let us go down, and confuse their language there, so that they will not understand one another's speech." (8) So the LORD scattered them abroad from there over the face of all the earth, and they left off building the city. (9) Therefore it was called Babel, because there the LORD confused the language of all the earth; and from there the LORD scattered them abroad over the face of all the earth.

THE STORY SHOWS NO awareness of Noah's three sons, implying that people are a unified folk migrating from the east. Commentators suggest this short story was a separate oral tradition or creative composition by the biblical author with special religious and political meaning. If one harmonizes the account with the previous narratives, the conclusion must be that the descendants of the three sons have not separated yet. But why not at least mention them? If they were still alive, and if they were righteous enough to survive the flood (except for Ham, now), why did they not stop this building activity? We must not be too logical with these stories, lest we create problems that are not really in the accounts. This story requires that we not work with the model of the three sons and their descendants. The narrative is a parable with a particular message, and the plot line did not require reference to Noah's three sons. It could be that the author deliberately places Genesis 10 with its testimony of human diversity in language prior to Genesis 11 with its monolithic unity of one language to imply that Genesis 10 testifies to the natural human condition that must be restored by God when the divine intervention diversifies the languages. If so, this is criticism of the Assyrian and Babylonian attempts to make all people speak one language (Middleton 224–27).

Commentators several generations ago assumed there were originally two stories woven together: an early account about the building of a tower with a subsequent dispersion of the people, and a later narrative about the building of a city and the confusion of tongues (Gunkel 94–103; Westermann 536–38). More recent commentators view the narrative as a unity and as a well-balanced composition.

They come to Shinar. Shinar is the Semitic way of pronouncing Sumer, the name of the southern part of Mesopotamia. Sumerians were culturally predominant in southern Mesopotamia in the third millennium BCE, but the land would continue to be called the "land of Sumer" or the "land of Sumer and Akkad" down into the first millennium BCE by Assyrians and Chaldean Babylonians. "Sumer" generally referred to the deep southern part of Mesopotamia and "Akkad" referred more to the central or north-central regions of Mesopotamia. Our biblical author implies that the people came to the deep southern part of Mesopotamia, for the historical consciousness of Mesopotamians in the first millennium BCE was that in the deep southern part of Mesopotamia the oldest cities in the world were founded. (Historically that was not true; the earliest simple villages were in the north, the more developed urban centers arose in the south subsequently.) The people come from the "east." Where is this eastern land from whence they come? The mountains of Ararat are actually to the northwest of the land of lower Mesopotamia. So they are not coming from the region of the Ark. Some

The Tower of Babel and Beyond 259

Mesopotamian traditions, especially old Sumerian traditions, spoke of their origin in the east, that is, the mountains of Persia, the Zagros. Most Sumerian and later Mesopotamian traditions, however, spoke of their origin on the sacred island of Dilmun (modern-day Bahrain) in the Persian Gulf, or of their origin from the coastlands on the southwestern side of the Persian Gulf. So we are a little puzzled by the reference to the "eastern" origin. But from the perspective of the biblical author, whose home was in the far west of Palestine, the reference to the origin in the east may be simply a loose generic reference to places "over there" in and around the Mesopotamian valley.

The people build the tower, which by itself is a significant statement. In the *Enuma Elish* vi.59–64 the gods build the first ziggurat or temple for Marduk after his victory over Tiamat. They mold these bricks for a full year. (Gods are rather slow; no wonder they "invent" people to do work.) This first "ziggurat" is built by people according to the biblical author. Even though their actions are not a good thing, nonetheless the story debunks the Mesopotamian gods, because this activity is attributed to human hands not to divine beings. Perhaps it also implies that the biblical builders of the tower aspire to be like the gods (Blenkinsopp 2011:166–67). There are interesting similarities between the accounts. In both narratives there is a decision to make bricks, the building of a tower, and an emphasis on the tower's height. It seems that the biblical author yet again parodies and critiques the *Enuma Elish* and demythologizes the mythic worldview (Westermann 545; Lim 132; Kass 226).

The people use brick for stone and bitumen for mortar, thus reflecting our author's Palestinian perspective. In Palestine people built city walls and large buildings with stone and mortar, but in Mesopotamia brick and bitumen were used. Our author thus explains the construction materials to a Palestinian audience. Some commentators assume the author must be in Palestine speaking to Judeans, but our author could be in Babylon speaking to Judeans in exile, simply comparing the respective building practices of both regions.

In verse 4 we hear the builders speak, but we really hear the biblical author telling us how they sin by building this tower. The people say, "Come let us make brick, and burn them thoroughly," "Come, let us build ourselves a city, and a tower with its top in the heavens," and "Let us make a name for ourselves." Three times they say, "let us," a verb form common in the Hebrew Bible, which would not draw our attention, except for the fact that in Gen 1:26 God says, "Let us make humankind in our own image." Does the biblical author evoke for us the memory of the creation in this story about the tower? Now humanity seeks to "create" with the same language by which

God speaks (Cotter 68). In Gen 1:26 the verb is *'asah*, "to make," whereas here the verb is *banah*, "to build," and both verbs are in the cohortative first person plural form. Has humanity begun to usurp the role of God as creator? Elsewhere in Genesis 1–11 people create many things, the foundational elements of human culture, and it is not seen as evil. Is there something about this creative activity that is evil, does it usurp the role of God more than any other creative activity? Is it because with this creative act people seek to enter into the divine realm in some way? Are they attempting to return to the garden from which the man and the woman were exiled? We sense these people seek to blur the distinction between themselves and the divine by their actions, and we are reminded of how the boundary between the divine and the human is blurred in Gen 6:1–4 (Cotter 75). (We shall notice other similarities between these two stories again.) After the people say, "let us . . ." three times, then God will say, "let us . . ." and put an end to their work. One gets the impression that the author wishes us to see the efforts of the people and the response of God in juxtaposition.

Another hint that we should compare Genesis 1 and Genesis 11 is that both God and the builders of Babel work with dirt. God uses *'adamah*, the "red earth," to make man, the people use dirt or mud (the word is not used in the biblical text) to make "bricks." The Hebrew word for brick, *levenah*, comes from the word for "white," *lavan*. Red is the color of blood, or life, white is the color of corpses or death. (The word white is associated also with the worship of the moon, and moon worship is hinted at in conjunction with Abraham's family.) We have a contrast between the "red earth" used by God, and the "white bricks" used by people. Perhaps our author compares the creative activity of God with the reversal of creation undertaken by these people (Kass 225–26).

The people declare their intent to build a tower that will be so tall that its "top" will be in the heavens. It sounds as though they simply have ambitious architects until we realize what the idiom actually means. They want their building to reach into the "heavens" so that they will be able to go into the "heavens." It is no coincidence that the name of the Babylonian tower, the "Etemenanki," means the "House of the Foundation of Heaven and Earth," which implies the building connects the earthy realm with the heavenly realm. Temples were believed to have their foundations in the underworld and their tops in the heavenly realm. In their inscriptions both Nabopollasar and Nebuchadnezzar II claim that their building projects "rival the heavens" (Westermann 547; Wenham 1987:237; Kass 229). Our biblical author boldly criticizes imperial Babylonian penchant for great buildings, especially major temple building projects. Major building projects were the most impressive display of power and wealth in the ancient world.

Why would they want to go into the heavens? The ancients told stories of great heroes who went into the divine realm, and usually those heroes stole powerful gifts. In Mesopotamian mythology Etana ascends to the heavens and brings the institution of kingship to earth. In Greek mythology Prometheus steals fire from the gods and brings it to humanity and is punished by being chained to a stone forever while birds peck out his liver. The builders of Babel wish to storm the divine realm. The biblical author may imply that they are the heroes of old, like Etana. Perhaps, these builders think that they are returning to the Garden of Eden, which they believe is in the heavens. Many ancients believed the gods lived on top of a great mountain inaccessible to people. Eden, the place where people met God, as we recall, could be envisioned as being on a mountain. Perhaps the builders think they are reconstructing the divine mountain upon which Eden could be located, and thereby they might have contact with God. More likely, it is not simple, pious contact with God that they desire; they want the divine gifts of knowledge that brings power and immortality. If so, they want to storm the heavens and seize the divine prerogatives. That, of course, is what Etana does when he goes up to the divine realm and brings kingship to earth for the Mesopotamians. Commentators sense that building a tower whose top goes into the heavens is an act of human pride, which aspires to the gifts of the divine realm; they want to be like the gods, or they want to be gods.

Of similar ilk is the statement, "and let us make a name for ourselves." We could hear this expression and understand it to mean that they desire to have a good reputation for themselves in future years. Indeed, that was part of the understanding expressed in these words in ancient Mesopotamia. But in Mesopotamian literature, "making a name for oneself," also means to attain a certain degree of immortality, and perhaps even achieving a limited degree of divine status by becoming a great hero. In Mesopotamian culture the hope of an afterlife was not a cheerful thing; they expected their spirits or shades to descend to the underworld and slowly fade away in a rather dismal existence. Thus, in some of the literature, such as the *Gilgamesh Epic*, the attainment of a great reputation, or making a name for oneself, was another way for great people to achieve a long lasting legacy. Average people made a name for themselves by having children; kings made a name and lasting fame with their building projects and by waging war (Gunkel 96). Kings and great heroes were believed to be close to divine or semi-divine status, so their attempts to attain such a "name" that would last throughout the ages was considered appropriate. The builders of the tower say they wish to make a name that will last throughout the ages. Idioms like "to make a name for oneself" and a building with "its top in the sky" appear in Mesopotamian building inscriptions frequently (Kramer 1968:108–11; Lim 182), so one takes special notice when the same language appears in this story.

Kings of any age seek to do that which is powerful and heroic, and above all, they aspire to accomplish something semi-divine. All the more, we see the builders trespass upon the domain of God as they engage in the actions of kings and tyrants. Throughout the Primeval History our biblical author has naught but disdain for such people and their endeavors.

The builders declare that they build this tower lest they be scattered across the face of the earth. The earlier statements about building a tower into the heavens and making a name exhibit their arrogance and pride, their desire to aspire to divine status. But now they display absolute disregard for God. God told them to spread across the earth and reproduce so that the earth might be filled with people. This was the imperative in Gen 9:7 where the family of Noah was commanded, "be fruitful and multiply, abound on the earth and multiply in it." The builders disobey the primal command to scatter and reproduce. This was noticed by the famous Jewish historian Josephus (*Antiquities of the Jews* I.iv.1) in the first century CE (Wenham 1987:240; Fretheim 412). When they declare that they wish not to be scattered, they imply that God will scatter them. Ironically, at the end of the story God will do that.

The builders might also imply something more sinister about God. If they wish not to be scattered, what do they really fear? Were they to be scattered, would it be easier for God to kill them off individually by flooding once more? Perhaps they feel that there is strength and safety in numbers, especially if they have to defend themselves against God. They desire to build this tower to have high ground in case of another flood. The builders not only disregard the command of God to disperse, they exhibit a tremendous lack of trust in God.

What then are their sins in building the tower? They refuse to obey God's command of reproduction, they show lack of trust in God, perhaps even a willingness to fight back against God, and they seek immortality both by storming the divine realm and by their desire to make a name for themselves. To sum it up, their sin is over-weaning pride, the sin of so many people and rulers throughout history who brought themselves to ruin by overextending the reach of their own hands or the resources of their people. They have committed the sin of ultimate pride in their attempt to attain the divine, self-divinization (Clines 1976:495). The sin of pride or *hubris* is the sin of heroes in the ancient mythologies, such as Prometheus, who went beyond the boundaries and tried to enter into the domain of the gods, because they thought they were worthy to enter into such a domain. It is the sin of our modern leaders in the business, religious, and political realms, who seem to think that by their authority, leadership, or charisma they stand above the law, and so they transgress the law with impunity. They fail, and their followers suffer, and we suffer. Our biblical author has crafted a parable for all time. This sin of hubris impressed itself upon the biblical author as the great sin in Babylon, where monumental buildings claimed to be gateways to the divine realm for religious and political leaders.

If pride is the act of rebellion by the builders of the tower, the Primeval History has come full cycle. The sin of the man and the woman in the garden was one of pride, and the sin of the first ancestors has become the sin of corporate humanity acting in concert at the foot of the tower. The Primeval History begins and ends with the sin of pride, the sin of hubris. But that should come as no surprise. Not only the rich and powerful commit such sins of pride in our age, but people as a whole live with corporate hubris. We have hubris in our society over many things. We are proud and too confident of our way of life, our science and technology, our military strength, and our economic capacities. It is a pride borne of too much success, and it is a pride that has led us to believe that in the process of world globalization everyone else needs to be like us so that the world might be a better place. It is such hubris on our part that has engendered wrath against America throughout the world. Perhaps we are the workers standing at the foot of the tower, taking a little too much pride in the building we construct.

Sarcasm drips from our biblical narrative as the story continues. God comes down and sees what the people are building. What! Did God misplace the divine bifocals, so that God must come all the way down from the divine realm to peek at the tower on hands and knees? Does God really need to visit the eye doctor? Not really! The tower was designed to storm the heavens—to virtually knock on God's front door! Our author indicates that the building effort so arrogantly undertaken with the desire of upstaging God is really so tiny and insignificant, that God has to come down to take a closer look at what these creatures are doing, for their building project is really so very, very small. God is much bigger than the builders suspected (Wenham 1987:240). It could also be noted that God "comes down" in reference to Sodom in Gen 18:21, and that did not end well for people either. "Coming down" may be a prelude to divine judgment. (Wenham 1987:241). Some commentators also see this as another example of God's personal self-involvement in the human condition for both judgment and salvation (Fretheim 412).

This throws into relief the next statement, which so often has puzzled commentators. God says that if this building project goes through, "nothing that they propose to do will now be impossible for them." The word "propose" is used in Deut 19:19 in reference to what a false witness intends.

Further, in Job 42:2 Job says of God that, "no purpose of yours can be thwarted." Job may utter this with contempt. Thus, Gen 11:6 may contain a negative comment by God on the people's activity. Commentators wonder if the implication is that human endeavors may indeed challenge the divine realm. If so, then our biblical story reflects a very mythic way of thinking. Some authors suggest that this line might be a remnant of an earlier mythic version of this story, and the challenge of the builders, like that of the Sumerian Etana or the Greek Prometheus, was to be taken more seriously. Commentators are not comfortable with that conclusion, but they are not too sure what else to say.

Another possibility, however, is to throw this expression into relief with the image of the previous verse. If God has to come down to see what a small project is being constructed by humanity by which to challenge the divine realm, perhaps this expression by God is also sarcasm (McKeown 51). That is to say, the people will think "nothing will be impossible for them." In reality, compared to God, humanity will still be small and impotent. But they will think that they have power, and this will lead them to engage in even more tyrannical and oppressive behavior that is both self-destructive and destructive to other people. Perhaps our biblical author again is thinking of the activity of Babylonian kings and tyrants in their attempts at worldwide domination and their foolish endeavors at storming the heavens with their building projects, especially those of Nabonidus. In effect, God is saying that though their efforts are foolish and futile, nonetheless, they must be stopped, for their efforts will lead to further suffering of subject peoples, including the Judeans.

"Come, let us go down," says God. To whom is God talking? We discussed this complex debate in conjunction with Gen 1:26. We could assume that God is talking to divine beings who once were gods but now have been denigrated to a group of nameless angelic messengers by the process of emerging monotheism. However, when God says "let us," this divine cohortative contrasts vividly with the three human cohortatives, "let us make bricks," "let us build ourselves a city," and "let us make a name for ourselves." With one divine "let us" statement God undertakes an action that undoes three by humanity. The verb hearkens back to Gen 1:26 wherein God says, "let us make humankind in our image." Now God undoes something made by humanity, whereas earlier God started the process by making humanity. It all appears to be a way in which the biblical author connects the first account in Genesis 1–11 with the last account. So perhaps for the sake of a literary contrast the verb form "let us" is placed upon God's lips, and perhaps in our discussions we have made a mountain out of a molehill by trying to determine who is addressed.

The Tower of Babel and Beyond 265

God confused their language and scattered them all over the face of the earth, an appropriate punishment visited upon the people for their defiance of God. But the author may use this motif of scattering in a more significant way. It is the appropriate punishment for their act of pride that their unity is broken and they are scattered. Yet from the greater plot line we observe in all the stories of the Primeval History, we might also view this divine act as one of grace. It was gracious of God to scatter the people instead of killing them (Lim 183). By scattering them, God moved them in the direction they were supposed to go in the first place: they were to spread, reproduce, and rule the earth wisely. In the greater Primeval History we might view this divine act as punishment or grace, or perhaps both.

If there is a correspondence with history, and especially the history of the sixth century BCE Chaldean Empire, then the tower was actually built by slaves and prisoners of war dragged from all over the empire, who naturally spoke different languages already. Their language was not confused by God; it was already diverse. Nor were they scattered; they were released to return to their homes willingly and gladly. But the biblical author tells this story in parabolic fashion, so correspondence between actual history and symbolic plot line will not be a perfect match.

The difference between the historical experiences of people and the symbolic story line results from the theological message the author attempts to convey. The building of this tower is an act of human cooperation and technological achievement. It is logical in the story line to portray a unified humanity working together to create this grand piece of architecture; "stupendous undertakings" require an "undivided humanity" (Skinner 223). The biblical author implies that in building this monument the people act with pride and defiance. Thereby the author creates a parody on of the pride and power of the Babylonians and especially the Babylonian leaders, the king and the priests, who organize such great building activities. In the symbolic story the building activity symbolizes the arrogance of Babylonian leadership and satirizes Babylon's claim to be the center of the world.

Confusing the language of the people is symbolic of God's intervention in history to topple the tyranny of such an empire. Empires are held together by the will and the commands of the kings and other leaders. By confusing the "language" of the builders, the story implies that God "confuses" the command infrastructure created by the leaders of the empire. God topples the kings and priests by making their commands ineffective and destroying the basis of their leadership. That certainly seemed to be what happened, at least in the eyes of the Judeans in Babylonian Exile, when the great Chaldean Babylonian regime fell so quickly before the onslaught of the Persian king Cyrus in 540 BCE. It seemed as though God made the command structure of the Babylonian crumble; God "confused" the language and the entire regime literally went to pieces.

Within a year after seizing Babylon in 540 BCE, Cyrus the Great, the Persian ruler of most of the Middle East, issued a proclamation permitting Judeans to return home to Jerusalem and rebuild their city and Temple. Presumably Cyrus permitted deported exiles of other kingdoms to do likewise. This was Cyrus' way of currying the favor of the diverse peoples within his newly created empire. History and the story plot do not coincide perfectly; in the story the people apparently are scattered unwillingly, in real life exiles returned home joyously. But the story is told from the perspective of the empire with its arrogance and pride. The empire has collapsed, symbolized by the image of people trudging slowly away from the unfinished building the day after the great "confusion."

The tower is called the "Tower of Babel." The biblical author engages in a word play and also provides us with a hint to the historical background. The word "Babel" in Hebrew is a combination of two other words. It takes the consonants of the name from Babylon (*bbl*), which is *Bab-ili* in Babylonian (meaning "gate of God"), and it combines them with the vowels from the Hebrew word for "mix" or "confuse" (*balal*). These vowels indicate that a theoretic verb is envisioned that occurs only in the rare Hebrew verb form (or conjugation) known as the "polpal," and it means to "babble" like an idiot. This form of the word never occurs in the Hebrew Bible, though it might have existed in everyday discourse, and it does occur in related languages like Arabic and Aramaic (Simpson 565). So Babel is an artificial word. The vowels from "babble" give primary meaning to the word and to the story, for the people spoke to each other in diverse languages and it therefore sounded like "babble" to everyone else.

But the tower is in (or near) Babylon, and Babylon was the city in an empire that stood for human arrogance and pride. Babylon was capital for the Amorite Empire in the early second millennium BCE, the Kassite Empire in the later second millennium BCE, and the Chaldean Empire from 625 to 540 BCE. Our author humorously implies that the great city of Babylon is not really the "Gate of God," the center of the world, but the place of babble and confusion, a city of arrogance and oppression. Does this sound like any of our modern cities?

Babylon was the quintessential city of power, riches, and rule in the Mesopotamian valley. Chaldean Babylon destroyed Jerusalem in 586 BCE, and thus the word Babylon became a code word for any great evil empire in later Jewish and Christian literature (including the book of Revelation). The story of Babel's fall in Genesis 11 is a parable to describe not only the fall of Babylon in 540 BCE, but as a parable it is a hopeful statement about the fall of any evil and arrogant empire that defies God and ultimately receives divine retribution. It is a story about the fall of tyrants and tyranny, and Babylon is the prototype of empires that defy God and engage in human exploitation. The prophets of Israel turned such rhetoric back upon the audience and spoke of Jerusalem and its kings in similar fashion (Richardson 124–25). So we must be ready to see that the words of judgment in the Babel parable can describe our society, too.

Mesopotamians viewed their building projects with pride. Nebuchadnezzar had his name inscribed on every fiftieth brick in the renovation of the buildings in Babylon (McKeown 71). In response to such architectural propaganda, the biblical author paints an account of human pride and concomitant divine punishment for such grand pretensions. The biblical author ridicules such religious and political propaganda which claims that a ziggurat is the "navel of the earth" and the sign of the pre-eminence and divine election of the people, city, empire, or king who construct it (Van Seters 184). God comes down to the tower, the ziggurat, the cosmic mountain, so small by divine standards that God must descend in order to see it. Though the account may be primarily a parable on the efforts of Chaldean kings like Nabopolasar, Nebuchadnezzar, and Nabonidus, the story really satirizes the policies of kings in any age. The sin of the builders is the desire to storm the heavens and make a name for themselves, which is their code language for immortality and fame. Such is the sin of kings, rulers, and presidents in any age who bestride their people and seek the immortality of power, wealth, and fame by means of tyrannical rule. Such immortality is fleeting, says the biblical author, for it is not in accord with the divine will. The tower was "symbolic of the ruthless power and oppression of the great empires that existed in the region" in the ancient time (Fritsch 50).

On a larger canvas the story is Israelite and Jewish polemic against the social and intellectual values of Mesopotamian society as they viewed those values from their perspective. The story criticizes the power of kings and the values of urban mercantile society; it attacks the religious values of Mesopotamian religious intelligentsia with their complex temple architecture and its ideological symbolism, their sacrificial cultus, their sophisticated techniques of divination, and their over-weaning power in society. The story of the tower of Babel implies that once a long time ago God came down to destroy just such a society and scatter them over the face of the earth, and that God will come down again to do the same to imperial Babylon, to its kings, to its priests, and to its entire social, political, and religious value system (Middleton 219–22).

The divine will was for this people to scatter, which they did not willingly do. Ultimately, the empire falls, the minions of the ruler scatter, and the great building accomplishments slowly fade into the sands of time, and with their demise the names of great kings are forgotten. The biblical story of Babel attempts to "lampoon the efforts of the Babylonian kings to complete it. It is not an etiology of a ruin" (Van Seters 184). The judgment that fell upon the builders and the kings in a primeval age can happen again to kings in the contemporary age. Indeed, such did occur when the Chaldean Babylonian empire fell before Persia in 540 BCE. Who ultimately will be remembered in the opinion of the biblical author? There will be one man who comes from Babel, be that Ur or Babylon, and he will become the father of a great people and he will be remembered through the ages. He will be remembered because he was obedient to God. He name was Abraham. Thus the story of the Tower of Babel becomes the springboard to tell the story of Abraham in Genesis 11 and thereafter.

The story remains a timeless parable about human pride and the use of technology for such activity that would vaunt human beings above God in their rule of the earth. Leon Kass said it nicely when he envisioned God's view of the tower.

> More generally, He (God) may not like the absence of reverence, the vaunt of pride, the trust in technique, the quest for material power, the aspiration for self-sufficiency, the desire to reach into heaven—in short, the implied will to be as gods, with comparable creative power. From God's point of view, the city of man is, in its deepest meaning, at best a form of idolatry and self-worship, and at worst a great threat to the earth. (Kass 219).

Hidden in this description one can sense that the characterization of the building of Babel and its tower is also a characterization for much of what happens in our modern world as people continue to have a vaunt of pride, an overweening trust in their technological technique, their business acumen, and their military might, and the desire to be inordinately self-sufficient from the divine realm. This text comes painfully close to describing us today. The great narrative of the primeval age appears to describe people of any age, especially the modern age.

The people trudge away from the unfinished structure. They wished to make a name for themselves. They wished for power, glory, and fame—a form of immortality, I suppose. They are no different than so many political leaders, business tycoons, and yes, even arrogant clergy, who wish to make a name for themselves today. But ultimately they all trudge away from the unfinished building. Do they hear the voice of God saying, "You fool, this night your soul shall be required of you!"? They made a name for themselves, but it was a name of shame.

Abraham' Family

Genesis 11:10–32

(10) These are the descendants of Shem. When Shem was one hundred years old, he became the father of Arpachshad two years after the flood; (11) and Shem lived after the birth of Arpachshad five hundred years; and had other sons and daughters. (12) When Arpachshad had lived thirty-five years, he became the father of Shelah; (13) and Arpachshad lived after the birth of Shelah four hundred three years, and had other sons and daughters. (14) When Shelah had lived thirty years, he became the father of Eber; (15) and Shelah lived after the birth of Eber four hundred three years, and had other sons and daughters. (16) When Eber had lived thirty-four years, he became the father of Peleg; (17) and Eber lived after the birth of Peleg four hundred thirty years, and had other sons and daughters. (18) When Peleg had lived thirty years, he became the father of Reu; (19) and Peleg lived after the birth of Reu two hundred nine years, and had other sons and daughters. (20) When Reu had lived thirty-two years; he became the father of Serug; (21) and Reu lived after the birth of Serug two hundred seven years, and had other sons and daughters. (22) When Serug had lived thirty years, he became the father of Nahor; (23) and Serug lived after the birth of Nahor two hundred years, and had other sons and daughters. (24) When Nahor had lived twenty-nine years, he became the father of Terah; (25) and Nahor lived after the birth of Terah one hundred nineteen years, and had other sons and daughters. (26) When Terah had lived seventy years, he became the father of Abram, Nahor, and Haran. (27) Now these are the descendants of Terah. Terah was the father of Abram, Nahor, and Haran; and Haran was the father of Lot. (28) Haran died before his father Terah in the land of his birth, in Ur of the Chaldeans. (29) Abram and Nahor took wives; the name of Abram's wife was Sarai, and the name of Nahor's wife was Milcah. She was the daughter of Haran the father of Milcah and Iscah. (30) Now Sarah was barren; she had no child. (31) Terah took his son Abram and his grandson Lot son of Haran, and his daughter-in-law Sarai, his son Abram's wife, and they went out together from Ur of the Chaldeans to go into the land of Canaan; but when they came to Haran, they settled there. (32) The days of Terah were two hundred five years; and Terah died in Haran.

If we count generations from Shem to Abraham we have ten generations, comparable to the ten generations of Sethites down to Noah. That might simple be a coincidence, but the biblical author did like symbolic numbers and balanced sequences (Blenkinsopp 2011:172)

In the past two generations historians have noted that some of these names sound strangely like north Mesopotamian and Syrian cities. The person Haran sounds like the city Haran. Sarug, a city near the major north Mesopotamian city of Haran, is the name of one of the ancestors, Serug. Terah's name may be found in the place name Turahi, another town near Haran. Nahor's name may be the name of a city mentioned not only in Gen 24:10, but also in the archives of the city of Mari, a place somewhat to the south of Haran on the Euphrates River. This city's name was Nachur or Nakhur (Speiser 1964:79–80; Vawter 162; Westermann 563; Hamilton 361). We might have some memory of cities in north Mesopotamia where not only Abraham, but also other clans related to the Abraham family, might have lived before they migrated south to Palestine. Years ago historians suspected that Abraham was part of a larger migration of peoples, called Amorites, who moved into Palestine in the early second millennium BCE. However, the Bible speaks only of Abraham and not those other migratory groups. Though this theory of Amorite migration is no longer advocated by scholars, some suspect that there were still a few migrants, in addition to Abraham, who came south and ultimately became part of later Israel. The memory of their existence might be recalled in the Joshua speech in Joshua 24 where the Israelites make a covenant with the people of the city of Shechem. Joshua refers to ancestors who lived on the other side of the great river, the Euphrates (Josh 24:2). If Joshua is speaking to not only the Israelites, but to the Shechemites also, he might imply that other families came to Palestine from Mesopotamia who are kin to each other. Evidence for such folk might be in the names of the ancestors, which are place names from whence they came.

Some scholars suspect that the name Terah might have other meanings. It could mean "ibex" or it might be one of the words for "moon." If the latter meaning is correct, an intriguing notion is raised. Chief cities where the moon god was revered were Ur and Haran, the two cities to where the families moved. One person, Haran, has the same name as one of these cities. Terah's name sounds like the name of the lunar month in Mesopotamia, Yerah, as well as the name for the moon in Hebrew. In the pantheon of the city, Haran, the title Sharratu, which would be close to Sarai's name, was given to the moon-goddess, Ningal, the consort of Sin. Laban, the brother of Rebekah, has a name that means white, which is a color that describes the moon. Malkatu was the daughter of the moon god, and her name sounds like Milcah, the wife of Nahor. On the other hand, Malkatu is also a title of the goddess Ishtar, so we may be fooled by names that sound alike. Perhaps, the names of several Mesopotamian deities are spoofed by the biblical author (Simpson 568–69; Hamilton 361; Wenham 1987:252, 273).

Later Jewish tradition assumed that Abraham's family members were devotees of the moon god before he went to Palestine. The moon god Sin was the personal deity of Nabonidus, the last king of Chaldean Babylon in the mid-sixth century BCE, and this king attempted to dramatically promulgate the worship of Sin in Mesopotamia. These coincidences incline me to suspect the Tower of Babel story is commentary on this era in history.

Perhaps, there were two memories about the origin of Abraham's family, one that placed them in Haran (in the north), the other which placed them in Ur (in the south). If so, the biblical author wove both of these traditions together by simply having the family move from one city (Ur) to the other (Haran) and reside in the latter city for some time (Simpson 570).

The existence of a genealogy after the Tower of Babel account is a sign of divine graciousness. People are elected by God to become the ancestral line of those who ultimately receive the covenant with God through Moses and obtain the blessing of land, descendants, and chosen calling. This particular line of people culminates with Abraham, who becomes the chosen ancestor of the later Israelites and Judeans. God did not desert humanity after Babel, but worked through a particular family and people.

There is also something somber about the direction of the story. It is as though God despairs about working with universal humanity; God decides to work with one family. God moves from concern with universal humanity to a particular humanity, the family of Abraham and ultimately Israel and the Judeans. The entire story moves in the direction of particularity: a particular people with a particular covenant created at a particular place (Sinai) and a particular time (after the liberation of slaves).

God turns from Mesopotamia and now focuses upon Palestine. The image of the failed tower speaks of the disobedience of Mesopotamians in the past and the continued disobedience of Mesopotamians in the time of the author, which gives God good reason to turn divine attention to a small group of people in the west, in Palestine. The movement of Abraham from Ur in south Mesopotamia to Haran in north Mesopotamia portrays the experience of a singular clan, called out of its cultural sphere to go to a new land. This new land ultimately is in the west, away from the failure and corruption of Mesopotamian civilization. Our biblical author may be aware that Mesopotamia was older and more sophisticated than the world of Palestine. So he told the story of how his people had to leave Mesopotamia years ago because God despaired of them. This may be satire against the Mesopotamians. But that should come as no surprise, since the Assyrians and the Babylonians crushed the Israelites politically and militarily, destroying the cities and the political entities of both the northern state of Israel (722 BCE) and the southern state of Judah (586 BCE).

The Primeval History really comes to an end with this final genealogy, a transition genealogy. We now turn to the family of Abraham. The scene moves to Palestine, where Abraham, Isaac, and Jacob will roam in a land that they hope someday will belong to them and their children.

The relative ages of these ancestors are shorter than the ages of folk in the earlier genealogies, especially the lists of people before the flood. Math games have been played with this particular list, but no special code or pattern seems to emerge. Rather, the biblical author's point simply may be that the quality of human life deteriorated after the flood because of human sin, and people simply did not live as long. This pattern of declining ages will continue through the patriarchal narratives and into the exodus narratives. The same pattern of declining ages among primordial personages is also found in the *Atrahasis Epic*. The patriarchs will live past the century mark, and so will Moses, but not by much. Eventually the lifespans begin to approximate the more normal, but blessed, figure of seventy years. Thus, the numbers appear to be artificial, but they testify to human finitude and sin and the subsequent need for divine blessing and grace.

A final point is that Ur in these passages is called Ur of the Chaldees. Historically the Mesopotamian city of Ur was never really known by that name. If the biblical author, however, were to call the city by that name, it would be appropriate to call it "Ur of the Chaldees" only when the Chaldean Empire was in power in the Mesopotamia valley, which was from about 625 BCE to 540 BCE. This becomes an argument for dating the final written form of these biblical narratives to that era. Furthermore, it is in this era that Nabonidus, the last king of Chaldean Babylon, revered the moon god Sin and built shrines to that deity in Haran and Ur, cities through which Abraham traveled. It seems that our narrative points to the sixth century BCE as the age in which Abraham should be symbolically located. This is the time when Judeans would return from Babylon to Palestine after their release by Cyrus the Great in 539 BCE, and they would follow the footsteps of Abraham back to Palestine.

How interesting that the Primeval History ends with the birth of the Hebrew people in Abraham and at the same time points to the era when the people would be reborn again after the Babylonian Exile. Both are symbols of grace, images of how God leads people to a new an exciting future. The Primeval History ends with a powerful image of divine grace. But as the Primeval History ends, a new and even bigger chapter in the life of God's people begins. But then, that is what believers still say about the presence of God in our midst today. When one great chapter in life ends, another begins, and the final word is always one of grace.

23

Conclusion

GENESIS 1–11 CONTAINS MASTERFULLY crafted and intellectually profound narratives. There are many insights to be derived from these accounts, far more than can be covered in any single commentary. I heard it said several years ago that a definitive commentary on Genesis or even simply on Genesis 1–11 can never again be written because the massive amount of scholarship is too vast for any one commentator to thoroughly master. I heartily concur. This commentary is not comprehensive, but it attempts to address significant theological issues and address concerns and questions about this material that people might have today.

If we were to summarize the important lessons to be gleaned from these accounts, they would be as follows: 1) The creation account in Genesis 1 is designed to proclaim that one God created the world without recourse to combat, for God is so powerful. Furthermore, the world is created good not evil. 2) The creation of humanity in Genesis 1 is a profound statement about human equality and dignity; all men and women are kings and queens. 3) People are to rule the world wisely, which means today that we should be sensitive to environmental concerns. 4) The creation of humanity in Genesis 2 proclaims that people are created to be free and morally responsible, not slaves of the gods and their minions, the priests and kings. 4) God graciously enables people to be co-creators in the world, another imperative to environmental sensitivity, for we are still co-creators of the world with God. 5) Sexual identity arises at the same time for men and women, the man is not superior because he is created first, and furthermore the woman is an *'ezer*, a powerful companion, not a subordinate. 6) People are created to be in loving, sexual unions, as a natural state, not a result of sin. 7) In Genesis

3 the snake is not the devil; people are responsible for sinning in their own free will. As a symbol for the fertility goddess, the snake is debunked and is simply a smart animal not a divine being. 8) The man and the woman sinned together; they are equally responsible for their actions. 9) The man and the woman symbolically represent us when we fail to act responsibly; that is why they have no names. 10) The greater sin for the man and the woman was to deny their responsibility and "pass the buck for their sin." The biblical author wished for Judeans in Babylonian Exile to sense that and accept responsibility for their exiled situation. 11) The curses upon the man and the woman describe a reality that already existed for them outside the garden in real life, in the adult world, but it is also a reality to be overcome someday. 12) The final word is grace, not punishment, as the couple leave the garden. 13) Cain is the ancestor of all humanity; God's protection of Cain is symbolic of God's grace in preserving a sinful humanity. The mark of Cain is a blessing, not a curse. 14) Genealogies are a subtle critique of kingship in the ancient world, as perhaps the story in Gen 6:1–4 may be also. 15) The flood narrative is a direct parody on many ancient Near Eastern flood accounts and it is designed to affirm monotheism and the gracious control God has over the power of the flood. 16) God is gracious, there will never be another flood, and this is a critique of Mesopotamian religionists who try to bring Judeans over to the worship of their gods in their futile attempts to forestall some envisioned cosmic catastrophe. 17) The curse on Ham does not exist; the curse on Canaan has nothing to do with any justification of slavery or the supposed inferiority of a race of people. 18) The tower of Babel story is a parody on the arrogance of kings or a people who glorify themselves with their group's accomplishments. 19) These stories should never be used to justify the oppression of any one; all people are equal before God. 20) The ultimate message in the stories is grace, all the stories end with grace. 21) Out of this universal world history, God will call Abraham, the ancestor of later Judeans and ultimately Christians.

I remember the flip chart from first grade in my Lutheran grade school classroom with all the beautiful color pictures of the Old Testament story. It was early in the 1950s that I heard these stories told in conjunction with the pictures with enthusiasm by the teacher, who, by the way, was one of the best teachers I had in grade school. There was the picture of Eve talking to the snake, but Adam was not in the picture. There was the picture of the man and the woman hiding in the bushes from God. There was the picture of the man and the woman leaving the garden, naked but positioned discretely, while a ten-foot-tall angel held a six-foot long flaming sword. That should scare first graders enough to keep them in line! There were two men offering sacrifices of grain and a sheep. There was a huge ark floating on the water while people screamed for help from a nearby rock in the water, but received no assistance from the man in the ark. The man in the ark simply shook his hand at them so as to say that they could not be taken aboard the ark. That certainly did not teach first graders compassion! Finally there was the tall, circular, winding stairway up the outside of a tall building reaching into the clouds. Gee, did we miss the story of drunk Noah and Ham? Did we dwell enough on the fall narrative with three out of six pictures devoted to that subject? Two of those pictures were blatantly wrong: Eve was not alone and the couple did not leave the garden naked. But with those pictures went an oral narrative that was very flawed. I will not blame the teacher or even the creators of the fine color pictures for the misconceptions I was taught. I will blame an oral tradition of teaching piety among Christian laity that has been perpetuated for generations. Maybe I will blame preachers for perpetuating those misunderstandings with their casual allusions in sermons. How can a theological tradition that proclaims *sola scriptura* so loudly and boldly then develop so many misconceptions of these stories and others in the Bible?

Do we read the stories too quickly and quote biblical passages rather than reading them, or is it just theological stubbornness that says, "I know what I believe, don't bother me with the facts." I have taught Old Testament for over thirty five years to encourage people to look closely at the text, especially if they are teachers, so as to avoid misconceptions. Ultimately, my desire to oppose so many misconceptions has led me to write this book and others so as to reach a wider audience.

I tell my students repeatedly that if someone quotes the Bible to oppress other people, be they women, African Americans, or poor people, they have misused and abused the Bible. I tell them that the Bible as a document may reflect in the narratives that it comes from the first millennium BCE, an age of patriarchalism, slavery, and brutal wars, but the deeper message of the biblical text affirms the equality of all people before God and envisions a golden age in which that equality and freedom from the miseries of life will be realized. Too often we have domesticated this vision of hope by projecting it into heaven. The Bible envisions that somehow in this life some of those things will be realized; Christians certainly did. Paul was speaking of the Christian community in this life when he said that in Christ there is no longer Jew or Greek, slave or free, male or female (Gal 3:28). Christians in those early years certainly tried to actualize that in their communities. After the Roman Empire became the patron of the church, Christians seemed to forget their mission for egalitarianism in this world. They left this mission for Enlightenment figures in the seventeenth and eighteenth centuries to rediscover.

Genesis 1–11 contains such stories of human equality and dignity. The man and the woman are both created out of the Adam in Genesis 1, the man and the woman arise with gender identity together in Genesis 2, the critique of kings occurs throughout these passages in the Primeval History, and that last concern really unveils the attempt by biblical authors to assail the classes in society that divide people into the oppressors and the oppressed. Further, I hope I have shown in this book how the critique of polytheism is also the critique of the prerogatives of those in power. If there is no Tiamat, the role of the king in the New Year's Festival of Babylon is mindless folly. If there are no gods, then there are no semi-divine warriors of the ancient days from whom kings can claim descent. Nor are there flood heroes raised to semi-divine status who parallel kings aspiring to such a status. Finally, the story of the tower is a parody on all kings who bestride their people with oppressive power and reach to grasp the golden ring of immortality with their building projects. The passages of Genesis 1–11 sing the song of revolutionary ideals as they decry kings and therefore declare that all common folk are equal. That is why the narrative begins with the Adam, who is royal, yet at the same time is all of us.

Jewish intelligentsia created these sacred texts in the first millennium BCE. These people were scribes who learned to write by copying the pieces of literature of their age, texts created by other intelligentsia of the ancient world. The Jewish authors found ideas in other texts and advanced them. Their stories spoke of monotheism and human equality. They were intelligent and they were reflective; their stories reflect their brilliant insight into the human condition and their realization of the message that needed to be proclaimed for their people and for the ages. The "eye of faith" can see even more in these authors, for the devout Jew or Christian will declare that these scribes were "inspired," that they spoke for God, and that these texts were crafted by people inspired by God to move the human intellectual advance forward as well as the human social condition. That is a faith statement, but I hope that it is shared by many in the audience who read this book. If it is not shared, at least recognize that these scribes were the "cutting edge" intelligentsia of their age.

Hopefully, this book has communicated some insights to the reader about the message of these chapters. A wide range of topics have been covered, not all germane to the central thesis of this book concerning human equality. But to have a sensitive feeling for the message of this literature, it really is necessary to cover a wider range of issues. Nevertheless, the primary purpose of this work has been to discuss topics that speak of human equality and dignity, for that was one of the primary goals of the original authors, I believe. Too often that message has been lost in the clutter of human piety in the church. But hopefully we can hear it again in our modern age, when we especially need to heed those messages. The Protestant reformers of the sixteenth century wished to release the power of the biblical text for people in their age; we need to continue doing that in our own age.

Bibliography

Albertz, Rainer. 2003a. *Geschichte und Theologie*. Beihefte zur Zeitschrift für die alttestamentliche Wissenschaft 326. Berlin: de Gruyter.

———. 2003b. *Israel in Exile: The History and Literature of the Sixth Century BCE*. Translated by David Green. Studies in Biblical Literature 3. Atlanta: Society of Biblical Literature.

Amzallag, Nissim. 2009. "Yahweh, the Canaanite God of Metallurgy?" *Journal for the Study of the Old Testament* 33:387–404.

Anderson, Gary. 1988. "The Cosmic Mountain." In *Genesis 1–3 in the History of Exegesis*, edited by Gregory Robbins, 187–224. Studies in Women and Religion 27. Lewiston, NY: Mellen.

———. 2001. *The Genesis of Perfection*. Louisville: Westminster John Knox.

Bailey, Lloyd. 1989. *Noah: The Person and the Story in History and Tradition*. Columbia: University of South Carolina Press.

Bal, Mieke. 1987. *Lethal Love: Feminist Literary Readings of Biblical Love Stories*. Indiana Studies in Biblical Literature. Bloomington: Indiana University Press.

Barr, James. 1993. *The Garden of Eden and the Hope of Immortality*. Minneapolis: Fortress.

Barre, Michael. 1999. "Rabisu." In *Dictionary of Deities and Demons in the Bible*, edited by Karel van der Toorn et al., 682–83. 2nd ed. Leiden: Brill.

Batto, Bernard F. 1992. *Slaying the Dragon: Mythmaking in The Biblical Tradition*. Louisville: Westminster John Knox.

———. 2000. "The Institution of Marriage in Genesis 2 and in *Atrahasis*." *Catholic Biblical Quarterly* 62:621–31.

———. 2004. "The Divine Sovereign: The Image of God in the Priestly Creation Account." In *David and Zion: Biblical Studies in Honor of J. J. M. Roberts*, edited by Bernard F. Batto and Kathryn L. Roberts, 143–86. Winona Lake, IN: Eisenbrauns.

Beaulieu, Paul-Alain. 2007. "World Hegemony, 900–300 BCE." In *A Companion to the Ancient Near East*, edited by Daniel Snell, 48–61. Malden, MA: Blackwell.

Becking, Bob. 1999. "Cain." In *Dictionary of Deities and Demons in the Bible*, edited by Karel van der Toorn et al., 180. 2nd ed. Leiden: Brill.

Benjamin, Don C. 1997. "Stories of Adam and Eve." In *Problems in Biblical Theology: Essays in Honor of Rolf Knierim*, edited by Henry T. C. Sun and Keith Eades, 38–58. Reprinted, Eugene, OR: Wipf & Stock, 2011.

Berges, Ulrich. 1994. "Gen 11,1–9: Babel order das Ende der Kommunikation." *Biblische Notizen* 74:37–56.

Bertman, Stephen. 2003. *Handbook to Life in Ancient Mesopotamia*. Facts on File Library of World History. New York: Facts on File.

Beyerlin, Walter. 1978. *Near Eastern Religious Texts Relating to the Old Testament*. Translated by John Bowden. Old Testament Library. Philadelphia: Westminster.

Bird, Phyllis. 1981. "'Male and Female He Created Them': Genesis 1:27b in the Context of the Priestly Account of Creation." *Harvard Theological Review* 74:129–59.

Blenkinsopp, Joseph. 1992. *The Pentateuch: An Introduction to the First Five Books of the Bible*. Anchor Bible Reference Library. New York: Doubleday.

———. 2011. *Creation, Un-Creation, Re-Creation: A Discursive Commentary on Genesis 1–11*. New York: T. & T. Clark.

Bobrick, Benson. 2001. *Wide as the Waters: The Story of the English Bible and the Revolution It Inspired*. New York: Simon & Schuster.

Bremmer, Jan. 2003. "Brothers and Fratricide in the Ancient Mediterranean: Israel, Greece, and Rome." In *Eve's Children*, edited by Gerard Luttikhuizen, 77–92. Themes in Biblical Narrative 5. Leiden: Brill, 2003.

Brenner, Athalya. 1984. *The Israelite Woman: Social Role and Literary Type in Biblical Narrative*. Biblical Seminar 2. Sheffield: JSOT Press.

———, editor. 1998. *Genesis*. The Feminist Companion to the Bible 2/1. Sheffield: Sheffield Academic.

Brodie, Thomas L. 2001. *Genesis as Dialogue: A Literary, Historical, and Theological Commentary*. Oxford: Oxford University Press.

Brown, William P. 1999. *The Ethos of the Cosmos: The Genesis of Moral Imagination in the Bible*. Grand Rapids: Eerdmans.

———. 2010. *The Seven Pillars of Creation: The Bible, Science, and the Ecology of Wonder*. Oxford: Oxford University Press.

Brueggemann, Walter. 1968. "David and His Theologian." *Catholic Biblical Quarterly* 30 (1968) 156–81. Reprinted in Brueggemann, *David and His Theologian: Literary, Social, and Theological Investigations*, edited by K. C. Hanson, 1–28. Eugene, OR: Cascade Books, 2011.

———. 1982. *Genesis*. Interpretation. Atlanta: John Knox.

Carr, David. 1993. "The Politics of Textual Subversion: A Diachronic Perspective on the Garden of Eden Story." *Journal of Biblical Literature* 112:577–95.

———. 1996. *Reading the Fractures of Genesis*. Louisville: Westminster John Knox.

Clines, David. 1976. "Theme in Genesis 1–11." *Catholic Biblical Quarterly* 76:483–507.

———. 1978. *The Theme of the Pentateuch*. Journal for the Study of the Old Testament Supplement Series 10. Sheffield: Department of Biblical Studies, University of Sheffield.

———. 1979. "The Significance of the 'Sons of God' Episode (Genesis 6:1–4) in the Context of the 'Primeval History' (Genesis 1–11)." *Journal for the Study of the Old Testament* 13:33–46.

Cohn, Norman. 1961. *The Pursuit of the Millennium*. Rev. ed. New York: Oxford University Press.

Cohn, Robert. 1983. "Narrative Structure and Canonical Perspective in Genesis." *Journal for the Study of the Old Testament* 25:3–16.

Collins, Steven. 2013. "Where Is Sodom? The Case for Tall el-Hammam." *Biblical Archaeology Review* 39/2:30–41, 70–71.

Cotter, David W. 2003. *Genesis*. Berit Olam. Collegeville, MN: Liturgical.

Craig, Kenneth. 1999. "Questions Outside Eden (Genesis 4.1–16): Yahweh, Cain and Their Rhetorical Interchange." *Journal for the Study of the Old Testament* 86:107–28.

Croatto, José. 1996. "El relato de la torre de Babel (Génesis 11:1–9): Bases para una nueva interpretción." *Revista bíblica* 58:65–80.

Day, John. 2012. "The Sons of God and Daughters of Men and the Giants: Disputed Points in the Interpretation of Genesis 6:1–4." *Hebrew Bible and Ancient Israel* 1: 427–47.

DeWitt, Dale. 1979. "The Historical Background of Genesis 11:1–9: Babel or Ur?" *Journal of the Evangelical Theological Society* 22:15–26.

Dohmen, Christoph. 1996. *Schöpfung und Tod.* 2nd ed. Stuttgarter Biblische Beiträge 35. Stuttgart: Katholisches Bibelwerk.

Eslinger, Lyle. 1979. "A Contextual Identification of the *bene ha'elohim* and *benoth ha'adam* in Genesis 6:1–4." *Journal for the Study of the Old Testament* 13:65–73.

Exum, J. Cheryl, and H. G. M. Williamson, editors. 2003. *Reading from Right to Left: Essays on the Hebrew Bible in Honour of David J. A. Clines.* Journal for the Study of the Old Testament Supplement Series 373. Sheffield: Sheffield Academic.

Fitzpatrick, Paul E. 2004. *The Disarmament of God: Ezekiel 38–39 in Its Mythic Context.* Catholic Biblical Quarterly Monograph Series 37. Washington, DC: Catholic Biblical Association.

Fretheim, Terence E. 1994. "Genesis." In *The New Interpreter's Bible*, edited by Leander E. Keck, 1:319–674. Nashville: Abingdon.

Friedman, Richard Elliott. 1995. *The Disappearance of God: A Divine Mystery.* New York: Little, Brown.

Fritsch, Charles. 1959. *Genesis.* The Layman's Bible Commentary. Richmond: John Knox.

Frymer-Kensky, Tikva. 1992. *In the Wake of Goddesses: Women, Culture, and the Biblical Transformation of Pagan Myth.* New York: Free Press.

Gaster, Theodor. 1969. *Myth, Legend, and Custom in the Old Testament.* 2 vols. New York: Harper & Row.

Gervitz, Stanley. 1963. *Patterns in the Early Poetry of Israel.* Chicago: University of Chicago Press.

Gnuse, Robert Karl. 1984. *The Dream Theophany of Samuel: Its Structure in Relation to Ancient Near Eastern Dreams and Its Theological Significance.* Lanham, MD: University Press of America.

———. 1996. *Dreams and Dream Reports in the Writings of Flavius Josephus: A Form-Critical and Traditio-Historical Analysis.* Arbeiten zur Geschichte des antiken Judentums und des Urchristentums 36. Leiden: Brill.

———. 2002. "A Process Theological Interpretation of the Primeval History in Genesis 2–11." *Horizons* 29:23–41.

———. 2010. "The Tower of Babel in Genesis 11: A Parable of Judgment or Cultural Diversification?" *Biblische Zeitschrift* 54:229–44.

Good, Edwin M. 2011. *Genesis 1–11: Tales of the Earliest World.* Stanford: Stanford University Press.

Gros Louis, Kenneth. 1982. "Genesis 3–11." In *Literary Interpretations of Biblical Narratives 2*, edited by Kenneth Gros Louis and James S. Ackerman, 37–52. Nashville: Abingdon.

Gunkel, Hermann. 1997. *Genesis*. Translated by Mark E. Biddle. Mercer Library of Biblical Studies. Macon, GA: Mercer University Press. (3rd German ed., 1910.)

Hallo, William W. 1970. "Antediluvian Cities." *Journal of Cuneiform Studies* 23:57–67.

Hallo, William W., and Lawson Younger, editors. 2003. *The Context of Scripture*. Vol. 1, *Canonical Compositions from the Biblical World*. Leiden: Brill.

Hamilton, Victor P. 1990. *The Book of Genesis: Chapters 1–17*. New International Commentary on the Old Testament. Grand Rapids: Eerdmans.

Hartshorne, Charles. 1984. *Omnipotence and Other Theological Mistakes*. Albany: State University of New York Press.

Hasel, Gerhard, and Michael Hasel. 2000. "The Hebrew Term 'ed in Gen 2,6 and Its Connection in Ancient Near Eastern Literature." *Zeitschrift für die alttestamentliche Wissenschaft* 112:321–40.

Hepner, Gershon. 2003. "The Depravity of Ham and the Tower of Babel Echo Contiguous Laws of the Holiness Code." *Estudios bíblicos* 61:85–131.

Hinnells, John. 1985. *Persian Mythology*. Rev. ed. London: Hamlyn.

Hurowitz, Victor. 2005. "The Genesis of Genesis: Is the Creation Story Babylonian?" *Bible Review* 21/1:36–48, 52.

Jacobs-Hornig, B. "*Gan*" (garden). 1978. In *Theological Dictionary of the Old Testament*, edited by Johannes Botterweck and Helmer Ringgren, 3:34–39. Translated by Geoffrey W. Bromiley and David E. Green. Grand Rapids: Eerdmans.

Jacobsen, Thorkild. 1981. "The Eridu Genesis." *Journal of Biblical Literature* 100:513–29.

Kass, Leon. 2003. *The Beginning of Wisdom: Reading Genesis*. New York: Free Press.

Kawashima, Robert. 2004. "*Homo Faber* in J's Primeval History." *Zeitschrift für die alttestamentliche Wissenschaft* 116:483–501.

King, Philip J., and Lawrence E. Stager. 2001. *Life in Biblical Israel*. Library of Ancient Israel. Louisville: Westminster John Knox.

Kline, M. G. 1962. "Divine Kingship and Genesis 6:1–4." *Westminster Theological Journal* 24:187–210.

Kramer, Samuel Noah. 1963. *The Sumerians: Their History, Culture, and Character*. Chicago: University of Chicago Press.

———. 1968. "The Babel of Tongues: A Sumerian Version." *Journal of the American Oriental Society* 88:108–11.

Kramer, Samuel Noah, and John Maier, editors. 1989. *Myths of Enki, the Crafty God*. New York: Oxford University Press.

Kselman, John. 1988. "Genesis." In *Harper's Bible Commentary*, edited by James L. Mays, 85–128. San Francisco: Harper & Row.

Kugel, James L. 1997. *The Bible as It Was*. Cambridge, MA: Belknap.

Kugel, James L., and Rowan Greer. 1986. *Early Biblical Interpretation*. Library of Early Christianity 3. Philadelphia: Westminster.

LaCocque, André. 2006. *The Trial of Innocence: Adam, Eve, and the Yahwist*. Eugene, OR: Cascade Books.

———. 2008. *Onslaught against Innocence: Cain, Abel, and the Yahwist*. Eugene, OR: Cascade Books.

Lambert, Wilfrid. 1992. "Enuma Elish." In *Anchor Bible Dictionary*, edited by David Noel Freedman, 2:526–28. New York: Doubleday.

Lambert, Wilfrid, and Alan Millard, editors. 1969. *Atra-hasis: The Babylonian Story of the Flood*. Oxford: Clarendon.

Lanfer, Peter. 2012. *Remembering Eden: The Reception History of Genesis 3:22–24.* New York: Oxford University Press.
Levenson, Jon. 1985. *Sinai and Zion.* San Francisco: Harper & Row.
Levison, Jack. 1985. "Is Eve to Blame? A Contextual Analysis of Sirach 25:24." *Catholic Biblical Quarterly* 47:617–23.
L'Heureux, Conrad E. 1983. *In and Out of Paradise.* New York: Paulist.
Lim, Johnson T. K. 2002. *Grace in the Midst of Judgment: Grappling with Genesis 1–11.* Beihefte zur Zeitschrift für die alttestamentliche Wissenschaft 314. Berlin: de Gruyter.
Lind, Millard. 1980. *Yahweh Is a Warrior: The Theology of Warfare in Ancient Israel.* Scottdale, PA: Herald.
Lohr, Joel. 2011. "Sexual Desire? Eve, Genesis 3:16, and *teshukah*." *Journal of Biblical Literature* 130:227–46.
Löning, Karl, and Erich Zenger. 2000. *To Begin with, God Created . . . : Biblical Theologies of Creation.* Translated by Omar Kaste. Collegeville, MN: Liturgical.
Lowery, Daniel. 2013. *Toward a Poetics of Genesis 1–11: Reading Genesis 4:17–22 in Its Near Eastern Context.* Winona Lake, IN: Eisenbrauns.
Luttikhuizen, Gerard, editor. 2003. *Eve's Children: The Biblical Stories Retold and Interpreted in Jewish and Christian Tradition.* Themes in Biblical Narrative 5. Leiden: Brill.
Machinist, Peter. 2006. "Kingship and Divinity in Imperial Assyria." In *Text, Artifact, and Image: Revealing Ancient Israelite Religion*, edited by Gary Beckman and Theodore Lewis, 152–88. Brown Judaic Studies 346. Providence: Brown University Press.
Matthews, Victor H., and Don C. Benjamin, editors. 1997. *Old Testament Parallels: Laws and Stories from the Ancient Near East.* 2nd ed. New York: Paulist.
McCarter, P. Kyle. 1999. "Id." In *Dictionary of Demons and Deities in the Bible*, edited by Karel van der Toorn et al., 446. 2nd ed. Leiden: Brill.
McKeown, James. 2008. *Genesis.* Two Horizons Old Testament Commentary. Grand Rapids: Eerdmans.
Mettinger, Tryggve N. D. 2007. *The Eden Narrative: A Literary and Religio-historical Study of Genesis 2–3.* Winona Lake, IN: Eisenbrauns.
Meyers, Carol. 1988. *Discovering Eve: Ancient Israelite Women in Context.* New York: Oxford University Press.
Middleton, J. Richard. 2005. *The Liberating Image: The Imago Dei in Genesis 1.* Grand Rapids: Brazos.
Miller, J. Maxwell. 1974. "The Descendants of Cain: Notes on Genesis 4." *Zeitschrift für die alttestamentliche Wissenschaft* 86:164–73.
Miller, Patrick D. 1985. "Eridu, Dunnu, and Babel: A Study in Comparative Mythology." *Hebrew Annual Review* 9:227–51.
———. 2003. "Man and Woman: Toward a Theological Anthropology." In *Reading from Right to Left: Essays on the Hebrew Bible in Honor of David J. A. Clines*, edited by J. Cheryl Exum and H. G. M. Williamson, 320–28. Journal for the Study of the Old Testament Supplement Series 373. Sheffield: Sheffield Academic.
Moberly, R. W. L. 2009. *The Theology of the Book of Genesis.* Old Testament Theology. Cambridge: Cambridge University Press.

Moran, William L. 2002. *The Most Magic Word: Essays on Babylonian and Biblical Literature.* Edited by Ronald S. Hendel. Catholic Biblical Quarterly Monograph Series 35. Washington, DC: Catholic Biblical Association.

Mullen, Theodore. 1997. *Ethnic Myths and Pentateuchal Foundations: A New Approach to the Formation of the Pentateuch.* Atlanta, GA: Society of Biblical Literature.

Naidoff, Bruce. 1978. "A Man to Work on the Soil: A New Interpretation of Genesis 2–3." *Journal for the Study of the Old Testament* 5:2–14.

Neville, Richard. 2011. "Differentiation in Genesis 1: An Exegetical Creation *ex nihilo*." *Journal of Biblical Literature* 130:209–26.

Niditch, Susan. 1985. *Chaos to Cosmos: Studies in Biblical Patterns of Creation.* Scholars Studies in the Humanities 6. Chico, CA: Scholars.

Parker, Julie Faith. 2013. "Blaming Eve Alone." *Journal of Biblical Literature.* 132:729–47.

Pritchard, James B., editor. 1969. *Ancient Near Eastern Texts Relating to the Old Testament.* 3rd ed. Princeton: Princeton University Press.

Rad, Gerhard von. 1972. *Genesis.* Rev. ed. Translated by John Mark. Old Testament Library. Philadelphia: Westminster.

Rashkow, Ilona. 1998. "Daddy-Dearest and the 'Invisible Spirit of Wine.'" In *Genesis*, edited by Athalya Brenner, 82–107. The Feminist Companion to the Bible 2/1. Sheffield: Sheffield Academic.

Richardson, Alan. 1953. *Genesis 1–11.* Torch Bible Paperbacks. London: SCM.

Ruiten, Jacques van. 2003. "Eve's Pain in Childbearing? Interpretations of Gen 3:16a in Biblical and Early Jewish Texts." In *Eve's Children: The Biblical Stories Retold and Interpreted in Jewish and Christian Tradition*, edited by Gerard Luttikhuizen, 3–26. Themes in Biblical Narrative 5. Leiden: Brill.

Sanders, Theresa. 2009. *Approaching Eden: Adam and Eve in Popular Culture.* Lanham, MD: Rowan & Littlefield.

Sauer, James A. 1994. "A New Climatic and Archaeological View of the Early Biblical Traditions. In *Scripture and Other Artifacts: Essays on the Bible and Archaeology in Honor of Philip J. King*, edited by Michael Coogan et al., 366–98. Louisville: Westminster John Knox.

Sasson, Jack M. 1980. "The 'Tower of Babel' as a Clue to the Redactional Structuring of the Primeval History (Gen. 1–11)." In *The Bible World: Essays in Honor of Cyrus H. Gordon*, edited by Gary Rendsburg, 211–19. New York: Ktav.

Sawyer, John. 1986. "Cain and Hephaestus: Possible Relics of Metalworking Traditions in Genesis 4." *Abr-Nahrain* 24:155–66.

Scharbert, Josef. 1983. *Genesis 1–11.* Die Neue Echter Bibel. Würzburg: Echter.

Schmidt, Konrad. 2002. "Die Unteilbarkeit der Weisheit." *Zeitschrift für die alttestamentliche Wissenschaft* 114:21–39.

Scholz, Susanne, editor. 2003. *Biblical Studies Alternatively: An Introductory Reader.* Upper Saddle River, NJ: Pearson Education.

Schüngel-Straumann, Helen. 2003. "On the Creation of Man and Woman in Genesis 1–3: The History and Reception of the Texts Reconsidered." In *Biblical Studies Alternatively: An Introductory Reader*, edited by Susanne Scholz, 80–94. Upper Saddle River, NJ: Pearson Education.

Seely, Paul. 2001. "The Date of the Tower of Babel and Some Theological Implications." *Westminster Theological Journal* 63:15–38.

Sharon, Diane. 1998. "The Doom of Paradise: Literary Patterns in Accounts of Paradise and Mortality in the Hebrew Bible and the Ancient Near East." In *Genesis*, edited by Athalya Brenner, 53–80. The Feminist Companion to the Bible 2/1. Sheffield: Sheffield Academic.

Simkins, Ronald A. 1994. *Creator & Creation: Nature in the Worldview of Ancient Israel.* Peabody, MA: Hendrickson.

Simpson, Cuthbert. 1952. "The Book of Genesis." In *The Interpreter's Bible*, edited by George Arthur Buttrick, 1:439–829. New York: Abingdon.

Skinner, John. 1910. *Genesis.* International Critical Commentary. Edinburgh: T. & T. Clark.

Smith, Mark S. 2010. *The Priestly Vision of Genesis 1.* Minneapolis: Fortress.

Smith-Christopher, Daniel. 2002. *A Biblical Theology of Exile.* Overtures to Biblical Theology. Minneapolis: Fortress.

Soggin, Alberto. 1991. "Der Turmbau zu Babel." In *Prophetie und geschichtliche Wirklichkeit im alten Israel: Festschrift für Siegfried Herrmann zum 65. Geburtstag*, edited by Rüdiger Liwak und Siegfried Wagner, 371– 75. Stuttgart: Kohlhammer.

Sparks, Kenton. 2007. "*Enuma Elish* and Priestly Mimesis: Elite Emulation in Nascent Judaism." *Journal of Biblical Literature* 126:625–48.

Speiser, E. A. 1964. *Genesis.* Anchor Bible 1. Garden City, NY: Doubleday.

———. 1967. "In Search of Nimrod." In *Oriental and Biblical Studies*, edited by J. J. Finkelstein and Moshe Greenberg, 41–52. Philadelphia: University of Pennsylvania Press.

Stordalen, Terje. 2000. *Echoes of Eden: Genesis 2–3 and Symbolism of the Eden Garden in Biblical Hebrew Literature.* Biblical Exegesis and Theology 25. Leuven: Peeters.

Stratton, Beverly. 1995. *Out of Eden: Reading, Rhetoric, and Ideology in Genesis 2–3.* Journal for the Study of the Old Testament Supplement Series 208. Sheffield: Sheffield Academic.

Steck, Odil Hannes. 1970. *Die Paradieserzählung: Eine Auslegung von Genesis 2,4b–3,24.* Biblische Studien(N) 60. Neukirchen-Vluyn: Neukirchener.

Steinmetz, Devora. 1994. "Vineyard, Farm and Garden: The Drunkenness of Noah in the Context of the Primeval History." *Journal of Biblical Literature* 113:193–207.

Swidler, Leonard. 1979. *Biblical Affirmations of Women.* Philadelphia: Westminster.

Toorn, Karel van der. 1999. "God (I)." In *Dictionary of Deities and Demons in the Bible*, edited by Karel van der Toorn, et al., 352–65. 2nd ed. Leiden: Brill.

Toorn, Karel van der et al., editors. 1999. *Dictionary of Deities and Demons in the Bible.* 2nd ed. Leiden: Brill.

Trible, Phyllis. 1978. *God and the Rhetoric of Sexuality.* Overtures to Biblical Theology. Philadelphia: Fortress.

———. 2003. "Eve and Adam: Genesis 2–3 Reread." In *Biblical Studies Alternatively: An Introductory Reader*, edited by Susanne Scholz, 94–101. Upper Saddle River, NJ: Pearson Education.

Tsumura, David Toshio. 1989. *The Earth and the Waters in Genesis 1 and 2: A Linguistic Investigation.* Journal for the Study of the Old Testament Supplement Series 83. Sheffield: Sheffield Academic, 1989.

———. 1994. "Genesis and Ancient Near Eastern Stories of Creation and Flood." In *I Studied Inscriptions from before the Flood: Ancient Near Eastern Literary, and Linguistic Approaches to Genesis 1–11*, edited by Richard S. Hess and David Toshio Tsumura, 27–57. Sources for Biblical and Theological Study 4. Winona Lake, IN: Eisenbrauns.

———. 2005. *Creation and Destruction: A Reappraisal of the Chaoskampf Theory in the Old Testament*. Winona Lake, IN: Eisenbrauns.

Uehlinger, Christoph. 1990. *Weltreich und "eine Rede": Eine neue Deutung der sogenannten Turmbauerzählung (Gen 11,1–9)*. Orbus biblicus et orientalis 101. Göttingen: Vandenhoeck & Ruprecht.

Van Seters, John. 1992. *Prologue to History: The Yahwist as Historian in Genesis*. Louisville: Westminster John Knox.

Vanstiphout, Herman. 2003. *Epics of Sumerian Kings: The Matter of Aratta*. Writings from the Ancient World 20. Atlanta: Society of Biblical Literature.

Vawter, Bruce. 1977. *On Genesis: A New Reading*. Garden City, NY: Doubleday.

Vischer, Wilhelm. 1949. *The Witness of the Old Testament to Christ*, vol. 1. London: Lutterworth.

Wallace, Howard N. 1985. *The Eden Narrative*. Harvard Semitic Monographs 32. Atlanta: Scholars.

Walton, John. 2009. *The Lost World of Genesis 1: Ancient Cosmology and the Origins Debate*. Downer's Grove, IL: IVP Academic.

———. 2011. *Genesis 1 as Ancient Cosmology*. Winona Lake, IN: Eisenbrauns.

Wenham, Gordon. 1986. "Sanctuary Symbolism in the Garden of Eden Story." In *Proceedings of the Ninth World Congress of Jewish Studies Division A: The Period of the Bible*, 19–25. Jerusalem: World Union of Jewish Studies.

———. 1987. *Genesis 1–15*. Word Biblical Commentary 1. Waco, TX: Word.

Westermann, Claus. 1984. *Genesis 1–11: A Commentary*. Translated by John J. Scullion. Continental Commentaries. Minneapolis: Augsburg.

Wilson, Ian. 2002. *Before the Flood: The Biblical Flood as a Real Event and How It Changed the Course of Civilization*. New York: St. Martin's.

Wolde, Ellen J. van. 1989. *A Semiotic Analysis of Genesis 2–3*. Studia Semitica Neerlandica 25. Assen: Van Gorcum.

———. 1994. *Words Become Worlds: Semantic Studies of Genesis 1–11*. Biblical Interpretation Series 6. Leiden: Brill.

———. 1997. *Stories of the Beginning: Genesis 1–11 and Other Creation Stories*. Translated by John Bowden. Ridgefield, CT: Moorehouse.

York, Anthony. 1996. "The Maturation Theme in the Adam and Eve Story." In *"Go to the Land I Will Show You": Studies in Honor of Dwight W. Young*, edited by Joseph Coleson and Victor H. Matthews, 393–410. Winona Lake, IN: Eisenbrauns.

www.ingramcontent.com/pod-product-compliance
Lightning Source LLC
Chambersburg PA
CBHW021652230426
43668CB00008B/596